How Claims Spread

SOCIAL PROBLEMS AND SOCIAL ISSUES

An Aldine de Gruyter Series of Texts and Monographs

SERIES EDITOR
Joel Best, *University of Delaware*

HOW CLAIMS SPREAD

Cross-National
Diffusion of Social Problems

JOEL BEST

EDITOR

ALDINE DE GRUYTER
New York

ABOUT THE EDITOR

JOEL BEST
Professor and Chair, Department of Sociology and Criminal Justice,
University of Delaware.

ALDINE DE GRUYTER
A division of Walter de Gruyter, Inc.
200 Saw Mill River Road
Hawthorne, New York 10532

This publication is printed on acid free paper

Library of Congress Cataloging-in-Publication Data

How claims spread : cross-national dliffusion of social problems /
Joel Best, editor.
    p. cm. — (Social problems and social issues)
    Includes bibliographical references and index.
    ISBN 0-202-30653-4 (cloth : alk. paper) — ISBN 0-202-30654-2 (pbk : alk. paper)
        1. Social problems—Cross-cultural studies.   2. Social policy—Cross-
cultural studies.   3. Cultural relativism.   I. Best, Joel.   II. Series.

HN17.5 .S63 2001
361.1—dc21

                                                                    00-046926

Manufactured in the United States of America
10 9 8 7 6 5 4 3 2 1

CONTENTS

CONTRIBUTORS

Jun Ayukawa   Professor of Sociology and Dean, Graduate School of Humanities, Kinjo Gakuin University, Japan.

Andy Bennett   Lecturer in Sociology, University of Surrey, United Kingdom.

Joel Best   Professor and Chair, Department of Sociology and Criminal Justice, University of Delaware.

Mia Cahill   Member of the survey division, Mathematica Policy Research, Inc.; Visiting Scholar, Institute for Law and Society, New York University.

Véronique Campion-Vincent   Folklorist at Centre National de la Recherche Scientifique, Paris, France.

Frank Furedi   Reader in Sociology, University of Kent, United Kingdom.

Karim Ismaili   Assistant Professor of Criminal Justice and Fellow of the Center for Teaching and Learning, St. John's University, New York.

Philip Jenkins   Distinguished Professor of History and Religious Studies, Pennsylvania State University.

Ellie Lee   Professor of Sociology, Centre for Women's Studies, University of Kent, United Kingdom.

J. Robert Lilly   Regents Professor of Sociology, Northern Kentucky University.

Tarja Pösö   Professor in Social Work, University of Tampere, Finland.

vii

Vincent Sacco   Professor of Sociology, Queen's University, Kingston, Ontario.

Tadashi Suzuki   Doctoral student in Sociology, Southern Illinois University at Carbondale.

Grace Ellen Watkins   Assistant Professor of Sociology, Illinois College.

1

The Diffusion of Social Problems

JOEL BEST

In the 1970s, Herbert Blumer (1971) and Malcolm Spector and John I. Kitsuse (1977) urged sociologists to focus on how and why social problems emerged and evolved. Many researchers responded to this call for a new approach to social problems, and began exploring the *social construction* of social problems. This meant shifting their analytical focus away from the objective (the troublesome social conditions people call social problems) and toward the subjective (how people thought about and talked about social problems) (Loseke 1999). Constructionist analyses examined claims (the rhetoric used to define social problems and promote policy solutions for them), the claimsmakers who presented those claims, and the ways the public, press, and policymakers responded to claimsmaking.

CASE STUDIES AND CONSTRUCTIONISM

Typically, these constructionist researchers conducted case studies, each an account of how and why a particular problem came to national public attention (Schneider 1985; Best 1999). On occasion, researchers studied the construction of a local problem, such as a crime wave in a single city (e.g., Best 1991; Fishman 1978), but most approached social problems as though they were national phenomena. No doubt this reflected the relative ease of finding national sources of evidence. Because constructionist analyses focus on claimsmaking, researchers typically trace the record of claims made in such public arenas as the media or congressional testimony (Hilgartner and Bosk 1988). Traditionally, the evidence most accessible to researchers appears in national sources: only newspapers published in the largest cities were indexed thoroughly enough to allow analysts to retrieve stories; for the most part, the only magazines indexed have national audiences; although it is possible to locate and retrieve some programs shown on major television networks, it is nearly impossible to recover and study local news broadcasts; and federal government documents are thoroughly indexed, while state and local government documents are not.[1] Press reports and government documents are often key sources for constructionist researchers; national sources are the most visible, the most prestigious venues for social problems claims, and they are far more likely to be saved in library collections—and more far likely to be better-indexed—than local or regional materials. The relative ease of gathering such evidence insures that most case studies examine national campaigns to construct social problems.

Moreover, because most of the sociologists who did constructionist research lived and worked in the United States, their case studies tended to describe the construction of social problems in contemporary America. There were exceptions, of course. *Historical* case studies described social-problems construction in earlier times (in practice, this usually meant the late nineteenth or early twentieth centuries—again, about the only periods for which plentiful, accessible sources were available for study) (e.g., Adler 1996; Fine 1997; Fine and Christoforides 1991; Jenkins 1998; Loseke 1997; Margolin 1994; Neuman 1998; Rafter 1992; Trent 1995). Other case studies—often by foreign scholars describing events in their own countries—examined the construction of social problems in Canada (Croucher 1997; Harbison 1999; Lippert 1990), Great Britain (Furedi 1997; Jenkins 1992; Thompson 1994), Japan (Ayukawa 1995; Kitsuse et al. 1984; Yamazaki 1994), and a few other countries (Bammer and Martin 1992; Ross 1989, Simpura and Eremitcheva 1997).[2] Thus, studies of historical or foreign cases existed, but they were a small minority, greatly outnumbered by contemporary American case studies.

By definition, all these case studies—those set in contemporary America, as well as those describing events in other times or places—deal with particular social problems, with individual cases of social-problems construction. Researchers tended to concentrate on the specifics of their cases. They asked narrowly focused research questions: Who made the claims in this case? How did the claimsmakers characterize this problem? What solutions did they propose? How did the public, press, and policymakers respond to these claims?

This case-by-case approach had advantages, but they came at a cost. In particular, doing individual case studies shifted attention away from the connections that existed among social problems (Best 1999). Social-problems claims do not develop in a vacuum. Claims about one social problem often influence those about another: claimsmakers borrow rhetoric and tactics from one another; in some cases, experienced claimsmakers join efforts to call attention to other social problems; compelling images (e.g., the threatened child or random violence) link claims about different problems; and reactions to one set of claims often shape the responses to later claims (Best 1990, 1999; Jenkins 1992, 1999). Some social problems (such as gangs or sexual abuse) seem to manifest cyclical patterns: there are periodic waves of intense concern, interspersed with troughs of relative disinterest (Jenkins 1998). By limiting the focus to one construction of a social problem at a time, case studies make it difficult to recognize and study these connections. Also, significantly, sociologists of social problems have paid very little attention to the geographic spread—the diffusion—of social problems.

THE DIFFUSION OF SATANISM AS A SOCIAL PROBLEM

Consider satanism in the 1980s and 1990s. Satanism attracted the attention of a number of constructionist sociologists. In the late 1980s, claims about a million-member satanic blood cult that conducted 60,000 human sacrifices annually in the United States had become common. Although largely ignored by the prestige press, claims about the satanic menace appeared in the mass media: in television talk shows and even in a two-hour prime-time Geraldo Rivera documentary broadcast by NBC in 1989; in countless programs on religious radio and television stations; and in numerous popular nonfiction books from both secular and religious publishing houses (Johnston 1989; Larson 1989; Noblitt and Perskin 1995). Police and other professionals could attend training seminars warning about the blood cult and offering advice on detecting signs of satanism and investigating "occult crimes" (Hicks 1991a, 1991b). Therapists helped "survivors" recover their memories of satanic ritual abuse, and legislatures passed laws prohibiting occult crimes or extending the statute of limitations in cases involving recovered memories.

In addition to the attractions of studying an attention-grabbing topic, there were two important analytical advantages to studying the social construction of satanism. First, satanism could be viewed as a case of pure social construction, of claims that had no connection to objective social conditions. There is, very simply, no convincing evidence that a million-member satanic blood cult ever existed. Although there were a handful of homicides by disaffected teenagers who professed an interest in satanism, law enforcement officials found no evidence of a single case of human sacrifice, let alone 60,000 cases per year. Although therapists guided hundreds of individuals in recovering memories of childhood satanic ritual abuse, most psychologists became skeptical of the reliability of recovered memories. In some cases, survivors' accounts were demonstrably wrong. Although it is, of course, impossible to prove the negative proposition that a blood cult does not exist, the satanic menace stands as a social problem constructed from minimal evidence.

Constructionist analysts have long had a fondness for such cases, because they lay bare the process of social construction. By describing the emergence of a social problem constructed from thin air, analysts can argue for the importance of social construction (Best 2000). Traditional sociologists sometimes rejected constructionism by saying, in effect, that people worry about crime and other social problems because they are real problems, not because someone makes claims about them. But, constructionists could respond that an unsubstantiated problem like satanism demonstrates that concern can be aroused in the absence of any real problem. Such cases make objective conditions seem irrelevant, unnecessary for those making social problems claims. Hence, claims about satanism attracted numerous constructionist analysts.[3]

The second analytical advantage lay in the history of claims about satanism: it was possible to date when the problem emerged. Most social problems have somewhat murky histories; we may suspect that child abuse has occurred throughout human history but, precisely because people long took the exploitation of children for granted and did not consider it problematic, we lack detailed historical information about the extent and nature of child abuse. In contrast, the recent concern with satanism had its roots in the publication of one, originally obscure book. *Michelle Remembers* (Pazder and Smith 1980) described a woman who, in the course of psychiatric treatment, recovered memories of childhood abuse in a satanic cult. Gradually, knowledge of this book spread via talk shows and evangelists; additional accounts appeared that elaborated on the blood-cult theme. By the late 1980s, the belief was fairly widespread and had been articulated in some detail: there was a huge, completely secret conspiracy of satanists— often including powerful individuals in the local community who could help conceal the cult's existence—who held rituals featuring human sacrifice, child sexual abuse, and other terrible elements. By the mid-1990s, concern with the blood cult had peaked: journalists and social scientists began calling the mainstream media's attention to the moral panic over satanism; skeptics debunked various claims about satanism; and, because no evidence that could withstand close inspection came to light, fears about the satanic menace began to fade (Lanning 1989; Loftus and Ketcham 1994; Nathan and Snedeker 1995; Ofshe and Watters 1994; Richardson et al. 1991).

This concern with satanism was not confined to the United States. Researchers reported that the blood-cult story also aroused concern in other countries (Victor 1998). In other English-speaking countries, such as Canada (Lippert 1990), Great Britain (Jenkins 1992; La Fontaine 1998), and Australia (Richardson 1997), claimsmakers warned about a large conspiracy involved in ritualized sexual abuse. Similar claims appeared in other countries, such as the Netherlands (Rossen 1990) and Norway (Dyrendal 1998).

The spreading fears of satanism—fears, remember, unsupported by convincing evidence—raise interesting questions. How and why did this somewhat peculiar concern spread across international boundaries? Traditional sociological explanations for such phenomena (e.g., the prosecution of witches in various European countries) use terms that emphasize irrationality—collective delusion, hysterical contagion, craze, and the like (e.g., Ben-Yehuda 1980). But discounting the problem's spread as irrational ignores parallel processes. At roughly the same time that Americans exported concern with satanism, they also exported concerns about child sexual abuse. Just as Americans experienced a wave of heightened concern with sexual abuse in the 1980s, so did other countries (e.g., Jenkins 1992). Of course, we are less likely to see this as remarkable, let alone irrational. The problem of sexual abuse is widely understood to be real, serious, and commonplace; unlike the case of satanism, there is plentiful evidence that many children experience sexual abuse, and there is reason to presume that such abuse occurs in many—if not all—societies. So we find nothing remarkable in concern about sexual abuse spreading to many countries at roughly the same time.

Once again, we see the analytical advantage of studying the satanism problem. Because we know when this particular construction of the satanic menace took shape,[4] and because we know there is no evidence that an actual blood cult existed, it is particularly easy to trace the spread or diffusion of this social problem. Several social scientists have sought to explain how and why satanism arrived in Great Britain. The differences in their accounts of this process suggest some key questions about the diffusion of social problems.

Spreading Satanism to Britain

Philip Jenkins' (1992) book, *Intimate Enemies*, examines moral panics in 1980s Britain over sex killings, serial murder, pedophilia, missing children, and child abuse, as well as satanism. This is a striking list, because most of these topics also rose to considerable prominence in the United States during the same period (Best 1990). What accounts for these similar concerns in two nations an ocean apart? Jenkins notes several circumstances that facilitated diffusion. In the background were social, economic, demographic, and technological developments that, for example, fostered "idealist movements mainly composed of young people, with wide-ranging agendas for social reform" (p. 226). To the degree that different societies experienced similar trends, they might be susceptible to similar constructions of social problems. Important, too, was shared culture. In particular, Britain, the United States, and other English-speaking nations share a common language, making it relatively easy for information—ranging from popular culture (such as fiction, film, and popular songs) to news reports to academic studies—to spread across national boundaries. Finally, diffusion is facilitated by international social networks: British police had contact with American police; British feminists had connections to American feminists; and so on. Most of the major players in the construction of American social problems—social movement activists, government officials, the reporters, editors, and producers of mass media, and the various academic and professional experts—not only had counterparts in Britain, but they were in contact with those counterparts. In the case of satanism, several American advocates visited Britain and, in workshops, press interviews, and other venues, outlined how the problem was being constructed in the United States.

Yet, Jenkins notes, there are important obstacles to the diffusion of social problems from the United States to the United Kingdom. There is xenophobia: "Britain has long demonstrated an ambiguous attitude to America and its culture, and the admiration is tempered by fears of being 'swamped' by this alien presence" (p. 224). In addition, there are institutional differences: Britain has centralized, relatively homogeneous policing, where America's police are decentralized, making it far easier for a local agency to adopt a particular, peculiar concern; and Britain has fewer electoral offices and stronger party discipline, so that Americans find it easier to run for office on their records as moral entrepreneurs. The imitation or absorption of American social problems claims is by no means automatic. Although the British adopted claims about satanic ritual abuse:

> This example suggests that American concerns would be accepted and "naturalized" in Britain only if they struck a chord among a significant sector of British society. In most cases, there had to be some British interest group already organized over a particular issue . . . before it sought out an American "expert" to shape its campaign. The American influence might be found in the rhetoric and emphases of a British movement, but it could rarely initiate them altogether. (p. 225).

Victor (1998:557–58) offers a similar model. He characterizes satanism as a "moral panic," and argues that the diffusion of moral panics depends upon cultural similarities (particularly "ideologies containing the same demonologies") and social networks (especially "the existence of similar occupations"). He argues that, absent these parallels, diffusion is less likely:

> In France, SRA [satantic ritual abuse] accusations being made in American society and nearby England are regarded with ridicule, if they are known at

all. Journalists and popular writers are often quite critical of the foibles of American culture and often resistant to what they consider to be cultural fads coming from America. . . . Fundamentalist Protestantism has no political significance. French feminism, which centers its demonology upon a critique of the capitalist elite and socioeconomic injustice, is ideologically quite different from Anglo-American feminism. It is likely that cross-national, personal contacts between people in the same occupations, such as medical doctors, psychotherapists and police, are relatively uncommon, due in part to language and cultural differences.

In contrast, the British anthropologist J. S. La Fontaine (1998) argues that both people making claims about satanism and academic analysts tended to gloss over important differences in various constructions of the satanism problem. For claimsmakers, charging that many different victims made essentially the same reports about satanists' activities was powerful evidence that the reports must be true. In fact, La Fontaine notes, there were significant differences among claims: for instance, many American claims involved upper-middle class parents charging that their young, preschool-age children had been subjected to ritual abuse by satanists working in the children's day-care centers; in Britain, by contrast, it was more often social workers charging that lower-class parents were satanists who abused their own adolescent children; that is, the people making the charges, the alleged offenders, and the alleged victims were quite different in the claims made in the two countries. La Fontaine also criticizes analysts who failed to acknowledge that the evolution of the satanism problem in Britain involved three distinct stages: "the initial phase, in which religious activists are dominant and American influence most visible, a second period during which cases involving children are exposed and there is the greatest media interest and public controversy, focusing on social work and, finally, a third phase in which the victims are mainly adults and the public leadership has been taken over by members of the therapeutic professions" (p. 162). In her view, diffusion is not irrelevant: "Since historically the allegations began in the United States, it could also be said that their spread has reflected the dominant role of the United States in an international culture whose medium is English" (p. 12). Still, American claims "probably should be regarded as a precipitating factor, rather than a cause, of the British epidemic" (p. 19); that is, the diffusion of satanism claims depended upon the existence of compatible beliefs about the occult, satanists, and so on in Britain (cf. Ellis 1993). Once claims about satanism had a foothold in Britain, the problem evolved in directions different from those taken in the United States.

Satanism, then, offers an interesting case for beginning to think about the international diffusion of social problems claims. Several analysts have noted the spread of satanism concerns from the United States to the U.K.

They agree that cultural similarities and social networks play a part in this process, but they also agree that these are not sufficient, that claims must somehow "strike a chord" if they are to spread.

SOCIAL PROBLEMS AND STUDIES OF DIFFUSION

Diffusion refers to the process by which things spread among people. Social scientists usually characterize diffusion as involving four elements: (1) the people with whom diffusion originates—variously called sources, emitters, transmitters, and so on; (2) something—practices, information, material objects, or whatever—that is diffused; (3) people who adopt whatever that something is—called adopters, recipients, and so on; and (4) the means by which diffusion occurs—often referred to as channels, linkages, or networks (Lopes and Durfee 1999; Rogers 1995; Strang and Meyer 1993; Strang and Soule 1998). Diffusion, then, involves the spread of some innovation from transmitters to adopters via particular channels. This is a central process for understanding social change, and social scientists from a range of disciplines have published many hundreds of studies of diffusion. These studies focus on qualities of transmitters (e.g., what sorts of people are most effective in promoting diffusion?) and adopters (e.g., what sorts of people are most likely to accept—or resist—diffusion?), on the characteristics of whatever is being diffused (e.g., what sorts of innovations are more—or less—likely to spread?), and on the channels (e.g., what conditions foster or discourage diffusion?).

For constructionists, some of these questions may seem more interesting than others, but all have some relevance to the sociology of social problems.[5] All claimsmaking is a form of diffusion, in which claimsmakers (transmitters) try to persuade audiences (adopters) by making claims (via channels) about social problems (the object of diffusion). We tend to take this process for granted when examining the spread of claims in a particular society; however, spreading claims across national boundaries pose special problems.

Claims

Consider the claims—the object of diffusion. A social problem claim is basically an argument with four elements: (a) that some condition exists; (b) that it is problematic (i.e., that it is troubling and ought to be addressed); (c) that it has particular characteristics (e.g., that it is common, has known causes or serious consequences, or is a problem of a particular type); and (d) that some sort of action should be taken to deal with it. Successful diffusion of a claim would seem to require the transmission of all four elements. The first two are relatively straightforward. Certainly diffusion requires accepting the notion that the condition exists; a society whose members doubt the existence of some condition is unlikely to be receptive to claims about that problem (again, witchcraft offers an example with analytic leverage—being worried about witches requires believing in witches). Similarly, the condition must be seen as problematic: a society with a traditional aristocracy might view a decline in deference as troubling, but their claims will have little appeal to members of a democratic society, who might acknowledge the existence of the condition, but view it as a cause for celebration, rather than concern.

These first two elements highlight the importance of the societies to which claims might spread. Diffusion depends on the prospective adopters having cultures and social structures such that they can recognize that their society has the condition about which claims are being made, and their agreeing that that condition is problematic. Social-problems claims are unlikely to take root in societies very different from those in which claims originate. In particular, diffusion requires that adopters view their society as similar to the society where the claims originated: "the cultural understanding that social entities belong to a common social category constructs a tie between them. . . . Where actors are seen as falling into the same category, diffusion should be rapid" (Strang and Meyer 1993:490). When similarities are harder to recognize, diffusion becomes less likely.

The third element in all claims involves the claimsmakers arguing that the problem in question has particular characteristics. For example, they might characterize compulsive gambling as widespread, a disease or addiction, affecting people throughout the society, having serious consequences for the gamblers, their families, and the larger society, and so on. Often, a social problem may attract diverse claimsmakers who, while generally allied in their concern about the problem, disagree about the details of these characteristics. Such disagreements are especially likely as campaigns gather momentum. Imagine a lone claimsmaker who seeks to draw attention to some new problem. To the degree that this individual is successful, allies join the crusade. The more people join, the more we can anticipate differences in their claims. This will be particularly true when campaigns seek to enlist support in different sectors of society—within the media and government, among other activists and experts. These others may enlist in the crusade, but they bring their own interests and their own perspectives; when they add their voices to the claimsmaking, their messages are likely to feature subtle—or not so subtle—differences. Because most claims identify multiple—and sometimes contradictory—characteristics of problems, the diffusion of this third element tends to be forgiving. Adopters must accept the ideas that a condition exists, and that it is problematic, but they can, to some degree, pick and choose among the available characteristics presented in various claims, adopting some and ignoring others.

There is analogous flexibility in adopting the fourth element—calls to action. Just as claimsmakers may not agree about all of a problem's characteristics, they may advocate various actions. Many social movements include both moderates who call for minor reforms to address the problem, and extremists who demand more drastic changes (Benford 1993; Mann 2000). Diffusion requires adopting some calls for action, but the adopters can often choose among a variety of proposals. In short, social problems claimsmakers do not always speak with one voice. The effort to bring a problem to public attention often involves a debate or struggle over just how the problem (and its solutions) ought to be defined.

How do these differences within claims about problems' characteristics and their solutions affect diffusion? Too many differences threaten to make claims seem confusing, incoherent, contentious. Claims spread more easily when this cacophony can be simplified. Strang and Meyer (1993:492) argue that theorization—"the self-conscious development and specification of abstract categories and the formulation of patterned relationships such as chains of cause and effect"—aids diffusion. Theorization abstracts and simplifies. In the case of social-problems claims, theorization smoothes out the argument. It reduces specifics of limited, local relevance, and rephrases the claim in terms that make it more widely acceptable. The theoretical becomes significant, the practical less important: "actual practices are interpreted as partial, flawed, or corrupt implementations of theorized ones" (Strang and Meyer 1993:499). Thus, a theoretized claim is more easily spread to new societies, where it can be reformulated to take local culture and social structure into account.

Channels for Transmitting Claims

Diffusion must occur through channels. Theorists of diffusion make an analytic distinction between relational channels involving "direct, interpersonal contact between transmitters and adopters," and nonrelational channels, such as mass media, that do not involve personal ties (McAdam and Rucht 1993:59). A related distinction is between broadcast models of diffusion from an external source into a population, and contagion models involving diffusion from internal sources spreading within a population (Strang and Soule 1998:270). In practice, of course, most cross-national diffusion combines both relational and nonrelational channels, and both broadcast and contagion processes. Through informal ties (such as acquaintanceship) and more formal ties (such as membership in the same organizations), people in different countries know one another enough to establish relational channels: this one got to know people while attending school abroad; these met at international conferences for police officers, or social workers, or whatever. At the same time, information about social problems flows through nonrelational channels, through the press and entertainment media, through books and news broadcasts and the Internet. Relational and nonrelational channels are mutually reinforcing.

Diffusion researchers argue that a variety of conditions foster diffusion (Strang and Soule 1998). In general, the mass media and "change agents" (who deliberately seek to foster diffusion) play key roles in broadcast models. Contagion models, by contrast, argue that close social relationships (strong ties) foster diffusion within cohesive populations, but that weak ties enable diffusion to spread broadly across diverse populations, that structurally equivalent actors perceive themselves as competitors and therefore quickly copy one another, but that actors also emulate those they consider to have more prestige, and that spacial proximity encourages all sorts of diffusion. All of these considerations shape the channels through which diffusion flows.[6]

Transmitters and Adopters

While the nature of the available channels affects the ease with which social problems claims can spread, all diffusion ultimately depends on the actors in the process—the transmitters and, especially, the adopters. Transmitters may—but need not—make deliberate efforts to disseminate social-problems claims to other countries. Drawing attention to problematic conditions is of course central to social problems claimsmaking, and some claimsmakers explicitly seek to spread their message to other nations. This is particularly true with claims about large-scale, even global problems, such as population growth, ecological degradation, nuclear proliferation, and economic globalization.[7] Such claimsmakers become missionaries, seeking to spread their message abroad, either through relational or nonrelational channels. But other transmitters are more passive; their focus is domestic, even localized. Still, their claims may reach other countries, particularly via such nonrelational channels as media coverage, professional publications, and the like.[8]

While claims, channels, and transmitters are all necessary, the key actors in diffusion are adopters. Prospective adopters must engage in some "social construction of similarity," that is, defining conditions in their society as sufficiently like those depicted in the transmitters' claims: "All instances of diffusion depend on a minimal identification of adopter with transmitter" (McAdam and Rucht 1993:60). Claimsmakers sometimes take it for granted that their claims will gain acceptance; they often see themselves as purveying new knowledge, correcting the neglect or prior, erroneous interpretations of social conditions. But adopters must do their own social-problems work (Holstein and Miller 1993; Snow and Benford 1999); they must recognize the relevance of foreign claims, acknowledging parallels between the claimsmakers' society and their own.

Incorporating Diffusion Concepts in the Sociology of Social Problems

The literature on diffusion, then, offers an array of concepts that can be applied to analyses of social problems construction. Earlier, we noted that analysts such as Jenkins (1992), Victor (1998), and La Fontaine (1998) had examined how claims about satanism spread from the United States to Great Britain. If we apply some of the terminology used in diffusion research, we see that, for the most part, their explanations tended to focus on the channels that made diffusion possible: recent social changes, common language, and networks of contacts (Jenkins), shared ideologies (Victor), and compatible beliefs (La Fontaine). (Diffusion theorists might argue that several of these elements (e.g., social changes, ideologies, and beliefs) also may have affected prospective adopters' readiness to define Britain as similar to the United States. Although all three analysts emphasize the roles American antisatanists played in visiting Britain and spreading their message (a fairly clear example of transmitters actively establishing or exploiting relational channels to disseminate claims), La Fontaine warns that the Americans' message was not simply adopted, but had to be reworked to fit British culture and social structure (i.e., La Fontaine offers evidence that theorization—the transmission of a relatively abstract, simplified version of antisatanist claims—was necessary for the process to succeed).

This example suggests that concepts from the diffusion literature can indeed enrich discussions of the social construction of social problems. Sociologists of social problems need to recognize that spreading claims demands explanation, that this process is not simply natural, routine, or inevitable. Many claims fail to spread. Perhaps they never come to the attention of prospective adopters, through some combination of a lack of activity by potential transmitters, or insufficient channels for diffusion. Or perhaps the claims are known but not adopted, because prospective adopters deny that their society resembles the transmitters'. And, of course, other claims are picked up in some—but rarely in all—societies that might adopt them. These processes demand explanation. The chapters in this volume begin this task.

PLAN OF THE BOOK

The chapters examine cases of the diffusion of claims about social problems and social policy. The first set of studies deals with the diffusion of social problems between the United States and some other country. Thus,

Sacco and Ismaili consider the conditions that foster—or discourage—the diffusion of social problems between Canada and the United States; sharing a common border and (at least with most of Canada) a common language, the channels for communication between these two countries are extensive, yet not all claims originating in the United States spread to Canada, and Canadian claims have modest success in the United States.

The next four chapters concern diffusion between the United States and Great Britain; interestingly, none of these case studies describes simple, straightforward diffusion from the United States to the U.K.. Lee traces antiabortion activists' efforts to spread claims about "postabortion syndrome" (i.e., arguing that women who have abortions suffer enduring psychological trauma) from the United States to the U.K., and shows how abortion's place within British law and medicine made diffusion of these claims difficult. In contrast, Lilly's chapter suggests that blaming notorious episodes of gun violence on American influences (i.e., claiming that an American-induced problem was contaminating Britain) made it easier for the British to enact stiff gun-control measures. Furedi shows how and why the problem of workplace bullying rose to considerable prominence in Britain, yet efforts to spread these claims to the United States have had only modest success. Finally, Best and Furedi review the curious history of road rage claims, which spread to the United States without acknowledgment of their British origin. In the last chapter in this cluster, Suzuki examines diffusion between the United States and Japan; he argues that recent Japanese constructions of pornography as a social problem combine rhetoric originating in both nations.

Of course, diffusion need not be limited to exchanges between only two nations. Three chapters consider cases of diffusion spreading across several countries. Jenkins shows how American concerns about sexual violence, and particularly child sexual abuse, raised alarm and inspired tougher penalties throughout much of Western Europe; this diffusion was facilitated by the declining importance of national boundaries. Similarly, Bennett sketches how young people's musical subcultures have become an important channel for constructing "risk" lifestyles and other social problems throughout Western Europe. Finally, the folklorist Campion Vincent compares the transmission of three implausible stories about the theft of human organs; this complex story shows claims flowing among—and occasionally being taken very seriously—in countries on six continents.

A final cluster of chapters emphasizes the role of diffusion in shaping social policy. Ayukawa describes how the Japanese government's vested interests in the tobacco trade (and U.S. efforts to open Japan to exports of U.S. tobacco) limit efforts to reduce smoking in Japan. Cahill explains why the U.S. government's policies toward sexual harassment not only helped define the need for a policy, but supplied the framework for Austria's sexual-harassment law. Watkins and Best try to understand why the United States continues to resist adopting the metric system of measurement (and how Canada changed measurement systems with relatively little difficulty). Finally, Pösö considers how Finland's definition of child protection as a problem of families and social welfare leads to a focus on parents, and relative disinterest in the children themselves.

These case studies describe very different processes, ranging from very deliberate attempts to disseminate social problems claims, to developments that were more inadvertent, from successes in which social problems constructions spread to new countries, to failures in which claims were sown, but failed to take root. They are intended to suggest that the diffusion of social problems is neither simple nor automatic. Ideally, these studies will encourage other analysts to incorporate diffusion into their research.

NOTES

1.   Certainly this was long the case. However, the advent of the Internet, full-text databases (such as NEXIS), and other forms for storing and retrieving electronic information is changing the ways researchers can study claims.

2.   Virtually all of the English-language constructionist studies that have come to my attention examine industrial countries—the United States, Canada, Australia, Japan, or Western Europe. I suspect that the perspective's appeal is relatively limited elsewhere; in Third World countries, for example, troubling social conditions are likely to command analysts' attention, while focusing on claims must seem to be an academic luxury.

3.   Rains (1975:6) offered a similar explanation for labeling theorists' fondness for using witchcraft as an example of deviance:

Witches have become interesting again not because of their renewed claim to existence in certain circles, but precisely because their claim to existence has been so thoroughly discredited. They stand now as the pure case of unwarranted imputation, the kind of ideal case in which *no actual* deviance is involved. The appeal of this subject matter clearly lies in the degree to which "actual" deviance can be portrayed as irrelevant *because* it is *actually* nonexistent. (emphasis in original)

4.   Of course, there had been earlier warnings about satanism (e.g., some claims in the 1960s linked satanic worship and drug use). But the constellation of beliefs that emerged in the 1980s, following the publication of *Michelle Remembers,* centered around a distinctive set of claims, involving ritual abuse in particular, but also heavy metal music, fantasy role-playing games, and so on.

5.   Although constructionist case studies sometimes examine the process of diffusion (e.g., Best 1999; Jenkins 1992), the topic has not received much systematic attention from sociologists of social problems. In contrast, scholars in the related area of social movements have begun developing theories to explain the cross-national

diffusion of social movements (McAdam and Rucht 1993; Snow and Benford 1999). Of course, many historical social movements, including democratization, antislavery, temperance, social purity, and women's rights, featured overt efforts to spread reform ideas among nations. Once again, historical cases offer opportunities to test sociological theories.

6. In *Random Violence* (Best 1999), I argued that the diffusion of social problems within the United States tends to flow from a core of major media centers (such as New York, Los Angeles, or Washington) to smaller communities on the periphery. An analogous process sometimes shapes cross-national diffusion, but assertions about the power of America's media hegemony predict more diffusion of social problems claims than actually occurs.

7. Consider the (generally nonconstructionist) recent calls for sociologists of social problems to concentrate on issues of global significance (e.g., Glynn, Hohm, and Glenn 1997; Mazur 1991).

8. Snow and Benford (1999) develop a typology of social-movement diffusion based on both transmitters and adopters being either active or passive. They refer to diffusion involving passive transmitters and active adopters as *adaptation*.

REFERENCES

Adler, Jeffrey S. 1996. "The Making of a Moral Panic in 19th-Century America: The Boston Garroting Hysteria of 1865." *Deviant Behavior* 17:259–78.

Ayukawa, Jun. 1995. "The Construction of Juvenile Delinquency as a Social Problem in Post World War II Japan." *Perspectives on Social Problems* 7:311–29.

Bammer, Gabriele, and Brian Martin. 1992. "Repetition Strain Injury in Australia: Medical Knowledge, Social Movement, and De Facto Partisanship." *Social Problems* 39:219–37.

Benford, Robert D. 1993. "Frame Disputes within the Nuclear Disarmament Movement." *Social Forces* 71:677–701.

Ben-Yehuda, Nachman. 1980. "The European Witch Craze of the 14th to 17th Centuries." *American Journal of Sociology* 86:1–31.

Best, Joel. 1990. *Threatened Children: Rhetoric and Concern about Child-Victims.* Chicago: University of Chicago Press.

———. 1991. "'Road Warriors' on 'Hair-Trigger Highways': Cultural Resources and the Media's Construction of the 1987 Freeway Shootings Problem," *Sociological Inquiry* 61:327–45.

———. 1999. *Random Violence: How We Talk about New Crimes and New Victims.* Berkeley: University of California Press.

———. 2000. "The Apparently Innocuous 'Just,' the Law of Levity, and the Social Problems of Social Construction." *Perspectives on Social Problems* 12:3–14.

Blumer, Herbert. 1971. "Social Problems as Collective Behavior." *Social Problems* 18:298–306.

Croucher, S. L. 1997. "Constructing the Image of Ethnic Harmony in Toronto, Canada." *Urban Affairs Review* 32: 319–47.

Dyrendal, Asbjorn. 1998. "Media Constructions of 'Satanism' in Norway." *FOAF-Tale News* 43:2–5.

Ellis, Bill. 1993. "The Highgate Cemetery Vampire Hunt: The Anglo-American Connection in Satanic Cult Lore." *Folklore* 104:13–39.

Fine. Gary Alan. 1997. "Scandal, Social Conditions, and the Creation of Public Attention: Fatty Arbuckle and the 'Problem of Hollywood.'" *Social Problems* 44:297–323.

———, and Lazaros Christoforides. 1991. "Dirty Birds, Filthy Immigrants, and the English Sparrow War: Metaphorical Linkage in Constructing Social Problems." *Symbolic Interaction* 14:375–93.

Fishman, Mark. 1978. "Crimes Waves as Ideology." *Social Problems* 25:531–43.

Furedi, Frank. 1997. *Culture of Fear.* New York: Cassell.

Glynn, James A., Charles F. Hohm, and James A. Glenn. 1997. *Global Social Problems.* Reading, MA: Addison Wesley Longman.

Harbison, Joan. 1999. "The Changing Career of 'Elder Abuse and Neglect' as a Social Problem in Canada." *Journal of Elder Abuse and Neglect* 11 (4):59–80.

Hicks, Robert D. 1991a. "The Police Model of Satanic Crime." Pp. 175–89 in *The Satanism Scare,* edited by James T. Richardson, Joel Best, and David G. Bromley. Hawthorne, NY: Aldine de Gruyter.

———. 1991b. *In Pursuit of Satan: The Police and the Occult.* Buffalo, NY: Prometheus.

Hilgartner, Stephen, and Charles L. Bosk. 1988. "The Rise and Fall of Social Problems." *American Journal of Sociology* 94:53–78.

Holstein, James A., and Gale Miller. 1993. "Constructionism and Social Problems Work." Pp. 131–52 in *Constructionist Controversies,* edited by Gale Miller and James A. Holstein. Hawthorne, NY: Adline de Gruyter.

Jenkins, Philip. 1992. *Intimate Enemies: Moral Panics in Contemporary Great Britain.* Hawthorne, NY: Aldine de Gruyter.

———. 1998. *Moral Panic: Changing Concepts of the Child Molester in Modern America.* New Haven: Yale University Press.

———. 1999. *Synthetic Panics: The Symbolic Politics of Designer Drugs.* New York: New York University Press.

Johnston, Jerry. 1989. *The Edge of Evil: The Rise of Satanism in North America.* Dallas: Word.

Kitsuse, John I., Anne E. Murase, and Yoshiaki Yamamura. 1984. "Kikokushijo: The Emergence and Institutionalization of an Educational Problem in Japan." Pp. 162–79 in *Studies in the Sociology of Social Problems,* edited by Joseph W. Schneider and John I. Kitsuse. Norwood, NJ: Ablex.

La Fontaine, J. S. 1998. *Speak of the Devil: Tales of Satanic Abuse in Contemporary England.* New York: Cambridge University Press.

Lanning, Kenneth V. 1989. "Satanic, Occult, Ritualistic Crime." *Police Chief* 56 (10): 62–83.

Larson, Bob. 1989. *Satanism: The Seduction of America's Youth.* Nashville: Thomas Nelson.

Lippert, R. 1990. "The Social Construction of Satanism as a Social Problem in Canada." *Canadian Journal of Sociology* 15:417–39.

Loftus, Elizabeth, and Katherine Ketcham. 1994. *The Myth of Repressed Memory: False Memories and Allegations of Sexual Abuse.* New York: St. Martin's.

Lopes, Paul, and Mary Durfee, eds. 1999. "The Social Diffusion of Ideas and Things." *Annals of the American Academy of Political and Social Science* 566:1–155.

Loseke, Donileen R. 1997. "'The Whole Spirit of Modern Philanthropy': The Construction of the Idea of Charity, 1912–1992." *Social Problems* 44:425–44.

———. 1999. *Thinking about Social Problems*. Hawthorne, NY: Aldine de Gruyter.

Mann, Ruth M. 2000. *Who Owns Domestic Abuse? The Local Politics of a Social Problem*. Toronto: University of Toronto Press.

Margolin, Leslie. 1994. *Goodness Personified: The Emergence of Gifted Children*. Hawthorne, NY: Aldine de Gruyter.

Mazur, Allan. 1991. *Global Social Problems*. Englewood Cliffs, NJ: Prentice-Hall.

McAdam, Doug, and Dieter Rucht. 1993. "The Cross-National Diffusion of Movement Ideas." *Annals of the American Academy of Political and Social Science* 528: 56–74.

Nathan, Debbie, and Michael Snedeker. 1995. *Satan's Silence: Ritual Abuse and the Making of a Modern American Witch Hunt*. New York: Basic Books.

Neuman, W. Lawrence. 1998. "Negotiated Meanings and State Transformation: The Trust Issue in the Progressive Era." *Social Problems* 45:315–35.

Noblitt, James Randall, and Pamela Sue Perskin. 1995. *Cult and Ritual Abuse*. Westport, CT: Praeger.

Ofshe, Richard, and Ethan Watters. 1994. *Making Monsters: False Memories, Psychotherapy, and Sexual Hysteria*. New York: Scribner's.

Pazder, Laurence, and Michelle Smith. 1980. *Michelle Remembers*. New York: Congdon and Lattes.

Rafter, Nicole H. 1992. "Claims-Making and Socio-Cultural Context in the First Eugenics Campaign." *Social Problems* 39:17–34.

Rains, Prudence. 1975. "Imputations of Deviance: A Retrospective Essay on the Labeling Perspective." *Social Problems* 23:1–11.

Richardson, James T. 1997. "The Social Construction of Satanism: Understanding an International Social Problem." *Australian Journal of Social Issues* 32:61–85.

———, Joel Best, and David G. Bromley, eds. 1991. *The Satanism Scare*. Hawthorne, NY: Aldine de Gruyter.

Rogers, Everett M. 1995. *Diffusion of Innovations*, 4th ed. New York: Free Press.

Ross, H. Laurence. 1989. "Lost and Found: The Drunk-Driving Problem in Finland." Pp. 177–88 in *Images of Issues*, edited by Joel Best. Hawthorne, NY: Aldine de Gruyter.

Rossen, Benjamin. 1990. "Moral Panic: The Story of Oude Pekela." (unpublished English translation of Dutch original)

Schneider, Joseph W. 1985. "Social Problems Theory: The Constructionist View." *Annual Review of Sociology* 11:209–29.

Simpura, Jussi, and Galina Eremitcheva. 1997. "Dirt: Symbolic and Practical Dimensions of Social Problems in St. Petersburg." *International Journal of Urban and Regional Research* 21:467–79.

Snow, David A., and Robert D. Benford. 1999. "Alternative Types of Cross-national Diffusion in the Social Movement Arena." Pp. 23–39 in *Social Movements in a Globalizing World*, edited by Donatella della Porta, Hanspeter Kriesi, and Dieter Rucht. New York: St. Martin's.

Spector, Malcolm, and John I. Kitsuse. 1977. *Constructing Social Problems*. Menlo Park, CA: Cummings.

Strang, David, and John W. Meyer. 1993. "Institutional Conditions for Diffusion." *Theory and Society* 22:487–511.

Strang, David, and Sarah A. Soule. 1998. "Diffusion in Organizations and Social Movements: From Hybrid Corn to Poison Pills." *Annual Review of Sociology* 24:265–90.

Thompson, Bill. 1994. *Soft Core.* London: Cassell.

Trent, James W., Jr. 1995. *Inventing the Feeble Mind: A History of Mental Retardation in the United States.* Berkeley: University of California Press.

Victor, Jeffrey S. 1998. "Moral Panics and the Social Construction of Deviant Behavior: A Theory and Application to the Case of Ritual Child Abuse." *Sociological Perspectives* 41:541–65.

Yamazaki, Atsushi. 1994. "The Medicalization and Demedicalization of School Refusal: Constructing an Educational Problem in Japan." Pp. 201–17 in *Troubling Children: Studies of Children and Social Problems,* edited by Joel Best. Hawthorne, NY: Aldine de Gruyter.

2

Social Problems Claims
and the Undefended Border
The Case of Canada and the United States

VINCENT F. SACCO and KARIM ISMAILI

Canadian social-problems texts and courses present their students with an array of issues that would be familiar to scholars teaching similar courses in the United States. Crime, addictions, race, and mental illness are typically among the assortment of social problems to which Canadian undergraduate students can expect to be exposed (Gomme 1998; Nelson and Fleras 1995; Synnott 1996). Other indicators suggest that both professionals and laypeople in Canada share with their American counterparts common views of what are or what are not considered the social problems that require attention. In the former respect, public opinion polls consistently reveal that despite their lower crime rates, Canadians, like Americans, continue to think about crime as among the more serious social issues in Canadian society (Ouimet 1999; Roberts 1997). Constructionist analysts in Canada have shown how problems such as satanism (Lippert 1990) and elder abuse (Leroux and Petrunik 1990) have emerged from claimsmaking processes remarkably similar to those that have been documented by scholars working south of the border.

How are the similarities between Canadians and Americans regarding what constitutes (and by implication, what does not constitute) a social problem to be explained? To what degree do these similarities reflect a diffusion of social problems claims between countries that seem, at least on the surface, to share so much in common?

THE MEANING OF DIFFUSION

The diffusion of cultural elements, including social problems, involves the spread or movement of those elements from one social setting to another (Strang and Soule 1998). For McAdam and Rucht (1993), diffusion involves four elements: (1) a person, group or organization that is the emitter; (2) a person, group or organization that is the adopter; (3) the item that is diffused, such as material goods, information, skills, and the like; and (4) a channel of diffusion that may consist of persons or media that link the transmitter and the adopter. Despite its apparent simplicity, the process by which social problems diffuse is complicated and subject to a variety of interpretations. Several relevant complexities may be identified.

First, while our principal concern in this chapter is the flow of social-problems claims, diffusion processes may also involve a flow of the conditions or behaviors about which problem claims are made. Thus, Fischer (1980) has postulated that violent criminal behavior is characterized by urban-to-rural diffusion. More recently, Best (1999) has argued that behaviors, fashions, and patterns of speech associated with Los Angeles gangs have diffused to other American urban areas and in so doing have become available as evidence of the diffusion of the gangs themselves. Indeed, academic arguments about media-induced violence in the form of "copycat crimes" are arguments about the extent to which problematic behaviors diffuse throughout social systems (Howitt 1998).

In contrast, and more central to present concerns, however, is the spread of social problems ideologies as well as claimsmaking strategies and tactics (Morris 1981; Oberschall 1989; Tarrow 1998). Both news and entertainment media can grant wide exposure to claims about conditions and graphically and dramatically portray the means by which these grievances are expressed (Spilerman 1970).

A second complication concerns the nature of the mechanisms by which the diffusion of social problems occurs. In some cases, diffusion reflects the deliberate efforts on the part of established claimsmakers to proselytize about a particular moral vision of society (Best 1999). In fact, claimsmakers seek a national forum in the form of network news coverage, certification from a daytime talk-show "expert," or the subject of the television docudrama, in large part because the exposure increases the likelihood that others will come to share their moral vision. Newsmakers and talk-show and movie producers cooperate in this process, not because of an intrinsic interest in the grievances being expressed, but because they derive organizational benefit from the exploitation of novelty. The dramatic presentation of novel issues is the lifeblood of much contemporary media (Koopmans 1993).

Although the spread of claimsmaking tactics such as strikes or sit-ins may appear to be a product of contagion, the process need not be conceptualized as irrational (Tarrow 1998). Instead, the spread of such tactics may be viewed as involving the transfer of information that raises awareness, defines occasions for action, or hints at the relative strengths and weaknesses of parties to a definitional conflict (Conell and Cohn 1995). As social-problem constructions diffuse, they provide opportunities for action on the part of "adopters" who are actively engaged in rational decision-making processes (Rogers 1962; Strang and Soule 1998). Thus social-problem constructions do not so much diffuse as they become available for utilization. Viewed in this way, decisions about the adoption of novel social-problem constructions relate to more general questions about the ways in which cultural resources are mobilized in the claimsmaking process (Williams 1995).

The diffusion of social-problems claims across international borders adds yet another level of theoretical and empirical complication. Perhaps most significant in this respect are questions relating to channels of diffusion. McAdam and Rucht (1993) distinguish between "relational" and "nonrelational" models of diffusion. The former model emphasizes the role that direct contact between emitters and adoptees plays in the diffusion process, while the latter focuses attention on more impersonal channels such as the media. McAdam and Rucht (also see Strang and Meyer 1993) suggest that cross-national cultural diffusion is likely to occur in the absence of high levels of direct contact, provided nonrelational channels are available. Thus, to the degree that adopters define themselves as similar to those who originate problem definitions or policy solutions, and to the degree they find such definitions or solutions relevant to their own experiences, cross-national adoption is likely. McAdam and Rucht see both types of channels as important and suggest that direct interpersonal contacts are perhaps most important at the earliest stages of diffusion in that they facilitate the adopters' identification with transmitters.

CANADA AND THE UNITED STATES:
SIMILARITIES AND DIFFERENCES

It has been argued that despite some very notable exceptions—such as the spread of "satanic panic" from the United States to Canada and several European nations—social problems claims do not travel well internationally (Best 1999; Jenkins 1992, Victor 1998). Of course, the cross-national diffusion of such claims is a variable process, its outcome dependent on a range of factors. It should be noted at the outset that our remarks focus primarily on diffusion between English Canada and the United States. The unique linguistic and cultural makeup of Quebec makes it a special case, especially when viewed in the larger context of North America, and we thus will exclude it from this analysis.

Greater cross-national diffusion is expected when nations do not differ markedly with respect to their cultures and languages and when they are in close proximity (Best 1999; Jenkins 1992; McAdam and Rucht 1993; Strang and Soule 1998). English is the language common to the United States and most regions of Canada (with the important exception of Quebec) and more than one-half of the population of Canada lives within 100 miles of the American border (Romanow and Soderlund 1996). This proximity and shared linguistic heritage suggest that claims about social problems should be expected to diffuse rather freely between the two nations, all other things held equal.

Another factor that facilitates cross-national diffusion is Canada's status as one of the most decentralized federations in the world. This decentralization—along with its constitutionally entrenched multiculturalism and official policy of bilingualism—has facilitated the growth of strong regional identities. Indeed, many Canadians identify more strongly with their region than with their nation. This fragmented national identity is significant because of Canada's proximity to the United States, a much larger nation with an extremely strong, assertive national presence. In their study of the diffusion of New Left political movements from the United States to Germany, McAdam and Rucht (1993) argued that German students may have been more receptive to influences from abroad due to "a certain lack of fixed national identity" (p. 71). We contend that the lack of a strong Canadian national identity, which at times manifests itself through the lack of a strong national consensus on social issues, weakens its ability to withstand the diffusion of U.S. social-problem claims.

It is also important to consider differences between Canada and the United States that might serve to militate against diffusion. While equality and achievement are valued in both societies, less emphasis has been placed on this in Canada than in the United States. Lipset argues that this difference reflects Canada's closer links with its European origins that have helped perpetuate an older set of beliefs and more conservative behavior (Lipset 1990:4). One area in which this difference manifests itself is in the role of government. For example, Canadians greatly value the benefits associated with the welfare state, including universal health care, a relatively generous unemployment insurance program, and access to higher education. Despite recent claims that such benefits are unaffordable and place a heavy burden on future generations, movements aimed at rolling back the welfare state have had mixed success. This is at least in part due to the widespread belief that such programs distinguish Canadians from Americans, and that any modification in existing arrangements would lead inexorably to the "Americanization" of Canada. Claims based on the virtues of unbridled free-market liberalism often fail to take root because they are met with vigorous opposition from trade unions. Indeed, the generally strong social democratic tradition that is entrenched in most of Canada represents a significant barrier to the diffusion of many social, economic, and cultural ideas that emanate from the United States.

Also of relevance in this respect are the historical and contemporary differences that exist with respect to patterns of immigration and ethnic stratification. The need in each country to affirm principles of national unity and legitimate cultural diversity has resulted in the employment of competing metaphors (Seiler 1993). While Americans speak of a "melting pot" Canadians prefer the image of a "mosaic." Each approach, it has been argued, is reflective of historical and economic realities unique to Canadian and American processes of nation building. The Canadian approach to ethnicity and immigration is a response to a counterrevolutionary and colonial history combined with the influence of a French Canadian culture and a formidable geography and climate. In comparison, the American revolutionary origins of nationhood and the commitment to individual rights have combined with abundant resources and a milder climate to foster the melting pot ideology. In the former case, the mosaic suggests tradition, stability, and the importance of boundaries, even though it constructs their character as horizontal rather than vertical. In the latter case, the melting pot is an inclusive, optimistic symbol that appears to validate equally diverse cultural expressions. In the American experience, more so than the Canadian one, race has figured prominently in the construction of social problems such as crime, poverty, housing, and drugs. To some degree, this consistent interweaving of ethnic realities and social-problem definition in the American context must be seen to express the ideological emphasis on the connection between individualism, entitlement, and the ideological resistance to a ready acknowledgement of cultural hierarchy.

Another essential difference between Canada and the United States that presents an obstacle to the diffusion of claims is the historical emphasis on the rights and obligations of the community in comparison to the individual. The former is a basic organizing principle of Canadian social life and is perhaps best exemplified by the constitutional commitment to provide "peace, order, and good government." The American stress on "life, liberty, and the pursuit of happiness" implies a greater commitment to individual rights (Lipset 1990:93). Claims diffusing from one country to another are unlikely to be successful if this fundamental difference is ignored or underestimated.

Religious differences between the two nations may also account for variations in the influence of particular claims and claimsmakers. Americans have been described as utopian moralists who "are much more prone to see conflicts as reflecting moral concerns" (Lipset 1990:79). In the United

States, religious activists press hard to institutionalize virtue; social and political dramas are morality plays to destroy evil people, and to eliminate wicked institutions and practices (Lipset 1990:77). Canadians, on the other hand, seem more likely to recognize the permanent imperfection of man, a national trait that "undermines any propensity to take part in a crusade against an immoral enemy" (Lipset 1990:79). The role of religion in civic life thus differs between the two nations. Claims rooted in morality are unlikely to be received in Canada in the same way they are received in the United States.

Despite these obstacles, it is probably the case that some kinds of constructions diffuse northward more easily than others. Problems that are framed in terms of individual-level deviation probably diffuse more easily than do those that speak to elements of the economic or political structure that are unique to the United States. For example, crime problems, which often draw on astructural, individualized accounts of villainy, are more likely to diffuse than are problems framed in terms that emphasize the relevant character of the American political, economic, or legal systems.

However, as Jenkins (1992) pointed out with respect to the British case, and as implied by a model that emphasizes the rational utilization of cultural resources, the process of diffusion is not synonymous with absorption. Differences in electoral practices and political structures will determine not only what gets imported but also how those imported claims are transformed and interpreted (Strang and Soule 1998). In addition, claims are more likely to be accepted when there already exists at least some minimal level of movement organization for problem construction (Oberschall 1989). Jenkins (1992) maintains that while tactics and ideology may be imported, some nascent recognition of the problem must already be in place.

It is also the case that in some circumstances, attempts to apply foreign constructions to Canadian problems are actively resisted. A kind of anti-Americanism and resistance to cultural domination by the United States expresses itself in variety of ways, one of which is to reject the assumption that we share common problems (Cullen et al. 1978; Orchard 1993). As has often been stated, it is sometimes difficult to define Canadian culture, except in opposition to American culture (Romanow and Soderlund 1996). Indeed, an important part of the Canadian identity is to deny actively that some problems (such as "violence," "guns," or "race"), that are seen as distinctly American, are problems in Canada at all. In a similar way Victor (1998) argues that while a moral panic about satanic ritual abuse diffused from the United States to several nations, it was not taken up by the French who are "quite critical of the foibles of American culture and often resistant to what they consider to be cultural fads coming from America" (p. 558).

THE ROLE OF CULTURAL DOMINANCE

Robertson Davies, the Canadian author and literary critic, has observed that "[c]ulture is ambience, a part of the air we breathe" (1989:47). Culture shapes and is shaped. Immune to boundaries, culture diffuses from place to place, mutating as it is exposed to new environments. The influence of culture can be benign, but it is often consequential. The diffusion of a particularly powerful culture can dramatically transform the objects it encounters, whether those objects are individuals, institutions, or societies. The greater the cultural dominance of one nation by another, the more likely the diffusion of social problem claims will be a one-way, rather than a reciprocal process. The domination of Canadian cultural industries by foreign—especially American—interests has been a subject of commentary and concern for decades (Ostry 1993; Portman 1993; Taras 1999; Winter and Goldman 1995).

Rooted in the history and political economy of the two nations, as well as in their geographic nature and demographic structures, this concern has been widely viewed as a rational response to the ever-present threat of Americanization. While evidence of Americanization can be found throughout the western world, it is more plentiful in Canada because contact with the United States is closer and more prolonged (Preston 1972:8). As the Canadian political scientist John Meisel (1989:285) has written:

> [Canadians] share a keen awareness of, interest in, and concern with all things American, that is, with the United States of America. Popular culture, sports, politics, even tourist attractions south of the border are part of the mental map of most Canadians and are frequently as important to us, if not more so, than corresponding indigenous realities. . . . The magnitude and effect of this American presence in us all varies considerably from person to person, but it is ubiquitous and inescapable.

American influences have penetrated virtually every aspect of Canadian life. Given America's greater population, along with its significant military, economic, and international influence, the power relationship between the two nations has been, and continues to be, overwhelmingly one-sided: "In few cases has a foreign neighbour exerted as much of an influence as the United States has exercised on Canada" (Preston 1972:6). Scholars from both nations have argued that this "American presence" has shaped both the articulation and implementation of Canadian public policy, far beyond any impact Canada may have had on the United States (Thompson and Randall 1994:300). And in the era of the North American Free Trade Agreement, differences between Canada and the United States are eroding further under pressures of economic and cultural harmonization (Granatstein 1996:283).

Popular Media

The dominance of American cultural content in the Canadian media marketplace has been extensively documented by Canadian academics (Orchard 1993; Romanow and Soderlund 1996; Winter and Goldman 1995). The images, ideas, and social constructs that permeate American popular culture are easily diffused to Canada through television, print, film, and music, reinforcing the well-grounded fear that Canada's cultural distinctiveness will vanish. It has been estimated that approximately 80 percent of magazines and books on Canadian store shelves are of foreign (principally American) origin. Moreover, foreign content accounts for 96 percent of videos and 85 percent of compact disks sold in Canada and 95 percent of drama on Canadian television. According to Statistics Canada, the national statistical agency, Canadians in 1995 spent almost as much time watching foreign drama and comedy on television as they did watching all forms of Canadian content combined (Gorman and Crompton 1997). To the extent that U.S. social-problems claims are rooted in popular news and entertainment, they are readily available as cultural resources for the construction of similar problems in Canada. Thus, for example, much of the ideological work relating to the construction of the "serial killer" problem in Canada in the 1980s had already been done by American cultural and crime-control industries. Jenkins (1994) found that villains such as Hannibal Lector and atrocity tales about "serial killing sprees" in the United States were as familiar to the average consumer of Canadian media as they were to the American consumer. The use of American news frames by Canadian journalists is extremely common, with one result of this practice being the absorption of Canadian stories into such frames. The shootings at an Alberta high school in 1999 took on an even greater sense of dread than might normally be expected given that they followed closely the Columbine high school shootings in the suburbs of Denver. In a related way, attempts by journalists to find the Canadian angle on major international (i.e., American) stories often results in the "discovery" of similar conditions and dangers in Canadian society.

Also important in this respect is the role of the expert, on whom contemporary news media have become so reliant. As discussed by several writers, journalists make extensive use of "experts" to contextualize news reporting and facilitate conformity to news values regarding balance and objectivity (Best 1999; Tuchman 1978). This reliance sometimes speeds the process by which social-problems claims diffuse across national boundaries. As social problems such as elder abuse, wife assault, and workplace violence emerged in the United States, an infrastructure consisting of experts, critics, and celebrity spokespeople quickly developed. Because a similar infrastructure did not exist in Canada at these earliest points of problem formulation, journalists sought the opinions of American experts. Thus, Lippert (1990) suggests, there is a "marriage of convenience" by which the search by Canadian journalists for expertise combines with the entrepreneurial spirit of American claimsmakers to ensure the northward diffusion of social-problem claims. With respect to the social construction of satanism in Canada, Lippert found that Americans were indeed more widely quoted than Canadians in Canadian newspapers and that much of this coverage emphasized the degree to which the Canadian case could be expected to resemble the American one.

There is another sense in which the U.S. domination of the cultural industries of North America probably influences social-problem construction in Canada. The much larger carrying capacity of American information channels—both mass and elitist—means that, in an absolute way, a great deal more social problem construction is attempted in the United States. While many of the campaigns result in successful problem construction, many more do not. The moral and ideological struggles that allow "winning" constructions to emerge serve as object lessons to interested audiences about what does and what does not work in the social-problem marketplace. To a considerable degree, social-problem imagery that is to be found in popular and elite media reporting, and that is available for use as cultural resources within the Canadian context, relates to claims' successes in the United States. Emulation would appear more likely when success rather than failure is observed (Strang and Soule 1998).

The Social Sciences

Significantly, it is not only in these "low" channels (Jenkins 1992) of popular media that such cultural domination is observed. In a related way, Canadian social science and policy development are sensitive to developments south of the border. Concern about the "Americanization" of Canadian universities emerged during the late 1960s and early 1970s (Butler and Shugarman 1970; Clark 1975). During the preceding decade, and owing in large part to "baby boom" demographics, Canadian universities had undergone a rapid, unprecedented rate of growth. From the mid-1950s to the mid-1960s, university student bodies in Canada increased by almost 400 percent (Granatstein 1996). The need for faculty was pressing and immediate; the small number of Canadian graduate schools was unable to train sufficient faculty to meet the need. While efforts were made to encourage Canadians living in the United States or elsewhere to return home, Canadian universities increasingly developed strategies intended to attract foreign academics to Canadian positions. These strategies, including generous terms of appointment and tax holidays, produced the intended consequences and the exponential growth in university faculty was largely accomplished through the recruitment of primarily American academics. In 1951, according to Granatstein (1996), there were 30 political scientists in all Canadian universities. Fifteen years later there were 200, and in 1973 there were 750.

Critics charged that the effects of adding non-Canadian faculty were most troublesome in the "culturally sensitive" disciplines of sociology, history, and political science. American academics, it was argued, were unfamiliar with—and in some cases uninterested in—Canadian society and their teaching and research reflected that. Students, critics charged, were more likely to learn about inner-city New York or Chicago than they were to learn about Quebec or Canada's Aboriginal people. American scholars were also accused of attempting to reproduce the departments they had left behind. Personal networks were a major source of continued recruitments, so that particular American graduate schools came to dominate particular Canadian social science departments (Granatstein 1996). Research traditions either ignored Canadian social reality or clumsily approached its study. Those opposed to the "American takeover" maintained that even when attention was focused on Canadian society, the interpretive lens was imported and the ideological content of models drawn from American social science distorted any meaningful understanding of Canadian social and political life (Crean 1976; Gurstein 1972). One prominent Canadian political scientist charged that the development of the discipline was largely "imitative, reflecting with a time lag the interests and approaches of American political science" (in Cairns 1975:206). Social problems research during the period suggests that the images of Canada and its social problems were significantly shaped by American scholarship.

More recent decades have witnessed a reversal of many of these trends. The recruitment of Canadians in Canadian schools is now both an accepted practice and, in most cases, a legislative requirement. However, critics argue that the problems on which Canadian social scientists focus their attention continue to reflect American influence. This influence expresses itself in several ways. First, although it has become customary to hire Canadian academics in Canadian universities, this is not necessarily the bulwark against foreign influence that it is sometimes thought to be. This is because the criterion most relevant to recruitment is citizenship rather than training. Canadians trained at prestigious, highly regarded American schools meet the legal criteria for recruitment, even though their social-scientific understanding of Canadian society may be no more developed than that of a scholar who holds foreign citizenship. Moreover, even those who received their graduate training in Canadian academic departments during the 1970s and 1980s found themselves trained by American scholars whose work often reflected these influences.

Second, judgments about professional careers and the quality of academic work in Canada typically reflect concerns about parochialism. Necessary assessments at the time of application for promotion or tenure that one has an "international reputation," that one's work is "widely read," or that one is an "important scholar" often mean in practice that scholarly work must address—or at least be read by—an American audience. In many subdisciplines, American journals are regarded as the "top" journals. Access to such outlets requires not only that the scholarly work in question be on the theoretical and methodological "cutting edge," but that it also reflect the types of concerns that are dominant in the journal at the time. In this respect, social problems that are salient in the American context can prove instrumental as organizing themes.

These influences are reflected in and reinforced by the political economy of textbook publishing (Ostry 1993). According to Granatstein (1996) foreign firms control about 80 percent of educational publishing in Canada. It is generally more profitable for publishers to adapt a successful American textbook to the Canadian market than to prepare the development of one that will meet the needs of only the latter market. Such adaptations typically involve content changes that tinker as little as possible with the successful formula and thereby encourage wrapping Canadian content around the existing skeletal structure. In this way, attention to theoretical models and substantive matters reflective of the American experience is reproduced across academic generations.

Third, academic disciplines in the United States are more likely to be institutionalized. Institutionalization here refers to the creation of structures through which the intellectual activity of a discipline takes place: professional journals, learned societies, publishers, funding agencies, libraries, and academic departments. This greater degree of institutionalization in the United States "serves to make ideas more readily available to potential recipients, it renders possible concentration of effort on them, it fosters interaction about them, and it aids in their communication" (Cairns 1975: 203). Institutionalization thus facilitates the consolidation, elaboration, and diffusion of ideas, enhancing their "radiative power."

Diffusion in the Policy Community and the Role of Interpersonal Communication

In an effort to explain the impact of the United States on the issues faced and policies adopted in Canada, Mildred Schwartz identified two types of processes that account for Canadian choices of political conduct. The "communication-diffusion model" emphasizes the choices made as a result of information spread through elaborate formal and informal communication networks. In such cases "the United States acts as an analogue to an 'opinion leader'; it is, for whatever reasons, the pace setter, the exemplar for action" (Schwartz 1972:101-102). A second model developed by Schwartz views harmonization between the United States and Canada as both inevitable and functional, reflecting the realities of "problem solving." This "problem-solving" model suggests that Canada emulates the United States because the information and skills often at issue are similar in the two countries, as are the problems. Since the United States and Canada often confront common problems with a relatively restricted range of alternatives, it should not be surprising that they reach similar conclusions. Viewed in this light, what may appear to be U.S. influence is simply the result of a common fate.

Schwartz notes that both the communication-diffusion and problem-solving models reveal a central paradox in the relationship between the United States and Canada:

> Despite the many genuine barriers to the adoption of American political styles [in Canada], the flow of information about these cannot be eliminated. ... This suggests that almost every time a problem arises in Canada that had previously been dealt with in the United States, the latter's experiences will likely have some bearing on the decision made in Canada. To be sure, those American experiences will often be rejected or at least modified to conform to the Canadian situation, but their existence cannot be denied. And if they exist, there is at least some chance that they will have an impact (Schwartz 1972:112).

Preston (1972:8) has argued that the American impact on Canada can generate a conscious or unconscious transference of ideas and institutions. This transference is facilitated through policy communities that cross-national boundaries. According to Pross (1986:98), a policy community "is that part of a political system that—by virtue of its functional responsibilities, its vested interests, and its specialized knowledge—acquires a dominant voice in determining government decisions in a specific field of public activity, and is generally permitted by society at large and the public authorities in particular to determine public policy in that field." It includes all actors or potential actors with a direct interest in the particular policy field, along with those who attempt to influence it—government agencies, pressure groups, media people, and individuals, including academics, consultants, and other "experts." We contend that it is in the policy community where a great deal of American influenced communication-diffusion and problem-solving takes place.

Paul Rock provides an excellent example of this process in his study of the evolution of Canadian policies for victims of crime (1986). Rock traces the origins of Canadian policy to a number of "little histories" that were underway in the late 1970s and early 1980s. One of those histories brought Canadian politicians, policy officials and academics into the orbit of American criminal justice policymakers who were themselves preoccupied with addressing the needs of crime victims. Canadians, confronted with a problem, looked to the Americans for assistance. And the Americans, familiar with many of the Canadian actors, were more than willing to assist their neighbors to the north. Indeed, during this period "the work and business in America simply spilled over into Canada without planning" (Rock 1986: 97). This process of communication diffusion and problem solving between the United States and Canada is not unique; it occurred because:

> Canadian criminology and politics are awash with American influences and it is quite impossible to draw boundaries or separate bundles of thought. As an official [from Canada] reflected rhetorically, "where do Canadian criminologists go to school? What books do they read? Canadians—including scholars—watch American t.v. etc." Canadians thus swim in an American sea. And then officials often seek out Americans when projects are contemplated (Rock 1986:97).

It is in this sense that "the American criminal justice system represents a kind of animated panorama of possibilities, warnings and influences" for Canadians (Rock 1989:265). Rock's study sheds light on the impulse of Canadian policymakers and academics to scan the American policy environment and, where appropriate, import and put to strategic use what they have uncovered and learned. In a similar way, Beare (1996) documents the role played by American policymaker and legal scholar G. Robert Blakely in the development of Canadian responses to the problem of organized crime. According to Beare, Blakely, the author of the American RICO statutes, was invited at least twice to Ottawa to advise on the possible creation of Canadian "proceeds of crime" legislation. At one of the symposia attended by Professor Blakely, other invited guests included a representative of the Office of the Chief Counsel, DEA, an Acting Attorney-in-Charge of Strike Force 18, and a member of the American Bar Association Committee on the Prosecution and Defence of RICO cases. These examples suggest that American social, political, and cultural ideas filter into Canada in ways that are subtler than the obvious popular influence exerted through television and film. The routine work of Canadian policymakers, academics, consultants, activists, and media workers is submerged in American realities.

The role of interpersonal relationships and communications has often been underemphasized in the study of cross-national diffusion. However, the linguistic commonalities between (English) Canada and the United States and the proximity of the two nations combine to make the interpersonal dimensions of the diffusion process particularly significant. The means by which these relationships are forged are many and various, and reflect similarities in the ways that the occupations concerned with the construction of social problems are structured in the two nations (Victor 1998). Canadian academics, for instance, often attend American conferences. The Society for the Study of Social Problems, the American Society of Criminology, and the Academy of Criminal Justice Sciences claim large Canadian memberships, and the annual meetings of such associations attract large numbers of Canadians. On occasion, American conferences are held in Canada. At some Canadian universities, for purposes of travel funding, attendance at an American conference is, ironically, not even considered "international travel." Similarly, physicians, therapists, policymakers, and members of policing and social-service systems in the two nations are linked by a variety of personal associations that emerge from workshops and conferences, service on association committees, and various collaborative undertakings.

In a similar way, Canadian conferences and workshops organized around emerging social problem themes often invite American speakers whose media profiles and published works suggest that they are "high profile." Randy Lippert (1990) has documented how American "satanism experts" in the 1980s established consultative and other professional relationships with Canadian claimsmakers. Thus one American evangelist/author travelled the church circuit in Canada, while American police cult experts conducted seminars at Canadian colleges and for members of Canadian policing agencies. If we are to believe Davies (1989:46) when he says that "the United States assumes it must dominate, that its political and moral views are superior to all others," then it stands to reason that this constant interaction likely has a profound impact on the perceptions, values, ideas, and priorities of Canada (Meisel 1989:286).

The conceptualization of social-problems diffusion in terms that emphasize the mobilization of cultural resources, then, facilitates an understanding of the disproportionate influence of American claimsmaking on Canadian social-problem construction. Ideological constructions that originate in the United States are readily available, underwritten by the imagery of popular culture, and tried and tested in competitive struggles in the social problems marketplace. This is not to suggest, however, that there is anything automatic about the process of cultural diffusion (Flaherty and Manning 1993).

DIFFUSION FROM CANADA TO THE UNITED STATES

The historic domination of Canadian cultural industries by American conglomerates explains why there is less diffusion from Canada to the United States than from the United States to Canada. In comparison to the situation discussed above, Canadian political and social life tends to be largely invisible in American popular culture (Feldthusen 1993). This is perhaps most evident in the most public media of film and television (Williams et al. 1990). Of course, Canadian writers, directors, and performers figure very prominently in the American cultural industries, although it is unlikely that from an American viewpoint their contributions are associated with a perspective that is in any sense distinctly Canadian. In a related way, it is interesting to note that an increasingly large number of films and television productions that promote social-problems claims about crime, poverty, or other urban problems are filmed in Canadian cities such as Toronto or Vancouver. Most typically, however, the locale is either unidentified (but portrayed as a generic American city) or supposed to represent some specific major American city such as New York or Chicago. It can be argued that not only does the use of such locales render Canadian urban realities invisible, but it also communicates subtly to Canadian viewers (who are more likely to recognize the locales) how similar the problems of the two societies really are.

While Canadian social-problem claims may be less available for use by American claimsmakers, examples of their use in the construction of American social problems do exist. For instance, the construction of the health-care debate in the United States frequently includes claims about the virtues (or evils) of universal health care in Canada. In addition, stories about Canadian constitutional crises and political unrest in the province of Quebec were readily available to U.S. claimsmakers in the 1990s who wished to convince others of the need to tread cautiously with respect to bilingualism. In reference to the debate about English language laws in the United States, one essayist for a national newsmagazine referred to the situation as the "Quebecification of America" (Gray 1993:70). Another commented on the French-English conflict in Canada: "The main lesson we should learn from our neighbor's troubles is not to import them here. Multiculturalism and bilingualism, once planted, grow like kudzu. Our struggles over our racist problem have lasted 200 years and included a Civil War. Let's not add problems that have made even Canada interesting" (Brookhiser 1992:78).

CONCLUSIONS

That Canadians are subject to a considerable degree of American cultural influence is undeniable. This influence seems to find expression in a variety of "high" and "low" culture channels. In a sense, such channels reflect Best's (1990) distinction between "insider" and "outsider" claimsmaking. The connections between Canadian and American policy and political communities provide a rather direct means by which Americanized problem definitions enter Canadian discourse. At the same time, popular American media speak to the Canadian viewing, reading, and voting publics and thereby suggest a more indirect channel by which American views of social problems enter public discussion north of the border.

However, despite what many critics regard as "American cultural imperialism," the process by which American social-problems claims diffuse northward is not straightforward. While several factors encourage such diffusion, others actively support resistance. For this reason, it is perhaps most useful to conceptualize the diffusion process as one of cultural resource utilization. The dominance of American culture on the continent makes available resources for the claimsmaking process in Canada. Not all such resources are used, and those that are used are not always used successfully. The lack of symmetry between the two nations suggests why Canadian constructions figure less prominently in the case of social-problem construction in the United States.

To be sure, the diffusion process is difficult to unravel. The discovery of similar problem constructions in two societies does not necessarily imply that it is meaningful to talk in terms of diffusion. An alternative hypothesis would contend that if the societies are at similar stages of historical development and undergoing similar processes of social and economic change, they may end up discovering similar kinds of problems. While there may be a sharing of problem imagery, this may have more to do with shaping the outcome than with constructing the problem in some more fundamental way.

While it may be difficult in specific cases to detail the importing and exporting of social-problems claims, there would appear to be at least one broad manner in which the American cultural understanding of social problems has increasingly come to influence Canadian views on such issues. An important theme in the scholarship on cultural differences between Canada and the United States is the degree to which "individualism" represents a central American value (Alston et al. 1996; Goldberg and Mercer 1986). It can be argued that, just as Americans understand legal rights and economic achievement in individualist terms, so they understand their social problems. Traditionally, much social-problems rhetoric has drawn on melodramatic imagery that emphasizes the roles of victims and villains (Best 1999; Nelson-Rowe 1995). Crime, poverty, homelessness, mental illness, addictions, and other problems are typically framed in ways that emphasize individual failing or blame, and that render structural factors irrelevant. This view is so implicit in media representations such as crime films, television drama, and news reporting that it is almost invisible. In recent years, the cult of the celebrity, and the movement toward more tabloid styles of news reporting have only accentuated these tendencies (Best 1999).

It may be that it is at this broad ideological level that American culture exerts its most subtle but also its most profound influence on claimsmaking in Canada. As a theme in all forms of cultural content to which Canadians are exposed, it is inescapable. As a way of understanding social problems, it is consistent with the images of the world that bombard all North Americans steadily.

ACKNOWLEDGMENT

This research was supported in part by a grant from the College of Professional Studies, St. John's University.

REFERENCES

Alston, J. P., T. M. Morris, and A. Veditz. 1996. "Comparing Canadian and American Values: New Evidence from National Surveys." *American Review of Canadian Studies* 26:301–14.

Beare, M. E. 1996. *Criminal Conspiracies.* Toronto: Nelson Canada.

Best, J. 1990. *Threatened Children: Rhetoric and Concern about Child-Victims.* Chicago: University of Chicago Press.

———. 1999. *Random Violence.* Berkeley: University of California Press.

Brookhiser, R. 1992. "Canada Might Get Interesting." *Time* 139 (March 9):78.

Butler, M., and D. Shugarman. 1970. "Canadian Nationalism, Americanization and Scholarly Values." *Journal of Canadian Studies* 5(3):12–28.

Cairns, A. C. 1975. "Political Science in Canada and the Americanization Issue." *Canadian Journal of Political Science* 8:191–234.

Clark, S. D. 1975. "Sociology in Canada: An Historical Overview." *Canadian Journal of Sociology* 1:225–34.

Conell, C., and S. Cohn. 1995. "Learning from Other People's Actions: Environmental Variation and Diffusion in French Coal Mining Strikes, 1890–1935." *American Journal of Sociology* 101:366–403.

Crean, S. M. 1976. *Who's Afraid of Canadian Culture?* Don Mills: General Publishing.

Cullen, D., J. D. Jobson, and R. Schneck. 1978 "Anti-Americanism and its Correlates." *Canadian Journal of Sociology* 3:103–20.

Davies, R. 1989. "Signing Away Canada's Soul: Culture, Identity and the Free Trade Agreement." *Harpers* 278 (January):43–47.

Feldthusen, B. 1993. "Awakening from the National Broadcasting Dream: Rethinking Television Regulation for National Cultural Goals." Pp. 42–74 in *The Beaver Bites Back: American Popular Culture in Canada,* edited by D. H. Flaherty and F. E. Manning. Montreal: McGill-Queen's University Press.

Fischer, C. S. 1980. "The Spread of Violent Crime from City to Countryside, 1955 to 1975." *Rural Sociology* 45:416–34.

Flaherty, D. H., and F. E. Manning (eds.). 1993 . *The Beaver Bites Back: American Popular Culture in Canada.* Montreal: McGill-Queen's University Press.

Goldberg, M. A., and J. Mercer. 1986. *The Myth of the North American City: Continentalism Challenged*. Vancouver: University of British Columbia Press.

Gomme, I. D. 1998. *The Shadow Line: Deviance and Crime in Canada*. Toronto: Harcourt Brace.

Gorman, T., and S. Crompton . 1997. "Canadian Television in Transition." *Canadian Social Trends* 44 (Spring):19–23.

Granatstein, J. L. 1996. *Yankee Go Home? Canadians and Anti-Americanism*. Toronto: HarperCollins.

Gray, P. 1993. "Official or Not, English Reigns Supreme." *Time* 142 (Dec. 2):70.

Gurstein, M. 1972. "Towards the Nationalization of Canadian Sociology." *Journal of Canadian Studies* 7(3):50–58.

Howitt, D. 1998. *Crime, the Media and the Law*. New York: Wiley.

Jenkins, P. 1992. *Intimate Enemies*. Hawthorne, NY: Aldine de Gruyter.

———. 1994. *Using Murder*. Hawthorne, NY: Aldine de Gruyter.

Koopmans, R. 1993. "The Dynamics of Protest Waves: West Germany, 1965 to 1989." *American Sociological Review* 58:637–58.

Leroux, T. G., and M. Petrunik. 1990. "The Construction of Elder Abuse as a Social Problem: A Canadian Perspective." *International Journal of Health Services* 20: 651–63.

Lippert, R. 1990. "The Social Construction of Satanism as a Social Problem in Canada." *Canadian Journal of Sociology* 15:417–40.

Lipset, S. M. 1990. *Continental Divide*. London: Routledge.

McAdam, D., and D. Rucht. 1993. "The Cross-national Diffusion of Movement Ideas." *Annals of the American Academy of Political and Social Science* 528:56–74.

Meisel, J. 1989. "Escaping Extinction." Pp. 285–303 in *Partners Nevertheless*, edited by N. Hillmer. Toronto: Copp Clark Pitman Ltd.

Morris, A. 1981. "Black Southern Student Sit-In Movement: An Analysis of Internal Organization." *American Sociological Review* 46:744–67.

Nelson, E. D., and A. Fleras. 1995. *Social Problems in Canada Reader*. Scarborough, Ont.: Prentice-Hall Canada.

Nelson-Rowe, S. 1995. "The Moral Drama of Multicultural Education." Pp. 81–99 in *Images of Issues*, 2nd ed., edited by J. Best. Hawthorne, NY: Aldine de Gruyter.

Oberschall, A. 1989. "The 1960 Sit-Ins: Protest Diffusion and Movement Take-Off." *Research in Social Movements, Conflict and Change* 11:31–53.

Orchard, D. 1993. *The Fight for Canada*. Toronto: Stoddart.

Ostry, B. 1993. "American Culture in a Changing World." Pp. 33–41 in *The Beaver Bites Back: American Popular Culture in Canada*, edited by D. H. Flaherty and F. E. Manning. Montreal: McGill-Queen's University Press.

Ouimet, M. 1999. "Crime in Canada and the United States: A Comparative Analysis." *Canadian Review of Sociology and Anthropology* 36:389–408.

Portman, J. 1993. "And Not by Bread Alone: The Battle over Canadian Culture." Pp. 343–63 in *Canada and the United States: Differences that Count*, edited by D. Thomas. Peterborough, Ont.: Broadview Press.

Preston, R. A. 1972. "A Plea for Comparative Studies of Canada and the United States and the Effects of Assimilation on Canadian Development." Pp. 3–31 in *The Influence of the United States on Canadian Development*, edited by R. A. Preston. Durham, NC: Duke University Press.

Pross, A. P. 1986. *Group Politics and Public Policy.* Toronto: Oxford University Press.

Roberts, J. 1997. *Public Opinion, Crime and Criminal Justice.* Boulder CO: Westview.

Rock, P. 1986. *A View From the Shadows: The Ministry of the Solicitor General and the Making of the Justice for Victims of Crime Initiative.* Oxford: Clarendon Press.

———. 1989. "Victims and Policy in Canada: The Emergence of the Justice for Victims of Crime Initiative." Pp. 261–88 in *From Crime Policy to Victim Policy,* edited by E. A. Fattah. London: Macmillan.

Rogers, E. M. 1962. *Diffusion of Innovations,* 2nd ed. New York: Free Press.

Romanow, W. I., and W. C. Soderlund. 1996. *Media Canada,* 2nd ed. Mississauga, Ont.: Copp Clark.

Schwartz, M. A. 1972. "American Influences on the Conduct of Canadian Politics." Pp. 99–112 in *The Influence of the United States on Canadian Development,* edited by R. A. Preston. Durham, NC: Duke University Press.

Seiler, T. P. 1993. "Melting Pot and Mosaic: Images and Realities." Pp. 303–25 in *Canada and the United States: Differences that Count,* edited by D. Thomas. Peterborough, Ont.: Broadview Press.

Spilerman, S. 1970. "The Causes of Racial Disturbances: A Comparison of Alternative Explanations." *American Sociological Review* 35:627–49.

Strang, D., and J. W. Meyer. 1993. "Institutional Conditions for Diffusion." *Theory and Society* 22:487–512.

Strang, D., and S. A. Soule. 1998. "Diffusion in Organizations and Social Movements: From Hybrid Corn to Poison Pills." *Annual Review of Sociology* 24:265–90.

Synnott, A. 1996. *Shadows: Issues and Social Problems in Canada.* Scarborough, Ont.: Prentice-Hall Canada.

Taras, D. 1999. *Power and Betrayal in the Canadian Media.* Peterborough, Ont.: Broadview Press.

Tarrow, S. 1998. *Power in Movement,* 2nd ed.. Cambridge: Cambridge University Press.

Thompson, J. H., and S. J. Randall. 1994. *Canada and the United States: Ambivalent Allies.* London: University of Georgia Press.

Tuchman, G. 1978. *Making News.* New York: Free Press.

Victor, J. S. 1998. "Moral Panics and the Social Construction of Deviant Behavior: A Theory and Application to the Case of Ritual Child Abuse." *Sociological Perspectives* 41:541–65.

Williams, R. H. 1995. "Constructing the Public Good: Social Movements and Cultural Resources." *Social Problems* 42:124–44.

Williams, T. M., S. Phillips, L. Travis, and D. Wotherspoon. 1990. "Windows on the World: Canadian versus US Television Voices." *Canadian Journal of Communications* 15:19–44.

Winter, J., and I. Goldman. 1995. "Mass Media and Canadian Identity." Pp. 201–20 in *Communications in Canadian Society,* 4th ed., edited by B. D. Singer. Toronto: Nelson Canada.

3

Reinventing Abortion as a Social Problem
"Postabortion Syndrome" in the United States and Britain

ELLIE LEE

The announcement that the British-based Marie Stopes Clinics would begin providing an abortion service so simple that a woman could end her pregnancy during her lunch break had a predictable outcome: a flurry of news stories, followed by a heated debate about "lunchtime abortion." The debate began with a comment by Tim Black, Marie Stopes' chief executive, that a new abortion technique would make "early abortion a minor procedure that could quite easily be completed during a working woman's lunchtime break" (Brown 1997:2). Using this technique for abortions performed during the first twelve weeks of pregnancy with a local anesthetic, a woman can enter a clinic, undergo the abortion, and leave within two hours.

The most forceful opposition to the new service came from representatives of antiabortion organizations. Those who oppose abortion were outraged by the argument that it should be made as easy as possible for a woman to end a pregnancy. However, the terms in which abortion opponents framed their argument against "lunchtime abortion" were noteworthy. Jack Scarisbrick, speaking for the British antiabortion organization Life, called the service "bad news for women because abortion violates women." He claimed that "Post abortion trauma is becoming a major women's disease when they try to come to terms with the guilt, grief and anger at the loss of life" (Brown 1997:2). This claim, that abortion leads to the disease of postabortion trauma, is the subject of this chapter.

Over the past decade, British antiabortion groups have publicized the claim that abortion leads to a "woman's disease" called "postabortion trauma" or "Postabortion Syndrome" (Thorpe 1996). Both of the main British antiabortion organizations, Life and the Society for the Protection of Unborn Children (SPUC), have produced and distributed leaflets and briefing documents that discuss the psychological effects of abortion in these terms. They contend that a specific "psychiatric illness," "disease," or "condition" with definable "symptoms" can result from abortion. Both organizations also advertise and provide "abortion counseling" to women seeking abortion, and after abortion. British antiabortion groups argue that a woman needs a particular form of counseling before abortion, to "inform" her about the psychological trauma the procedure causes. After abortion, antiabortion groups contend that women need to be counseled to help them deal with the symptoms of Postabortion Syndrome (PAS).

This contention that abortion causes psychiatric problems is an interesting development in the abortion debate. The more familiar argument made by abortion's opponents has been that abortion is a social problem and morally wrong because it destroys an already existing human life. The antiabortion movement has therefore presented itself as a movement that exists to oppose legal abortion, and to defend the "right to life" of the "unborn child."

The claim that abortion destroys a human life, an existing person, has been framed in both religious and medical terms. The fetus has been deemed a person both on the grounds that God said it is so, and also more recently through claims that medicine has proved this is the case (Franklin 1991). Antiabortionists make extensive use of ultrasound images to show that a developing fetus looks like a baby. They also emphasize medical facts (e.g., the fetal heart starts beating at six weeks gestation, or a fetus can respond to stimuli such as sound), and on this basis contend that medicine has proved the fetus is a living person. All of these arguments focus on the fetus's "personhood."

It might be expected that abortion opponents would frame their response to "lunchtime abortion" in similar terms. Easier and quicker abortion could be opposed on the grounds that it would lead to the immoral destruction of more "unborn babies." Instead, criticism of lunchtime abortion emphasized the harm to women's mental health.

In discussing framing abortion in these terms, my first aim is to ask how and why British antiabortion organizations came to make this claim. What factors led abortion opponents in Britain to reconstruct their argument against abortion in terms of a "disease" that they claim afflicts women's minds following abortion? Second, to what extent have British proponents of the PAS claim influenced others not associated with antiabortion organizations?

THE CONTEXT FOR THE CLAIM

The term "Postabortion Syndrome" first appeared in Britain during the 1987 parliamentary debate about the Alton Bill, which sought to restrict the legal time limit for abortion in the U.K. to 18 weeks. The bill's sponsor David Alton described postabortion trauma as "the psychiatric morbidity experienced by a woman after an abortion" (Steinberg 1991:181). Three years later, during a debate about the Human Fertilisation and Embryology Bill[1] in the House of Lords, Dame Elaine Kellett-Bowman claimed that research carried out in the United States showed that 82 percent of women who had had a pregnancy terminated suffer from PAS. By the end of the 1980s, both main British antiabortion groups, SPUC and Life, were distributing leaflets and briefings about PAS, and had begun offering counseling to women before and after abortion. Newspaper articles at this time began to refer to PAS when they included comment from antiabortion groups (Legh-Jonson 1989; Johnson 1992; *Scottish Catholic Observer* 1992; *Guardian* 1992; Macdonald 1992).

Why did the PAS claim emerge at this point? First, the antiabortion campaigners and their parliamentary supporters found it difficult to gain support for restrictive reform legislation following abortion's legalization in 1967. Despite numerous attempts, the antiabortion movement failed to bring about any changes to British abortion law during the 1970s and 1980s. Adopting new arguments against abortion can be understood as a response to this failure.

Cultural context is a second factor: Britain and other Western societies feature a longstanding concern with abortion's psychological effects. This concern is expressed by parties unrelated to the antiabortion movement or any campaign to restrict the availability of abortion. The PAS claim can be understood as an attempt to co-opt this concern and, in doing so, to problematize the availability of abortion.

Third, throughout the 1980s, U.S. antiabortionists argued that abortion can lead to PAS. By the decade's end, this claim generated a high-profile debate in the United States involving politicians of major stature, and provoked substantial media discussion of PAS. British antiabortion activists then adopted the claim for themselves, perhaps hoping that the same degree of attention would be paid to their argument as to that of their American counterparts.

Much of this chapter's discussion of PAS's emergence in Britain will concentrate on the third factor, "the American dimension." I will consider the PAS claim as presented by U.S. antiabortionists, its impact on the American abortion debate, and its diffusion to Britain. However, it is first necessary to spend some time discussing the first two factors, to provide the context within which British abortion opponents responded to the claim, and to clarify some distinctive features of the abortion debate in British society.

THE ABORTION DEBATE IN BRITAIN

Abortion was made legal in Britain in 1967, but on grounds strikingly different from those laid down in the *Roe v. Wade* ruling in the United States, and indeed in European legislatures. The dominant feature of British abortion law is that it medicalizes abortion. Under British law, unlike that in the United States, women have no right to abortion. In contrast, the right to decide whether a woman can legally end a pregnancy rests in the hands of two doctors, who can agree to the request for abortion on medical grounds. The 1967 Abortion Act has been amended only once, in 1990, through Section 37 of the Human Fertilisation and Embryology Act. The terms of the Abortion Act 1967 (as amended) are as follows:

A person shall not be guilty of an offence under the law relating to abortion when a pregnancy is terminated by a registered medical practitioner if two registered medical practitioners are of the opinion formed in good faith—
(a) that the pregnancy has not exceeded its twenty-fourth week and that the continuance of the pregnancy would involve risk, greater than if the pregnancy were terminated, of injury to the physical or mental health of the pregnant woman or any existing children of her family; or
(b) that the termination is necessary to prevent grave permanent injury to the physical or mental health of the pregnant woman; or
(c) that the continuance of the pregnancy would involve risk to the life of the pregnant woman, greater than if the pregnancy were terminated; or
(d) that there is substantial risk that if the child were born it would suffer from such physical or mental abnormalities as to be seriously handicapped.

The key feature of this law is that it does not have any clear moral basis (Radcliffe-Richards 1982). British law is not based on stated principles regarding the moral appropriateness, or inappropriateness, of legal abortion. As a result, there is no clear ascribing of rights to either the pregnant woman, or the fetus. Under British law, at no stage in pregnancy does the woman have the right to end a pregnancy. Equally, at no stage in pregnancy is a fetus consistently deemed a "person," worthy of legal protection. Rather, throughout pregnancy, the abortion decision reflects medical judgment. It is the judgment of two doctors that is primary in deciding whether a woman's request for abortion complies with the terms of the Abortion Act.

Empowering doctors to make abortion decisions through this kind of law does not necessarily make it difficult for women to get abortions. Rather, the law can, and in practice does, at the current time at least, give liberally minded doctors the ability to judge just about any abortion, carried out in early pregnancy, lawful. Under clause (a), a doctor can argue that any pregnancy carried to term represents more of a threat to a woman's physical health than any abortion. In practice, women access abortion relatively easily in Britain at present. But it is the particular interpretation of the law by doctors, rather than any legal recognition of woman's rights, that makes this possible.

The construction of the terms under which women can legally terminate abortion in Britain as a matter best decided by medical discretion has been termed the "medicalisation of abortion" (Sheldon 1997:3). Framing of the law in "medicalized" terms means that medical authority, rather than moral imperative, becomes decisive. Claims that can be justified on health grounds carry most weight. Such "demoralization" of abortion, by eliminating from the law any recognition of moral claims for women's or fetal rights, has had two important effects on the British abortion debate.

First, it restricts the terms under which antiabortion campaigners can frame their case and gain a hearing. Framing British abortion law in medical rather than rights-based terms constrains debate about moral, legal, and social aspects of abortion, certainly compared with debate in the United States. A medicalized abortion law has meant that certain issues that have been important in the U.S. debate have been limited, if not eliminated in Britain. Most significantly, claims based on the "right to life" of the "unborn child" tend to fall outside the terms in which the abortion debate has been constructed. Claims for the "right to life" of the fetus can be relatively easily dismissed, because abortion decisions are made by medical practitioners on the grounds of the effects of continuing or ending a pregnancy for a woman's health.

Fetal rights claims are most likely to find support when they focus on the fetus after "viability." Arguments that abortion should not be allowed after this point (when medical science can enable a fetus to survive outside the womb), are likely to be most successful (Furedi 1998). In contrast, arguments not constructed in medical terms—for example, arguing for the "right to life" of a fetus at six weeks' gestation—are less likely to succeed. Given that British law makes the effect of continuing a pregnancy on a woman's health the key question, claims for the "right to life" of a nonviable fetus cannot trump the medical imperative.

For the same reason, British law also leaves little room for the discussion of the rights of male partners. If abortion is conducted in the interests of women's health, there is little scope for men to claim that their interests should hold sway (Nolan and Furedi 1995). The medicalization of abortion has therefore meant that, where the U.S. antiabortion movement has been able to claim that abortion constitutes a social problem, its British equivalent has been less able to do likewise.

A second, linked effect, increasingly evident after 1967, is for debate about abortion to be excluded from the public, political arena and limited to the private sphere, where the response to a woman's request for an abortion is deemed best dealt with through medical discretion (Sheldon 1997). To put it crudely, politicians in general and incumbent governments in particular have delegated decisions about abortion to the medical profession. Abortion has been construed as outside politics.

This does not mean there have not been heated debates about abortion in the British parliament. Between 1967 and 1992, 16 parliamentary bills sought to restrict abortion (Moore 1992). What is interesting about these bills, however, is that all were brought by backbench MPs and, while they did succeed in generating an unusually full debating chamber and much heated discussion, none was given sufficient parliamentary time or support by MPs to bring about legal change.

Antiabortion opinion was perhaps most influential in Parliament during the early 1980s under the Thatcher government. At this time there were more MPs in Parliament who wanted to see abortion law made more restrictive than at any other time since 1967. However, the antiabortion campaign was "not part of a Thatcherite offensive but, on the contrary, was an attempt to force Thatcherism to move in a direction it was plainly unwilling to go" (Durham 1991:38). Even at its most influential, the antiabortion movement was not able to convince sufficient numbers of politicians to pass legislation to protect the rights of the "unborn child."

The cumulative effect of the medicalization of abortion has been to marginalize the opinion of those who disagree with the existing abortion law on rights-based grounds:

> whatever disagreement or struggle there is regarding abortion [in Britain] . . .
> has become increasingly muted. . . . It appears a status quo with regard to the
> regulation of abortion services has been established, and those who continue
> to kick against it—be they pro- or anti-choice activists—are cast as marginal
> extremists. (Sheldon, 1997:2)

Those who disagree with existing law, either on the grounds that it fails to protect the rights of the child (or on the grounds that it fails to give rights to women), are deemed extremists. Given the marginalization of the claim that the fetus should have legal rights, abortion opponents have had to develop alternative arguments against abortion.

It is therefore unsurprising that antiabortion claims that do not rely on the fetus's alleged "right to life" but that rest rather on abortion's alleged negative effects on women's health have emerged with increasing regu-

larity over the past ten years. Various claims, centering on an alleged relationship between abortion and damage to women's health, have become
central to British antiabortion arguments: antiabortion activists have alleged that a link exists between abortion and breast cancer, and that abortion contributes to future infertility, as well as that abortion leads to mental
ill health.

Such claims, if they can be substantiated, potentially offer antiabortion
claimsmakers two main benefits. First, they confer legitimacy through
medical authority: an argument against abortion grounded in medical fact
is likely to seem authoritative; while moral arguments against abortion can
be dismissed, medically based arguments can be presented as incon-
testable fact. If it has been "medically proven" that abortion damages
women's health, who could still argue that abortion should be available to
women on the grounds that it is beneficial to their health?

Second, claims that abortion damages women's health can address the
antiabortion movement's "rhetorical Achilles heel" (Hopkins, Reicher and
Saleem 1996:541). Moralistic arguments against abortion leave abortion
opponents unable to respond effectively to charges that they ignore the
woman's needs. There is widespread agreement that a woman's personal
circumstances and feelings about a pregnancy should be taken into account in deciding whether abortion should be allowed (Furedi 1998). Consequently, arguments that focus purely on the fetus are problematic
because they contradict such concern for the woman with an unwanted
pregnancy; only those people who believe that abortion is sinful are likely
to, in all circumstances, discount the needs and interests of the woman who
finds herself in this situation. Claims that construct abortion as a social
problem because it is bad for women can therefore be understood as an attempt to repair this "Achilles heel." Thus, the British antiabortion organization Life uses the slogan "pro-woman, pro-life" on its leaflets and
publicity materials. British Victims of Abortion claims that abortion always
has two victims, "the unborn child and the mother."

The claim that abortion leads to mental ill health is not, however, simply
a response to the difficulties associated with morally based claims. It can
also be understood as an attempt to address concerns that abortion is psychologically problematic for women, concerns that preceded the PAS claim.

ABORTION IS LIKE NO OTHER OPERATION

During the debate about "lunchtime abortion," antiabortion organizations were by no means the only commentators to draw attention to abortion's alleged psychological effects. The then Minister for Health, Tessa
Jowell, argued that while she supported the development of abortion ser-

vices, this particular innovation appeared to "trivialise what for many women will be almost inevitably be a difficult and distressing decision" (Borrill 1997). One journalist wrote that while she believes in a woman's right to choose an abortion, abortion is always followed by "sadness and an aching sense of loss" (Miles 1997:23). Another contended: "Although intended to help women, it's likely that presenting the procedure as so minor will inevitably add to their feelings of guilt and inadequacy when they find they need more than 'half an hour's recovery time' to get over it" (Everett 1997). An editorial in the newspaper *Scotland on Sunday* (1997:14) argued that "the speed of the operation does not diminish its psychological dangers" and suggested that the service "risks trivialising abortion operations if they can be carried out during a lunch break."

These commentators construed abortion as carrying emotional costs for women. Where the risks of other medical procedures can be assessed according to the impact they have an physical health, abortion's risks must also weigh its negative psychological effects. The contention that abortion is or could be a "minor procedure" consequently seems problematic, in that it fails to take these effects into account.

According to feminist psychologist Mary Boyle (1997), the negative presentation of abortion's psychological effects draws attention to powerful ideas about maternity. Where the "psychological risks" of abortion and childbirth have been assessed, childbirth has been found to present a greater degree of risk. Boyle cites research that found a five to six times greater risk of psychosis after childbirth than after abortion. Other research reported fairly serious psychological distress in around 20 percent of women in the first year following childbirth. The popularity of the term "baby blues" suggests that negative feelings after birth are common. Yet public discussion highlights the "trauma" associated with abortion, rather than the psychological effects of maternity.

Boyle argues that the perception that abortion is psychologically problematic for women rests on powerful ideas concerning the desirability and "naturalness" of motherhood. Her account of the debates about abortion in Britain and the United States emphasizes the effects of positive discourses surrounding motherhood and negative discourses about its alternatives. Maternity has over many years been powerfully represented by the law, the medical profession, and the media as the desirable, natural outcome of pregnancy. The perception that abortion will generate emotional or psychological problems therefore rests on a construction of abortion as being against women's nature.

The argument that abortion leads to psychological problems because it represents a rejection of motherhood was made most directly in the years before legal abortion. Taking attitudes to abortion in the medical profession as their example, Sarvis and Rodman showed that a perceived connection between the psychological risks of abortion and the naturalness of motherhood was dominant in the 1950s and 1960s. They suggest the view of the American doctor Galdston was typical of medical opinion when he argued in the 1958 that "woman's main role here on earth is to conceive, deliver, and raise children. . . . When this function is interfered with, we see all sorts of emotional disorders. . . . This is not just textbook theory, as all who practice psychiatry very well know" (Sarvis and Rodman 1973:109). In its 1966 report, "Legalised Abortion," the highly influential Royal College of Gynaecologists and Obstetricians also framed the psychological effects of abortion in terms of the rejection of maternity: "There are few women, no matter how desperate they may be to find themselves with an unwanted pregnancy, who do not have regrets at losing it." The report suggested that this regret is a "fundamental reaction, governed by maternal instinct" (Simms and Hindel 1971:52).

Such views about abortion were based on a perception that the woman seeking abortion was "abnormal." Within the framework of Freudian psychology, dominant at the time, a rejection of the wish for motherhood indicated abnormal psychological adjustment, that would lead to mental disturbance (Zimmerman 1981:66). Thus, commentaries at this time often pathologized women seeking abortion as abnormal or sick, with both their reasons for abortion and their likely psychological response characterized as forms of mental illness.

Following the legalization of abortion in the United States, and its partial decriminalization in Britain, this pathologization of the effects of abortion diminished. It became more difficult in the face of new research findings to sustain the argument that psychiatric illness would result in women who aborted unwanted pregnancies. Research that measured women's psychological state after abortion challenged claims, based on anecdotal evidence, that negative psychological responses were inevitable. Later studies of the psychological response to abortion in larger groups of women found that psychological or emotional problems following abortion were not as common as had been thought, and where they existed were due to problems present before the abortion, rather than to the abortion itself (Zimmerman 1981:67–68).

The publication of such research did not mean that concern about the psychological effects of abortion disappeared. Rather, findings that suggested that abortion had negligible psychological effects "brought expressions of concern that perhaps the extent of abortion-related psychological distress was being underestimated" (Zimmerman 1981:68). This concern was justified on the grounds that studies of the psychological effects of abortion were still methodologically flawed: in most, a substantial share of women dropped out between the original and postabortion assessments of their psychological state. The continued interest in the psychological effects of abortion may also have reflected a conviction that abortion must have some negative psychological effects. While this conviction was by this time not always expressed in terms of women's instinctual or natural desire for motherhood, a sense that abortion must carry particular "psychological risks" remained.

One feminist psychotherapist's account of the need for continued concern about the psychological effects of abortion emphasizes that while the desire for motherhood may not be natural, it is nevertheless deeply ingrained in a woman's psyche (Dana 1987). This results in part from socializing girls to expect that motherhood is part of their future. In addition, society demands from women—and glorifies—their caring for and nurturing children and other family members. After abortion, Dana therefore contends, it is to be expected that women will experience psychological difficulties. She argues that the conflict between a woman's conscious decision to end a pregnancy and the unconscious acceptance of the value of motherhood will generate negative emotions. Women need not the "right to choose" abortion but "the right to feel." Other writers on abortion also argue that the psychological effects of abortion should not be underestimated and that counselling or therapy may be necessary to allow a woman to integrate the experience of abortion into her life (Lodl, McGettigan and Bucy 1987).

Another argument for the psychological effects of abortion is that, while some women may cope well with abortion, others are nevertheless "at risk" psychologically. Factors that increase this risk are isolation, lack of support, desertion by the male partner, cultural or religious antagonism to abortion, the woman's own beliefs about abortion, young age, termination of pregnancy at later gestations, and previous history of psychological disturbance (Brien and Fairbairn 1996).

However the concern is justified, abortion remains "psychologized." It is conceptualized by many significant opinion formers in society, including medical professionals, feminists, and journalists, as a procedure that can have important psychological or emotional effects. Against this background, antiabortion groups asserted that women suffer from serious psychological problems after abortion. However, the PAS claim does not simply draw attention to the possibility that a woman can experience negative feelings after abortion. Rather, this claim frames the psychological effects of abortion in terms of a "syndrome" or specific psychiatric disorder, so that the psychological effects of abortion are repathologized.

THE AMERICAN DIMENSION

The PAS claim, as a specific representation of the psychological effects of abortion, emerged first in America during the 1980s. The claim achieved significant visibility in the American abortion debate at the end of the 1980s, prior to its diffusion to Britain.

There are significant differences in the effects of the PAS claim in the United States and Britain. In both countries, PAS remains a putative rather than an accepted diagnosis of abortion's psychological effects. That a woman can suffer from a specific "women's disease" or "syndrome" following abortion has not been established as a medical fact but remains a contentious claim clearly associated with abortion opponents. The prominence of the debate over the claim in the United States, as compared to the U.K., indicates important differences between these two countries, which are significant in considering diffusion of the PAS claim.

The Claim

American abortion opponents Vincent Rue and Anne Speckhard have been credited with first developing the PAS "diagnosis" (Doherty 1995). Rue's first public presentation in America about PAS was in 1981. During the 1980s he gave papers at antiabortion conferences and published a number of articles about PAS.[2] Rue and Speckhard's work is frequently referred to by other abortion opponents in the United States: their argument about PAS has been adopted by most major American antiabortion organizations, and it has shaped the formation and campaigns of specific U.S. organizations dedicated to publicizing abortion's negative psychological effects—e.g., American Victims of Abortion and Women Exploited by Abortion.

In this view, the psychological effects of terminating pregnancy should not be underestimated; rather, it is "possible that the decision to elect abortion can generate significant resulting psychosocial distress" (Speckhard and Rue 1992:96). That is,

> while abortion may indeed function as a "stress reliever" by eliminating an unwanted pregnancy, other evidence suggests that it may also simultaneously or subsequently be experienced by some individuals as a psychosocial stressor, capable of causing posttraumatic stress disorder (PTSD). . . . We suggest that this constellation of dysfunctional behaviors and emotional reactions should be termed "Postabortion syndrome (PAS)" (Rue 1995:20).

According to the American Psychiatric Association's *Diagnostic and Statistical Manual of Mental Disorders* (the *DSM)*, the symptoms of PTSD—a condition first named by psychiatrists following the return of soldiers from the Vietnam war [Scott 1990, Young 1995]—include persistent reexperience of the traumatic event, avoidance of stimuli associated with the trauma, and increased arousal (e.g., hypervigilance). The *DSM* states it is possible for someone to develop the symptoms of PTSD:

following a psychologically distressing experience that is outside the range of usual human experience (i.e., outside the range of such common experiences as simple bereavement, chronic illness, business losses, and marital conflict). The stressor producing this syndrome would be markedly distressing to almost anyone, and is usually experienced with intense fear, terror, and helplessness. . . . The most common traumata involve either a serious threat or harm to one's children, spouse, or other close relatives and friends; sudden destruction of one's home or community; or seeing another person who has recently been, or is being, seriously injured or killed as the result of an accident or physical violence (American Psychiatric Association 1980: 247–48).

According to the *DSM*, a person cannot therefore be diagnosed as suffering from PTSD unless the traumatic event fits the above description. The criterion that that the trauma has to be "outside the range of usual human experience" has been described as the "gatekeeper" to the PTSD diagnosis (Joseph, Williams and Yule 1997). On these grounds, marital conflict or simple bereavement have been excluded as events sufficiently traumatic to lead to PTSD. Regardless of how upsetting the individual concerned finds a divorce or the death of a loved one, or how they respond psychologically to that experience, they cannot be diagnosed as suffering from PTSD.

On this basis, Henry David (1997), a U.S. expert on medical aspects of abortion, contends that the PAS diagnosis makes no sense. He argues that given the numbers of women who have had abortions (an estimated one-third of American women and one-quarter of British women will have an abortion), it is difficult to see how abortion can be defined as an event that is "outside the range of usual human experience." For David, abortion is part of everyday experience for so many women that it simply cannot be defined as a potentially traumatic experience.

In contrast, Speckhard and Rue maintain that abortion can legitimately be defined as a "trauma" on the grounds that many women perceive it that way. They argue that "stress begins with one's perception of it" (Speckhard and Rue 1992:106). Hence, there can be no generally applicable definition of what events can be traumatic; a more subjective definition of stress should be accepted. While some women may not perceive abortion as a stressor, others will. When abortion is perceived as stressful by the woman, symptoms characteristic of PTSD are likely to emerge, and these women can legitimately be diagnosed as suffering from PAS.

A Wide Range of "Symptoms"

A noteworthy feature of the PAS claim is the representation of its "symptoms." Rue explicitly compares them with those of PTSD: "the symptoms are the same: flashbacks, denial, lost memory of the event, avoidance of the subject" (Rourke 1995: E-1). He has developed "diagnostic criteria" for PAS, along the lines of the criteria for PTSD given in the *DSM*. According to these criteria, the abortion experience is defined as a stressor, sufficiently traumatic to cause the symptoms of reexperience, avoidance, and impacted grieving. To be diagnosed as having PAS, the woman has to reexperience the abortion trauma in one of four listed ways (e.g., recurrent, distressing dreams of the "unborn child"); she has to show three (of a possible seven) manifestations of avoidance (such as avoiding thoughts about abortion or feeling detached from others); and she has to have two of a possible eleven "associated features" (such as difficulty in falling asleep or eating disorders) (Rue 1995:27-28). The PAS claim is therefore formally modeled on the accepted psychiatric criteria for PTSD.

However, the writings of PAS claimsmakers reveal a shift from a definition of PAS symptoms where the proposed comparison with PTSD is made clear, to a much broader collection of symptoms that could perhaps more accurately be described as negative feelings. Rue (1995:20) lists a wide range of feelings and behaviors that he argues might be evident in women who have had an abortion, including feelings of helplessness, hopelessness, sadness, sorrow, lowered self-esteem, distrust, regret, relationship disruption, communication impairment and/or restriction, and self-condemnation. Similarly, the U.S.-based Elliott Institute includes as symptoms of PAS: sexual dysfunction (comprising loss of pleasure from intercourse, an aversion to males in general, or promiscuity), increased cigarette smoking, child neglect or abuse (including "replacement pregnancies"—i.e., becoming pregnant after an abortion), reduced maternal bonding with children born after the abortion, divorce, and repeat abortions (having another abortion in the future).[3] Associating this broad range of symptoms with a diagnosis of PAS lets claimants argue that large numbers of women may suffer from the syndrome. As the "diagnostic criteria" for PAS become broader, it is easier to claim that many women may suffer from the "syndrome."

In their contribution to the special issue of the *Journal of Social Issues* on the psychological effects of abortion, Speckhard and Rue (1992:104–5) formalize this elastic definition of PAS symptoms: "as a psychosocial stressor, abortion may lead some women to experience reactions ranging from mild distress to severe trauma, creating a continuum that we conceptualize as progressing in severity from postabortion distress (PAD) to PAS to Post abortion psychosis." Positing reactions to abortion as a continuum is significant, in that it creates a link between mild and severe responses: all become less serious versions of the same response. Feelings a woman might have after abortion, such as sadness or regret, become seen as a less serious version of a psychiatric disorder.

Denial

The most significant "symptoms" of PAS named by Rue and Speck-hard are "denial" and "repression." Rue (1995:10) suggests that, in coping with the trauma of abortion, women employ "a mechanism known as 'psychic numbing.'" This means that women deny the trauma of the abortion, and repress memories of it, "thus enabling the persons to present a reasonably calm exterior." However, there is every possibility that "a degree of anxiety and depression may re-emerge later." Similarly, Randall argues:

> Early psychological studies on the aftermath of abortion reported some damage, but found it in only small minority of women. This does not contradict our experience of PAS, because symptoms of repressed grief are most likely to surface from six months to two years after the trauma occurs. . . . Most of those we see and counsel have had their abortions between 8 and 35 years ago. (Randall 1996: xvii)

In this construction of women's psychological response to abortion, the absence of evidence for PAS in the present does not invalidate the claim. The Elliott Institute (n.d.) argues: "many women who have had an abortion use repression as a coping mechanism." There may be a long period of denial before a woman seeks psychiatric care, and "indeed for many women, the onset or accurate identification of PTSD symptoms may be delayed for several years." Hence, while there may not be large numbers of women with PAS now, there will be many PAS sufferers in the future.

Moreover, any of the many symptoms listed above, whenever they appear following an abortion, can be evidence of PAS. Since the woman has denied and repressed her feelings, they can emerge much later in her life, and appear to her and to other people to be unrelated to the abortion experience. Thus any future depression, or other more or less severe negative feelings experienced by a woman who has had an abortion can be attributed to having ended a pregnancy earlier in her life.

Presenting denial as a significant response to abortion permits the claim that large numbers of women have in fact experienced abortion as trauma, whether they know it or not. The president of the U.S. National Right to Life Committee has used Rue's argument to contend that even women "damaged" by their abortion experience can in good faith claim to have no negative psychological reactions, because they have suppressed them, and therefore have no conscious awareness of them (Franz n.d.).

The emergence of PAS as a public-health problem can then be projected into the future: "It took the Vietnam veterans over 10 years to convince the American Psychiatric Association that there is such a thing as post-traumatic stress syndrome. . . . We believe PAS is experiencing a similar journey" (Brotman 1990:4). Rue claims PAS will come be recognized by the APA as a form of PTSD, as the symptoms of "repressed trauma" emerge in women who have had abortions.

DIFFUSION

How did the PAS claim diffuse from the United States to Britain? One mechanism was relational diffusion (McAdam and Rucht 1993:59), that is, via direct contact between American PAS claimsmakers and their British counterparts. At the end of the 1980s, a number of speaking engagements were organized in Britain by the Society for the Protection of Unborn Children (SPUC), featuring prominent American PAS claimsmakers. In 1985, Olivia Gans, the director of American Victims of Abortion, spoke at an SPUC conference in Britain. Two years later, SPUC set up British Victims of Abortion (BVA). In 1988, Gans again visited Britain at the invitation of SPUC, and toured the country "sharing from her own abortion experience, and speaking on the research into damage resulting from abortion" (Bowman 1996: xv).

In the same year, antiabortion parliamentarians with links to Life and SPUC invited Vincent Rue to speak at the House of Commons. He told MPs that women who have had abortions may experience "the same kind of guilt and misery as Vietnam war veterans who cannot shake off the nightmare of life under fire" (Illman 1989). During his visit he also spoke to other British audiences, asserting that "postabortion trauma" exists, and is a variant of PTSD (Birth Control Trust 1989).

This mechanism for the diffusion of claims, through direct contact between members of an identifiable social movement in different countries, is especially important at the beginning of diffusion. McAdam and Rucht (1993:60) suggest that: "such ties are especially critical at the outset of the process in helping to encourage the identification of adopters with transmitters [of social movement ideas]." It is certainly the case that some British adopters of the term "PAS" from the outset relied on the claim's American originators: the Americans were "experts" in the study of women's psychological responses to abortion, who could be referred to in British claimsmaking.

British abortion opponents' use of American "experts'" writings also contributed to the claim's diffusion. BVA distributes PAS literature written by American antiabortionists. In 1994, BVA was invited to give evidence to the Rawlinson Commission (discussed below) about abortion's psychological effects. They submitted the leaflet "What is Postabortion Syndrome?" by the then president of the National Right to Life Committee (Franz n.d.), Speckhard's paper, "Summary of the Psycho-Social Aspects of Stress Following Abortion," and the National Right to Life Committee's report on the psychological aftermath of abortion as references (Rawlinson 1994). The commission report also listed other American sources.

While Life does not directly distribute leaflets written by American PAS claimsmakers, Life's own literature is clearly influenced by Rue's putative "diagnosis" of PAS. For example, a Life briefing paper describes PAS as "a form of Post Traumatic Stress Disorder, first described in Vietnam war veterans," and emphasizes the importance of the "defence mechanism . . . denial" in explaining "why the condition is difficult to recognise and diagnose" (Jarmulowicz 1992:9). Comparisons between PTSD and women's psychological response to abortion reappear in Life's literature.

The influence of their American counterparts also shapes the activities of British antiabortion organizations. These organizations have adopted the approach, first developed in the United States, of offering "counseling" and "support" to women before and after abortion. Similarly, British efforts to use the psychological effects of abortion to effect legal change through campaigns for "informed consent" legislation (under the rubric of "a woman's right to know") borrow from American PAS claimsmakers. Such legislation would compel abortion service providers to inform women requesting abortion of the procedure's allegedly deleterious psychological effects. In the mid-1990s, BVA identified one of its aims as working with "parliamentarians in an attempt to have informed consent legislation enacted" (British Victims of Abortion n.d.). More recently, the American tactic of encouraging women to sue abortion providers for emotional damage caused by abortion appeared in Britain. BVA launched a PAS national helpline to encourage women to come forward and speak publicly about their experiences, and Life announced that it would set up a free phone line to persuade women to sue doctors over the side-effects it alleges result from abortion (Birth Control Trust 1998).

Another mechanism for diffusion of the PAS claim is reciprocation. This kind of diffusion involves a mutual interest on the part of transmitters and adopters in the object of diffusion, and produces reciprocal engagement in the diffusion process (Snow and Benford 1999:27–28). Members of the antiabortion movement in both the United States and Britain were equally enthusiastic about the project of internationalizing the PAS claim from the United States to Britain. However, while American and British PAS claimsmakers may have been equally engaged with the diffusion process, this did not guarantee that the claim would generate the same response in both countries. Other social-problems claims have had different impacts in the United States and Britain (Jenkins 1992:224–28), and the national differences in the response to the PAS claim are the most striking aspect of its diffusion to Britain. While the claim generated a heated debate in the United States, the response to the claim in Britain was muted.

THE AMERICAN DEBATE: A DISPUTED CLAIM

The PAS claim had its greatest influence in the United States between 1987 and 1989. It was during this time that C. Everett Koop, then Surgeon General of the United States, undertook, at the behest of President Ronald Reagan, an inquiry into abortion's health effects (both physical and psychological). Gary Bauer, the President's Advisor on Domestic Affairs and an "ardent pro-life advocate," proposed the inquiry, believing that "the campaign against legal abortion could be broadened by a government campaign stressing the health consequences of abortion" (Wilmoth 1992:2)

The context for the Koop inquiry was a "stalemate" on the abortion issue in the United States, where "pro-life advocates were unable to expand their political goals beyond the successes of the early 1980s" (Wilmoth 1992:2). Through the 1970s and 1980s, the abortion debate had focused largely on the morality of abortion, the rights of the fetus versus the rights of the woman. This moral focus had succeeded in generating much debate about *Roe v. Wade*, but no consensus in favor of overturning the law. Turning the focus to the health effects of abortion was an outcome of this stalemate. White House advisors concluded that it would in fact be impossible to muster an antiabortion consensus on moral grounds, so they decided to follow the model supplied by the antismoking campaign and develop a case on public-health grounds (Holden 1989).

Given that Koop, like Reagan, was known for his opposition to legal abortion,[4] many assumed that the inquiry results would emphasize abortion's deleterious health consequences. The stalemate would then be resolved in favor of abortion opponents. However, the outcome of the inquiry was quite different: the stalemate was not resolved, but rather reproduced, in relation to abortion's mental-health effects.

The Koop Inquiry

There were two main components of the Koop investigation into the health effects of abortion. The first was an investigation by the Surgeon General and his staff, that took a year and a half to complete. This involved staff in several agencies of the Public Health Service evaluating 250 pieces of research, as well as meetings and discussion "with a variety of groups representing pro-life, pro-choice, and professional perspectives" (Wilmoth 1992:2). Koop met privately with 27 groups, including representatives of the Association of State and Territorial Health Officials, the Alan Guttmacher Institute, the American Public Health Association, the American College of Obstetricians and Gynecologists, the National Right-to-Life Committee, Planned Parenthood Federation of America, the Southern Baptist Convention, and the U.S. Conference of Catholic Bishops (U.S.

House 1989). Following this inquiry, Koop and a range of experts on the psychological effects of abortion presented written and verbal statements at a 1989 hearing before a subcommittee of the House Committee on Government Operations. The Reagan administration's decision to support antiabortion advocates' demand that attention be paid to the health effects of abortion then led to government officials spending a significant amount of time, energy, and resources investigating the issue.

However, the outcome of the Koop inquiry was not what PAS claimsmakers had envisioned. The issue of the physical health effects of abortion proved uncontentious; all available evidence indicated that abortion is a relatively safe medical procedure. Moreover, the Koop inquiry did not find evidence to support the PAS claim; rather, it led to a heated public debate about the psychological effects of abortion.

The Koop report was completed in January 1989, but not made public. Instead, Koop sent a letter to President Reagan that, apparently against Koop's wishes, was released to the press. The letter said that there was insufficient evidence about the psychological effects of abortion to draw conclusions and that research in this area was flawed. Koop's inquiry found that "the scientific studies do not provide conclusive data about the health effects of abortion on women" (Holden 1989). His assessment was that "we have two groups of people saying very honestly and very sincerely different things" (Madigan 1989), and that "the available scientific evidence . . . simply cannot support either the preconceived beliefs of those pro-life or those pro-choice" (Holden 1989).

It seems that, regardless of his own views on abortion, Koop did not want to draw conclusions that would aid either side in the abortion debate. He stated, "My position [on abortion] is well known to everybody in this country. I'm opposed to it. But I also took an oath to uphold the law of the land. That's why I walk a tightrope and why I prepared the report as I did" (Okie 1989).

Counterclaims

Koop's report was finally released at the congressional hearing, which did not draw any conclusions or make suggestions with regard to abortion law or policy. However, it did generate comment in the media; they reiterated Koop's findings that studies about the psychological effects of abortion were flawed, and his call for further research into the subject (Okie 1989; Leary 1989). In addition, the views of the PAS claim's opponents who gave evidence to the Koop inquiry against this "diagnosis" achieved a high degree of prominence.

The American Psychological Association (APA) was the most prominent opponent of the PAS claim. Prior to the hearing, but following Koop's letter to Reagan, Brian Wilcox of the APA, who contributed a literature review to the Koop study, declared, "Although we searched and searched and searched, there was no evidence at all for the existence of the 'post-abortion syndrome' claimed by some right-to-life groups" (Holden 1989). The press quoted other APA spokespeople: "there is no evidence for PAS" (Kotulak and Van 1989); and "abortion inflicts no particular psychological damage on women" (Thompson 1989).

Following the hearing, PAS opponents continued to get favorable publicity. In April 1990, a study carried out by the APA countered the contention of antiabortion groups that many women suffer severe trauma that surfaces years after an abortion: "Severe negative reactions after abortions are rare and can best be understood in the framework of coping with a normal life stress" (Brotman 1990). In an often-quoted article, psychologists associated with the APA and other influential scientific bodies argued that "A review of methodologically sound studies of the psychological responses of U.S. women after they obtained legal, nonrestrictive abortions indicates that distress is generally greatest before abortion and that the incidence of severe negative responses is low" (Adler et al. 1990). The article also noted that Koop did in fact testify at the congressional hearing that the development of significant psychological problems after abortion was "miniscule from a public health perspective."

The APA was the professional body that most actively criticized the PAS claim, but it was not alone. In May 1990, a panel of leading psychiatrists at the American Psychiatric Association's annual meeting made the news; the panel argued that government restrictions on abortion were far more likely to cause women lasting harm than the procedure itself would, and that Association officials absolutely rejected the definition [PAS], on the basis there was no evidence to support it (Specter 1990). In testimony before Congress on behalf of the American Public Health Association, Henry David also disputed the claim that abortion has severe negative effects on women's mental health. The American Medical Association did not give evidence to the Koop inquiry, but in 1992 published an article that characterized PAS as a "myth," which became a reference point in subsequent reporting (Vogt 1992; Boodman 1992). It began: "This is . . . about a medical syndrome that does not exist," and suggested that the only evidence is support of the claim that there is such a syndrome is to be found in a "small number of papers and books based on anecdotal evidence and stressing negative effects have been presented and published under religious auspices and in the nonspeciality literature" (Stotland 1992). Further, while women may experience abortion as a loss, and thus feel sad afterward, this feeling is "not equivalent to a disease," and negative feelings should always be distinguished from psychiatric illness (Stotland 1992). An article by the AMA's Council on Scientific Affairs reported,

Until the 1960s, many assumed that serious emotional problems following induced abortion were common. In 1989, after reviewing more than 250 studies of the emotional aftermath of abortion, Surgeon General C. Everett Koop concluded that the data were "insufficient . . . to support the premise that abortion does or does not produce a postabortion syndrome." He noted, however, that emotional problems resulting from abortion are "miniscule from a public health perspective" (Council on Scientific Affairs 1992).

The Koop inquiry, then, did not lead to legislative changes in abortion law on the basis that abortion damages women's health. This failure reflected the opposition to the PAS claim by the American Psychological Association and other important scientific organizations. Support for the PAS claim on the part of President Reagan and the White House ensured there was a high-profile debate about PAS, but without support from key professional bodies, it was impossible for PAS claimsmakers to achieve the consensus they needed.

PAS and "Informed Consent" Laws

After 1992, political debate at the federal level about the public-health consequences of abortion appeared to have ended, but the public and political debate continued at the state and local levels. Missouri and Pennsylvania enacted legislation in the early 1990s requiring that women seeking abortion be informed of the medical and psychological risks of abortion (Wilmoth 1992:3–4). Lobbying for the passing of "informed consent" abortion legislation at a state level became a relatively important tactic for the American antiabortion movement in the 1980s. The movement aimed to influence state politicians and lawmakers, and was aided by "preexisting networks of conservatives who had successfully fended off state approval of the proposed Equal Rights Amendment" (O'Connor 1996:96).

The 1992 Supreme Court ruling in *Planned Parenthood of Southeastern Pennsylvania v. Casey* further encouraged this approach. In its decision in *Casey,* the Court weakened the standard for determining the constitutionality of certain abortion restrictions. The Court made it clear that individual states might not impose restrictions on the right to choose that have the "purpose or effect of placing a substantial obstacle in the path of a woman seeking an abortion" and adopted the "undue burden" standard, ruling that state laws could burden, but not unduly burden, a woman's abortion decision. On this basis, the Court decided to uphold a Pennsylvania law as not posing an undue burden. The law required a 24-hour waiting period and giving certain information to a woman considering abortion. This included the provision that the attending doctor "orally describe the commonly employed abortion procedures, the medical risks associated with each, [and] the 'possible detrimental psychological effects of abortion'" (Center for Reproductive Law and Policy 1999).

Since *Casey*, 19 states have passed requirements that women must receive certain information before they can consent to abortion, and these requirements are in force in 13 states at the time of writing.[5] Sometimes termed "Right to Know" legislation, these laws have been subject to successful challenge by abortion providers. The inclusion of the provision that women should be informed of their possible risk of suffering from psychological problems after abortion has been successfully defeated in some states.[6] Nevertheless, the introduction of legislation that requires women to be informed of the possible psychological risks of abortion indicates that U.S. advocates continue to find ways to pursue the PAS claim.

The story of PAS in the United States draws attention to two important issues. First, while claimsmaking against abortion on the grounds of its mental health effects might appear to provide a mechanism through which abortion's problems can be established as "fact," such claims are also subject to counterclaims. Opposition to abortion based on mental-health grounds proved to be contentious and was disputed as strongly as arguments based on morals.

Second, the PAS claim of success in achieving a high degree of prominence in the U.S. media, as well as a limited legislative effect, resulted from the significant political support offered to claimants. Support for the claim given by the Reagan administration in particular proved vital in transforming it into a publicly debated issue. The support of high-ranking government officials for the PAS claim ensured that it would be extensively debated. The Koop inquiry utilized state resources, involved senior officials and members of the U.S. political establishment, elicited a response from key organizations and individuals with expert knowledge about the psychological effects of abortion, and led to coverage in American media.

Given their own marginalization from the abortion debate, it is no surprise that antiabortionists in Britain would look to their American counterparts for inspiration and ideas. How far has the PAS claim enabled the British antiabortion movement to overcome its lack of influence?

PAS IN BRITAIN: MARGINALIZATION CONTINUED

The lasting effect of the diffusion of the PAS claim to Britain has been to reorient the activities of antiabortion organizations. They developed, funded, and staffed a network of counseling centers, and produced leaflets, briefing documents, and books to substantiate the claim that abortion leads to PAS. However, the claim has not as yet been adopted and endorsed by parties outside the British antiabortion movement. The claim remains identified with—and confined to—its original owners. PAS claimants have failed to influence others who might give prominence to the claim.

The most significant attempt to promote the PAS claim in Britain took place in 1994, with the report of the Rawlinson commission on the physical and psycho-social effects of abortion on women (Rawlinson 1994). The Rawlinson commission stands as an interesting contrast with the Koop inquiry. It reveals the problems that confront British PAS claimsmakers who attempt to gain authority for the claim through means similar to those adopted in the United States.

The commission was headed by Lord Rawlinson of Ewell, and administered by Christian Action Research and Education (CARE). Its stated aim was to carry out an investigation into the physical and psychosocial effects of abortion, rather than to discuss the ethics of abortion (Rawlinson 1994:1). Lord Rawlinson was a respected member of Parliament. A life member of the House of Lords, he had been the Attorney General under the Conservative administration during the 1980s. While Lord Rawlinson's chairmanship of the commission gave it some credibility, it is important to note that, unlike the Koop inquiry, there was no governmental involvement in the commission. Of the seven members of Parliament who were members of the Rawlinson commission, none was close to the government or held a position in policymaking on health. Where the Koop inquiry involved government officials at the highest level, the British Department of Health "did not feel it appropriate" to give evidence to the Rawlinson commission, agreeing only to "respond to a specific question" that arose from evidence that was given (Birth Control Trust 1994). The commission was therefore, in parliamentary terms, unofficial.

Where U.S. pro-choice organizations were determined to respond to the PAS claim in the course of the Koop inquiry, in Britain their response was quite different. The 34 Rawlinson commission members included representatives of the organizations Feminists Against Eugenics, Life, SPUC, Doctors Who Respect Human Life, Labour Life, and CARE. Members who were parliamentarians included the veteran antiabortion MP David Alton and Rev. Martyn Smith, MP. It was reported that at the press conference to launch the report, Alton confirmed that "no members [of the commission] were drawn from individuals or organizations with a pro-choice perspective" (Birth Control Trust 1994). According to press reports, the commission "involved 25 prominent antiabortionists . . . and pro-choice experts refused to participate" (Lacey 1997).

In comparison with the Koop inquiry, the publication of the Rawlinson commission's report produced negligible debate. A small number of prochoice organizations issued press releases (National Abortion Campaign 1994; Pro-Choice Alliance 1994). Unlike the extensive media coverage of the Koop report, reporting about the Rawlinson commission was restricted to a small number of articles that stated the Commission's findings. According to the *British Medical Journal* (1994), the report recommended that centers providing abortion "should initiate independent and long-term follow up of those clients considered to be most at risk of emotional distress." A short article in the *Evening Standard* (1994) highlighted the "traumatic" emotional consequences of abortion, and the *Sunday Telegraph* noted that the report contended that women can suffer long-term depression after abortion (Rogers 1994). British journalists did not treat the report's publication as of great significance.

The response of medical and scientific bodies to Rawlinson was also low-key. Only one organization, the Royal College of Psychiatrists (RCP) responded, to dispute a statement made in the commission report about the RCP's position on abortion (Royal College of Psychiatrists 1994). In its press release about its findings, the Rawlinson commission claimed that the RCP had given written evidence that there are "no psychiatric indications for abortion," and went on to assert that this "raises serious questions given that 91 per cent of abortions are carried out on the grounds of the mental health of the mother." The RCP's statement characterized this as "an inaccurate portrayal of the College's views on abortion" and asked for a public retraction. The RCP also choose to restate its opinion that "There is no evidence of an increased risk of major psychiatric disorder or of long lasting psychological distress [following abortion]" (Royal College or Psychiatrists 1994). This was the only public statement issued by a British medical association or college.

Given the importance of medical opinion in framing the abortion debate in Britain, the ability to influence these bodies is vital for those with an interest in abortion. Yet the British medical profession has either not noticed the PAS claim, or has largely chosen to ignore—rather than respond to—it. In contrast with U.S. scientific and medical bodies, the most striking feature of the British medical profession's response to the PAS claim is therefore its absence. The argument that abortion is a social problem because of its alleged serious psychological effects has not generated a response from medical bodies with an interest in abortion.

Following the diffusion of the PAS claim to Britain, no statements or research findings that mention the claim have been issued by the Royal College of Obstetrics and Gynaecology (RCOG). The *Medline* index cites a number of articles and commentaries about "Post-Abortion Syndrome," but all are from American or Canadian medical journals. While the *Journal of the American Medical Association* has published a debate about the issue, no equivalent articles appeared in the *British Medical Journal*. During the 1988 debate about the Alton Bill, some antiabortion MPs made reference to "postabortion syndrome." In response, some doctors made it clear that they did not believe PAS was a credible diagnosis; respected British gyne-cologist Wendy Savage argued, "Postabortion trauma is another condition dreamt up in the US and flown over here to add weight to the [antiabor-tion] argument. Studies of women (including one I did myself) do not show that long term regret after legal abortion is at all common" (McNeil 1991:158).

CONCLUSIONS: THE LIMITS TO DIFFUSION OF ANTIABORTION CLAIMS

While abortion opponents in the United States and Britain hoped that claims against abortion on health grounds would avoid the degree of op-position generated by moral claims, this has proved not to be the case. In both countries, medical and scientific bodies have, to a greater or lesser de-gree, disputed the PAS claim. Given that this claim rests on a contention that abortion is bad for women's mental health, the failure to gain support from these bodies has proved decisive. As long as experts from the APA and the AMA in the United States and the RCOG and the RCP in Britain refuse to endorse the claim, it has little chance of sustained influence in abortion law and policymaking.

While the influence of the PAS claim in both the United States and Britain is currently limited, there is nevertheless a significant difference be-tween these two countries. The PAS claim achieved a prominence in the United States that could not be reproduced in Britain. The key difference between these two societies is the degree of influence the U.S. antiabortion movement exerts in politics. The size and degree of popular support at-tained by the U.S. antiabortion movement has allowed it to play an agenda-setting role in American politics. In contrast, the British antiabor-tion movement has not played a significant role. While the Reagan admin-istration, and later state-based legislators and politicians, were prepared to support the PAS claim, there was no comparable source of political sup-port for the British antiabortion movement.

It is ironic that the adoption of the PAS claim by British abortion oppo-nents was motivated by a need to overcome their political marginalization. However, as the comparison between the Koop inquiry and the Rawlinson commission demonstrates, the adoption of the PAS claim in Britain served to expose this marginalization further. This suggests that a failing move-ment in one country cannot adopt an argument from a more successful one elsewhere and expect to achieve a similar result. The outcome to date of the PAS claim in the U.K. reveals profound differences between this move-ment and its counterpart in the United States that diffusion cannot resolve. Regardless of how effective an argument may be for the American antiabortion movement, there is no guarantee it will have the same impact in Britain.

However, the limited impact of the PAS claim in Britain should not be taken to mean that concern about the psychological effects of abortion has diminished. For those inside medical professions, and in the media, a representation of abortion as having particular emotional risks is pervasive. But there is currently little prospect of this concern being transformed into acceptance that women suffer from a particular "syndrome" following abortion, and that their access to abortion therefore should be restricted. In Britain at least, the PAS claim did not have a decisive effect on the abortion debate, outside of reorientating the British antiabortion movement itself.

NOTES

1. The primary focus of this bill was to regulate experimentation on human embryos. However, one amendment concerned abortion.

2. Rue (1997) says that he first identified and presented evidence for PAS as a type of Post-traumatic Stress Disorder (PTSD) in 1981 when he gave testimony about PAS to the Subcommittee on the Constitution, U.S. Senate Judiciary Committee, 97th Congress, Washington, D.C. Some of Rue's 1980s talks have been published (1984, 1986). Anne Speckhard's (1985) unpublished doctoral dissertation is referred to in a range of writings by antiabortion commentators (cf., Doherty 1995).

3. Discussion of PAS "symptoms" can be found on the Elliott Institute (n.d.) website. The website describes the Elliott Institute as "a non-profit tax exempt corporation that was founded in 1988 to perform original research and education on the impact of abortion on women, men, siblings and society. The Elliot Institute publishes research and educational materials and works as an advocate for women and men seeking postabortion healing." Its main publication is the newsletter *Postabortion Review*. David Reardon (n.d.), director of the Elliott Institute, has explained why he believes it is important for "pro-life forces" to emphasize the negative psychological effects of abortion: "While efforts to educate the public about the unborn's humanity may help to motivate pro-lifers, such efforts will have no effect on those who support abortion. . . . The only way to reach them is for us, too, to focus on the woman. This point is absolutely crucial for pro-lifers to understand."

4. Koop had coauthored an antiabortion book that suggested that legal abortion had led to "the devaluation and destruction of innocent human lives on a massive scale" (Koop and Schaeffer 1983).

5. The Center for Reproductive Law and Policy (1999) lists the following states where "informed consent" laws are currently enforced: Idaho, Indiana, Kansas, Louisiana, Mississippi, Nebraska, North Dakota, Ohio, Pennsylvania, South Carolina, South Dakota, Utah, and Wisconsin. Such requirements passed, but have been blocked in Delaware, Kentucky, Massachusetts, Michigan, Montana, and Tennessee.

6. In a 1997 challenge to Wisconsin's restrictive state law, the judge concluded that if a physician believes that no psychological trauma is associated with the

abortion procedure to be used, "that is what the statute requires him or her to tell the patient" (*Karlin v. Foust*, 975 F. Supp. 1177 [W.D.Wis.1997]).

REFERENCES

Adler, Nancy E., H. P. David, B. N. Major, S. H. Roth, N. F. Russo, and G. E. Wyatt. 1990. "Psychological Responses after Abortion." *Science* 248 (April 6):41.

American Psychiatric Association. 1980. *Diagnostic and Statistical Manual of Mental Disorders*, 3rd ed. Washington: APA.

Birth Control Trust. 1989. *Abortion Review* (Autumn).

———. 1994. *Abortion Review* (Summer).

———. 1998. *Abortion Review* (Autumn).

Boodman, Sandra G. 1992. "Postabortion Trauma Existence Questioned." *Washington Post* (October 27):Z5.

Borrill, Rachel. 1997. "UK Antiabortion Protesters Angry at 'Lunch-hour Termination' Offer." *Irish Times*, June 30.

Bowman, Phyllis. 1996. *And Still They Weep: Personal Stories of Abortion*. Great Britain: SPUC Educational Research Trust.

Boyle, Mary. 1997. *Re-thinking Abortion: Psychology, Gender, Power and the Law*. London: Routledge.

Brien, Joanna, and Ida Fairbairn. 1996. *Pregnancy and Abortion Counselling*. London and New York: Routledge.

British Medical Journal. 1994. "Headlines." 309:8.

British Victims of Abortion. n.d.. "British Victims of Abortion." (leaflet).

Brotman, Barbara. 1990. "Both Sides in Abortion Issue Also Remain Divided over Post-operation Stress." *Chicago Tribune* (April 15):4.

Brown, Gerald. 1997. "Women Need Advice on Quickie Abortions." *Manchester Evening News* (June 28):2.

Center for Reproductive Law and Policy (CRLP). 1999. "Abortion, Mandatory Delays and Biased Counseling Requirements." CRLP factsheet (April 2—available at www.crlp.org).

Council on Scientific Affairs. 1992. "Induced Termination of Pregnancy Before and After Roe v Wade: Trends in the Mortality and Morbidity of Women." *Journal of the American Medical Association* 268:3236.

Dana, Miri. 1987. "Abortion—a Woman's Right to Feel." Pp. 152–77 in *Living with the Sphinx: Papers from the Women's Therapy Centre*, edited by Sheila Ernst and Marie Maguire. London: Women's Press.

David, Henry P. 1997. "Postabortion Psychological Responses." Pp. 341–47 in *Abortion Matters: Proceedings of the 1996 Amsterdam Abortion Conference*, edited by E. Ketting and J. Smit.

Doherty, Peter, ed. 1995. *Postabortion Syndrome: Its Wide Ramifications*. Dublin: Four Courts Press.

Durham, Martin. 1991. *Sex and Politics: The Family and Morality in the Thatcher Years*. Basingstoke: Macmillan.

Eliott Institute. n.d. "A list of the Major Psychological Sequelae of Abortion." Elliot Institute factsheet (available at www.abortionfacts.com).

Evening Standard. 1994. "Tyranny of Freedom of Choice." (April 28):11.

Everett, Flic. 1997. "Grieve . . . But Just Don't Take Too Long." *Manchester Evening News* (July 3).

Franklin, Sarah. 1991. "Fetal Fascinations: New Dimensions to the Medical-scientific Construction of Fetal Personhood." Pp. 190–205 in *Off-Centre: Feminism and Cultural Studies,* edited by S. Franklin, C. Lury, and J. Stacey. London: Harper Collins.

Franz, Wanda. n.d. "What is Postabortion Syndrome?" Factsheet distributed by British Victims of Abortion.

Furedi, Ann. 1998. "Wrong But the Right Thing to Do: Public Opinion and Abortion." Pp. 159–71 in *Abortion Law and Politics Today,* edited by Ellie Lee. Basingstoke: Macmillan.

Guardian. 1992. "Why Deciding Is Not Easy." (October 27):10.

Holden, Constance. 1989. "Koop Finds Abortion Evidence 'Inconclusive.'" *Science* 243:730.

Hopkins, Nick, Steve Reicher, and Jannat Saleem. 1996. "Constructing Women's Psychological Health in Antiabortion Rhetoric." *Sociological Review* 44:539–64.

Illman, John. 1989. "'Vietnam-like Guilt' of Women Haunted by their Abortions." *Daily Mail* (October 20).

Jarmulowicz, Michael. 1992. "The Physical and Psychological Effects of Abortion." Briefing at Leamington Spa:9.

Jenkins, Philip. 1992. *Intimate Enemies: Moral Panics in Contemporary Britain.* Hawthorne, NY: Aldine de Gruyter.

Johnson, Angella. 1992. "Aftermath of Abortion." *Guardian* (September 18):29.

Joseph, S., R. Williams, and W. Yule. 1997. *Understanding Post-traumatic Stress: A Psychosocial Perspective on PTSD and Treatment.* Chichester: John Wiley.

Koop, C. Everett, and Francis A. Schaeffer. 1983. *Whatever Happened to the Human Race?* Rev. ed. Westchester, IL: Crossway.

Kotulak, Ron, and Jon Van. 1989. "Study Shoots Down 'Abortion Syndrome.'" *Chicago Tribune* (February 19):7.

Lacey, Hester. 1997. "Does Abortion Really Ruin Your Life?" *Independent on Sunday* (August 8):32.

Leary, Warren E. 1989. "Koop Says Abortion Report Couldn't Survive Challenge." *New York Times* (March 17): A12.

Legh-Jonson, Alison. 1989. "Abortion: What Are the After-effects?" *Woman* (April 29):28.

Lodl, Karen M., Ann McGelligan, and Janette Bucy. 1987. "Women's Responses to Abortion: Implications for Postabortion Support Groups." Pp. 397–408 in *The Psychology of Women: Ongoing Debates,* edited by Mary Walsh. New Haven, CT: Yale University Press.

Macdonald, Katy. 1992. "The Agony of the Abortion Backlash." *Daily Mail* (September 24):27.

Madigan, Charles M. 1989. "Abortion on Trial, Supreme Court Review Sparks Adversarial Emotions." *Chicago Tribune* (January 15):1.

66

Ellie Lee

McAdam, Doug, and Dieter Rucht. 1993. "The Cross-national Diffusion of Movement Ideas." *Annals of the American Academy of Political and Social Science* 528:56–74.

McNeil, Maureen. 1991. "Putting the Alton Bill in Context." Pp. 149–59 in *Off-Centre: Feminism and Cultural Studies*, edited by S. Franklin, C. Lury, and J. Stacey. London: Harper Collins.

Miles, Rosalind. 1997. "I Used to Believe in Abortion But This Is an Insult to Humanity." *Daily Mail* (June 30).

Moore, Suzanne. 1992. "Looking for Trouble: Unwanted Pain of an Unwanted Pregnancy." *Guardian* (October 8):32.

National Abortion Campaign. 1994. "Leading Antiabortionists Head 'Private Commission.'" News release: February 12.

Nolan, David, and Ann Furedi. 1995. "Fighting a Battle of Ideas: Conflict on Abortion in the U.K." *Planned Parenthood in Europe* 24 (3):7.

O'Connor, Karen. 1996. *No Neutral Ground? Abortion Politics in an Age of Absolutes.* Boulder, CO: Westview.

Okie, Susan. 1989. "Abortion Report Koop Witheld Released on Hill." *Washington Post* (March 17).

Pro-Choice Alliance. 1994. "Private Commission of Inquiry on Abortion." Press release (March 1).

Radcliffe-Richards, Janet. 1982. *The Sceptical Feminist: A Philosophical Enquiry.* London: Routledge.

Randall, Peter. 1996. "Introduction." Pp. ix–xiv in Phyllis Bowman, *And Still They Weep: Personal Stories of Abortion.* Great Britain: SPUC Educational Research Trust.

Rawlinson, Lord. 1994. "The Physical and Psycho-Social Effects of Abortion on Women." Report by the Commission of the Inquiry into the Operation and Consequences of the Abortion Act. Annex 3:22–23.

Reardon, David. n.d. "A New Strategy for Ending Abortion: Learning the Truth—Telling the Truth." Elliott Institute website (www.afterabortion.org).

Rogers, Lois. 1994. "Living with Choice." *Sunday Telegraph* (July 3):6.

Rourke, Mary. 1995. "Forgive—But Not Forget." *Los Angeles Times* (July 19): E-1.

Royal College of Psychiatrists. 1994. "The Royal College of Psychiatrists' Response to the Rawlinson Report on 'The Physical and Psychosocial Effects of Abortion.'" Press release (July 1).

Rue, Vincent. 1984. "The Victims of Abortion." Proceedings of National Right to Life Committee Convention, Kansas City, MO.

———. 1986. "Post-Abortion Syndrome." Proceedings of the First National Conference on Post-Abortion Counseling, University of Notre Dame.

———. 1995. "Post-Abortion Syndrome: A Variant of Post-traumatic Stress Disorder." In *Post-Abortion Syndrome: Its Wide Ramifications*, edited by Peter Doherty. Dublin: Four Courts Press.

———. 1997. "The Psychological Safety of Abortion: The Need for Reconsideration." *Post-Abortion Review* 5 (Fall):7–10.

Sarvis, Betty, and Hyman Rodman. 1973. *The Abortion Controversy.* New York: Columbia University Press.

Scotland on Sunday. 1997. "Editorial." (June 29):14.

Scott, Wilbur J. 1990. "PTSD in DSM-III: A Case in the Politics of Diagnosis and Disease." *Social Problems* 37:294–310.

Scottish Catholic Observer. 1992. "Abortion Claims 3.5 Million Child Victims—and 350,000 Mothers." (September 25):3.

Sheldon, Sally. 1997. *Beyond Control: Medical Power and Abortion Law.* London: Pluto Press.

Simms, Madeleine, and Keith Hindel. 1971. *Abortion Law Reformed.* London: Peter Owen.

Snow, David A., and Robert D. Benford. 1999. "Alternative Types of Cross-national Diffusion in the Social Movement Arena." Pp. 23–39 in *Social Movements in a Globalizing World,* edited by Donatella della Porta, Hanspeter Kriesi, and Dieter Rucht. Basingstoke: Macmillan.

Speckhard, Anne. 1985. "The Psycho-social Aspects of Stress Following Abortion." Unpublished Ph.D. dissertation, University of Minnesota.

Speckhard, Anne, and Vincent Rue. 1992. "Postabortion Syndrome: An Emerging Public Health Concern." *Journal of Social Issues* 48 (3):95–119.

Specter, Michael. 1990. "Psychiatric Panel Condemns Abortion Restrictions." *Washington Post* (May 16): A03.

Steinberg, Deborah Lynn. 1991. "Adversarial Politics: The Legal Construction of Abortion." Pp. 175–89 in *Off-Centre: Feminism and Cultural Studies,* edited by S. Franklin, C. Lury, and J. Stacey. London: Harper Collins.

Stotland, Nada L. 1992. "The Myth of the Abortion Trauma Syndrome." *Journal of the American Medical Association* 268:2078–79.

Thompson, Dick. 1989. "A Setback for Pro-Life Forces." *Time* 133 (March 27):82.

Thorpe, Vanessa. 1996. "'Abortion Wrecks Your Life' Claims Group." *Independent on Sunday* (December 29):3.

U.S. House. 1989. Subcommittee on Human Resources and Intergovernmental Relations, Committee on Government Operations. *The Medical and Psychological Impact of Abortion.* 101st Congress, 1st sess., March 16.

Vogt, Amanda. 1992. "Doubt Cast on Trauma in Abortions." *Chicago Tribune* (October 23):5.

Wilmoth, Gregory H. 1992. "Abortion, Public Health Policy, and Informed Consent Legislation." *Journal of Social Issues* 48(3):1–17.

Young, Allan. 1995. *The Harmony of Illusions: Inventing Post Traumatic Stress Disorder.* Princeton, NJ: Princeton University Press.

Zimmerman, Mary K. 1981. "Psychosocial and Emotional Consequences of Elective Abortion: A Literature Review." Pp. 65–75 in *Abortion Readings and Research,* edited by Paul Sachdev. Canada: Butterworth and Co.

4

Constructing a "Dangerous Gun Culture" in Britain
New Gun Control Laws, 1997

J. ROBERT LILLY

One of the more puzzling aspects of gun issues in the United States is that legislatures seem to accomplish very little that could be confidently termed progressive, or preventive in nature. Yet the body count continues to grow, including at the time of this writing a Michigan first grader shooting and killing a classmate. By contrast, after the 1996 killing of sixteen schoolchildren and a teacher in Dunblane, Scotland, Britain quickly passed legislation that banned small-caliber guns. This paper provides a claims-making/constructionist analysis of this law—the Firearms (Amendment No. 2) Act 1997.

GUN TRADITIONS BEFORE HUNGERFORD: 1700–1987

Firearms in Britain are not new cultural artifacts. They are part of the nation's most recognizable traditions that include military defense, imperialistic policies, and domestic and international sporting events. Not surprisingly, these traditions and the importance of firearms to their existence are deeply embedded in the cultural contours of class-based interests. The old customs of riding to the hounds and shooting game came from the upper echelons and the landed gentry.

Target shooters trace the beginnings of the sport of rifle and pistol shooting in Britain to the country's unexpected and ignominious early failures in the Boer War (1899–1902). This experience and the specter of potential German and/or French invasions of the homeland, contributed to a post–Boer War movement to beef up what some observers termed the nation's sagging martial arts. The superior marksmanship of the enemy, for example, influenced the military to encourage establishing civilian shooting clubs in hopes of a better performance in the next war. Lord Salisbury, who was Prime Minister during the Boer War, is credited with saying he could see the day when there would be a rifle in every English cottage (Elliot 1996:1). Other efforts established the Boy Scouts (1909), and later an emphasis was placed on teaching women how to shoot rifles (Ryan 1980:10).

The post–Boer War concern about Britain's martial preparedness was preceded nearly sixty years earlier by another "war scare." Immediately after Louis Napoleon (later Napoleon III) seized power in France in an 1852 coup d' etat, Alfred Lord Tennyson wrote a poem, "Rifle Club," that was widely read when it was published later in the *Times* (May 9, 1859) as "Form, Form, Riflemen Form." It appealed to the fear that Britain was "no match for the large conscript army of the Second Empire" (Clarke 1992). This publication predated the long-rifle clubs that later were seen as providing the genesis of the Home Defense Force.

The sport of shooting pistols at targets competitively became an event in the first modern Olympic games, held April 6–15, 1896, in Athens, Greece. One of the modern Olympic games founders, Baron de Coubertain, was himself a pistol shooter. Sumner Paine, from the United States, won the games' first "Free Pistol and Rapid Fire" gold medal. In 1901, Britain's National Small-bore Rifle Association was organized. Later, during the early post–World War years when the British Empire changed its moniker to the British Commonwealth, it sponsored pistol shooting at the Manchester Commonwealth Games. And in the 1950s the British Shooting Sports Council was established, having evolved from an informal meeting of shooting notables. For some years they had been known as the Long Room Committee, a reference to the meeting place on the premises of one of London's firearms dealers. Tory Michael Colvin explains: "This country has a long and honourable tradition in the sport of pistol shooting, the sport that Britain invented and has dominated for the past one hundred years. It is a sporting success story for Britain" (Macdonell 1997b).

Gun clubs, where "shooters" could practice their aim, became popular, and by 1996, there were reported to be 2,118 gun clubs in Britain (Lederer 1996). The selective membership of gun clubs, as well as the government's stringent licensing procedures that required all applicants for gun ownership to submit a recommendation from someone of high esteem, served to solidify gun ownership as a privilege for the relatively influential and wealthy. Those who qualified for a license based on their apparent respectability enjoyed the sport of shooting.

The possession of firearms has been heavily regulated in Britain since 1824, when soldiers brought guns back from the Napoleonic Wars and the police were given the right to arrest anyone holding a weapon with the intent to commit a crime (Moore 1996). In 1920, gun controls were tightened: anyone holding a firearm was required to obtain a license because people were terrified of a Bolshevik revolt. In the wake of the American "gangster" era seventeen years later, machine guns were banned (*Economist* 1994:69). Gun-control measures were expanded with the 1968 Firearms Act, which further regulated licensing procedures. Generally speaking, throughout history, Britain has experienced great control and confidence about guns within her borders. That confidence has been seriously challenged by new constructions of gun culture in Britain.

THE EMERGENCE OF A "DANGEROUS GUN CULTURE," 1987–1997

While Britain has well-established gun traditions, today some Britons think that a recently developed gun culture is a scourge among the people. The term "gun culture" does not appear in the earlier discourse describing the *respectable* sport of shooting, but it is now used to criticize the role of guns and their owners. These critics perceive guns and the people who own them as dangerous and not worthy of a full measure of respect. Two major, somewhat similar events contributed to this newfound fear of firearms in Britain, the 1987 Hungerford and the 1996 Dunblane incidents.

In August 1987, a young man named Michael Ryan went on a six-hour random shooting spree in and around the 800–1,000-year-old, sleepy market town of Hungerford. He first killed his dog and his mother, then set her house ablaze. Next he shot at firemen and killed two neighbors. He then drove 25 miles to Savernake Forest, where he killed a woman finishing a picnic with her two toddlers. After next driving to Hungerford, he walked down High Street shooting more people, including, among others, a policeman, a couple parked in a car, and a 63-year-old woman taking in the sunshine in a wheelchair. He entered a school that was empty for the summer, and after talking with police, shot himself. Counting Ryan, seventeen people were killed.

Often reported as the worst shooting incident in British history, the Hungerford "massacre" was treated as an anomaly by the British media.[1] The mass murder of sixteen people by a man with a gun was a phenomenon the British believed might happen elsewhere, but certainly not in their country. It was constructed as a "freak tragedy," committed by a young man who, according to his neighbors, simply needed more love and sympathy in his life (Wynn-Jones 1997).[2] In response to this incident, 48,000 firearms were voluntarily surrendered to the government, and automatic weapons were banned by the 1988 Firearms Act.[3] Between the time of the Hungerford and the 1996 Dunblane tragedies, government officials, academics, and the media reported little about gun problems in Britain, although a few stories attracted notice.

An August 1987 *St. Petersburg Times* article with a London dateline was titled, "Massacre in Britain Called U.S.-style Violence." It contributed to the Americanization of Ryan's crimes by describing him as a "combat-jacketed Rambo" whose killings were a form of an "American disease" (O'Connor 1987). In the same article, a psychology lecturer and former English police superintendent claimed that Ryan could be said to form part of the gun culture that was quite specific to the United States. Dr. Paul Devonshire, a clinical psychologist at a London hospital, was quoted: "There are many similarities between ourselves and America. I think it's something we could see within our own tradition" (O'Connor 1987).

In July 1987, police in London ambushed a payroll robbery gang, killing two. Among the gang's arsenal were two shotguns (O'Connor 1987). Within two years of Hungerford there were at least three incidents involving shootings similar to Ryan's. At the end of 1987, Kevin Weaver murdered four people in Bristol. When he was arrested, he was found to have a pump-action shotgun, a sawn-off shotgun, and up to 800 rounds of ammunition. In January 1988, a deputy headmaster and four schoolboys were injured when a youth went on a rampage with a double-barreled shotgun in school. In September 1988, 18-year-old Tony Bhaskett is reported to have "gone berserk" in Walsall, wounding three other youths before killing himself (Holden 1989). Later, the *Economist* stated that the number of armed robberies rose 127 percent between 1982 and 1992 (*Economist* 1994). Claims about these other incidents, indicating that a dangerous gun culture was already in Britain, helped raise popular anxiety over firearms and crime (Taylor 1996).

But the fear that Britain had developed a gun culture did not fully materialize until 1996, with the qualitatively different Dunblane incident. Here, Thomas Hamilton gunned down sixteen children and one schoolteacher at one of the ostensibly safest places for the young, a *primary school*. These deaths were systematically planned and there was no doubt that Thomas wanted to kill *children*. Like Ryan, the murderer committed suicide and denied a traumatized and grieving public the incalculable, expressive benefits of a trial where blame could be assessed, punishment assigned, and closure assisted (Lilly and Ball 1982).

Responses to the Dunblane deaths reflected and extended the earlier claims about gun violence made after Hungerford. In some circles, people began to see a *pattern* emerging—of unprecedented violence involving guns. In light of the Dunblane incident, Hungerford was no longer viewed as an anomaly, but as a precursor or a symptom of a "disease" or "cancer" running rampant throughout the land. An August 10, 1997, news report recalled Hungerford: "Something also died in Britain that day, as gun culture and mass killings . . . abruptly arrived" (Wynn-Jones 1997:5).

Newspapers repeatedly printed statistics concerning gun ownership and gun violence, and they fanned the spark into a fire of outrage. The *New Statesman* reported a 142 percent increase in the use of handguns in crimes (Squires 1996:12). The *Economist* (1995:40) reported: "Between 1983 and 1993, the number of offenses recorded by police in which firearms were involved nearly doubled, to 14,000." The chief constable of Grampien police stated: "Shootings are now an everyday occurrence in Manchester, Glasgow, and Merseyside" (quoted in *Economist* 1995:40). According to Kevin Dunn, correspondent to the television show, "News," there is one gun for every twenty people in Britain—an estimated 200,000 to 250,000 legally owned handguns, and one million illegal guns. Another estimate is that there are 1.9 million legally held guns in the United Kingdom, and between 200,000 and one million illegally held guns (Moore 1996).

Only days after the Dunblane incident, senior police officers also voiced strong concern for the growing number of guns in Britain. A year before Dunblane they had written to the Home Secretary recommending a gun amnesty. They were concerned because the number of weapons in circulation was alarming. More than 800,000 firearms certificates were issued annually, but the officers estimated that as many as 3 million firearms were in circulation (Campbell 1996). A spokesman for the Association of Chief Police Officers reinforced this position by saying that gun amnesty had been under active discussion for more than a year. Sir Paul Condon, London's Metropolitan Police Commissioner, also expressed fears about a gun culture emerging on the streets of Britain's inner cities (Timmins 1996).

These statistics implied that Britain was a country with an advanced problem of gun violence far worse than it was ten short years earlier. The Hungerford incident was rapidly re-constructed as a stepping stone to Dunblane, one that had been previously *misunderstood*. Michael Ryan too was re-constructed. No longer was he depicted as an anomaly, or as an individual deserving pity. On the tenth anniversary of Hungerford, the local vicar, Rev. Andrew Sawyer, described the former soldier, Michael Ryan, as "'raw evil'" (Holiday 1997:15). Now he was seen as a product of a culture that supported such violence. Hungerford and Dunblane were now viewed, not as transient tragedies for which there was no explanation, but as cultivated realities.

CLAIMS CONCERNING GUNS AND GUN OWNERS

In the marketplace of ideas, there are many competing claims vying for attention from the media, government officials, and the general public. Constructionist analysts suggest that the most successful claims contain "cultural resonance," or threaten the mores and values of a society. This approach can be used to explain why the most recent social construction

of a dangerous gun culture in Britain has been so successful. Though un-
defined, the term "gun culture" has been linked to many elements considered undesirable in British society, resulting in increased emotional fervor
over the issue and the mobilization of groups on both sides of the issue.

A Sense of Community and Xenophobia

As an island nation, Britain is well known for its claims to uniqueness,
solidarity, community, and tradition. In recent years, such traits have been
demonstrated by a consistent resistance both to new immigrants and to becoming a "good citizen" of the European Community. Examples abound;
two will suffice. In August 1989, it was announced that John Major, then
the new Foreign Secretary, was going to Hong Kong. His mission was to
reassure residents about their future and the possible resettlement of 3.5
million dependent-territory passport holders, in England. The *Sunday Telegraph* published a five-column critical response that termed the language
used by some of the Thatcher government's statements that described
Hong Kong's people as "our fellow citizens" and "hard working British
subjects," as "disingenuous references" that could not conceal Hong Kong
citizens' "profound foreignness" and "fervent patriotism" for China (Lovibond 1989:16). The column elaborated by arguing that almost weekly the
homeland was retreating from its Englishness, in large measure because of
the "pernicious doctrine of multi-racialism." Troublesome developments
included 20,000 Muslims who burned the Union Jack in London; the appointment of a Nigerian as Lord Mayor of a northern city; and the announcement that the majority of students in London schools were from
immigrant families. The columnist lamented that barely a generation ago,
"these islands were occupied by a single people, who despite differences
by region, background and expectation were bound by common loyalties
and affections, by a shared history and memory" (Lovibond 1989:16). In
1989, this sense of loss was not unique to the British Isles. A similar theme
resounded across much of Europe whenever the implications of the forth-
coming European Community were discussed. Professor Chris Mullard,
head of ethnic studies at the University of Amsterdam, observed: "The
states in Europe are fiercely nationalistic" (Alibhai 1989). The worry was
that a respectable xenophobia was mushrooming all over the continent,
one that was white, racist, and very powerful.

This view of Britain was twice reinforced in late 1999 and early 2000, first
in a political statement, and then in a policy. When former Prime Minister
Thatcher spoke at the annual Conservative party conference, almost a
decade to the day since the fall of the Berlin Wall, she fervently stated, "We
are quite the best country in Europe. In my lifetime all the problems have
come from mainland Europe, and all the solutions have come from the English-speaking nations across the world" (Hoge 1999:A1). Four months

later, Britain put into effect perhaps the strictest limits on asylum in Europe in hopes of stemming the tide of immigrants (Lyall 2000).

Part of maintaining British self-proclaimed uniqueness and solidarity is the disapproval of most anything foreign taking residence. For those who oppose gun ownership, this is a marketable fear that has proven to be unmatched in its effectiveness. Less than a year before Dunblane, the *Economist* (1995:40) stated there had been reports of "a flood of cheap firearms leaking into Britain through the EU." The same publication had made a similar comment a year earlier: "The pool of illegal arms is growing ... since border controls between European Union states were relaxed" (*Economist* 1994:69). In one instance, France was identified as the place where gun-runners could buy cut-price weapons and ship them to Britain by slipping them past tired Customs staff (Osward 1996). British soldiers were also said to have smuggled arms back from Bosnia and the Falklands.

Claimsmakers also attributed Britain's new gun culture to the importation of Jamaican crime gangs, known as "yardies," and their involvement in the manufacture and sale of drugs. "Yardies" are said to have started out as political factions formed to protect communities, but as researcher John Davison claimed, "Having tasted the power of the gun, these young men took the short step from political gangsterism into armed crimes" (quoted in Coughland 1997). The lucrative nature of these crimes eventually led them to running drugs into other countries, Britain among them. Davison's (1997) book on the subject, *Gangsta*, has been described by journalists as a "well-documented account" and a "chilling read": "This account of the yardies' impact on cities thousands of miles apart offers a cautionary tale of the far-reaching consequences once guns are fed into a society" (Coughlan 1997).

A Crisis in Masculinity

Yardies and some of the organizations opposing gun control were also linked to "a rather desperate crisis in masculinity" (Taylor 1996:8). This claim, based on a form of literary criticism, asserted that when the routine domination of men within the gender order is challenged, defensive discourses emerge. For Britain, the "crisis of masculinity" was triggered by the "condition of continuing and long-term poverty born of the crisis of mass manufacturing" (Taylor 1996:8). This argument claimed that because men were deprived of cultural capital generated by skilled and unskilled employment, crime markets serve as alternative sources for confirmations of masculinity. Guns were linked to this source of masculinity as organizational tools, not unlike the mythical role of guns used to tame the United States' Wild West.

The most frequent accusations found in news articles concerning gun ownership was that Britain was developing an "American-style" gun culture (Evans 1997a). America, "where guns are ubiquitous," was often pointed to as an instigator of the growing gun culture in Britain (*Economist* 1996:57). American movies, television, literature, advertisements, and magazines were charged with promoting gun ownership and gun violence to the citizens of Britain. Some claimsmakers were quick to stress the large numbers of people murdered by guns in the United States (for 1994: 15,463 in America, 75 in Britain), and to attribute those numbers to the United States' liberal gun-control policy and its uncivilized culture (Taylor 1996, 1998; Witkin 1996:44). Still others claimed that gun licenses were harder to obtain in Japan than in Britain, and that Japan had proportionately fewer handgun murders (*Economist* 1996:69). These critics argued for stringent gun controls. One British government official, in an attempt to save his Victims of Crime bill, stressed to the public that it was not intended to create an American-style gun culture, but to protect victims' rights (Macdonell 1997a). Claimsmakers also argued that California Governor Pete Wilson's veto of a bill that would have "banned quickly-manufactured, unsafe, 'Saturday night specials' is a demonstration of how entrenched United States gun culture is" (Reed 1997). Such statements indicted people from the United States and Jamaica as uncivilized outsiders and held them responsible for the pollution of Britain's streets, largely removing the responsibility from the British people, and placing it on feared foreigners.

The Sexualization of the Gun

Claimmakers also made an extended effort to link firearms with improper sexual mores. This was done by attacking the image of the gun itself in the media and the individual values of shooters. Advertisers were often accused of developing "pornographic" advertisements featuring guns to sell movies, television shows, gun magazines, and guns themselves, including toy guns. An article entitled "Shooters Aren't Sexy" argued:

> In the cinema, the car chase has been replaced by explicitly choreographed gun play. Guns have become sexy, powerful, and addictive. In the younger market brutal gunplay is the common denominator of the fantasy comics which brought us Pamela Anderson's *Barb Wire*. Newsagents should apply discretion to the stocking and display of "hard-core" US-style gun magazines, just as they do with hard-core pornography. (Squires 1996:12)

Great attention focused on the sexual activities of Thomas Hamilton, the Dunblane murderer. The *Cullen Inquiry*, the official report on the incident, dedicated three chapters to documenting Hamilton's mental state, including his apparent long-standing sexual preoccupation with young boys. The document meticulously detailed Hamilton's involvement with various boys' clubs for a period of many years, and the rumors that circulated about him concerning his intentions toward the boys that he mentored. In the report, Lord Cullen argued that various complaints had been lodged against Hamilton by parents and other concerned citizens. According to County Commissioner Brian D. Fairgrieve,

> While unable to give concrete evidence against this man, I feel that too many "incidents" related to him such that I am far from happy about his having any association with Scouts. He has displayed irresponsible acts by taking young favourite Scouts for weekends during the winter and sleeping in his van. . . . The lack of precautions for such outdoor activities displays either irresponsibility or an ulterior motive for sleeping with the boys. (quoted in Cullen 1996:Section 4.6)

The accusations did not result in either a reprimand or incarceration of Hamilton for sexual misconduct, nor did he sexually assault any of the Dunblane children before they were killed. What claimsmakers managed to do was link acts that the British found repulsive and abnormal to gun ownership, thereby tainting guns by association. A newsmagazine article managed to link pedophilia with guns by arguing that the families of the Dunblane victims are "owe[d] . . . an acknowledgment . . . that we are perilously soft on persistent paedophiles." (Riddell 1996)

ORGANIZATIONAL PROMOTION AND REMEDIES

If the social construction of a new problem is to survive in the marketplace of ideas, it requires support from organized groups. In order to obtain policies that successfully address the problem, there must be organized pressure to propose, pass, and implement new policies (Lowney and Best 1995:51). Organized groups, who eventually won their battle for more intense gun-control measures, heavily supported claims of a developing or existing gun culture in Britain.

Governmental Remedies Arrive

There was a general consensus that stricter gun laws were in order; according to a 1988 Gallup Poll, 75 percent of the British people favored a ban on all guns in Britain (Gabb 1988:2). Public consensus, coupled with little protest from any gun lobby, resulted in the Firearms Act of 1988, which banned semiautomatic and automatic guns and also tightened the licensing regulations. Still, some argued that a strong gun lobby prevented a total ban from being realized. Former cabinet minister David Mellor criticized the gun lobby for watering down the 1988 Firearms Act (Mcgregor 1996:7).

But another argument could be made to explain why there was not a complete ban. The British simply did not view guns as the problem in 1988. They did not think of Hungerford as an expression of a violent gun culture in Britain. They sympathized with the shooter, they blamed themselves for not anticipating Michael Ryan's troubles, and they certainly did not view Hungerford as a precursor to Dunblane. Their disbelief that a second such incident would occur on English soil prevented them from lobbying heavily for a ban on all handguns, and therefore against the sport of shooting. The gun-control measures of 1988 went largely uncontested and were therefore passed into law within a short time.

The Dunblane incident produced a different reaction from many British people, however. As previously discussed, Dunblane altered the way that Hungerford was viewed, and it also altered the way the British viewed guns. In the eyes of many British people, Dunblane typified a very violent pattern that set them into action. The measures taken after Hungerford suddenly seemed ineffective. It was apparent to many citizens that a more extreme approach was warranted to battle the gun culture in Britain.

One claim made to demonstrate the existence of a gun culture in Britain was that anyone could secure a license for a gun. The families of Dunblane victims, the government, and Parliament—in fact, most of the British population—were especially outraged that Thomas Hamilton was able to secure a gun license when he was, in their opinion, so obviously unstable. What followed was great emphasis on devising procedures that would allow the licensing authorities to evaluate the mental health of all applicants and impose longer waiting periods before one could secure a gun. The senior police officers' Superintendents' Association for England and Wales was one of many groups that proposed that applications for gun licenses should be supported by a psychological profile approving the applicant's mental health (Butler 1996). The Shooting Sportspersons Liaison Committee (SSLC) argued in October 1996 that the criminal records of applicants should be checked, and that applicants should submit a form signed by a qualified doctor demonstrating that they were of sound mind before their probationary period (of at least six months) began. Only upon successful completion of the probationary period would gun owners be permitted to keep their guns at home. The SSLC also proposed that a minimum attendance requirement for gun clubs be instituted, and that an independent licensing authority be appointed (Booth 1996).

Official Inquiry

Unlike Hungerford, Dunblane had its own official inquiry headed by a lord. On March 21, 1996, Britain's Secretary of State requested that Scottish judge Lord Cullen conduct an inquiry into the Dunblane incident and offer suggestions for preventing such tragedies in the future (Cullen 1996: Foreword). In addition to exploring Hamilton's mental state in great detail, the *Cullen Inquiry* attempted to ascertain why he was given a license in light of his apparent mental instability. While the vetting procedures established by the 1968 Firearms Act (and reaffirmed by the 1988 Act) required that an applicant be a "suitable person to hold a firearm certificate" (Cullen 1996:6.8), it did not require the applicant to submit proof of his mental competence. Nor did licensing authorities attempt to gauge the applicant's mental competence. The procedure did require complete criminal background checks, however, and this was the litmus test used to determine whether an applicant was suitable.

Better Police Training

The *Cullen Inquiry* was submitted to the government on October 16, 1996, only seven months after Hamilton's murderous rampage. It suggested that police officers responsible for the licensing system be better trained to recognize character flaws, that at least two letters of recommendation should be provided at the time of application, and that a body should be convened to discuss the involvement of doctors in assessing the mental health of applicants. If such precautions were taken, the perpetuation of a gun culture might be halted. The report also suggested that self-loading pistols and revolvers be disabled and secured at gun clubs, where membership rosters should be closely monitored, thereby keeping tight rein on the gun problem.

The *Cullen Inquiry* took a middle-of-the-road approach to the problem, one that was criticized by many. The government chose not to take Lord Cullen's advice, calling it "impractical" (Travis 1996), and took the position that handguns should be banned, the position taken by most citizens of Britain. The only question that remained was how far the ban would extend.

Ban Guns

In 1996, Prime Minister John Major and the Conservative government pushed for a ban on all higher-caliber handguns, exempting the single-shot .22 and all those of lesser caliber. This proposal would have resulted in banning those kinds of weapons used by Hamilton, while allowing gun owners to continue their sport shooting, although requiring that all handguns of .22 caliber and below be kept at fortified gun clubs. Michael Howard, the Home Secretary, said that such requirements were "the minimum conditions for the continuation of handgun shooting in Britain" (Travis 1996).

Sympathizers and Families Organize

Unlike the aftermath of Hungerford, supporters of the families of the Dunblane victims formed the Snowdrop Campaign (also known as the Snowdrop Petition). It called for a complete ban, saying: "We have argued all along that this is an issue on which there must be no compromise. What we have before us is exactly that—a compromise that . . . will result in the deaths of more innocent people" (Lederer 1996:2A). The *St. Louis Dispatch* (1996) quoted the parents: "Any decision to continue to permit lawful possession of firearms implies a willingness by this government to tolerate gun crime."

The influence of the Snowdrop Campaign organization is hard to overestimate. Its themes struck a resonate chord, "mak[ing it] stand out amongst single-issue campaigns" (Thomson, Stancich, and Dickson 1998). It was organized within a few days of the killings. By March 22, 1996, less than two weeks after the massacre, its organizers attended the Scottish Grand Committee and met with Dr. Mick North, an articulate professor and widowed single parent who had lost his only child, a daughter, to Hamilton. At this time, the organizers decided that contrary to their initial desires, they could not remain anonymous. By May, the Snowdrops had begun collecting signatures and handing out antigun literature during the first days of the 26-day public Cullen Inquiry. In July, the group traveled with victims' parents to Parliament and handed over a petition with more than 700,000 signatures calling for a complete handgun ban. Three months later, in October, Ann Pearston, one of the Snowdrop organizers and a Conservative, made an emotional, but tightly measured speech with great affect, at the Labour party's annual conference (Smith 1997). During the time of these concerted efforts, an impressive memorial monument was planned for the Dunblane victims. The school building was razed and the monument constructed on the very spot where the victims died. (In contrast, it took ten years before Hungerford held its first commemoration event and placed its victims' names on a modest plaque.)

The Labour party supported the families of Dunblane victims. Gordon Brown (1996:8), member of Labour, argued that banning all handguns was essential because legally held weapons were used in both Hungerford and Dunblane, and .22-caliber guns have equally lethal effects as larger-caliber guns. The families of Dunblane victims and the Labour party were unable to convince the Conservative government to proceed with a ban on all handguns. The Firearms Act of February 1997 did not ban all guns, but it did ban all handguns above .22 caliber and required that gun clubs heighten their security so that they could safely house all guns not banned. Those who owned any of the exempted guns were to temporarily turn them in to the police until the gun clubs could meet the restrictions. The provisions of the act began in June 1996, and all phases were to be completed by October 1, 1996. In January 1997, there was a proposal to extend the proposed ban to include all handguns. It was accepted in the Commons, but failed in the Lords, 215 to 81 (Evans 1997b). In May 1997, a second proposal to extend the 1997 Act to include all handguns, including those below .22 caliber, was introduced in the Commons; it was approved in June. The 1997 Act and the proposed amendment generated even more controversy and, subsequently, more organizational mobilization.

There was great support for the complete ban of all handguns from a cross-section of people. Gill Marshall-Andrews of the Gun Control Network supported the complete ban and argued that shooters had "no conception of the encroaching American gun culture"; she accused them of resisting legislation "that is patently in the interests of public safety" (Evans 1997a). She claimed that the shooters had "narrow sectional interests," and "that if the Lords did not approve the ban, the people should ask if the Upper House has a purpose in modern Britain."

The ban also received support from the police. The Police Federation chairman claimed that the Lower House's approval of the complete ban in May of 1997 was a "victory for common sense" (Deane 1997). The British police force had just recently begun to arm themselves with guns in response to their fears of a raging gun culture and, reportedly, of high gangster drug activity. The London police reported having twelve cars on the streets of London, each equipped with three officers and three guns, a practice that was uncommon ten years earlier (*Economist* 1995:40). One report related: "The public is feeling increasingly insecure" (*Economist* 1994:69).

The proposal for a complete ban was heartily supported by the new British [Labour] government and Parliament, with the exception of the Tories and the House of Lords. Home Office Minister Alun Michael applauded the proposed amendment, saying that .22-caliber guns are portable, easy to conceal, and lethal in their effect, and to make exceptions would make nonsense of the Bill (Macdonell 1997b). Michael also argued that: "The commitment to this legislation given by the Prime Minister and the Home Secretary has won support from those who campaigned for the ban and from the police, including the Police Federation and the Association of Chief Police Officers, who have to deal with the effects of the 'gun culture'" (Cordon 1997). Lord McNally, a Liberal Democrat frontbencher, claimed: "This is the piece of legislation that can say, as a country we are going to combat the gun culture" (Macdonell 1997b).

The shooting industry, its supporters in the Tory party, and the House of Lords, fought these claims to prevent the ban on all handguns. Viscount Slim expressed a common argument among proshooters when he warned:

"Nothing in this Bill, when enacted, will stop evil people from getting hold of guns and committing evil acts of murder" (Evans 1997b). It was also argued that anyone truly wanting a gun could secure one by illegal means, and therefore the bill was unwarranted. John Dyer (1997:1) of the Sporting Shooters Association asked, "Is the problem guns, or those who are clearly in need of help but simply don't get it?" Pat Johnson, secretary of the British Shooting Sports Council, also argued: "This Bill will not prevent criminals from using guns, nor will it stop maniacs from getting hold of whatever weapon they choose. The only individuals who will be affected are target shooters who were looking forward to competing in the Sydney Olympics and the Manchester Commonwealth Games. Their sport is now gone" (Deane 1997:66). Tory Michael Colvin claimed that the bill was being considered in the "highly emotive atmosphere" following Dunblane and would penalize competition shooters (Macdonell 1997b).

David Maclean, former Home Office Minister, laid the responsibility on other elements of British society when he proclaimed: "They should tackle television and let them tackle the influence of films in those areas which promote the gun culture. They shouldn't be tackling the Commonwealth team, the British Olympic Team and those who are legitimately handling firearms safely in gun clubs" (Macdonell 1997b). C.C.C. Cheshire, the chief executive of the National Rifle Association, echoed the sentiment a month later when he argued: "Neither of those men [Michael Ryan and Thomas Hamilton] would have had weapons if the police had done their job" (Hoge 1997:2).

Despite the objections, the 1997 Firearms Act was amended in November 1997 to include a ban on handguns, including the .22 caliber and those below. Sportsmen exported their guns to foreign gun clubs where they may still compete, or surrendered them to the British government for destruction. The number of lower-caliber handguns was believed to have been 40,000, and by November 3, 1997, 26,000 of those had been handed into the government in anticipation of the amendment's passage (Cordon 1997). The shooting teams for the Olympics and the Commonwealth Games must train outside of Britain if they wish to continue participation in the competitions.

Efforts to ban all guns in Britain continue. Following its successful campaign and amid internal rancor, the Snowdrop organization folded. Dr. Mick North, with the support of the Gun Control Network, took this topic to the U.N.'s crime prevention and criminal justice division. They hoped to get a declaration on gun-related violence similar to that on human rights. And they wanted the UN to give them "consultative status," which the National Rifle Association acquired after it opened a European office in Brussels (McAlpine 1997).

CONCLUSIONS

It is instructive to view social problems as matters of definition dependent upon changing constructions of reality, where more can be learned through examination of claims and counter-claims than through studying conditions themselves (Spector and Kitsuse 1977; Ball and Lilly 1982). Yet, it is essential to examine conditions because they influence the activities involved in problem definition.

It was the misfortune of guns and their owners to become entangled in an obscene tragedy at the same time Britain was experiencing a structural transition from one social order to another. A society that a mere generation prior was relatively isolated and white, by the time of Dunblane had become multicultural and racially diverse. Traditions, however defined, were pressured into changes often initiated by global developments far beyond Britain's ability to control.

Gun owners, especially those shooting for sport and who were members of shooters' clubs, were the recipients of expressive redefinitions. Rather than being viewed as respectable and solid representatives of tradition, they were now identified as nutters. This change accompanied the shift from Britain being isolationist to becoming a vulnerable member in a post-1989 New Europe without borders. In the face of this transition and the Dunblane incident, lobbying against gun control was then seen in some circles as nothing more than a political strategy used by a marginalized population, composed primarily of men. They were not helped by the appearance on TV of some of spokespeople dressed in camouflage, whose verbal skills identified them to some observers as "nutters," better watched than listened to.

A different sense of victimization also existed post-Dunblane compared to post-Hungerford. In part this can be explained by how the two events were dramatized in the media. In terms of drama, Hungerford was *new*.[4] There was nothing with which to compare it within Britain. At this time, a discourse had not been developed to make sense out of what had happened, except that it was a horrible tragedy caused by a nutter. But by Dunblane, Britain had had nine years to develop a new discourse about guns and crimes. If Hungerford had been anomalous, Dunblane was an obscene tragedy involving different, less disparate, unimaginable victims, innocents murdered by a local under foreign influence. Who could be more innocent than children?

The presentation of Dunblane as a community added considerably to the drama. While Hungerford and Dunblane are relatively anonymous places, that had little purchase in collective consciousness until each tragedy, they were presented as being very different. Compared to the southern England, old style, foxhound, sleepy community that was Hungerford, Dunblane represented an idyllic version of the best of Scottish rural life "to which we all aspire" (Hastings 1996:9). One observer interpreted how the two communities differed:

> Dunblane is a prosperous, upper middle class town, with more than its fair share of movers and shakers, and a certain symbolic significance in Scotland, a bulwark of conservative Scottishness. The murders were all the more harrowing for occurring there than in say, Aberdeen, which has elements of a rough oil town now. Hungerford is a provincial English backwater in comparison. One might expect a more robust, empowered response from the people of Dunblane. (Nellis 2000)

In some eyes, Dunblane was an extension of the dramatic shadow that hung over Lockerbie, the Scottish community that, after an airliner was bombed out of the sky during the 1988 holiday season, proved it could rally round, cope with the impossible, and would not be destroyed by the madness of others. From this perspective, the aftermath of Dunblane was not about guns. It was about how communities cope with tragedy, about parental outrage over an issue with which a whole nation, perhaps the world, could identify—school security. In the absence of the killers who could be tried and punished, guns and gun owners became the villains to be blamed. If the victims wanted gun control, they could hardly be denied.[5] In the face of the considerable influence garnered by the Snowdrop campaign during a preelection campaign that saw the demise of nearly two decades of Conservative dominance, the small-bore shooters were overwhelmed.

The lack of a total gun ban suggests an important point. Nearly one million legal long guns are still in private hands in Britain, and perhaps more than this number in illegal hands. In a very fundamental way, gun traditions are still very much alive and growing in Britain, helped to a still unknown extent by the loose borders that have come with post-1989 developments in the New European community. What was banned represents more of a Pyrrhic win than a total, new, scorched-earth, antigun victory.

The speed with which the ban was generated, however, does speak to two fundamental differences between the United States and Britain. Gun control efforts in these two countries are in some ways separated by a common tongue. Both countries cherish their communities, but each approaches this subject with different ideas about its core. In the United States, the community represents a place where "individual rights" are protected, enjoyed, and debated. Among these rights is the contested, but protected, place of guns as constructed by the language of the U.S. Constitution's Second Amendment. No such contested barrier exits in Britain; it has no constitution, hence nothing like the Second Amendment.

The British legislation prohibiting private possession of handguns embodied a "community consensus" about conflicting values. It came out on the side of the greater freedom of public safety from gun-related crimes. Closely allied to the basic differences in the two nations' histories and forms of government is the fact that in Britain judges are not empowered to overturn legislation. One reason for this tradition is the belief that the hardest questions about rights and liberties have no answer in law. According to one interpretation, they are essentially political questions in which judges have no special competence (Gray 1997). To require judges to arbitrate such questions would implicate them in political conflict. In the United States, this is much less an issue. Its judges are ostensibly "politically free," but they are full-blown politicians because most of them are elected. In Britain, for the most part, judges are appointed.

Because of the emphasis placed on individual rights in the United States, the sense and presence of community in Britain stands out in relatively stark relief. Governmental, gun-lobby, and law-enforcement responses to gun tragedies in the United States rarely mention community. By comparison, after examining more than 500 British-based articles for this chapter, I found that language about community was paramount.

It is helpful to think of this in terms of issues other than gun killings. Currently, in the United States, an organization called "Be an Angel" *asks* car drivers to indicate their willingness to donate their body parts should they be involved in a fatal wreck. They can do so by marking a box on their license. In England, new driver's licenses have a place to mark if drivers *do not* want to donate organs if an accident is fatal. The assumption is that few would refuse. Last, in 1999, the British government proposed allowing the detention of psychopaths and pedophiles who have never been convicted or held as suspects, as a crime-prevention measure. The proposal was made by the Home Secretary, Jack Straw, who said that people coming under the new measure would have "regular quasi-judicial reviews" about two years apart (*Agence France Presse* 1999; Watts 1999). Such a suggestion in the United States would very likely be heresy and political suicide because it would violate a number of laws protecting individual rights.

New crimes offer the mass media, activists, government officials, and experts fresh stories. The Dunblane deaths of the schoolchildren are a classic example of a new crime. It provided the platform for restructuring past public shootings, mobilizing numerous interests, and passing new laws. This occurred within a rapidly shifting national context, which raised questions about deep cultural traditions involving national identity, and the intrusion of cultural elements defined as foreign and undesirable. This facilitated overlooking the domestic bases supporting an indigenous "dangerous gun culture."

NOTES

A previous version of this paper was presented at the annual meeting of the American Society of Criminology, 11–14 November 1998, Washington, D.C. The author is grateful for comments made by Michael C. C. Adams, Mike Nellis, Dick Hobbs, and Ian Taylor.

1. The media made no mention of previous "shooting incidents," often by the homeland military, that had occurred in what had been British colonies. Only one media source mentioned that the Hungerford death toll was not the largest amassed by a single British killer. Mary Ann Cotton, hanged in 1873, poisoned 19 people over 20 years. The record for the highest toll of the twentieth century had been owned by Dennis Nilsen, who strangled and drowned 16 men in north London (*Facts on File World News Digest* 1987).

2. Neighbor Linda Lepetit was quoted as saying maybe she should have spoken to Ryan more over the garden fence, "because if he hadn't been such a loner, who knows?" Journalist Ros Wynne-Jones also argued that the town of Hungerford still feels guilty about the incident because Michael Ryan was one of their own" (Wynne-Jones 1997).

3. Though Ryan was carrying an automatic weapon—a Kalishnikov (AK 47)—his 9 mm Beretta handgun was responsible for the deaths of more people (Wynne-Jones 1997).

4. I thank Dick Hobbs for this insight.

5. Mike Nellis deserves credit for this important point.

REFERENCES

Alibhai, Yasmin. 1989. "Community Whitewash." *Guardian* (January 23).

Agence France Presse. 1999. "Britain Considers Jailing Psychopaths Without Charges." (February 15).

Ball, Richard A., and J. Robert Lilly. 1982. "The Menace of Margarine: The Rise and Fall of a Social Problem." *Social Problems* 29:488–98.

Booth, Jenny. 1996. "Gun Group Calls for Club Clampdown." *Scotsman* (October 6):2.

Brown, Gordon. 1996. "We Must have a Total Ban." *Daily Record* (October 17):8.

Butler, Jo. 1996. "Police to Demand Profiling of Gun Applicants." *Press Association Newsfile* (March 25).

Campbell, Duncan. 1996. "Dunblane Massacre: Gun Control: Police Urged Amnesty on Howard as Firearms Numbers Grew." *Guardian* (March 14):3.

Clarke, Peter. 1992/3. "The Charitable Status of Rifle Clubs: Out With a Bang?" *Charity Law and Practice Review* 1:137–45.

Cordon, Gavin. 1997. "Home News." *Press Association Newsfile* (November 3).

Coughlan, Sean. 1997. "Book Review: Shots from the Crack Wars." *Times Newspaper Limited* (March 29).

Cullen, The Honorable Lord. 1996. *The Public Inquiry into the Shootings at Dunblane Primary School on 13 March 1996.* London: HM Stationery Office.

Davison, John. 1997. *Gangsta: The Sinister Spread of Yardie Gun Culture.* London: Vision.

Deane, John. 1997. "Handgun Ban Outlined in New Bill." *Press Association Newsfile* (May 22).

Dyer, John. 1997. "Stricter laws Will Be Detrimental." *Waikato Times* (August 22):1.

Economist. 1994. "Guns: Firing Up." 7856 (March 26):69.

———. 1995. "Guns—Capital Offences." 7925 (July 29):40.

———. 1996. "Gun Control—Shots in the Dark." 7958 (March 23):56–57.

Elliot, Christopher. 1996. "Guns Aim Abroad." *Guardian* (November 23):1.

Evans, Andrew. 1997a. "New Compensation Challenge on Guns Bill." *Press Association Newsfile* (February 19).

———. 1997b. [no title] *Press Association Newsfile* (June 30).

Facts on File World News Digest. 1987. "Hungerford Gunman Kills 14, Self." August 21:610:B2.

Gabb, Sean. 1988. *Gun Control in Britain.* Political Notes No. 33. London: Libertarian Alliance.

Gray, John. 1997. "MPs, Not Judges Should Have the Final Say." *Guardian* (July 15):15.

Hastings, Max. 1996. "Nightmare That Shattered an Idyll." *Evening Standard* (March 13):9.

Hoge, Warren. 1997. "Target Shooters Blast Pistol Restrictions." *International Herald Tribune* (July 18):2.

———. 1999. "Thatcher's Back and She Hasn't Changed a Bit." *New York Times* (October 7): A-1.

Holden, Wendy. 1989. "Shootings Recall Horror of Hungerford." *Daily Telegraph* (May 1):2.

Holiday, Richard. 1997. "10 Years On Hungerford Still Suffers Its Demons." *Evening Standard* (August 19):15.

Lederer, Edith M. 1996. "Britain Plans to Ban Most Handguns after School Killings." *Memphis Commercial Appeal* (October 17):4.

Lilly, J. Robert, and Richard A. Ball. 1982. "A Critical Analysis of the Changing Concept of Criminal Responsibility." *Criminology* 20:69–184.

Lovibond, David. 1989. "Will This Be The Death of England." *Sunday Telegraph* (August 13):16.

Lowney, Kathleen S., and Joel Best. 1995. "Stalking Strangers and Lovers: Changing Media Typifications of a New Crime Problem." Pp. 33–57 in *Images of Issues*, 2nd ed., edited by Joel Best. Hawthorne, NY: Aldine de Gruyter.

Lyall, Sarah. 2000. "Britain Raises Barriers High Against Asylum Seekers." *New York Times* (April 3): A1.

Macdonell, Hamish. 1997a. "Self Defence Bid Launched for Crime Victims." *Press Association Newsfile* (February 18).

———. 1997b. "Government Urged to Think on Handgun Ban." *Press Association Newsfile* (June 16).

McAlpine, Joan. 1997. "Dunblane Father in UN Campaign." *Sunday Times* (September 21).

Mcgregor, Stephen. 1996. "Mellor Sets Sights on Gun Lobby." *Herald* (March 18):7.

Moore, Emily. 1996. "Schools: Lay Down Your Guns." *Guardian* (October 15):10.

Nellis, Mike. 2000. Personal communication.

O'Connor, Robert. 1987. "Massacre in Britain Called U.S.-Style Violence." *St. Petersburg Times* (August 23):15A.

Osward, Louise. 1996. "Dear Mr. Howard, We have Blown a Hole in Your Gun Amnesty!" *The People* (April 28):12.

Reed, Christopher. 1997. "Governor Blocks Gun-Control Bill: California's Move to Ban 'Saturday Night Specials' Fails." *Guardian* (September 29):3.

Riddell, Mary. 1996. "I Have No Love for the Shooting Lobby." *New Statesman* (October 18):7.

Ryan, W. Michael. 1980. "The Invasion Controversy of 1906–1908: Lieutenant-Colonel Charles a Court Repington and British Perceptions of the German Menace." *Military Affairs* 44 (February):8–12.

Smith, Graeme. 1997. "Snowdrop in Danger of Withering." *Scotland on Sunday* (March 30):8.

Spector, Malcolm, and John I. Kitsuse. 1977. *Constructing Social Problems.* Menlo Park, CA.: Cummings.

Squires, Peter. 1996. "Shooters Aren't Sexy." *New Statesman* (September 27):12.

St. Louis Dispatch. 1996. Editorial. (October 27):3.

Taylor, Ian. 1996. "Firearms Crime—at the time of the Cullen Inquiry." *Salford Papers in Sociology,* No. 20. Salford: Institute for Social Research of the University of Salford.

———. 1998. "'Behavioral Science' and Firearms." *Theoretical Criminology* 2:471–79.

Thomson, S., L. Stancich, and L. Dickson. 1998. "Gun Control and Snowdrop." *Parliamentary Affairs* 51:329–44.

Timmins, Nicholas. 1996. "Are We Hostages to Gun Culture?" *Independent* (March 14):13.

Travis, Alan. 1996. "Dunblane: The Cullen Report." *Guardian* (October 17):2.

Watts, Geoff. 1999. "Presumed Dangerous: Statistical Data Included." *British Medical Journal* 319 (July 31):326.

Witkin, Gordon. 1996. "A Very Different Gun Culture: Britain Plans a Near Total Ban on Handguns." *U.S. News and World Report* 121 (October 28):44.

Wynne-Jones, Ros. 1997. "Hungerford: The Day One Man Took Everything." *Independent* (August 10):5.

5

Bullying: The British Contribution to the Construction of a Social Problem

FRANK FUREDI

Let's face it, America has been in denial about bullying. International practitioners, unions, researchers and advocates are the pioneers in the antibullying movement.

—Campaign Against Workplace Bullying (1999)

On the "BullyBusters" web page of the Campaign Against Workplace Bullying (CAWB), there are material and resources on one of the most recent "hidden" problems discovered by moral crusaders in the United States. Run by the husband and wife team of Gary and Ruth Namie—they affectionately refer to themselves as the Drs. Namie—this small, but ambitious campaign self-consciously makes a virtue of its dearth of resources. One of its aims is to open an office so as to "return the living room to the Namies" (Campaign Against Workplace Bullying 1999). CAWB is committed to making workplace bullying an issue in North America.

Workplace bullying covers a multitude of sins. Virtually any negative, uncivil encounter can be and is defined as bullying. Richard V. Denenberg, a supporter of CAWB, has noted that bullying encompasses vandalism, gestures, witholding of important information, and making faces—"even smiling the wrong way." "It can be very subtle" (Thompson 1999:2). Another American expert, the academic Loraleigh Keashley, claims that bullying involves mainly "subtle types of aggression, including ignoring a person's contributions, flaunting status, pulling rank, making unwanted eye contact and openly belittling individuals" (Thompson 1999:2).

The Namies claim that their interest in this problem was the product of their personal experience. While working as a clinical psychologist for a health maintenance organisation, Ruth Namie faced relentless negative criticism from her female supervisor. Gary Namie, an organizational psychologist and employee advocate "began researching what Ruth was going through and tried to put a name on it." His search for a "name" took him on a global journey. Why? Because although "there was very little literature in the United States that addressed the type of workplace harassment his wife experienced[,] it was well known in Sweden, England, Australia and New Zealand by a term more often associated with the schoolyard in America: bullying" (Levine 1998).

For the Namies, the importation of the European term "workplace bullying" into the United States is part of their crusade to transform this problem into a major public issue. Just as "Anita Hill turned sexual harassment into a front-burner issue in workplaces across America" so Gary and Ruth Namie "want to do the same thing for harassment that has nothing to do with sex or gender" (DeBare 1998). Although the campaign has attracted a small number of committed activists, it has failed to achieve any significant profile in the United States—so far. To boost its authority, CAWB is forced to rely on an international network of academics, health professionals, and antibullying advocates. CAWB's web site proudly features its "Global Allies in the Campaign . . . against workplace mobbing, bullying, terrorization, assaults on employee dignity" (Campaign Against Workplace Bullying 1999). Campaigns based in Japan, Australia, New Zealand, Italy, Germany, South Africa, Sweden, and the United Kingdom are highlighted to underline the significance of this global cause.

American moral crusaders rarely are as dependent on international support as the promoters of the CAWB. On the contrary, they are often in the privileged position of exporting their successful causes to other parts of the world. Jenkins (1992:110) has persuasively shown that "the British encounter with child abuse" is a "reflection of American influences." In the case of workplace bullying, the diffusion of the problem is in the opposite direction. In contrast to most forms of victim advocacy, American crusaders against workplace bullying systematically rely upon their international contacts for affirmation and support. They continually point to the success of their cause abroad in order to validate their own efforts. Loraleigh Keashly, an academic based at Wayne State University, bemoans the fact that "the United States lags behind many western European nations in addressing workplace bullying" (Thompson 1999:4). Keashly and other advocates regard Sweden, which has enacted a "dignity at work" law, as a model for the United States to emulate. While Sweden offers a model of enlightened workplace practice, the unique success of the British campaign against bullying is regarded as the exemplar; American advocates continually rely on the authority of their British counterparts to gain recognition for their cause. British activists and experts are routinely featured in the few American publications that provide an outlet for CAWB's views.

British advocates of the antibullying cause also recognize the pioneering role of Sweden and other Scandinavian countries in the discovery of this social problem (Kaminski 1994). The social construction of the problem of workplace bullying originated in Scandinavia. Swedish academics and campaigners were in the forefront of placing emotional injury on the workplace agenda. According to Heinz Leymann (1999), the doyen of Swedish workplace bullying research, Scandinavian societies were particularly hospitable to the construction of this problem. Since the mid-seventies, a compromise deal between business and labor sought to minimize conflict by prioritizing issues of health and safety and the emotional well-being of workers. Leymann believes that it was the new work environment laws, enacted in the late seventies in Finland, Norway, and Sweden, that stimulated the growth of industrial psychology and a preoccupation with problems of the emotion. A 1991 amendment to the Swedish Work Environment Act that highlighted "the psychosocial aspects of practical work environment policy" played a particularly important role in focusing attention on this issue (Swedish National Board of Occupational Safety and Health 1994).

The institutionalization of workplace bullying within the regime of industrial relations and social life has probably gone furthest in Sweden. But, it is in Britain that the problem of workplace bullying has had the greatest impact on the perceptions of society. Consequently, this issue has had a far more prominent profile in Britain than in any other society. Advocates claim that workplace bullying is more prevalent there than elsewhere. According to a 1996 study carried out by the European Foundation for the Improvement of Living and Working Conditions, bullying in the European Union affected 8 percent of workers (Chappell and DiMartino 1998 :34). However, this figure pales in comparison to the far more dramatic incidence of bullying that researchers claim prevails in the United Kingdom. One study claims that in the United Kingdom, 53 percent of employees had been bullied at work, and that 78 percent had witnessed bullying at work (cited in Chappell and DiMartino 1998:45). This unusually high rate of bullying in Britain is confirmed by the largest survey on workplace bullying, funded by the British Occupational Health Research Foundation and supported by the Trade Union Congress and the Confederation of British Industry (CBI); it found reported rates that were significantly higher than elsewhere in Europe. One of the authors, Professor Cary Cooper, "linked the higher incidence compared with other European countries to the growth of long hours, job insecurity and the effects of 'downsizing' on workloads" (Milne 2000:7).

To a considerable extent, the high prevalence rates for workplace bullying in Britain are the outcome of the methodology used by surveys on bullying, which are prime examples of what is known as advocacy research.[1]

Now, however, there is widespread support for the contention that Britain suffers from an epidemic of bullying. Whereas in the United States, there has been little public recognition accorded to this issue, in Britain it has become headline news. In this essay I explore the emergence of this issue and why and how workplace bullying has been transformed into a major social problem in the United Kingdom. I also reflect on the prospects for this moral crusade in the United States.

THE BRITISH EXPERIENCE

The British public first heard of bullying in 1991. Andrea Adams, who is generally recognized as the pioneering crusader of this issue, succeeded in producing two BBC radio programs on workplace bullying and in placing a few articles in the British press. Her main concern was to gain recognition of the problem. As a skilled journalist, she was able to link the problem to the existing widespread public concern with the bullying of children in school. One of the key themes of her campaign was that bullying does not stop in childhood and that millions of adults suffer in silence from this affliction (Adams 1991). A small group of academic experts gravitated toward the promotion of this issue and were ready to affirm Adams' claim. Professor Cary Cooper, a psychologist based at the Manchester Institute of Science and Technology and one of Britain's best known media academics, claimed that childhood bullying can "cause lasting psychological damage" that can become a problem in adulthood and infiltrate the "world of work" (Adams 1991). Adams also regularly cited and collaborated with Neil Crawford, a psychotherapist and visiting tutor at the Tavistock Clinic in London. Crawford stressed the theme of negative childhood experiences continuing to shape adult behavior. Experts insisted that adult bullying had grave consequences. "Suicide attempts are not unknown, and bullying can even be a trigger for child abuse," argued Dr. Tony Baker, a child and family psychiatrist based in Surrey (Adams 1991).

Another important theme pursued by Adams was the association of workplace problems with bullying—particularly bullying management styles. Adams appealed to both trade unions (on the grounds of health and safety) and to employers (on the grounds of cost to industry). Her book (Adams and Crawford 1992) highlighted the claim that bullying cost millions of pounds to industry through absenteeism and reduced productivity. Newspaper reports widely publicized this burden on British industry (*Independent* 1992; BBC News Online 1999).

This small group of claimsmakers found influential allies in the British trade union movement. Unions associated with the International Labor Organization (ILO) became interested in the issue of workplace stress caused by "psychological violence" in the late eighties. Workplace bullying provided a new focus for raising the problem of stress (Chappell and Di Martino 1998:10). By 1994, British unions had begun to campaign around this newly discovered problem. A conference by the Manufacturing Science and Finance Union (MSF), titled "Bullying at Work," gained this union positive media recognition. Chris Ball, the head of the MSF's antibullying campaign was favorably cited in the press (Clement 1994). This conference, which brought together union activists and expert claimsmakers such as Andrea Adams, provided an important opportunity for gaining media publicity. Its success encouraged other unions to take up the issue.

By 1996, workplace bullying had entered the media vocabulary. Although reports and newspapers articles still referred to (and continue to refer to) this phenomenon as a hidden and unacknowledged problem, it acquired the status of one of the new abuse issues of the nineties. Claims made by antibullying activists were regularly recycled as headline news. "Bullying Bosses 'Cost £4 Billion a Year in Lost Labour'" headlined a report of a speech by Charlotte Rayner, the leading academic authority on workplace bullying, at a March 1996 teachers conference (Moore 1996). Rayner's survey results, suggesting that more than half of employees had been bullied, were presented by the media as straightforward fact. In September, the bullying of teachers by their senior colleagues emerged as a major issue. Newspapers reported on the "soaring number of teachers who are bullied and victimised by senior colleagues in the staffroom" (Durisch 1996). The Nottinghamshire education authority responded by introducing "formal measures to combat the problem." This problem was publicized through a survey conducted by a teaching union, which stated that up to 4,000 teachers face staffroom abuse and bullying by fellow teachers every day. Individual victims also began to frame their demands for compensation in the language of bullying. Helen Bamber, a Eurobond broker, sued her employer for sex discrimination. However, her successful case rested on the claim that her employers at Fuji International Finance had bullied her (White 1996). Individuals' claims of bullying were regularly validated by numerous surveys and reports that suggested that this was a very serious workplace problem. One such report, published by the Institute of Personnel and Development (1996), stated that one in eight people had been bullied at work and that half of those who have experienced bullying "say it is commonplace in their organisation and a quarter say the situation has got worse in the last year."

An important turning point in the social construction of the workplace bullying problem came in December 1997, when the Trade Union Congress (TUC) gained widespread publicity by launching its "bad bosses hotline." The TUC announced that it took almost 2,000 calls about bullying in just five days (Trade Union Congress 1998). The TUC asserted that the most frequent concern raised by callers was bullying (38 percent), well ahead of low pay (25 percent). The widespread publicity that the TUC gained from this initiative encouraged it to launch a national bullying campaign on October 5, 1998. The campaign was welcomed by employers' organizations and government and was widely reported in the media. The campaign—"No Excuse: Beat Bullying at Work"—claimed that a staggering 5 million people had been bullied at work. Since October 1998, the figure of 5 million has gained the status of an incontrovertible fact among professionals involved in human relations (*Personnel Today* 1999). The 1998 campaign was repeated in 1999. Newspaper articles continue to echo the consensus among labor, employers, and government. Headlines such as "Warning: Bullies at Work—Five Million Live in Fear of a Colleague as the Toll Soars" confirm the specter of a British industrial epidemic (Walker 1999).

The astonishing success of the antibullying crusade is recognized by the claimsmakers themselves. Lynn Witheridge (2000), the head of the Andrea Adams Trust, is delighted by the formidable media and official recognition that her campaign enjoys. She is proud of the fact that her organization is actively supported by the Cabinet Office and of the attendance of a government minister at a conference organized by the Trust.

A Valence Issue

Active lobbying by antibullying campaigners has been unusually effective and has met with virtually no resistance. Although the campaign was based on a small network of advocates and professionals, its impact on British opinion makers and the media was formidable. In less than a decade, a hitherto unknown issue succeeded in winning widespread recognition as a major social problem. One reason why this campaign was so successful was that the issue of bullying was framed in a way that was unlikely to raise controversy. Campaigners carefully avoided targeting any vested interests and attempted to appeal to all the relevant interest groups. Bullying was defined as a disease that afflicted the whole of society and from which no one gained. The victims of workplace bullies were presented as normal, everyday people entitled to society's sympathy. As a form of antisocial behavior, bullying fed into a more general concern with incivility in British society. In many respects, the problem of bullying strongly resembled what some American political scientists characterize as a valence issue. This term originated in American research into voting behavior; valence issues possess a strong symbolic character and are therefore unlikely to face opposition. "A valence issue such as child abuse elicits a single, strong, fairly uniform emotional response and does not have an adversarial quality" (Nelson 1984:26). The two principal characteristics of valence issues are their lack of specificity and their affirmation of the ideals of civic life. Since no one can publicly claim to support child abuse, child protection advocates could appeal to a wide consensus. An easily forged consensus meant that child abuse would be swiftly transmitted into the public domain; no political interests felt threatened by defining child abuse as a social problem, and the claims provided good human-interest copy for the media.

The public recognition accorded to childhood bullying provided an important platform from which to launch claims about adult bullying. Bullying experts projected adult bullying as the inexorable outcome of negative childhood experiences. Consequently, the antibullying campaign could tap into the existing public concern about the abusive behavior children suffered from both their peers and adults. Time and again, activists warned that bullying was not confined to children: "Bullying is still seen as a problem for children in schools and most people never suspect the range, severity and depth of misery created every day, nearly everywhere, by the bullying of adults by adults" (Randall 1997:1). "Could it really be that the trivial behaviour we usually associate with the school bully was terrorising men and women at their place of work?" asked radio producer Cathy Drysdale in her foreword to Andrea Adams' book (Adams & Crawford 1992:4).

Workplace bullying, like school bullying, became a valence issue that posed no threat to any interests. The issue was framed in general, diffuse terms. Virtually any form of negative behavior that offends contemporary social etiquette can be encompassed by the definition of bullying. Its only distinguishing feature is that it is not a singular event but a form of long-term, negative behavior. There is little consensus on how to define this negative behavior. Some of the leading British academic experts on the subject are so vague as to suggest that "bullying at work is not necessarily an all or nothing experience" (Rayner et al. 1999:12). One international study contends that bullying "can occur in a number of different ways" and that "some are obvious" while others are "subtle and difficult to explain" (Chappell & Di Martino 1998:11). Bullying serves to affirm the ideals of civic life, often expressed by the equally diffuse term "appropriate behavior."

Unlike many other workplace problems, bullying did not raise the question of conflicting interests. Whereas the problematization of sexual harassment could raise tension between men and women and racial discrimination could provoke controversy between blacks and whites, the question of bullying was presented as a problem for everyone. Although it was often used as part of a critique of "macho" management style, business had no problem with accommodating to the issue because it blamed the individual manager rather than the company itself. This individualized focus, along with the problematization of worker-to-worker relations was clearly not perceived as a threat by employers. Indeed, many employers welcomed the discovery of the workplace bully since it provided a widely accepted explanation for personnel problems. From an early stage, antibullying crusaders were able to gain the co-operation of many employers and their organizations. The Industrial Society actively endorsed this campaign and played an important role in promoting it in the public arena. They organized a major conference on the subject and provided a platform for leading antibullying experts Andrea Adams and Tim Field (Dobson 1995). The Institute of Personnel and Management (1996) adopted an active stance and was instrumental in raising awareness of the scale of this industrial disease; it published a report that claimed that one in eight workers was a victim of bullying. The Confederation of British Industry (CBI), the most influential British employers' organization actively collaborated with the TUC in the production of a series of surveys on bullying (Milne 1998). Human-resources professionals were quick to identify bullying as problem requiring their expert attention.[2]

The rise of the issue of bullying coincided with the increased recognition accorded to stress as a symptom of a more widespread malaise afflicting the workplace. In the aftermath of the shakeout of British industry, human resources experts emphasized stress and problems of the emotions as negative outcomes of this process. A 1993 report published by one employer organization, the Industrial Society, claimed that bosses listed stress, emotional, and personal problems as the most important reasons for sick leave after colds and the flu (O'Neill 1996). Three years later the TUC launched a publicity campaign against "this new industrial epidemic" (Trade Union Congress 1996). Numerous reports covering education, banking, the health sector, public-sector manual workers, and telephone companies offered alarming figures suggesting that 50 to 60 percent of employees suffered from stress (O'Neill 1996). Antibullying activists were quick to link their cause to the issue of stress. Andrea Adams presented bullying as the principal cause of the emotional malaise that dominated the workplace. "Bullying is the most stressful, destructive, humiliating and financially undermining factor in the UK employment scene," she informed a conference of trade unionists (Manufacturing Science and Finance Union 1994b). Workplace stress now had an active human cause: it was an emotional injury inflicted by a bully. Professor Cooper forcefully drew attention to this causal relationship: "Bullying is one of the biggest contributory factors" to workplace stress; his "researchers have talked to thousands of people in 70 occupational areas and believe bullying accounts for a third to half of all stress-related illness" (Kaminski 1994).

Politicians and government officials readily accepted the argument that something had to be done about workplace bullying. Guidelines on stress at work issued by the Health and Safety Executive Unions (1995:11) provided official recognition of this new social problem: "People can accommodate to most styles of management, but they can not easily cope with inconsistency, indifference or bullying." In October 1998, Public Health Minister Tessa Jowell officially backed the TUC's antibullying campaign. Antibullying policies were swiftly adopted in the public sector and informal pressure was placed on private enterprise to follow suit. Because the main promoters of this issue were the trade union movement and individuals closely allied to it, antibullying policy tended to be more widespread in workplaces that were unionized.

At a time when Britain was in the middle of assimilating and politicizing problems of emotion such as abuse and harassment, the media were quite hospitable to new claims of psychological hurt. Virtually any claim of workplace bullying was assured of national media publicity. The media did not interrogate any of the research upon which highly alarmist claims were based. Indeed, it is difficult to find any examples of journalists questioning assertions about the epidemic of workplace bullying. The claims made about the dimensions of the problem were faithfully reported as uncontroversial facts. The only aspect of the problematization of workplace bullying that was subject to media questioning was the litigation that ensued. The highly influential *Daily Mail* published several articles criticizing the large compensation payouts received by bullied employees (Alleyne 2000). However, the same newspaper regularly lent credibility to alarmist claims about the epidemic of workplace bullying.

The media played an important role in the construction and amplification of the bullying problem. Two BBC radio programs produced by Andrea Adams in 1990 and 1991 were instrumental in constructing the problem, which hitherto had had no name. On June 2, 1994, a BBC television program broadcast the first major alarmist report on the subject, a survey carried out by Staffordshire University claimed that 53 percent of employees (of a sample of 137) were bullied at work (Manufacturing Science and Finance Union 1994a). Three years later, the BBC launched a documentary series "Bully" and published a "Bullying Survival Guide" for its viewers (Furedi 1997b). This 11-part series lent credibility to the idea that bullying is just as much a problem of adulthood as it is of childhood. Numerous newspaper articles echoed this theme: "It's not something confined to the schoolyard: bullying is widespread in the workplace and can lead to breakdown and even suicide" (Luxton 1998); "Bullies in the schoolyard are bad enough, but this intimidation can also cast its shadow on the workplace" (Hilpern 1998).

The recognition that British society accorded to the adult bully encouraged new groups of victims to frame their problems in the language of bullying. In March 1998, civil servants demanded a cross-government policy to counter "the growing problem of bullying in Whitehall" (Elliott 1998). Research carried out by the MSF church workers section revealed that four out of ten female priests had been "verbally insulted by dog-collar bullies" (Luxton 1998). Even staff working for unions jumped on the bullying bandwagon. During the summer of 1999, Ken Gregory, a General and Boilermakers' Municipal (GMB) union official charged with protecting his members from bullying bosses was himself accused of "belittling and humiliating staff" (Clement 1999). The GMB faced more problems when its leader, John Edmonds, was accused of bullying by two female staff members (Leake 1999). Considerable media attention was devoted to a bullying scandal in the BBC's weather forecast unit: Bill Giles, a nationally prominent forecaster was accused of bullying other weather forecasters (Gilfeather & Whitaker 1999).

Victims of bullying and their lawyers were quick to convert the sympathy accorded to their plight into a demand for compensation. For their part, the British courts were distinctly responsive to the demands of those suffering from this newly discovered form of psychological injury. A number of landmark court cases lent weight to the claim that the victims of bullying suffered grave psychological harm. In July 1999, Cath Noonan, a council worker who quit her job on the ground that she suffered from stress after being bullied, won £84,000 in an out-of-court settlement (Vasagar 1999). The growth in litigation in both the courts and also in Industrial Tribunals led the Advisory, Conciliation and Arbitration Service (ACAS) to publish two advisory leaflets on bullying in July 1999. "More and more people are using ACAS Public Enquiry Points to ask questions about bullying at work," stated ACAS chairman John Hougham (Advisory, Conciliation and Arbitration Service 1999).

The Union Link

Social problems do not simply appear out of nowhere. From the standpoint of a constructionist sociology of social problems, the emergence of a social problem like that of workplace bullying is most usefully understood as the outcome of "the activities of individuals or groups making assertions of grievances and claims with respect to some putative conditions" (Spector and Kitsuse 1977:75). In Britain, the activities of an energetic group of skilled claimsmakers played a crucial role in the problematization of bullying. Like the leading proponents of workplace bullying in the United States, many of the British activists claimed to have gained their expertise from their own experience of victimization: many of them insisted that personal experience encouraged them to embark on the road to discovery of this particular problem. Tim Field personifies the victim-expert.

Field continually refers to his own victimization in his publications in order to explain why he has chosen to devote his life to this crusade. According to Field, it was the experience of being forced out of the company he had worked for for more than 15 years that inspired him to tackle this issue. His new manager's constant criticism led to a nervous breakdown that in turn motivated him to become a campaigner (Gosling 1996). Field runs *Bully OnLine,* one of the most authoritative web sites on the subject, and also coordinates the UK National Workplace Bullying Advice Line. Lynn Witheridge, cofounder of the Andrea Adams Trust, has also been the victim of bullying. She contends that she was unfairly dismissed as personnel and administration manager by her employer, the Sun Alliance Group, after a "three year campaign of unreasonable and malicious treatment, stress and bullying" (Witheridge 1997). She "suffered a stress breakdown" after her case was dismissed by an employment tribunal in 1995. After this event, she went on to launch the Andrea Adams Trust (Witheridge 1997).

From the outset, antibullying experts were able to draw on therapeutic professionals to give credibility to their diagnosis of the problem. Through their informal network, the experts succeeded in gaining recognition for their campaign. Therapeutic culture today assigns an important role to victim authority (Furedi 1998). Victim-experts are expected to speak out and are treated as recognized authorities on many of the major problems facing society. Joel Best (1990:12) contends that they possess the power to "own" and define social problems; this is a significant source of influence because "once claims-makers own a problem, they have a far better chance of controlling how the issue will evolve." However, professional antibullying experts on their own could not have succeeded in gaining such formidable national recognition for their cause. It was the adoption of this problem as their own by the trade union movement that underwrote the success of the antibullying campaign.

The adoption of workplace bullying as a cause by sections of the British trade union movement led to its transformation into a widely recognized social problem. Most of the early antibullying activists had close links with the trade union movement. Union officials actively relied on their expertise to provide authority for their antibullying drive. Unions sponsored many of surveys carried out by bullying experts. The Manufacturing Science and Finance Union (MSF), the first labor organization to campaign actively on this subject, had close links with Andrea Adams. She was the main speaker at a 1994 MSF conference, "Bullying at Work," the first conference of this kind. (Manufacturing Science and Finance Union 1994b). Other experts carried out surveys and wrote reports for union campaigns. Speakers at the October 1998 TUC conference that launched the first high-profile, national, antibullying campaign—"No Excuse: Beat Bullying at Work"—included Charlotte Rayner of the Staffordshire University Business School, Neil Crawford, psychotherapist at the Tavistock Clinic, and Helge Hoel, Research Fellow at the University of Manchester. All three had played an active role in the construction of this social problem through their research and publications (Trade Union Congress 1998).

Other unions swiftly emulated the MSF initiative. In 1994, the Public and Commercial Services Union of civil servants approached the Contributions and Benefits Agencies and demanded that bullying be made a disciplinary offence. This request was quickly accepted (O'Neill 1996). Other unions published reports and launched campaigns. The National Association of Schoolmasters Union of Women Teachers (NASUWT 1995) published a survey that claimed that 72 percent of its members were either subject to bullying or had witnessed it. The issue gained greater prominence when a motion condemning "the spread of bullying and hectoring management styles" was passed by the 1995 national TUC conference. In 1996, concern with the problem was echoed by the University and College Lecturers Union. Its report claimed that more than half of college staff had admitted they had been bullied at work, and stated that a "new style of macho management" had caused a "stress epidemic" (O'Neill 1996). A survey of union representatives in 1997 stated that 75 percent of them had witnessed or experienced bullying (Trade Union Congress 1998:3). Later that year, the TUC launched its "bad bosses hotline" (TUC 1998:2). Union-sponsored surveys and reports continue to be transmitted through the media to this day. In November 1999, a survey of 200 nurses across the U.K. concluded that almost 50 percent of them reported that they had been victims of bullying at work (BBC News Online:1999).

A closer inspection of the claim that the workplace has become traumatized by an epidemic of bullying indicates that what is under discussion is what used to be called office politics, assertive management, or the compulsion to get the job done. Trade union reports link the pressure to meet targets to the creation of an environment in which "intimidation and victimisation are almost unavoidable" (O'Neill 1996). The key focus of trade union activists is the pathologizing of workplace stress. Their reports claim a phenomenal rise of workplace stress. An increase in workload, combined with a more bullying style of management, is held accountable for the prevalence of this disease. For example, an MSF survey carried out in 1995 claimed that 60 percent of the respondents suffered from stress due to pressure of work. A report indicated that 87 percent of nurses believed that their stress levels had increased over the preceding years, 60 percent of union members at Barclays Bank had found their job more stressful than previously, and 22.7 percent had received treatment for a stress-related illness that they blamed on work. A 1996 union study indicated that manual workers were more stressed-out than previously; 63 percent of the respondents said that their jobs were more stressful than in the past. According to the National Association of Teachers in Further and Higher Education, eight out of ten lecturers at institutions of further education stated that their stress levels were unacceptable, and one out of four had taken time off to deal with their stress. The report concluded that college lecturers were being driven to the verge of a nervous breakdown (O'Neill 1996).

Trade union activists have been able to draw on a wide consensus that defines stress as harmful by definition. This medicalization of stress by health activists and the therapy lobby has helped union activists gain widespread sympathy for their claim. In April 1996, an important legal precedent was set when John Walker, a senior social worker, received £175,000 compensation for the "psychiatric damage to a normally robust personality." The High Court ruled that an "impossible workload" placed on Walker was the cause of his nervous breakdown. His employer's refusal to reduce his workload or his stress convinced the judge of the legitimacy of Walker's claim. The case set a precedent for other victims of a stressful working environment (Furedi and Brown 1999). Consequently, claims for compensation because of stress at work are on the increase. According to a TUC report published in September 1998, stress tops the list of cases that unions are taking to the courts. By linking stress to bullying, unions have sought to portray this disease as the outcome of psychological violence (Trade Union Congress 1998).

The adoption of bullying as a major focus for its activities by the union movement was also part of its reorientation toward a new-look, consumer-oriented approach. This development was integral to the trade union response to the crisis it faced in the early eighties. During that decade, union leaders found it increasingly difficult to forge an effective role for themselves. The decline of collective solidarity and the weakening appeal of union activism diminished the movement's influence. Union leaders responded by adopting the role of workplace advocates for the individual problems facing employees. The issue of health and safety emerged as a central theme in union politics. In order to play an effective role as the advocate for the workplace victim, trade unionism has become a high-profile advocate of therapeutic services. Whereas unions were once noted for their shop-floor activism and organizing, today they are far more likely to be known for their campaigns against workplace stress and bullying and for the help lines they run for those facing management bullying. "Unions offer cheapest and best legal services," boasts the TUC (Trade Union Congress 1999a). British unions now offer their members stress counseling and run workshops on how to cope with the demands of a busy workplace. Buying into the culture of emotionalism has given unions a new rationale for their existence (Furedi & Brown 1999:77).

BULLYING AND THE NORMALIZATION OF ABUSE

From the previous discussion, it is evident that the trade union move-ment, a nationally influential institution, played a crucial role in placing workplace bullying on the national agenda in Britain. American campaign-ers have failed to attract the support of an organization whose influence is comparable to the TUC. It is the absence of a comparable constituency of support that explains the restricted diffusion of the problem of work-place bullying in the United States. American claimsmakers also face a further obstacle. The role of trade unions in the national life of the United States is far less significant than in Britain. Consequently, this potential body of support is unlikely to be as effective as the TUC in influencing the American media and a wider body of opinion. American proponents of workplace bullying are also confronted with a reality in which there are already well-established workplace problems that touch on issues raised by their cause—sexual harassment, racial discrimination, and discrimi-nation on grounds of disability have gained widespread recognition. It is far from clear whether the social-problems market has a place for a more general form of psychological injury. As Loraleigh Keashley noted, U.S. government officials place a far greater emphasis on "racial and sexual harassment" than on "generalized workplace harassment" (Thompson 1999).

Experience suggests that workplace bullying is far more likely to be-come a social problem in societies where trade unions enjoy widespread legitimacy. One question raised by the experience of the past decade is why workplace bullying managed to gain greater prominence in Britain than in other Western European societies. As noted previously, research and pol-icy making around this issue first emerged in Scandinavia, yet workplace bullying has entered the British public imagination with far greater force than in other European societies. The skill and effectiveness of British moral crusaders no doubt played a part in the popularization of this issue. But probably the most significant variable has been the unique receptivity of British society to claims of abuse. Britain stands out as the European so-ciety that has most thoroughly assimilated American social problems such as child abuse, elder abuse, stalking, hate crimes, violence against women, and various forms of harassment. This has led to what I described else-where as the normalization of abuse (Furedi 1997a:73–85). From the start, campaigners oriented themselves to this development and promoted their cause as the most pervasive form of abuse in the workplace.

These campaigners sought to link their issue to more widely recognized abuses. The definition of bullying imitated the diffuse definitions adopted for other abuses. "As with sexual harassment and stress, there is no agreed definition of bullying" (Rayner et al. 1999). Others used the term bullying synonymously with other forms of harassment. For example, the 1999 TUC Women's Conference survey report, "No Excuse—No Harassment at Work," links the issue of bullying to harassment and the terms are used interchangeably (Trade Union Congress 1999b). It notes that there is "still a lack of information available about more complex issues in relation to sexual harassment and bullying, and in particular why workers are sexually harassed and bullied and how they react." A 1999 survey on workplaces noted that two-thirds of all the organizations in its study had some kind of written policy, statement, or guidelines on bullying at work. It added that most often "this takes the form of a broader harassment policy into which bullying has been slotted as one form of harassment" (*Employee Health Bulletin* 1999). Bullying was thus swiftly assimilated as yet another form abuse.

Widely accepted definitions of harassment, stalking, and bullying insist that these acts are determined by the victims' feelings rather than by the intention of the person who has caused the offense. Many British companies have adopted policies on bullying that allow the recipient to determine whether he or she has been injured. For example, the policy of the leading clothing chain, Marks & Spencer, states that individuals "have different levels of sensitivity and it is up to the recipient to decide whether they [sic] are experiencing behaviours unacceptable to them" (Industrial Data Services 1999:5). As the notion of unacceptable behavior is typically left rather vague, the range of individual acts that it can encompass becomes infinite. It is the individual's emotion, rather than any objectively defined criteria, that ultimately defines an act or an experience as harmful. This subjective interpretation of what constitutes a harmful act indicates that the heightened sense of injury that pervades contemporary society relates principally to harms that violate emotions.

The argument that bullying is not just about what children do to one another also resonated with the prevailing culture of abuse. Bullying, an all-purpose form of harassment, makes sense in a society that systematically anticipates psychological injury in human relations. During the nineties the meaning of bullying expanded to cover a bewildering variety of troublesome relations. It is also came to be used to characterize the harms that children inflict on their adult teachers. One survey claimed that at least half of all teachers in Midlands comprehensives who were interviewed had been bullied at least once in the past term by some of their pupils (*Daily Telegraph* 1998). Nor is it only children who can bully their teachers. In recent years, teachers have begun to accuse their colleagues of bullying. In one case, a primary school teacher was awarded £100,000 in an out-of-court settlement because he was traumatized by an "inappropriate joke" made by his headmistress at his expense. This award was enthusiastically greeted by other teachers who felt that they too had been bullied by colleagues. "I've been teaching for 18 years and I am leaving my latest post in a primary school after just two terms because I'm not happy with the way the head teacher has been treating me," wrote one aggrieved teacher in support of this award. Others echoed this sentiment: "I was a patient in a psychiatric hospital for most of last year, with a major depressive illness directly consequent on my experiences in school," reported another bullied teacher (*Guardian* 1998).

The campaign around the issue of workplace bullying has found a rich reservoir of support in a culture intensely preoccupied with the problem of abuse. That is why, in contrast to other parts of Europe, workplace bullying has become one of the defining social problems of the turn of the millennium. The United States shares many of the cultural preoccupations of Britain, but the absence of a credible and influential movement ready to take up this crusade continues to consign workplace bullying to the margins of American society.

NOTES

1.   This is a form of research that knows its findings in advance. The researchers' aim is as much to "raise awareness" about a problem as it is to find out its prevalence. Advocacy research is an exercise in propaganda. Take a report published on bullying inside the Merseyside Fire Brigade. The report states that it had a twofold object: "Firstly to raise awareness of bullying as an issue within the workforce and secondly to assess the degree of bullying that exists." In other words, the survey was an instrument for encouraging firefighters to buy into the culture of bullying. The report did succeed is raising awareness and in getting 30 percent of the firefighters to define themselves as victims of bullying (Merseyside Fire Brigade 1998).

2.   Interviews with human resources managers indicate that they regard workplace bullying as one of the key workplace issues of our time (interviews, March–April 1999).

REFERENCES

Adams, Andrea. 1991. "Another Totally Humiliating Day at the Office: Bullying Terrifies Adults, Too." *Independent* (January 31).
———, and Neil Crawford. 1992. *Bullying at Work: How to Confront and Overcome It.* London: Virago Press.
Advisory, Conciliation and Arbitration Service. 1999. "Stop Bullying." Press release (July 29).
Alleyne, R. 2000. "£200,000 for Man a Woman Boss 'Bullied into a Breakdown.'" *Daily Mail* (January 12).
BBC News Online. 1999. "Nurses Complain of Bullying at Work." (November 28): www.bbcnewsonline.co.uk.

Best, Joel. 1990. *Threatened Children*. Chicago: University of Chicago Press.

Campaign Against Workplace Bullying. 1999. www.bullybusters.org/home/bullybust.html.

Chappell, D., and V. Di Martino. 1998. *Violence at Work*. Geneva: International Labor Organization.

Clement, Barrie. 1994. "Workplace Bullying Attacked." *Independent* (November 7).

———. 1999. "Anti-bullying Union Faces Charge of Bullying." *Independent on Sunday* (August 1).

Daily Telegraph. 1998. "Bullying Takes its Toll." (June 22).

De Bare, Ilana. 1998. "Getting Bullied at Work: Two Psychologists Initiate Campaign to Tackle Problem." *San Francisco Chronicle* (October 19).

Dobson, Roger. 1995. "Corporate Bullies Make Life a Misery for Workers." *Independent* (September 3).

Durisch, Peter. 1996. "Teachers Win Protection from Staffroom Bullies." *Daily Telegraph* (September 15).

Elliot, Valerie. 1998. "Civil Servants Urge Action on Bullying." *London Times* (March 26).

Employee Health Bulletin. 1999. "Bullying at Work: A Survey of 157 Employers." Vol. 8 (April):4–20.

Furedi, Frank. 1997a. *The Culture of Fear: Risk-taking and the Morality of Low Expectations*. London: Cassell.

———. 1997b. "I Bully, You Bully, We Are Victims." *Independent on Sunday* (August 24).

———. 1998. "New Britain: A Nation of Victims." *Society* 35 (March):80–85.

———, and Tracy Brown. 1999. "Complaining Britain." *Society* 36 (May):72–78.

Gilfeather, Paul, and Thomas Whitaker. 1999. "TV Giles Rapped for Bullying Weathermen." *Sun* (October 22).

Gosling, Paul. 1996. "Workplace Bully Under the Cosh." *Independent on Sunday* (January 28).

Guardian. 1998. "Letters." (July 28).

Health and Safety Executive Unions. 1995. *Stress at Work: A Guide for Employers*. London: Health and Safety Executive Unions.

Hilpern, Kate. 1998. "Sticks and Stones." *Guardian* (July 13).

Independent. 1992. "Bullying at Work 'Costs Millions.'" (October 20).

Industrial Data Services. 1999. "IDS Studies: Personnel Policy and Practice, Harassment Policies." London: Industrial Data Services.

Institute of Personnel and Development. 1996. "One in Eight UK Workers Are Victims of Bullying Reveals New IPD Survey." Press release (November 28).

Institute of Personnel and Management. 1996. Press release (November 28).

Jenkins, Philip. 1992. *Intimate Enemies: Moral Panics in Contemporary Britain*. Hawthorne, NY: Aldine de Gruyter.

Kaminski, Julia. 1994. "Low Blows in the Name of High Performance: Bullying Triggers Stress." *Independent on Sunday* (May 29).

Leake, Christopher. 1999. "GMB Boss Faces More Claims of Bullying." *Mail on Sunday* (September 19).

Levine, D. S. 1998. "A Conversation [sic] Gary Namie, The Work Doctor" www.disgruntled.com (February).

Leymann, Heinz. 1999. "The Mobbing Encyclopaedia." www.leymann.se.

Luxton, Tim. 1998. "When Bullies Get to Work." *Guardian* (April 25).

Manufacturing Science and Finance Union. 1994a. "Tackling Bullying at Work." London: Manufacturing Science and Finance Union.

———. 1994b. "Bullying at Work." London: Manufacturing Science and Finance Union.

Merseyside Fire Brigade. 1998. "Bullying Survey." Liverpool: (CFO/41/98).

Milne, Seamus. 1998. "Managers Under Stress 'New Workplace Bullies.'" *Guardian* (December 1).

———. 2000. "Insecurity 'Fuels Job Bullying Epidemic.'" *Guardian* (February 15).

Moore, Toby. 1996. "Bullying Bosses 'Cost £4 billion in Lost Labour.'" *Daily Telegraph* (March 8).

National Association of Schoolmasters Union of Women Teachers. 1995. "No Place to Hide." London: National Association of Schoolmasters Union of Women Teachers.

Nelson, Barbara J. 1984. *Making an Issue of Child Abuse.* Chicago: University of Chicago Press.

O'Neill, Rory. 1996. "Stress at Work: Trade Union Action at the Workplace" (unpublished report). London: Trade Union Congress.

Personnel Today. 1999. (Cited in Walker, 1999).

Randall, Peter. 1997. *Adult Bullying: Perpetrators and Victims.* London: Routledge.

Rayner, Charlotte, Michael Sheehan, and Michelle Barker. 1999. "Theoretical Approaches to the Study of Bullying at Work." *International Journal of Manpower* 20:11–15.

Spector, Malcolm, and John I. Kitsuse. 1977. *Constructing Social Problems.* Menlo Park, CA : Cummings.

Swedish National Board of Occupational Safety and Health. 1994. "Swedish Work Environment Legislation." www.arbsky.se/aml/lagenin.htm (October 1).

Thompson, Robert. 1999. "Workplace Violence Experts See Lessons from Littleton." *HR News ONLINE* (June 14):1–4.

Trade Union Congress. 1996. "TUC Launches Campaign Against Stress, 'the New Industrial Epidemic.'" Press release (October 7).

———. 1998. "No Excuse: Beat Bullying at Work." London (media pack).

———. 1999a. "Unions Offer Cheapest and Best Legal Services." London.

———. 1999b. "No Excuse—No Harassment at Work." Women's Conference Survey Report. London.

Vasagar, Jeevan. 1999. "£84,000 for Bullying." *Daily Mail* (July 8).

Walker, Kirsty. 1999. "Warning: Bullies at Work." *Express* (August 5).

White, Claire. 1996. "Broker Tells of 'Bullying' by Employers She Sued." *Daily Telegraph* (March 27).

Witheridge, Lynn. 1997. "The Andrea Adams Trust: Sun Alliance Bullying Case To Be Reheard." News release (February 12).

———. 2000. Interview (March 9).

6

The Evolution of Road Rage in Britain and the United States

JOEL BEST and FRANK FUREDI

The term "road rage" began to spread in the United States in the summer of 1996,[1] although it took another year to achieve widespread currency. In early June 1997, road rage became a fairly prominent U.S. social problem: the American Automobile Association (AAA) released a report on road rage that attracted coverage in two of the major newsweeklies—*Newsweek* carried a full-page story (Adler 1997), while *U.S. News & World Report* presented five pages on the topic and made road rage its cover story (Vest, Cohen, and Tharp 1997); the following month, there was a congressional hearing on the subject (U.S. House 1997). However, virtually none of the American commentators who pontificated about road rage's significance acknowledged that road rage had first become a celebrated social problem in Great Britain.

This chapter traces the somewhat tangled history of road rage,[2] first in Britain, and then in the United States. Road rage offers a particularly clear—albeit complex and somewhat atypical—example of the international diffusion and evolution of a social problem.

ROAD RAGE IN BRITAIN

British newspapers first used the term "road rage" in 1994—two years before it would be widely applied in the United States. The first article to use the term appeared in the June 5, 1994 *Sunday Times;* it linked a dramatic news story (an elder of the United Synagogue had been convicted and fined for leaping from his gold Mercedes and punching a Buddhist monk sitting in his Nissan Micra) to other incidents, and argued that these cases revealed a new social problem—road rage. However, this article noted:

"Other observers say that 'road rage' is a phenomenon that has spread to Britain from abroad. In the United States the problem has reached epidemic proportions, with 1,500 being killed and injured as a result of traffic disputes last year" (Burrell 1994).[3]

The term captured the press's imagination: two months later, Pavilion Services offered massages by trained beauty therapists at M6 highway rest stops to help motorists overcome road rage; in November, a 24-year-old man—jailed for four years for assault and dangerous driving—was described as a "road rage driver," and other disturbing reports of aggressive driving or violence spoke of road rage (Coren 1994; Fleet 1994; *Independent* 1994). The media began to quote a new group of road-rage experts; one— the Royal Automobile Club's (RAC) Edmund King—claimed that "it is a very frightening time to be a motorist" (Harlow 1995). Members of Parliament called for government action (e.g., a publicity campaign, mandatory psychiatric treatment for convicted motorists [Harlow 1995]), and automobile manufacturers presented their own publicity and advertising campaigns focused on aggressive driving (Cook 1995). The media cited surveys to the effect that nine out of ten drivers experienced road rage (Gwyther 1995), and that almost three-quarters of drivers reported having been victims of others' road rage (Langley 1996).

British commentators offered an array of explanations for the new problem. One psychologist writing in the *Police Journal* suggested: "The improvement in driving conditions concerning safety engineering and comfort may have the unforeseen consequence of worsening driver behaviour" (Reinhardt-Rutland 1996:287). Another psychologist "believes there are too many cars competing for too little road space which means we grow as agitated as rats in an over-populated cage" (Gwyther 1995). A psychotherapist claimed: "There is an idealization of self expression to the extent that almost anything goes. We are encouraged to express ourselves physically" (Spillious 1995). The usual causal suspects made appearances: women pointed to male aggression (Moorhead 1996); the left blamed the changing labor market and difficulties obtaining social services (Campbell 1996); the right blamed the meritocracy's failure to serve as moral exemplars (Waugh 1995). These explanations were embedded in a widely held assumption about growing violence; according to two road-rage experts: "People perceive that society as a whole is becoming more violent, and our behavior behind the wheel is no exception" (Connell and Joint 1996:1).

Other stories identified additional "rages." The emergence of road rage was quickly followed by: "trolley rage"—conflicts between shoppers maneuvering supermarket shopping carts (called trolleys in Britain) (Mullin 1995); "golf rage"—concerned reaction to news of a shot driven over the heads of other players (Tredre 1995); "alarm rage"—directed at car alarms going off (Boseley 1995); and so on. Similar claims continued to appear throughout the remainder of the decade: "computer rage"—frustrated workers battering computing equipment (Sanghera 1999); "hotel rage"— angry guests (Harrington 1999); and "pool rage"—swimmers failing to share lanes (Goodbody 1998). "Air rage"—disorderly passengers in airliners—received considerable publicity (Thomas 1998), and "ground rage"— incidents of verbal and physical abuse hurled at airline staff by irate passengers—followed. The Manufacturing Science and Finance Union (1999), which represents some ground staff, organized a publicity campaign to protect its members, and Transport Minister Helen Lidell wrote airline executives asking them to reduce delays in order to minimize passenger frustration (Harper 1999). The decade ended with "lollipop rage," a "new and more violent form of road rage": an RAC survey suggested that lollipop ladies (wardens who help schoolchildren cross streets) had become the targets of drivers' rage; one city council even proposed teaching lollipop ladies self-defense techniques (RAC Foundation 1999).

Commentators took these "rage" problems seriously; they worried that these phenomena revealed a change in British culture, a decline in traditional civility. Again, there was a general assumption that these problems originated in the United States. Furedi (1997:24) noted that: "In the USA publicity about road rage has helped fuel paranoia.... During the late 1980s, 1200 road-rage-related deaths were reported." A business psychology consultant referred to "road rage, trolley rage, and all the other rage-isms imported from America" (Davidson 1995). Diffusion was freely— albeit mistakenly—acknowledged; having cultivated and nurtured the term, the British continued to insist that they had imported road rage from the United States.

Road Rage's British Proponents

The discovery of road rage was preceded by intensive media coverage of driving-related violence. The 1988 murder of Marie Wilkes (after her car had broken down on a highway) provoked widespread discussion about the risks of violent crime faced by women drivers, and this concern gained momentum over the next several years. Car associations, insurance companies, and manufacturers began to target women's anxieties and market their products as providing extra security. In 1990, the RAC launched its high-profile "knights of the road" advertising campaign: television ads featured a female driver whose car breaks down on a lonely road in the pouring rain, and the RAC promised that its recovery (roadside repair) services would give priority to lone women in distress. By the time the term "road rage" was invented, the British public had been exposed to a barrage of publicity concerning the alleged increase in driving-related violence, especially as it affected women.

Two leading competitors—the RAC and the Automobile Association (AA)—in the car-breakdown recovery business were early proponents of the danger of road rage. Most experts quoted in the media were linked to these organizations: Edmund King, RAC campaign spokesperson, emerged as a road rage expert in November 1994; a month later, the AA's Rayner Peet began providing regular comments to the media. In March 1995, the AA scored a major triumph in its publicity battle with the RAC when it published a survey, by Matthew Joint, on the incidence of road rage (Joint 1995). This report, which claimed that nine out of ten drivers experienced road rage, was seized by the British media and frequently cited.

In later years, other car-related businesses used surveys as public relations tools. Predictably, these surveys emphasized the high incidence of and growing public fear over driving-related violence. For example, a survey of 1,158 women by Norwich Union Insurance reported that seven out of ten locked all car doors while driving, that one in two were frightened to drive at night, and that two in three were afraid of parking in multistory car parks (parking ramps). The survey blamed the increase in road-rage incidents and attacks on women in car parks for the women's anxieties (Norwich Union Insurance 1995).

An unusually broad assortment of other claimsmakers sought to link their agendas to the new, highly visible problem. The Suzy Lamplugh Trust (one of the most visible organizations involved in highlighting problems associated with personal safety) jumped on the road-rage bandwagon at the outset. Psychologists, such as David Lewis, Conrad King, and Geoff Scobie, provided the expert authority needed to transform road rage into a social problem (Gwyther 1995; *Independent* 1994; Perry 1995). Conservative politicians regarded road rage as confirmation of their apprehensions about the breakdown of law and order. The Conservative MP Cheryl Gillian played a leading role in raising the issue in Parliament, and expressed concern about the erosion of civility. In May, 1996, Michael Howard (a former Conservative Home Secretary) promised to crack down on road rage.

Environmentalists portrayed road rage as symptomatic of Britain's unhealthy love affair with the car. British road-safety advocacy is animated by an intense hostility to what is disparagingly termed "car culture." Opponents of car culture object to the individualistic ethos associated with car ownership; as one critic puts it: "Driving is quick, private and selfish in the 1990's" (Fowler 1996). Hostility to car culture became a theme of the anti-Thatcherite reaction of the nineties; it was often linked to an environmentalist critique of a materialistic society driven by individual greed. Daniel McCarthy, Devon County Council's road safety officer, who taught courses to help road ragers involved in accidents, pointed to a "growing awareness that cars are bad for the environment and that roads are wrecking the countryside" (Harrison 1996). The environmentalist lobbying group Friends of the Earth argued that the growing incidence of road rage demonstrated that driving was a threat to people's security, that within the broad problem of antisocial behavior on the highways, "Road rage is the tip of the iceberg in that it is merely the unacceptable form of behavior by motorists" (Wolmar 1997). During the nineties, the environmentalist critique of car culture gained strength. Opponents of car culture argued that one benefit of curbing driving was that it would contain road rage. Ben Plowden, the director of the Pedestrian Association and a vociferous critic of car culture, claimed: "With a little imagination we can be free of traffic jams and road rage" (Plowden 1998). Other advocates deployed the feminist critique of masculinity to interpret road rage as essentially a male crime against vulnerable women; Di Haigney of the Royal Society for the Prevention of Accidents stated: "There is no doubt that young men are some of the most aggressive drivers on our roads" (Moorhead 1996). On a lighter note, the feminist comic Jo Brand quipped: "Road rage? Isn't that blokes being arseholes in cars as well as everywhere else?" (Turner 1996). Academic experts also promoted the idea that road rage was an expression of destructive masculinity (Groombridge 1998).

In Britain, then, no single group assumed ownership of the road-rage problem. Although industry initially used it as an advertising gimmick, road rage became integrated into a critique of car culture and, more broadly, anti-Thatcherite criticism of the selfish, uncaring, materialistic 1980s. The rapidly growing therapeutic industry became a major beneficiary of attention to road rage, and expanding the concern about rage from the road to other aspects of social life provided a compelling argument for therapeutic intervention.

ROAD RAGE IN THE UNITED STATES

Unlike the British, who invented road rage but claimed it came from the United States, Americans borrowed the term from the British—but never acknowledged its foreign origins. The American press covered road rage as though it was a new, all-American problem. Although a few early stories used the term in 1996, it was not until 1997—three years after the problem emerged in Britain—that road rage attracted extensive, prominent coverage.

A month after the AAA released its report and *U.S. News & World Report* made road rage its cover story, the Congressional Subcommittee on Surface Transportation held a July 17, 1997, hearing on road rage (U.S. House 1997). The hearing featured testimony from various traffic-safety experts, law enforcement officers, antispeeding activists, and psychologists. While road rage never became the predominant focus of media attention (the major television news programs devoted only two stories totaling less than three minutes to the topic in 1997 [NBC August 28, 1997; CNN November 25, 1997]), it began receiving considerable attention in many of the standard media—*People* magazine (1997), newspaper columns, specialty magazines aimed at business executives, women, and automobile hobbyists, comic strips, and so on.

Part of road rage's attraction may have been its vague definition. It was not clear precisely which driving behaviors counted as road rage. As in the construction of other new crimes, extreme examples of criminal violence typified the problem (Best 1999). Consider these examples from the opening paragraphs of major newsmagazine stories:

> Alfieri . . . attempted to pass [Andrews] on the right shoulder, then pulled around Andrew's car on the left, cut in front and hit the brakes—causing Andrews to swerve into a stopped tractor-trailer, resulting in multiple injuries and the loss of the 6-month-old fetus she was carrying. [Alfieri was] convicted on May 2 of aggravated vehicular homicide (against the fetus). (Adler 1997:70)

> In Colorado Springs, 55-year-old Vern Smalley persuaded a 17-year-old boy who had been tailgating him to pull over; Smalley decided that, rather than merely scold the lad, he would shoot him. (Vest et al. 1997:24)

Some claims restricted the term to such violent incidents: "where actual physical assaults take place. . . . The vigilante further escalates abuse and punishment of another combative driver by seeking to physically injure the other driver's vehicle, person, or passengers" (Larson 1999:26, 28). However, most definitions of road rage were far broader. Some equated it with expressing anger:

> It's where one driver lets another know that he or she is angry because of something that the other driver did. In expressing that anger, the driver might make obscene gestures, scream, honk, put on the brakes, cut in front or brandish a weapon. Or even use the weapon. (*People* 1997:59)

Others equated road rage with "aggressive driving"; thus, the congressional hearing transcript's title was: "Road Rage: Causes and Dangers of Aggressive Driving" (U.S. House 1997). Still other claims focused on problematic driving that might lead others to experience road rage: "Troopers are especially looking for drivers engaged in the kind of activities that anger fellow motorists and spur what has come to be known as 'road rage,' such offenses as speeding, tailgating, driving while under the influence and improper lane use" (Wuerz 1998:3A). Thus, some claimants equated road rage with "aggressive driving," while others defined it as hostile re-actions to others' driving.

Road Rage's American Proponents

Compared to Britain, road rage had fewer advocates in the United States. The July 17, 1997, congressional hearing brought together a con-stellation of advocates involved in promoting road rage as a social prob-lem.[4] The hearing was intended to generate support for two pending bills: the National Economic Crossroads Transportation Efficiency Act of 1997 (NEXTEA); and the 1997 reauthorization of the Intermodal Surface Trans-portation Efficiency Act (ISTEA). Like other earlier campaigns against drunk driving and speeding, road rage offered an attention-grabbing issue to which a variety of traffic safety proposals could be appended. Several congressional representatives and federal bureaucrats spoke to the impor-tance of safety issues, although some offered variant interpretations: "Ve-hicle miles traveled in America have increased 35 percent, but the road capacity has increased by 1 percent. . . . There are solutions to ameliorate this problem, and that is [sic] to . . . build more modern and safer high-ways" (Representative Bud Shuster in U.S. House 1997:3).

Representatives of groups with interests in traffic safety also testified. These included Advocates for Highway and Auto Safety (affiliated with the Ameri-can Insurance Association), the Insurance Institute for Highway Safety, and the American Automobile Association Foundation for Traffic Safety. The AAA pre-sented results of three studies assessing the extent and nature of aggressive driving and road rage: one of these—the so-called Mizell study discussed be-low—used American data; the other two were British studies. Also repre-sented at the hearing were members of a social movement organization—Citizens Against Speeding and Aggressive Driving, local (Fairfax County, Virginia) law enforcement officers who reported on the effectiveness of an enforcement program, and two psychologists.

The psychologists confirmed that road rage was a serious problem. Leon James, a professor at the University of Hawaii (who billed himself as "Dr. Driving") reported that: "Road rage is ubiquitous in America today. . . . Driving and habitual road rage have become virtually inseparable" (U.S. House 1997:92, 95). James argued for a broad array of solutions, in-cluding establishing QDCs (Quality Driving Circles) and CARR (Children Against Road Rage). Arnold Nerenberg, a clinical psychologist, testified: "I consider road rage to be a mental disorder of the 'adjustment reaction type.' It involves clearly expressing the anger directly to other drivers at least twice per year. . . . Fifty-three percent of all drivers have a road rage disorder" (U.S. House 1997:113–14). James, Nerenberg, and a third psy-chologist—John Larson (1999)—gave frequent interviews to the press; in

1998, Nerenberg announced formation of the International Association of Road Rage Experts.

For most of these advocates, road rage offered a newsworthy hook, a way to make the familiar, mundane issue of traffic safety seem fresh and compelling. The label "road rage" had succeeded where other, rival terms for the same behavior—such as motormania, predatory driving, and highway madness—had failed to catch the public imagination. Road rage offered an opening for promoting other safety issues; claims about improving drivers' training, lowering blood alcohol content standards, or increasing seat-belt usage could be piggybacked onto warnings about road rage. A Chicago Transit Authority billboard promoted mass transit: "Stop Road Rage Before It Starts." Even routine traffic enforcement efforts became newsworthy when reporters characterized them as campaigns in the war against road rage (Wuerz 1998). In 1997 and into 1998, road rage followed the trajectory taken by many contemporary new crimes (Best 1999): advocates presented a package of terrible examples and frightening statistics; the news media covered these claims; and as road rage became widely recognized, popular culture began to exploit the theme.[5] The AAA and other organizations with a commitment to traffic safety assumed ownership of the problem and continued to keep the issue alive.

SKEPTICS AND STATISTICS

One potentially awkward problem for claims about road rage was that official statistics gave little evidence that aggressive driving was causing terrible, increasing harm. Britain had "one of the world's lowest accident rates; 3,621 people died here in traffic accidents in 1995, the lowest toll since 1926" (Montalbano 1996:A1). The British crusade against road rage came under continuous questioning by skeptical officials and commentators. Police officials who specialized in traffic safety argued that road rage was just another name for "bad manners and bad driving" (Coren 1994). Jeremy Clarkson (1995), Britain's best-known media commentator on cars, launched a one-man campaign to deride the problem of road rage. The journalist Emma Cook (1995) accused road rage's proponents of opportunistically trying to scare women into purchasing safety-related products. Numerous other journalists concluded that road rage was a media creation. One leading transport editor called road rage a "convenient myth" used to describe routine, road-related violence; he noted that, in October 1996, one of Britain's largest insurance brokers had forced 52,000 customers to buy road-rage coverage, yet a year later, there had not been a single related claim (Moore 1997).

Briefly in 1996, road rage seemed to have the potential to inspire a major crime panic in Britain. Two separate road-related murders—the killings of Stephen Cameron and Lee Harvey—were heavily publicized and viewed as symptoms of escalating road rage. However, it soon became clear that neither killing involved road rage. After Cameron's fiancée was convicted of his murder, the road rage crusade became the target of considerable media skepticism (Moore 1997). Yet, in spite of these doubts, road rage became well established in British public discourse, and both therapeutic entrepreneurs and critics of a transportation policy based on private cars and car culture continued to refer to road rage as symptomatic of an emotional malaise afflicting British society.

Skepticism took a somewhat different form in the United States. U.S. figures showed that fatality rates fell substantially during the 1990s to a level that the administrator of the National Highway Traffic Safety Administration conceded was "an all-time low" (Richardo Martinez in U.S. House 1997:103). While some skeptics (e.g., Fumento 1998) considered these statistics proof that the road-rage crisis was unfounded, other apparently skeptical commentators hedged their bets. A *USA Today* feature story based on an analysis of "more than 500,000 accidents over the past decade shows that aggressive driving imperils the average driver no more today than it did 10 years ago. . . . Aggressive driving is neither a new nor a worsening problem." Yet, the story added "it may be on the verge of becoming worse" (Bowles and Overberg 1998:17A). The *Washington Post*'s story calling the claims into question also noted that: "aggression could be on the rise even though it hasn't shown up in statistics [because] . . . improved safety features such as air bags and better roads could be causing such a drop in injuries and crashes that they mask any other trend"; the story went on to quote an AAA official: "Is there more aggressive driving on the road? There has to be. We have more drivers. We have more congestion" (Davis and Smith 1998:B1).

One possibility was that road rage came to public attention precisely because fatality rates had fallen so markedly. The National Highway Traffic Safety Administration's Ricardo Martinez testified:

> Highway fatalities have decreased from 50,984 in 1966 to 41,907 in 1996, despite an enormous increase in travel. The fatality rate—fatalities per mile of travel—decreased by 69 percent during this period, from 5.5 fatalities per hundred million miles traveled to 1.7, an all-time low. Alcohol involvement in fatal crashes has dropped from 57 percent to 41 percent over this same [sic] 15-year period. Seat belt use has grown from 11 percent in 1982 to 68 percent in 1996. (U.S. House 1997:103)

In other words, as a result of a variety of reforms—improving roadways, designing safer vehicles, reducing the national maximum speed limit to 55 mph in 1974 (Congress did not return the right to set speed limits to the states until 1995), cracking down on drunk drivers, and mandating seatbelt use—there had been great improvements in traffic-safety statistics. However, these reforms could not be expected to continue to reduce death rates. For example, with a growing proportion of cars equipped with air bags and most people in cars using seat belts, fatalities of unrestrained drivers and passengers must approach their lower limit. Further improvements will require focusing on previously neglected causes of traffic deaths—such as road rage and aggressive driving. This is an example of a familiar paradox: solving major social problems invites the recognition of many minor social problems; problems once easy to overlook seem larger, more visible.

Still, road rage's proponents argued that it was a large and growing problem. There were two primary sources for these claims. First, NHTSA Administrator Ricardo Martinez testified:

> In 1996, 41,907 people died and over 3 million were injured in police-reported crashes. . . . We estimate that about one-third of these crashes and two-thirds of the resulting fatalities can be attributed to behavior associated with aggressive driving. The more serious the crash, the more likely aggressive behavior is involved. (U.S. House 1997:10)

Calculating that 28,000 was two-thirds of 41,907, the press began repeating the figure. Critics later commented that the two-thirds estimate was just an estimate; NHTSA was not reporting research results. Moreover, Martinez relied on a broad definition:

> He defined aggressive drivers as individuals who are more likely to: "speed, tailgate, fail to yield, weave in and out of traffic, pass on the right, make improper and unsafe lane changes, run stop signs and red lights, make hand and facial gestures, scream, honk, flash their lights, be impaired by alcohol or drugs, drive unbelted, or take other unsafe actions." Given the kitchen-sink inclusiveness of this list, whatever in the world causes the 13,000 or so traffic deaths that Dr. Martinez does not attribute to aggressive drivers? (Csaba 1997:43; see also Fumento 1998)

The second source for American claims was an AAA-commissioned study by Louis Mizell, Inc., "a Bethesda, Maryland-based firm which specializes in tracking crime and terrorism trends" using a "proprietary database of newspaper and police reports on all kinds of crime dating back to January, 1990" (U.S. House 1997:153—the Mizell report is reprinted on pp. 167–78). The Mizell study defined "aggressive driving" narrowly: "An incident in which an angry or impatient motorist or passenger intentionally injures or kills another motorist, passenger, or pedestrian, or attempts to injure or kill another motorist, passenger, or pedestrian, in response to a traffic dispute, altercation, or grievance. It is also considered 'aggressive driving' when an angry or vengeful motorist intentionally drives his or her vehicle into a building or other structure or property" (U.S. House 1997:170). The study "consulted 30 major newspapers, reports from 16 police departments, and insurance company claim reports to construct the database" (U.S. House 1997:170). The study identified 10,037 incidents, involving 218 deaths, over a period of nearly seven years; the number of incidents grew each year, suggesting that the problem was growing worse (cf. Harding et al. 1998).[6] However, critics generally ignored the Mizell study's unusual definition, and remarked instead that the 218 deaths were a tiny fraction of all traffic-related deaths during the same period (e.g., Fumento 1998; Glassner 1999). Others argued that the study misidentified the problem: "Coverage of road rage . . . shamelessly disregarded the import of firearms, even though the AAA study found that offenders in road rage incidents often use guns to kill or injure their victims" (Glassner 1999:8); and although alcohol continued to be involved in nearly half of traffic fatalities, "by the mid-1990s groups like MADD were finding it difficult to be heard in the media over the noise about road rage" (Glassner 1999:9).

In other words, the American response to road rage was inconsistent. On the one hand, the media promoted the problem as a serious, growing problem—an epidemic. At the same time, critics in the press were sophisticated enough to realize that the evidence supporting these claims was thin. This led to subversive, humorous interpretations of the road-rage campaign.

THE RAGE MOTIF AND PROBLEMS OF EMOTION

Contemporary social-problems claims often build upon a core notion, such as abuse or rights. Early claims about child abuse not only subdivided into categories of physical abuse, sexual abuse, emotional abuse, ritual abuse, and so on, but they spun off chains of claims about wife abuse, elder abuse, peer abuse, work abuse, and other forms of abuse experienced by victims who were not children. Similarly, the civil rights movement inspired campaigns for women's rights, gay and lesbian rights, children's rights, disability rights, prisoners' rights, victims' rights, animal rights, and rights for other populations that could articulate their grievances in terms of interference with their rights. Scholars of social movements speak of "master frames"—generic ways of articulating social issues that can be used to mobilize different social movements (Snow and Benford 1992; Williams and Williams 1995). Notions of abuse or rights can be seen as influential contemporary master frames that can both mobilize adherents around new causes, and that also attract critical analyses (e.g., Alan Dershowitz's [1994] concern about the "abuse excuse," or Michael Schudson's [1998] argument that the citizenship in the late twentieth century became reconfigured around the "rights-bearing citizen").

While the notion of master frame implies that claims about different social problems will share some fairly elaborate underlying theory of political and social relationships, social problems can share little more than similar names. This was the case with the "rage" family of problems. As noted earlier, once road rage became a familiar concept, British commentators began labeling other displays of inappropriate anger as "____ rage."

In the United States, air rage was the only other rage problem to attract substantial serious press coverage. Instead, the prospect of identifying other rage problems attracted humorists. A September 21, 1997, Sunday comic strip, "Dave," asked: "Road rage . . . an isolated case of aggressive driving gone too far *or* part of a growing national media-induced trend? Is no one safe? Are we on the verge of a 'rage epidemic'?" It then showed frames with people experiencing old rage, reader rage, web rage, smoker's rage, nonsmoker's rage, and rhetoric rage (frustration at a televised politician proposing "more freedom-limiting legislation to make all America safe from this dreaded 'road rage'!"). A similar February 28, 1998, strip for "Troubletown" (syndicated to alternative weekly papers) began "Everybody knows about road rage, but what other kinds of rage are equally serious?!", then featured fifteen frames showing other forms of rage (e.g., rejection rage, bad cellular reception rage). And the popular syndicated humorist Dave Barry wrote a February 1998 column noting that "opinion-makers in the news media have decided that [road rage] is a serious problem, currently ranking just behind global warming and several points ahead of Asia"; he went on to describe "parking lot rage" (waiting for other cars to vacate parking spots) and "shopping cart rage" (caused by supermarket congestion) (Barry 1998).

The responses of these humorists are revealing. First, they obviously recognized the possibilities for constructing claims about new forms of rage ("Are we on the verge of a 'rage epidemic'?"); part of their jokes depended on their audience understanding that rage, like abuse or rights, was a motif or frame that could be used to construct other social problems. Naming problems "____ rage." offered a formula for claimsmaking—and that formula's possibilities presented a recognizable target for humor. This was not an inevitable response. Recall that British commentators treated trolley rage as a genuine problem, whereas Americans found the notion of shopping-cart rage funny. Second, the humorists were implicitly skeptical about the claimsmaking process; they mocked the way politicians and "opinion-makers in the news media" brought new problems to public attention and ranked their seriousness ("all the other kinds of rage that are equally serious," "currently ranking just behind global warming"). Third—and least obvious—it is important to note that the humorists recognized that frustration and anger were at the core of all "rage" problems, and their humor acknowledged that frustration and anger were, after all, common experiences.

Even apparently serious discussions of road rage hinted that the problem had a comic side. Both *Time* and *U.S. News & World Report* printed lengthy, five-page feature articles on road rage: neither story included photographs; rather, both featured large cartoon-like illustrations of outsized, grimacing drivers looming from their vehicles (these comic portraits of drivers behaving badly—reminiscent of Ed "Big Daddy" Roth's classic hot-rodder cartoons—filled more than two pages in each case). Although the stories' text treated road rage as a serious problem, the pictures belied that message (Ferguson 1998; Vest et al. 1997).

Road rage and its attendant rages (created in both serious and comic claims) resemble the contemporary concern with hate crimes. Both hate crimes and road rage have names that suggest that inappropriate emotion—particularly anger—is central to these problems. These are problems of emotion—troubling feelings that need to be brought under social control. Most hate-crime laws address behavior (e.g., assault) that is already criminal; they add additional penalties for acts motivated by hatred of some racial or other category to which the victim belongs. It is the evidence of hatred as a motivation that makes the crime a *hate* crime. Similarly, claims about road rage adopt a traditional frustration-aggression model of psychology: drivers become enraged when frustrated by roadway congestion, or by the actions of other drivers. Road rage is bad driving and other acts of hostility—acts already, remember, prohibited under existing traffic and criminal codes—motivated by anger.

The experts that Congress and the media asked to interpret road rage were psychiatrists and clinical psychologists who medicalized road rage by defining inappropriate anger as symptomatic of psychological disorder, a problem of emotion management.[7] They medicalized bad driving: in their view, the flawed emotional reactions of individuals caused the problem, and the solution was treatment that taught anger management:

> We regard aggressive driving behaviors as symptoms of the underlying problem.... Most of the individuals I treat have a stress disorder.... Stress hormones race through the blood of every driver who holds strongly to any of the five stressful driving attitudes.... We introduce aggressive drivers to five alternative attitudes that they find more appealing than the stressful ones, and convince them to adopt the new attitudes. (Larson 1999:73–74)

Such therapies turned troubling social behavior into manifestations of psychological problems, deviant actions caused by rogue emotions (Glassner

1999). Almost completely absent was any sort of sociological imagination; through 1998, there was only a single scholarly study—by a team of criminologists in West Australia—exploring the social patterns in road rage (Harding et al. 1998).[8]

In Britain, road rage—and the extended family of rage problems—were less often subjects of humor. Critics worried that the construction of rage as a social problem reflected the ascendancy of a culture of emotionalism. They pointed to the shift from the traditional approval of keeping a "stiff upper lip" to a new emotionalism. A major feature story in the *Sunday Times* referred to the "angry nineties" as "Britain's Age of Rage" (Norman 1999). Increasingly, social problems formerly subject to philosophical or socioeconomic interpretations, are now explained from a perspective that highlights emotional damage and emotional deviance. When the *Guardian* published a major report on the crisis in Britain's education system, its emphasis was the emotional damage suffered by poor children, rather than on their social conditions or the failure of the system of education: "Poverty does its worst damage with the emotions of those who live with it" (Davies 1999). Academics find it easier to get funding for, say, research on "Unemployment and Mental Health" than for a study of structural unemployment. British society seems more comfortable dealing with poverty as a mental health problem than as a social issue. There is a widely held assumption that even relatively banal adverse circumstances induce stress and cause trauma and other forms of mental illness. This is a form of medicalization: it redefines social problems in psychological terms, meaning that their solution lies in therapy.

This shift of emphasis from the social to the therapeutic is particularly striking in British discussions of well-established social problems, such as racism. Whereas in the past critics of racism emphasized the importance of economic inequality, discrimination, and violence, today's tendency is to adopt the therapeutic language of victimization. A recent study by the Joseph Rowntree Foundation (1999) focused on the "devastating stress" suffered by victims of racial harassment. The report self-consciously sought to win public sympathy for victims of racism by playing the emotion card; its focus was on the "anger, stress, depression, sleepless nights" of the survey's respondents. Thus, the language of therapy provides a new vocabulary for talking about an old problem.

The therapeutic turn in Britain has encouraged the reinterpretation of crime as the violation of victims by people who have lost control over their emotions. In Britain, recently constructed, high-profile crimes—stalking, hate crimes, road rage, bullying, date rape—are perpetrated by psychologically destructive individuals not quite in control of their own emotions. In Britain, the problems of rage build upon a cultural foundation that views social problems as rooted in psychologically destructive behavior. Proponents of the therapeutic ethos contend that British society needs to confront its emotional deficit if it is to avoid a major crisis; one prominent psychologist warns: "The materialist aspirations of today's youth condemn them to an emotional holocaust" (James 1999). From this perspective, road rage is only one of the traumatic experiences inflicted on people by a materialistic society, insensitive to the needs of human emotion.

British critics view this culture of emotionalism as a reflection of foreign influence. The decline of stiff-upper-lip reserve in favor of public displays of emotion (e.g., the grieving surrounding the death of Princess Diana) is part of the Americanization of Britain. According to the journalist Philip Norman (1999), a road-rage incident "rightfully belongs to the New York streets in summertime when scorching heat melts brains along with the Tarmac." The new emotionalism—including the emphasis on the emotional aspects of social problems—is imported. No wonder the British found it easy to believe that road rage—a crime of emotion—had been transplanted from the United States (Burell 1994).

DISCUSSION

The different reactions to road rage in Britain and the United States are revealing. The problem first achieved notoriety in Britain, yet British commentators insisted that road rage had originated in the United States, that it had arrived in Britain via diffusion. The British were also quick to identify several other rage problems—trolley rage, air rage, and the like—and the commentators who invented these terms were generally serious. British commentators saw road rage and the larger family of rage problems as evidence of a foreign, corrupting influence—in particular, the spread of American emotionalism and its violence and materialistic car culture. Thus, traditional British civility seemed threatened by an invasion of foreign impropriety. Yet the concept of road rage also expressed a very distinct British perception regarding the negative consequences of car culture. At least for a section of British society, road rage symbolized all that was wrong with private car transportation. This link to the politicalization of car driving suggests that references to road rage are likely to continue as part of the ongoing British debate over car culture.

In contrast, the United States imported the notion of road rage, yet never acknowledged the term's British origins. For example, when the AAA presented three studies of road rage to Congress, it glossed over the fact that two of the three were from Britain. This reluctance to mention foreign influences may reflect Americans' notions of their nation's preeminence. At the same time, Americans responded to claims about road rage in two distinct ways. On the one hand, concerns about road rage (and air rage) received serious attention from Congress, law enforcement, the press, the AAA and various other organizations concerned with traffic safety, and some psychological experts. On the other hand, there were competing attempts to discount the road-rage problem, either by debunking the claims or by treating rage problems humorously. For Americans, the essence of road rage was not a decline in manners, but *anger*. Treated seriously, anger—like hate—was a negative emotion that reformers believed needed to be brought under control. Anger had destructive consequences, not only for society, but for the individual. But for humorists, anger had a comic quality: they pointed to the myriad frustrations of contemporary life, and viewed the resulting anger—and road-rage proponents' concern with that anger—as at least somewhat funny. The ease with which humorists dismissed road rage suggests that the problem is unlikely to endure as a focus for public attention in the United States.

ACKNOWLEDGMENT

Bruno Waterfield helped with the collection and analysis of many of the British materials.

NOTES

1.   NEXIS-LEXIS Academic Universe includes a full-text database for many U.S. and some foreign newspapers. It is a powerful tool for determining when terms begin to have widespread usage. The database lists only seven U.S. newspaper articles published before 1996 that contain the term "road rage"; three of these (all published in 1994 or early 1995) specifically refer to British concerns about road rage. The earliest reference was in a six-sentence, 1988 item in the *St. Petersburg (FL) Times:* the headline read "Highway driver accused of 'road rage' shooting"; and the piece began: "A fit of 'road rage' has landed a man in jail, accused of shooting a woman passenger whose car had 'cut him off' on the highway" (*St. Petersburg Times* 1988:1B). Although this article apparently led some British observers (e.g., Bressler 1996)—and even some Americans (e.g., Fumento 1998; Larson 1999:25)—to assume that road rage was a familiar term in the U.S. after 1988, it is important to understand that there were only three other references to American road rage appearing in U.S. newspapers or magazines indexed in LEXIS-NEXIS during 1988–95. These data hardly support the notion that the term was generally familiar or widely used. Far more common during the same period were references to "roid rage" (violent reactions by steroid users); 55 U.S. newspaper articles mentioned roid rage during 1987–94. The relative levels of media coverage make it seem more likely that the 1990s label "road rage" was a spin-off of "roid rage,"

rather than that one brief 1988 newspaper article in a regional newspaper inspired intense claimsmaking six years later.

Full-text databases, such as LEXIS-NEXIS, are new research tools, and many analysts fail to grasp their limitations. For example, Michael Fumento, often an insightful critic of others' use of evidence, uses NEXIS to document the "proliferation of the term 'road rage'": "It was, apparently, coined in 1988, and appeared in up to three stories yearly until 1994, when it began to catch on. After twenty-seven mentions that year, the numbers escalated sharply, to almost 500 in 1995" (Fumento 1998:12). Although results of NEXIS searches depend upon the precise search strategy adopted (and possibly on the particular NEXIS service being searched and the date when the search is conducted), our analysis located only a single newspaper story in 1988, two in 1991, 15 in 1994, and 270 in 1995. Of these 288 stories in our sample, 277 appeared in British newspapers, only seven appeared in the United States (including the three referring to events in Britain), while the remaining four appeared in Canadian or Asian newspapers. In other words, it is not enough to simply count citations; attention must be paid to the location of the publications being cited.

2. Obviously, we mean to survey only the history of the label "road rage." The various behaviors that came to be called road rage have, of course, much longer histories.

3. The origin of the figure of 1,500 U.S. deaths and injuries is unknown; we know of no U.S. agency that keeps track of "traffic disputes" or their consequences. However, the number took on a life of its own in Britain, where it appeared in several newspaper articles (e.g., Spillious 1995). These reports circulated before road rage began attracting attention in the United States. As will be seen, many of the eventual American estimates for road rage's prevalence in the United States were far higher.

The claim that the origins of road rage were American, made by commentators in Britain and elsewhere (e.g., Lupton 1999), probably referred to the 1987 media coverage of what was then called "freeway violence" in Los Angeles (Best 1991).

4. Several participants in the hearing referred to a locally notorious incident: "The 1996 high-speed duel two motorists held on the George Washington Parkway. . . . This senseless act resulted in the death of two innocent motorists and one of the participants" (U.S. House 1997:1). This incident, although it had not attracted national attention, obviously typified road rage's seriousness for many in Washington.

5. Road rage inspired a range of popular cultural creators. The British mystery author, Ruth Rendell (1997), published *Road Rage* featuring her series character Inspector Wexford (the title was a pun; the book concerned environmentalists opposed to highway construction through a wooded area—it did not feature traffic-related violence). In 1997 and 1998, at least seven artists performing rather different types of music—Adam X, Catatonia, Civil Tones, George Duke, Hillbilly Hellcats, James Taylor Quarter, and Macka-B—recorded songs called "Road Rage." The packaging for the CD-ROM game "Grand Theft Auto" (1997) promised: "Murder, road rage, pimping, bank raids, . . . unlawful carnal knowledge, and double parking."

6. Although the Mizell study found roughly 1,500 cases per year, it is important to appreciate that this could not have been the basis for British claims that U.S. road-rage casualties numbered 1,500 annually. The British claims circulated years before the Mizell study was completed in 1997.

7. These psychologists promoted remarkably inclusive definitions for diagnosing road-rage problems. Nerenberg argued that "expressing anger directly to other drivers at least twice per year" qualified as "road rage disorder" (U.S. House 1997:113–14). Similarly, Larson's Driver Stress Profile includes ten items each for anger, impatience, competing, and punishing. The anger items ask how often one gets angry at other drivers, at fast drivers, slow drivers, etc.; respondents get 0 to 3 points for each item (e.g., 1 point is assigned if the item is "true for you only once in a while"). However, a score of 9 or more (out of a possible 30—that is, conceding that one feels angry at other drivers, etc. once in a while) is scored as indicating high levels of anger. Someone with total of 35 points (out of a possible 120 on all four parts of the scale) is a "high scorer . . . very likely to be involved in a road rage incident" (Larson 1999:32–34). One can only suspect that applying Nerenberg's or Larson's criteria would lead to identifying a large very proportion of drivers as experiencing problematic emotions.

8. Road rage is only beginning to attract scholarly attention. Lupton (1999), another Australian, offers a cultural studies interpretation:

"Road rage" has emerged as a social problem in contemporary Western societies because of a constellation of factors. These include the sociocultural meanings invested in cars via their design and function and such products as advertising, news media representations and popular film, the psychodynamic meanings produced by cars' potential to be both "good" and "bad" objects", and the norms and expectations concerning the meaning and management of social relations and emotions such as anger, frustration and rage. Central to many of these aspects is the ontology of the cyborg body that is produced when a human is driving a car.

In contrast, Jack Katz (1999) presents an interactionist interpretation of drivers' expressions of anger with one another.

REFERENCES

Adler, Jerry. 1997. "'Road Rage': We're Driven to Destruction." *Newsweek* 129 (June 2):70.

Barry, Dave. 1998. "Our Next Epidemic: Get Set for Shopping Cart Rage." *St. Louis Post-Dispatch* (February 8): D2.

Best, Joel. 1991. "'Road Warriors' on 'Hair-Trigger Highways': Cultural Resources and the Media's Construction of the 1987 Freeway Shooting Problem." *Sociological Inquiry* 61:327–45.

———. 1999. *Random Violence: How We Talk about New Crimes and New Victims.* Berkeley: University of California Press.

Boseley, Sarah. 1995. "Rage Rises at Car Alarms." *Guardian* (November 1):5.

Bowles, Scott, and Paul Overberg. 1998. "Aggressive Driving: A Road Well-Traveled." *USA Today* (November 23):17A.

Bressler, Fenton. 1996. "Motoring: What the Courts Will Do with Road Ragers." *Telegraph* (December 7).

Burrell, Ian. 1994. "Motorists Go Armed for War on the Roads." *Sunday Times* (June 5):1,5.

Campbell, Duncan. 1996. "What Is This Thing Called Rage?" *Guardian* (October 28):22.

Clarkson, Jeremy. 1995. "Raging Bulls One, Mad Cows Zero." *Sunday Times* (March 5).

Connell, Dominic, and Matthew Joint. 1996. *Driver Aggression*. London: Road Safety Unit Group Public Policy.

Cook, Emma. 1995. "Motor Hype That Plays on Fear." *Independent on Sunday* (August 6): Real Life 20.

Coren, Giles. 1994. "When Rage Has Wheels." *Times* (December 30).

Csaba, Csere. 1997. "Ravings about Road Rage." *Car and Driver* 43 (October):43.

Davidson, Andrew. 1995. "Year of Rage." *Sunday Telegraph* (December 31).

Davies, Nick. 1999. "Crisis, Crisis, Crisis: The State of Our Schools." *Guardian* (September 14).

Davis, Patricia, and Leef Smith. 1998. "A Crisis That May Not Exist Is All the Rage." *Washington Post* (November 29): B1.

Dershowitz, Alan M. 1994. *The Abuse Excuse*. Boston: Little, Brown.

Ferguson, Andrew. 1998. "Road Rage." *Time* 151 (January 12):64–68.

Fleet, Michael. 1994. "Road Rage Driver Jailed for Attack on Two Motorists." *Daily Telegraph* (November 12).

Fowler, Rebecca. 1996. "End of Our Love Affair with the Car?" *Independent* (May 25).

Fumento, Michael. 1998. "'Road Rage' Versus Reality." *Atlantic Monthly* 282 (August):12, 14, 16–17.

Furedi, Frank. 1997. *Culture of Fear: Risk-Taking and the Morality of Low Expectations*. London: Cassell.

Glassner, Barry. 1999. *The Culture of Fear: Why Americans Are Afraid of the Wrong Things*. New York: Basic Books.

Goodbody, John. 1998. "Pool Rage." *Times* (October 24).

Groombridge, Nic. 1998. "Masculinities and Crimes Against the Environment." *Theoretical Criminology* 2:249–67.

Gwyther, Matthew. 1995. "Motoring: The Car in Front Is Driving Me Mad." *Independent* (May 7).

Harding, Richard W., Frank H. Morgan, David Indermaur, Anna M. Ferrante, and Harry Blagg. 1998. "Road Rage and the Epidemiology of Violence: Something Old, Something New." *Studies on Crime and Crime Prevention* 7:221–38.

Harlow, John. 1995. "Road 'Ragers' to Face Mental Test." *Sunday Times* (May 7):1.

Harper, Keith. 1999. "Airlines Are Ordered to Reduce Delays." *Guardian* (July 12).

Harrington, Anne. 1999. "A Tip for the Porter, Beware Hotel Rage." *Herald* (Glasgow) (February 16):1.

Harrison, David. 1996. "Driving Toward Desperation." *Observer* (December 8).

Independent. 1994. "Motorway Massage to Combat 'Road Rage'." (August 18).

James, Oliver. 1999. "Up to Nothing." *Guardian* (December 11).

Joint, Matthew. 1995. *What Is "Road Rage"?* London: Automobile Association.

Joseph Rowntree Foundation. 1999. Press release (June 21).

Katz, Jack. 1999. *How Emotions Work.* Chicago: University of Chicago Press.

Langley, John. 1996. "Road Rage Is Driving Britain to Distraction." *Telegraph* (January 24).

Larson, John. 1999. *Road Rage to Road-Wise.* New York: Forge.

Lupton, Deborah. 1999. "Monsters in Metal Cocoons: 'Road Rage' and Cyborg Bodies." *Body & Society* 5:57–72.

Manufacturing Science and Finance Union. 1999. "Ground Rage—Scourge of the Holiday Season." Press release, July 12.

Montalbano, William D. 1996. "Britain Reels from a Rise in Bad Manners." *Los Angeles Times* (June 3): A1.

Moore, Toby. 1997. "Why Road Rage Is Just a Convenient Modern Myth." *Express* (July 31).

Moorhead, Joanna. 1996. "Driving Forces." *Guardian* (December 5):4.

Mullin, John. 1995. "Court Hears How Checkout Fracas Brought Trolley Rage to Safeways." *Guardian* (August 3):3.

Norman, Philip. 1999. "Why John Bull Has Exchanged a Stiff Upper Lip for a Stiff Upper Cut." *Sunday Times* (February 13).

Norwich Union Insurance. 1995. Press release (August 21).

People. 1997. "Make Their Day." 48 (September 1):59–60.

Perry, Simon. 1995. "RAC's Nervous Breakdown Service." *Daily Telegraph* (December 20).

Plowden, Ben. 1998. "The Car Can Be Curbed." *Independent on Sunday* (November 29).

RAC (Royal Automobile Club) Foundation. 1999. "Lollipop Aggression: Beyond the Call of Duty?" (October 28).

Reinhardt-Rutland, Tony. 1996. "Road-Rage: Have Cars Become Too Safe and Comfortable?" *Police Journal* 69:285–88.

Rendell, Ruth. 1997. *Road Rage.* New York: Crown.

Sanghera, Sathnam. 1999. "Computer Rage Staff Are Venting their Anger on Workplace." *Financial Times* (May 28):13.

Schudson, Michael. 1998. *The Good Citizen.* New York: Free Press.

Snow, David A., and Robert D. Benford. 1992. "Master Frames and Cycles of Protest." Pp. 133–55 in *Frontiers in Social Movement Theory,* edited by Aldon D. Morris and Carol McClurg Mueller. New Haven: Yale University Press.

Spillious, Alex. 1995. "Why Do We Flip Our Ids?" *Guardian* (October 28):22.

St. Petersburg Times. 1988. "Highway Driver Accused of 'Road Rage' Shooting." (April 2):1B.

Thomas, Richard. 1998. "Air Rage." *Observer* (November 1):20.

Tredre, Roger. 1995. "Aggression: Suddenly Losing Your Cool Is All the Rage." *Observer* (October 15):14.

Turner, Liz. 1996. "Rage Against the Machine." *Guardian* (February 10).

U.S. House. 1997. Subcommittee on Surface Transportation, Committee on Transportation and Infrastructure. *Road Rage: Causes and Dangers of Aggressive Driving: Hearings.* 105th Congress, 1st sess., July 17.

Vest, Jason, Warren Cohen, and Mike Tharp. 1997. "Road Rage." *U.S. News & World Report* (June 2):24–25, 28–30.

Waugh, Auberon. 1995. "Way of the World: Not Polite." *Telegraph* (October 18).

Williams, Gwyneth I., and Rhys H. Williams. 1995. "'All We Want Is Equality': Rhetorical Framing in the Fathers' Rights Movement." Pp. 191–212 in *Images of Issues*, 2nd ed., edited by Joel Best. Hawthorne, NY: Aldine de Gruyter.

Wolmar, C. 1997. *Unlocking the Gridlock: The Key to a New Transport Policy.* London: Friends of the Earth.

Wuerz, Scott. 1998. "State Police 'See Everything'." *Southern Illinoisan* (February 15):3A.

7

Frame Diffusion from the U.S. to Japan: Japanese Arguments Against Pornocomics, 1989–1992

TADASHI SUZUKI

Japanese claimsmakers sometimes borrow social problems claims from other societies, especially the United States and Western European countries. The diffusion of social problems usually involves claims that originate in the United States and spread to Japan, rather than vice versa. For example, sexual harassment and stalking are two problems that originated in the United States and then became recognized—and within a few years the subjects of laws—in Japan. Their Japanese names—*sekuhara* (sexual harassment) and *sutookaa* (stalking)—reveal their American origins. Both problems have become well established in Japan. In these cases, the construction of social problems in the United States inspired efforts to construct the same problems in Japan.

In other cases, different countries may independently construct the same social problems. Pornography is one problem with a long history in both Japan and Western countries. Histories of Japanese pornography often begin with woodblock prints, called *shunga* (literally "spring pictures") that appeared by the middle of the seventeenth century. Shunga include *makuru-e* ("pillow pictures"), *koshokubon* ("sexual books"), and *warai-e* ("laughing [or masturbation] pictures"). Because they typically depict sexual intercourse or masturbation, shunga can be called pornography (Akagawa 1996; Screech 1999). Shunga emerged during the Edo [Tokugawa] period (1603–1867) when the Edo shogunate kept a policy of seclusion, so it is unlikely that Westerners influenced the emergence of shunga. In fact, Screech (1999:13) notes: "In 1615, shock was registered in London when the first import of 'certaine lasciuious bookes and pictures' were briefly seen before being summarily burned."

As in the West, pornography periodically became the subject of a "cycle of outrage" (Gilbert 1986) in Japan. Traditionally, Japanese antipornography critics argued that shunga threatened *fuzoku* (manners and customs). The initial attempt to control shunga was made by the Edo magistracy in 1722. The publication of shunga may have temporarily terminated, but it was revived in the early 1760s. One edict issued by the eighth shogun, Yoshimune, stated: "Whereas, among material heretofore published by houses of edition there have been books on sexual matters some of which are not conducive to good mores, and all of which are constantly changing, these are no longer to be produced." (quoted in Screech 1999:43).

More recently, Japanese claims about pornography reflect the diffusion of Western—and particularly American—constructions of the pornography problem. This chapter examines the diffusion of antipornography claims and frames from the United States to Japan in 1990–92, during the construction of "harmful" comics or "pornocomics" as a social problem. I begin by summarizing American constructions of pornography as a social problem during the 1970s and 1980s. Then I examine how these rhetorical frames contributed to constructing the Japanese harmful comics problem. Finally, I discuss the process by which claims and frames diffuse from one society to another.

ANTIPORNOGRAPHY CLAIMS IN THE UNITED STATES DURING THE 1970S AND 1980S

American antipornography claimsmakers traditionally based their arguments on morality. After the 1940s, a series of court decisions gradually began liberalizing obscenity law, generally on the grounds that laws against pornography violated the First Amendment's guarantee of freedom of the press. By the late 1960s, pornography was becoming increasingly available in the United States, and political conservatives were vocal in calling for the restoration of moral standards. In 1967, President Lyndon Johnson established the Commission on Obscenity and Pornography, charged with recommending new, constitutionally defensible legal standards for regulating pornography. The commission sponsored numerous research projects on the extent of pornography and its influence, and concluded that there was no reliable evidence linking pornography and sexual crimes (Nunamake and Beasley 1990). The commission recommended that there be no restrictions on pornography's availability to adults.

The commission's recommendations outraged moralists. Existing antipornography organizations, such as Morality in Media and Citizens for Decency Through Law, expanded during the 1970s and 1980s. In addition, new conservative antipornography groups formed in the 1980s, including Morality in America, the National Federation for Decency, Citizens Concerned for Community Values, and the National Consultation on Obscenity, Pornography, and Indecency (Downs 1989).

Underlying their opposition to pornography was the conservatives' fundamental view of "human frailty, defined as the propensity to sin, as the most significant feature of the moral landscape" (Berger et al. 1990:31). They feared that "pornography is morally corrupting and that it reduces people's sexual inhibitions," and they insisted that "the primary harms of pornography include the corruption of children's moral development. . . . Pornography is a sin and an offense against God" (Berger et al. 1990:31). In this view, pornography is "an apocalyptic, religious, and moral symptom of social and moral decline" (Downs 1989:27). In making these claims, conservatives echoed earlier critics who had denounced pornography in moralistic terms.

Traditionally, women's organizations had paid little attention to pornography. However, the emergence of the new women's rights movement in the 1970s led to the establishment of feminist antipornography organizations, such as Women Against Pornography, Women Against Violence Against Women, and the Pornography Resource Center (Downs 1989). These groups downplayed the traditional moral rhetoric of conservatives, and emphasized pornography's role in objectifying and exploiting women, and in causing rape and other forms of sexual violence. In the early 1980s, feminist activists, led by Andrea Dworkin and Catharine MacKinnon, promoted antipornography ordinances in Minneapolis, Indianapolis, and other cities. By arguing that women deserved protection from the exploitation and objectification caused by the production, distribution, and consumption of pornography, they insisted that women's freedoms under the First Amendment required restricting pornography.

Feminists had several, interrelated objections to pornography. First, they saw it as a reflection of gender inequality, as a form of "systematic oppression or disadvantaging of women [that] . . . reflects and causes the subordination of women by eroticizing power and domination" (Downs 1989:xix). Second, pornography objectified women; that is, it stripped them of their humanity and individuality, and turned them into sexual objects. In this view, pornography causes various harms: women forced to make pornography are sexually exploited; other women suffer from acts of sexual violence inspired by men's exposure to pornography; and there are more general harms to society caused by "repeated displays of negative images of women" (Downs 1989:xix). For feminists, the rise of pornography was accompanied by an increase in sexual violence (Lederer 1980) and, more generally: "pornography is the principal medium through which cultural sadism is diffused into the mainstream culture and integrated into the fantasies and sexual practices of individuals" (Berger et al. 1990:33).

By the mid-1980s, conservative moralists and feminists had become allies in a new antipornography movement that combined moralistic and feminist rhetoric. In 1984, the Reagan administration's Attorney General, Edwin Meese III, formed a new federal commission—the Attorney General's Commission on Pornography, intended to challenge the findings of the earlier commission appointed by Johnson. As expected, the new commission issued a report denouncing pornography; it incorporated arguments borrowed from both conservative moralists (suggesting that pornography encouraged deviant behavior) and feminists (suggesting that pornography exploited women).

The antipornography movement ultimately had minimal influence on American social policy. In the 1980s and 1990s, technology was transforming the pornography industry; the spread first of videotapes, and later the Internet, effectively destroyed the adult cinemas that had often been the focal points for antipornography protests. Pornography could now be acquired in the back room of the local video store, or through the privacy of one's computer. It was now so readily available that it was difficult to devise policies to bring it under control. However, the antipornography rhetoric of both conservative moralists and feminists continued to flourish. Their arguments were familiar and widely available for use by claimsmakers in the United States—and elsewhere.

THE "HARMFUL" COMICS PROBLEM IN JAPAN, 1990–1992

In the early 1990s, a new cycle of Japanese concern about pornography became focused on the problem of "harmful" comic books. A combination of incidents seems to have led to the emergence of this problem.

In 1988–89, four girls aged 4–6 were murdered in a suburb of Tokyo. Although every homicide is reported nationwide in Japan, these serial killings received especially heavy coverage in the press. In August 1989, a suspect was arrested and confessed. However, his father, who did not believe the charges, opened the suspect's room to media reporters in an attempt to prove the suspect's innocence. Many media reports noted that the room contained as many as 6,500 horror videotapes; tapes were stacked high enough to block light from coming through the room's window. This huge collection offered police, media, and citizens a way to explain the murders. The media ran stories that treated the video collection as the key to the suspect's personality, implying that the police saw a relationship between his crimes and his horror film collection. In response, several prefectures revised their juvenile ordinances to control youths' access to horror films.

The media then turned their attention to pornocomics. In the United States, comic books aim largely at children, and adult Americans rarely read them. On the other hand, Japanese comics (*manga*) come in a variety of genres—science fiction, sports, comedy, horror, love stories, pornography, and so on, much as American novels do. The mangas' main readers are teenagers, but some adults in their thirties and older read manga intended for their age groups, such as dramas depicting businessmen's daily lives. Pornocomics refer to a genre of comics, that features sexual content, including masturbation, nudity, and sexual intercourse. A genre of pornocomics called "*bishojo-kei* comics" (literally "beautiful-girl comics," although the actual meaning is "cute," rather than "beautiful") became a new trend in the 1980s. They often included sexualized drawings of women with childlike heads featuring huge eyes and round faces (like the females in "Sailor Moon"), yet with the sexually mature bodies of adults. Although these characters' breasts were revealed, their genitals were covered or shaded. Pornocomics, including bishojo-kei comics, subsequently led to claims about the "harmful" comic problem. ("Harmful" was a term used by those who sought stricter censorship to criticize pornocomics in the 1990s. Not everyone agreed that pornocomics were harmful, so the quotation marks were usually added.) The term has additional significance: publications can be officially specified as harmful under the juvenile ordinances, meaning that the publication (1) hinders the juvenile's sound upbringing by markedly stimulating juveniles' sexual emotions or / and; (2) hinders the juvenile's sound upbringing by markedly promoting juveniles' rudeness or misbehavior.

For example, an *Asahi Shimbun* (1989) news story focused on so-called *rolikon zasshi* ("Lolita-complex magazines"), because those magazines, too, had been found in the suspect's room. Rolikon magazines are a genre of adult magazines featuring sexualized images of little girls. They include some pornocomics, as well as magazines containing photographs of young girls (e.g., peeping shots of girls' underwear, or nude photos [these became defined as the social problem of child pornography in late-1990s Japan]). Soon the media's focus shifted almost completely from horror films to rolikon zasshi. Because the murder victims had been little girls, it was easy to make the link between these magazines and the crimes, and to argue that something had to be done.

In addition, on September 19, 1989, the Supreme Court dismissed a final appeal from a publisher who had been charged with selling pornographic magazines (designated as "harmful" publications) in vending machines; the court agreed that the juvenile ordinance of Gifu prefecture (which restricted such sales) did not violate freedom of speech and was constitutional. This judgment may have encouraged antipornocomics claimsmakers, including police, to start campaigns against comics.

The beginning of the campaign against pornocomics was signaled on

August 9, 1990, when two letters complaining about comics appeared in the reader's column of *Kishu-shinpo* (a small, local newspaper in Waka-yama prefecture). Two weeks later, the Tokyo Bureau of Life and Culture (1990) issued a report, "The Study on the Objectification of Sex." On September 4, sixteen comics, including some issued by major publishing companies, were specified as "harmful" publications in Fukuoka prefecture. On the same day, *Kishu-shinpo* began an antipornocomics campaign. Although it may have been a coincidence that the newspaper's attention coincided with the Fukuoka action, official reports often provide the media with an informational hook to catch the public's attention. The leading newspaper, *Asahi Shimbun* (1990a) also took up the report on September 4, running an editorial titled "Too Many Poor *Manga*." In early September, "The Club to Protect Children from Comic Books" was organized in Waka-yama prefecture. It began a petition campaign against pornocomics, and eventually collected 56,381 signatures.

Subsequently, the antipornocomics campaign spread nationwide. Organizations, such as self-government organizations, Parent-Teacher Associations, and women's organizations submitted petitions to local governments. For example, petitions submitted in Tokyo advocated four reforms: (1) amend the juvenile ordinance; (2) prohibit selling pornocomics in vending machines; (3) add an article to the emergency designation by which a publication could be designated as harmful soon after an issue appeared; and (4) add a reporting system so that citizens could report "harmful" comics. In addition, some petitions called for a prohibition on publishing pornocomics, or for passage of a national law to control comics (Yajima and Yamamoto 1994).

The Japanese government's General Affairs Bureau repeatedly required the publishing industry's Council of Publication Ethics to enforce stricter self-regulation of pornocomics. In December 1990, the council decided to add a mark or symbol on pornocomics' covers to show that they were aimed at readers 18 years old and over, and to establish a special committee to oversee issues regarding comics. The number of comics specified in each prefecture as harmful jumped from 771 for the entire year between October 1989 and November 1990, to 756 for the single month of December 1990 (because the same titles could be labeled "harmful" in several prefectures, these figures reflect increases in official activity, rather than any change in what was being published) (General Affairs Bureau cited in Nagaoka 1993).

In February, 1991, 75 politicians from the governing Liberal Democratic party met to discuss pornocomics. A week later, the Tokyo Metropolitan Police Board arrested five owners and staff members in three Tokyo bookstores for the possession of obscene drawings for sale. The following month, a bookstore in Kumamoto prefecture was declared as in violation of the juvenile ordinance prohibiting the sale of harmful publications—the first use of such ordinances against comics in Japan. On May 8, petitions on comics' control were adopted in the 120th National Diet (subsequently, these petitions would be sent to a cabinet, and the relevant departments were supposed to examine those petitions' requirements.) The 121st, 122nd, and 123rd National Diets also adopted petitions on comics' control.

By 1992, many local governments had amended their ordinances in various ways: (1) three more prefectures adopted the individual designation clause by which publications could be designated as harmful under their juvenile ordinances (making a total of 46 of the 47 prefectures); (2) four prefectures adopted the emergency designation clause by which publications could be designated without an examination by a deliberative council (a total of 41 prefectures); (3) five prefectures adopted the blanket clause by which publications could be designated automatically according to some specific standard (e.g., if one-third of an issue's total pages contain sexual content, such as pictures of nudity or intercourse) instead of an examination of the individual publication (a total of 21 prefectures); (4) the Tokyo metropolitan government began to designate pornocomics as harmful; (5) five prefectures adopted a fine or raised the highest amount for fines (a total of 45 prefectures); and (6) six prefectures adopted a reporting system (a total of 25 prefectures) (Nagaoka 1993). Local governments, such as Kyoto and Osaka, that had had relatively loose ordinances came to have rather strict ones. In addition to these official changes, the publishing industry brought comics under stricter self-regulation, through labeling (i.e., applying the "adult comic mark") and the oversight of the comics special committee.

However, these new laws also met with opposition: in 1991, feminists, comic editors, journalists, children's rights activists, and others held numerous meetings against using juvenile ordinances to increase control of comics. Also, local bar associations and organizations related to the publishing industry, such as labor unions and bookstore associations, submitted opinions to local governments against amending the ordinances. On March 13, 1992, comic writers, editors, and bookstore owners established the Organization to Protect the Freedom of Comics' Expression, and began activities opposing the amendment of the ordinances, by publishing advertisements in comic magazines, holding conferences, petitioning, and so on.

The anticomics campaign adopted two frames: the harm frame, and the feminist sexual discrimination frame. These paralleled—but were not precisely the same as—the two frames used by antipornography advocates in the United States.

The Harm Frame

According to the harm frame, pornocomics victimized children. In Japan, children were traditionally considered as beings close to *chikusho* (brutes) who, therefore, needed protection, since they tended to be steeped in vice (Hashizume 1995). On the other hand, after 1910, the Japanese Christian Organization to Correct Manners and Customs started invoking a harm frame (i.e., warning that children were corruptible innocents) by emphasizing the mother's role in protecting children from harmful environments, such as the licensed brothel district (Mori 1998). So, although the harm frame has Japanese—particularly Confucian—origins, there also was Western influence. In this view, children and juveniles are vulnerable to sexual depictions in the media that can lead them into sexual misconduct. They need to be protected from this harm.

In the 1990s, the police, the mothers' association, politicians, and psychiatrists warned that pornocomics were a harmful influence on children:

> [Some manga] express sex indecently with shocking depictions, so children who are immature should not be exposed to such comics. . . . It is our responsibility to protect children, who will carry the future of Japan on their shoulders, from a bad influence in this society, and to raise them properly. (Reader's column in *Kishu-shinpo*, August 9, 1990, reprinted in *Tsukuru Monthly* 1991.)

> Those [porno] comics depict sexual scenes. So, they will possibly hinder children's sound upbringing. For example, those comics may strikingly stimulate children's sexual senses and promote their rudeness and brutality, and eventually induce children to commit crimes and so on. (Tanabe Daini Shogakko [The Tanabe Second Elementary School] et al. October 20, 1990, letter reprinted in *Tsukuru Monthly* 1991.)

> Pornocomics hinder sound development of very vulnerable children and youth who do not have enough judgment. (Request on editing magazine for boys and girls, *Mayor of Tanabe-city Ikoma et al.* October 23, 1990, letter reprinted in *Tsukuru Monthly* 1991)

The Tokyo Metropolitan Assembly adopted "A Resolution on Regulation of Harmful Publications." The resolution emphasized the publications' influence on children and youth: "Harmful publications for children, which arouse pointlessly their sexual curiosity, have been in flood recently. They have been a social problem as one of the serious obstacles against wholesome education of children" (July 11, 1991, reprinted in *Tsukuru Monthly* 1991). The vice chairman of the Juvenile Problem Special Committee of Osaka insisted that there was a causal relationship between pornocomics and sexual crimes by juveniles: "Crimes which imitated pornocomics and porno-video films increased rapidly this year. No doubt there is a causal relationship between pornocomics and sexual crimes" (*Yomiuri Shimbun* 1991c).

Critics warned that harmful comics were difficult to distinguish from less troubling publications. The Japanese government's General Affairs Bureau sent the Council of Publication Ethics a letter: "Because many pornocomics make their covers look like those of common books on sale in book stores, convenience stores, and so on, even children and youth can buy those comics because of the current method of sale" (November 8, 1990, reprinted in *Tsukuru Monthly* 1991).

In short, the harm frame focused on the danger that pornocomics could corrupt children and youth, that the young had access to harmful materials, and that exposure might lead them into deviance. The harm frame is moralistic; as such, it resembles traditional conservative critiques of pornography in Japan. The Japanese harm frame resembles, but is not precisely the same as, the claims made by conservative moralists in the United States. For many U.S. moralists, pornography is in part a religious problem, linked to the idea of sin. In contrast, Japanese concerns focused on damage to youth (and therefore to the society which would be harmed by harming the young).

The Sexual Discrimination Frame

The sexual discrimination frame views pornography as an expression of sexual discrimination and violence against women that victimizes women. The women's movement spread in many countries during the last three decades of the twentieth century; in many cases, U.S. feminist analyses were disseminated to other countries. In Japan, the sexual discrimination frame used by pornography's opponents reflected this diffusion from Western countries, particularly from the United States.

Pornography was not the first Japanese issue to be framed in feminist language. After Western ideas, including humanism, progressivism, and pragmatism were introduced into late-nineteenth-century Japan, some intellectuals, such as Yukichi Fukuzawa, charged that inequality between men and women was an obstacle to Japanese civilization. They identified women—whose lower status had been taken for granted during the Edo period—as oppressed beings and, after the Meiji Restoration in 1868, advocated their liberation (Sugihara 1992).

Feminism had shaped earlier Japanese debates over prostitution (Akagawa 1996). Although there were claims criticizing prostitution for the objectification of sex as early as 1890, these claims emphasized monogamy and chastity, rather than contemporary feminism. For example, the Japanese Christian Organization to Correct Manners and Customs submitted a petition to prohibit husbands' adultery in 1890, when only wives' adultery was illegal, claiming that the toleration of men's adultery was a relic of the past's objectification of women (Mori 1998). After the Second World War, feminist rhetoric about sexual discrimination shaped the debate over prostitution in the officially licensed brothel districts, although the harm frame also was used to support claims that the districts endangered children's sound upbringing (Mori 1998). (Prostitution became illegal in 1956.)

Feminists came to use the term *Sei no Shohin-ka* (sexual objectification) to criticize prostitution at least by the early 1970s, and they started applying this frame to beauty contests and pornography in the 1980s (Akagawa 1995). Japanese feminists writing about pornography noted MacKinnon's and Dworkin's critiques, and discussed their applicability to Japanese pornography and Japanese society (Kamiya 1987, Kimura 1987, Funabashi 1990, Suzuki 1990, Yamasaki 1989, 1990). In particular, the argument that pornography objectified women became influential in 1980s Japan. For example, the feminist Active Women's Club focused on the issue of sexual objectification in the media, especially after 1986. In 1989, they succeeded in getting some companies they had accused of sexual objectification and discrimination to remove billboards and television advertisements (Kimura 1987, Active Women's Club (ed.) 1990). Feminists' criticism of the depiction of women in the media began attracting public attention. The term for sexual objectification became better known through feminists' antipornography activities. For example, a newspaper editorial argued that pornocomics commercialized women, treating them as a commodity, and thereby implying that women's personalities were irrelevant, that their purpose was to satisfy men's sexual desire: "Many manga studied treated men as the central figures. There are not a few stories in which women are depicted conveniently for men's dirty minds, for example, some stories depicted women as figures who feel pleasure even in forcible sex" (*Asahi Shimbun* editorial 1990a).

Since feminists view pornocomics as a form of pornography, their rhetoric flows from the specific form (pornocomics), to the general form (pornography), to the broader problems (sexual discrimination). In a roundtable talk concerning pornocomics, a member of the feminist Active Women's Club stated: "Our ultimate goal is to remove sexual discrimination in Japan. Pornography is the manifestation of the discrimination, and the antipornogaphy movement is a movement to change the sexually discriminatory society" (Hasegawa in Sakamoto et al. 1991:203). This rhetoric often incorporated a version of the harm frame, as well. Thus, pornography is harmful to children because it leads them to accept sexual discrimination against women:

Recent comics' depictions are certainly violent, and violence is used always against women. As people are exposed to such expressions of sexual discrimination since their childhood, they come to feel that such discrimination is common sense, and they become implanted with the notion of discrimination against women, like "that's the way women are." ... But, it does not mean that adults can be allowed to indulge in such discriminatory expression. So, I think that only saying that (pornocomics are) harmful to children is nonsense. (Hasegawa's comment in Sakamoto et al. 1991, 204)

Still, the feminists' master frame is "women's rights." They argue that pornography's sexual discrimination and objectification violates women's rights. Pornography reflects the reality of men's dominance of women. For feminists, pornography's main problem is its expression itself, rather than its harmful effects on children or men.

Thus, many ideas that originated with Western feminists found their way into Japanese antipornography claims, including the charges that pornography objectifies women and constitutes a form of sexual discrimination. Especially after the Meese Commission issued its report in 1986, Japanese feminists became increasingly familiar with American antipornography movements and their frames.

However, the Japanese did not adopt the entire U.S. feminist antipornography frame. For example, they did not advocate the sort of antipornography ordinances American radical feminists, such as MacKinnon and Dworkin, tried to enact. Rather, they were critical of antipornography ordinances. For example, the Active Women's Club opposed legal restrictions on pornography (Kimura 1987). Instead, Japanese feminists adopted a nonlegal strategy, promoting publishers' self-regulation without state censorship, much as liberal American feminists opposed the antipornography ordinances as threats to free speech.

Thus, Japanese feminists did not join conservatives in demanding stricter national laws to limit juveniles' access to pornocomics. Feminists and conservatives had different victims to protect: the conservatives' harm frame focused on children, while the feminists' sexual discrimination frame focused mainly on women. Therefore, it was the conservatives who were the major advocates for enforcing the Sound Upbringing Ordinance to prohibit selling pornocomics to those under age 18. But revising this law could not address feminists' concerns, because restricting youth's access to pornography tolerated the continued existence of pornography. Feminists preferred to encourage publishers to stop producing pornography, even as they allied themselves with publishers in opposing censorship. (For example, feminists, publishers, and other anticensorship groups established the "Organization to Consider the 'Harmful' Comics Problem," which held a symposium on September 28, 1991.)

SELECTION AND DIFFUSION OF FRAMES

In the diffusion of social problems frames to other societies, not all claims are necessarily accepted. Claimsmakers in the receiving society sift through claims and select some for their own use. When the sexual discrimination frame spread to Japan in the 1980s, Japanese feminists were influenced by the antipornography arguments of American radical feminists, yet the Japanese did not adopt all of their arguments, such as the model ordinances proposed in Minneapolis and Indianapolis. They adopted American feminists' frames to criticize Japanese pornographic culture, but no Japanese feminist seems to have advocated state censorship of pornography. Obviously, there was a process of selection, filtering the diffusion of American frames into Japan.

Fine (1979) offers a model of cultural innovation that may be applicable to the diffusion of frames. He identifies five analytical filters through which potential cultural items must pass in order to enter a group's own culture: cultural items must be Known, Usable, Functional, Appropriate, and Triggered by some experienced event. The relative numbers of potential items that meet each criterion can be expressed by a Venn diagram: K>U>F>A>T. That is, Known culture filters out the fewest potential elements, while relatively few pass through the Triggering events filter. Fine's model offers a framework for interpreting the diffusion of feminist claims from the United States to Japan.

Known: Claims and frames must be known in a society before a social problem can be constructed. Frames and claims diffuse through media, academia, popular culture (e.g., films and novels), personal communication (e.g., travel and the Internet) and so on, undergoing selection in social-problems construction. The media and academia seem especially influential. The media can spread social problems claims nationwide, although the content of the communicated information tends to be superficial. Academia can convey more detailed knowledge and may lead to claims about additional problems. For example, the "objectification of sex" had been used in earlier claims about prostitution since the 1970s, and MacKinnon and Dworkin's critiques of pornography were frequently introduced in journals in the late 1980s by Japanese feminists (Kamiya 1987, Kimura 1987, Funabashi 1990, Suzuki 1990, Yamasaki 1989, 1990). That is, feminists' arguments against pornography were already known—at least among Japanese feminists. Feminists were ready to criticize pornocomics in advance.

Usable: The second precondition is that claims and frames must be usable by claimsmakers. This criterion depends on social meanings shaped by the claimsmakers' "personalities, religion, political ideology, or morality." (Fine 1979:739). Japanese feminists seem to have reached a basic agreement that sexual discrimination against women in society should be solved by enlightening men, not through legal prohibitions. Although they were familiar with the sexual discrimination frame as used by U.S. antipornography feminists such as MacKinnon and Dworkin, they did not find the radical feminists' political tactics usable. Rather, Japanese feminists favored American liberals' anticensorship arguments. For Japanese feminists, pornography was not the principal cause of sexual discrimination against women (although they saw it as contributing to women's subservience to men); therefore, they thought that legal prohibitions against pornography, even if they made pornography disappear, could not eliminate sexual discrimination in a patriarchal society.

On the other hand, in the twentieth century, the Japanese harm frame has often been influenced by parallel American claims about pornography's harms. However, to the degree that those American claims were based on religious assumptions about sin and the like, they were not usable—they could not be diffused to Japan, where there are few Christians.

Functional: A third criterion is that claims and frames must be perceived as congruent with the claimsmakers' goals and needs, and they are defined as promoting their influence. American arguments against pornography match Japanese feminists' goals (i.e., elimination of sexual inequality), and the sexual discrimination frame promoted their influence in the debate over pornography. Pro-pornocomics claimsmakers did not offer effective arguments against the sexual discrimination frame, so the sexual discrimination frame has remained influential during the problem's construction.

Claimsmakers also merge claims into frames that support their demands. The harm frame's advocates merged the sexual discrimination frame into their harm frame. Although the harm frame had a long history in Japanese discussions of pornography, the feminist frame was relatively new to Japan. In the early claimsmaking about pornocomics, the two frames were independent; when the Mothers' Association of Tanabe city started their campaign, the separation between the two frames was clear: feminists criticized conservatives. Nonetheless, the two frames eventually merged. For example, a typical petition calling for enforcement of Tokyo's juvenile ordinance argued that pornocomics would implant a troubling sexual ideology in youths' minds because pornocomics treated females as sexual objects. Thus, Japanese conservatives incorporated the feminists' frame into their own claims. One representative of the Club to Protect Children from Comic Books warned: "Extreme sexual depictions (in pornocomics) teach children even things needless to know, and depict women as sexual tools. Freedom of expression is important, but how about wholesome education of children and youth?" (*Asahi Shimbun* 1990b). Another argued:

> Pornocomics objectify the female sex and are aimed chiefly at amusing the reader. . . . It is a problem that such pornocomics are a bad influence in building children's character. . . . There is the possibility that pornocomics' depictions of violence used against women, or women depicted as objects to amuse men, may excite children's abnormal curiosity. . . . (Jiro Ishikawa in *Mainichi Shimbun* 1992)

Merging frames sometimes helps make the original frames more functional. Thus, a harm frame that incorporates medical language can easily merge with other frames sharing the same objective, e.g., criticizing pornocomics. Yet, merging frames can have ironic consequences. The sexual discrimination frame calls for greater equality between men and women, yet the harm frame seeks to increase inequality between adults and juveniles (by giving them unequal access to information). Thus, there is a tension between the two frames that might make them less compatible.

Appropriate: Claims have greater potential the more they support power structures in society. Claims hostile to the dominant institutions do not diffuse or become influential frames without changes in the larger social structure. American radical feminists' frame against pornography diffused to Japanese feminists. However, while the Americans focused narrowly on addressing pornography's harm through ordinances, Japanese feminists decried a broad range of sexual objectification and discrimination, including sexual imagery on billboards and television advertisements, and prostitution and other sex-related businesses, in addition to pornocomics. That is, Japanese feminists sought the eventual elimination of sexual discrimination in Japanese society, and thus larger, more profound changes in the politically and economically male-dominated society. In contrast, the harm frame focuses on the protection of the juvenile, and does not conflict with existing authority.

In addition, claims tend to diffuse and flourish when promoted by high status members of society, such as politicians, police, or other official personnel. Therefore, low-status claimsmakers always try to involve higher-status allies. When a few mothers took action against pornocomics in Tanabe city, they first went to the mayor's office and the police. The feminists' frame was not perceived as appropriate, while major claimsmakers adopting the harm frame were able to coordinate their campaigns with the police, at least in some prefectures (Saito 1992; Yajima and Yamamoto 1994).

Triggering events: An incident or series of incidents that attract the public's and claimsmakers' attention sparks diffusion of claims and frames. However, the meaning assigned these events depends on interpretations by claimsmakers who may be looking for incidents that can illustrate their claims. Thus, the serial murders of young girls in 1988–89 triggered the rise of the horror films problem. But, those serial murders became a triggering event, not because of some quality of the murders themselves, but because numerous videotapes were discovered in the killer's room, and police interpreted those films as motivating the murders, thereby easily reminding claimsmakers of available rhetorical frames, such as claims that some popular culture (e.g., films, comics, books) can lead to sexual crimes. This was followed by additional incidents clustered together during the next year—a Supreme Court decision that seemed to encourage the police to use the juvenile ordinances, the report on "The Study on the Objectification of Sex" by the Tokyo Bureau of Life and Culture that first used the sexual discrimination frame to criticize pornocomics, and two letters appearing in local newspapers that began the antipornocomics campaign. These events led people to recognize the social problem, and led the claimsmakers to make claims.

Police announcements identified typifying examples to support the harm frame, that triggered or facilitated the problem. That is, a leading newspaper, *Yomiuri Shimbun,* ran stories: "Sexual Crime: Boy Motivated by a 'Pornocomic' Book. Mother's Association in Osaka Petitions for Designation of Harmful Publications" (1991a), and "Western Tama, Tokyo: High School Student: Stimulated by 'Harmful Manga'—Thirty Cases of Molestation of Girls" (1991b), and so on.

CONCLUSION

The diffusion of claims and frames is not instantaneous or automatic; it involves a filtering process. Social problems may not spread immediately to new countries. However, even when they are not applied, frames and claims can gain acceptance in other societies, and become part of their stock of rhetorical resources. Later, triggering events can lead claimsmakers to mobilize these stocks.

These filters reflect the receiving society's culture and social structure. This means that the process of diffusion will take different forms in different societies. This is one reason diffusion is more likely to occur between societies with similar social and cultural structures. Diffusion from the United States to Japan does not occur as often as diffusion from the United States to European countries, especially Great Britain, due to differences of religion, ethnic structure, class structure, political system, education system, and so on. However, in spite of these differences, there are still similarities between the United States and Japan. Both societies share capitalism, free speech, a pornography industry, male dominant culture, juvenile delinquency, and so on. Also, since diffusion can involve a time lag, social problems that do not diffuse at once may diffuse later, particularly if the receiving society comes to have social and cultural structures more similar to the giving society. For example, as long as gun shootings occur only in the United States, guns may hardly draw the public attention as an issue in Japan. However, should these events occur repeatedly in Japan, the public's attention might well focus on guns, and American claims could be adopted in constructing the gun problem in Japan. Gun problems have not diffused so far in Japan, but rhetoric, claims, and frames are stored as cultural resources, vocabularies that could be mobilized and used to talk about the issue.

ACKNOWLEDGMENT

The author greatly appreciates Dr. Mark Schneider's numerous valuable comments and suggestions in the preparation of this paper.

REFERENCES

Active Women's Club, ed. 1990. *Porno Watching: Women's Sex in the Media*. Tokyo: Gakuyo-shobo.
Akagawa, Manabu. 1995. "Rhetorical Analysis of Discourse on Prostitution." Pp. 153–201 in *Feminism's Contention 2: The Objectification of Sex*, edited by Yumiko Ehara. Tokyo: Keiso Shobo.
———. 1996. *Freedom for Sexuality/Freedom from Sexuality: Historical Sociology of Pornography*. Tokyo: Seikyusha.
Asahi Shimbun. 1989. "The Book's Control: the Present Condition: Institution Exists in Most Prefectures." August 27.
———. 1990a. "Too Many Poor Manga" [editorial]. September 4.
———. 1990b. "Are Sexual Depictions in Manga Harmful?" December 20.
Berger, Ronald J., Patricia Searles, and Charles E. Cottle. 1990. "Ideological Contours of the Contemporary Pornography Debate: Divisions and Alliances." *Frontiers* 11:30–38.
Downs, Donald A. 1989. *The New Politics of Pornography*. Chicago: University of Chicago Press.
Fine, Gary Alan. 1979. "Small Groups and Culture Creation." *American Sociological Review* 44:733–45.
Funabashi, Kuniko. 1990. "Porno-Culture and Sexual Violence." *Gendai Shiso (Contemporary Thought)* 18 (January):148–56.
Gilbert, James. 1986. *A Cycle of Outrage*. New York: Oxford University Press.
Hashizume, Daizaburo. 1995. *Theory of Love and Sex (Seiai-ron)*. Tokyo: Iwanami Shoten.
Kamiya, Masako. 1987. "American Feminism and the Trend in Pornography's Control." *Liberty and Justice* 38 (12):44–53.
Kimura, Rieko. 1987. "Questioning Porno-Culture: Women's Movement Against Sexual Violence," *Liberty and Justice* 38 (12):36–43.
Lederer, Laura, ed. 1980. *Take Back the Night: Women on Pornography*. New York: Morrow.
Mainichi Shimbun. 1992. "What Is Freedom of 'Sexual Expression' in Manga?" March 29.
Mori, Naoko. 1998. "Rhetoric of Mothers Constructing Sexuality: Focusing on Anti-Prostitution Movements and Social Purity Movements in Modern Japan." *Komaba Studies in Society* 8:34–48.

Nagaoka, Yoshiyuki. 1993. "The Amended Juvenile Ordinances: What and How It Changed." Pp. 156–169 in *Battle Royal over Control of Comics (Shigaisen)*, edited by the Organization to Protect the Freedom of Comics' Expression. Tokyo: Tsukuru Shuppan.

Nunamake, Anne, and Maurine H. Beaseley. 1990. "Women, the First Amendment, and Pornography: A Historical Perspective." *Studies In Communications* 4:101–18.

Saito, Yoshifusa. 1992. "The Present Condition and Background of the Juvenile Ordinances' Revision." *Law and Democracy* 268:3–7.

Sakamoto, Nanae, Yoshiko Hasegawa, and Koji Hayashi. 1991. "A Round-Table Talk: The Expression of Sexual Discrimination That Should Be Questioned." *Tsukuru Monthly* 1991:202–7.

Screech, Timon. 1999. *Sex and the Floating World: Erotic Images in Japan, 1700–1820*. Honolulu: University of Hawaii Press.

Sugihara, Nahoko. 1992 "The Issue of 'Modernity' in Japanese Feminism." Pp. 233–61 in *Feminism's Contention*, edited by Yumiko Ehara. Tokyo: Keiso Shobo.

Suzuki, Shou. 1990. "What is the Problem of Pornography." *Gendai Shiso (Contemporary Thought)* 18 (January):70–75.

Tokyo Bureau of Life and Culture. 1990. *Study on the Objectification of Sex*.

Tsukuru Monthly, ed. 1991. *Discussing the "Harmful" Comics Problem*. Tokyo: Tsukuru-Shuppan.

Yajima, Masami, and Isao Yamamoto. 1994. "The Development of the Movement to Regulate Harmful (Yugai) Comics." *Japanese Journal of Sociological Criminology* 19:74–94.

Yamasaki, Kaoru. 1989. "Porno-Illusion." *Gendai Shiso (Contemporary Thought)* 18 (September):110–17.

———. 1990. "On the Problem of Porno." *Gendai Shiso (Contemporary Thought)* 18 (January): 54–58.

Yomiuri Shimbun. 1991a. "Sexual Crime: Boy Motivated by a 'Pornocomic' Book." June 19.

———. 1991b. "Western Tama, Tokyo: High School Student: Stimulated by 'Harmful Manga'—Thirty Cases of Molestation of Girls." June 28.

———. 1991c. "Pornocomics: Local Governments Shift from Self-control to Prohibition of Sale." December 2.

8

How Europe Discovered
Its Sex-Offender Crisis

PHILIP JENKINS

In response to the perceived danger from sex offenders, many jurisdictions have implemented registration systems, so that police and the community at large will be aware of the presence of a convicted individual in their community, and can take appropriate defensive measures. One problem with such laws is that lax criteria for registration can lead to the inclusion of many petty offenses, so that those listed might be minor, fairly harmless deviants. In one case in early 1999, an eleven-year-old boy was added to such a register for sexual contacts with a two-year-old girl cousin, acts that many societies might interpret as sex play rather than assault, and that in most instances would be unlikely to find their way into the criminal justice system (Roberts 1999). Nevertheless, the boy's inclusion on the register is likely to have lifelong consequences for him and his family, and perhaps blight a life unnecessarily and unjustly. At the least, for many years he will have to inform police agencies of changes of address, and ac cording to their discretion, they might pass this information on to schools or agencies dealing with children or women.

Such a case, with all its dilemmas, sounds very familiar in the modern United States, where the need to identify and control sex offenders has come to be seen as politically essential, even when the proposed policies threaten the civil liberties of the offender, to say nothing of destroying any hope of rehabilitation. Nevertheless, the case in question occurred not in the United States but in Great Britain, in the city of Newcastle-on-Tyne. Like America, Britain also has had intense debate over draconian policies such as community notification (in which neighbors are notified of the presence of a paroled sex offender) or "predator" laws (that allow offenders to be detained for long preventive terms after their formal sentences have expired). The whole legal apparatus that the United States acquired in the early and mid-1990s is now quite familiar to authorities in Britain, as well as other European countries. To quote a recent British commentator: "We are going to have a national Sex Offender Register and if your name is on it you must tell the police every time you change address. We are going for more DNA samples, longer sentences and extended supervision on release" (Thomas 1999).

These legal changes reflect a deeper underlying reality, namely that in Europe, as in the United States, conceptions of sex offenses have been radically transformed in the last ten or twenty years. Whereas in the 1970s, it was common to depict violators of sex laws as pathetic inadequates in need of treatment rather than punishment, and indeed to place some of the blame for their offenses on seductive victims, today's orthodoxy suggests a far grimmer portrait. The vague term "sex offender" can cover a very wide range of behaviors, predatory and consensual, physically dangerous or mildly disturbing, while victims can vary from vulnerable toddlers to experienced adults; the acts in question might be as diverse as child molestation, statutory rape, exhibitionism, voyeurism, incest, and bestiality. In today's lexicon, however, the term "sex offender" has become indistinguishable from other highly damaging concepts such as molester, pedophile, and predator, that collectively indicate the extremely persistent nature of the crimes, a lack of response to any treatment or deterrence, and above all, extreme dangerousness.[1] According to this stereotype, if the offender has not yet killed an innocent victim (usually a child), then it is only a matter of time before such an act occurs, and perhaps there will be many victims. Sex offenders are thus "serial" predatory offenders, with a strong connotation that the behaviors are somehow linked to the better-known concept of "serial murder." In the face of such a threatening image, it is scarcely surprising that both American and European jurisdictions felt a critical need to introduce draconian policies, or that the public has accepted them with scarcely a murmur of protest: indeed, most popular protests have denounced the laws' excessive leniency. Moreover, this sense of urgency has been quite marked in countries that had been among the most traditionally liberal on sexual matters.

Yet although public attitudes have changed violently, there is little evidence of the actual rate of sex crimes growing significantly in any European country over the last ten or twenty years. In Germany, for example, where both official agencies and experts on sexual delinquency systematically tend to overestimate the actual prevalence of both rape and child abuse, the number of recorded crimes of both sorts fell steadily during the 1980s (Pfafflin 1999). Although arrests and convictions have boomed across much of Europe, this is overwhelmingly an outcome of new and harsher policies by courts and police agencies, and does not necessarily reflect any change in offender behavior. Nor is there any suggestion of a change in the proportion of sexual crime committed by anonymous stranger "pedophiles" or "sex fiends," as opposed to family members and neighbors. The danger of incest, which was so powerful an element in earlier feminist rhetoric, has been largely subsumed in the contemporary campaign against faceless "fiends" (Jenkins 1998).

Also, although the new public fears were partly a response to particularly violent or horrific sexual crimes, these incidents have not suddenly become more common, and it should be emphasized how very rare they remain. Nor are they new: the horrific Moors Murders occurred in Great Britain in the mid-1960s, and even these notorious events failed to ignite a sex-crime panic anything like that of the modern era. The real change in recent years is in the nature of reporting, and the interpretations that the media impose upon crimes. In particular, this has meant reading perverse sexual motives into crimes, so that a child killer is now viewed not just as a monster but as a "murderous pedophile." Even if such individuals do exist, it was by no means inevitable that they should have served as the sole focus for concern over the maltreatment of children, sexual or otherwise. The new severity is not a simple or objective response to a sudden crime wave, but should rather be seen as a classic moral panic of the sort often described by sociologists, and its roots must be sought in underlying social conditions.

Americans, too, experienced a panic over sex crimes in the mid-1990s, the era of Megan's Law and the Polly Klaas murder, of sexual predator laws, and the media furor over serial molesters and sex killers. The strong resemblance between American and European circumstances requires explanation. To some extent, similar conditions prevailed on both sides of the Atlantic, in that both America and Europe have shared parallel demographic developments and a similar expansion in the social role and status of women. Both factors might well have led to a dramatic rise of concern about vulnerable women and children, and thus a need to respond to threats from sex criminals. In both societies, too, politics were profoundly affected by the moral revolutions of the 1960s and 1970s and the subsequent conservative reaction. Even so, it is remarkable that both Americans and Europeans formulated the policies they did in precisely the same years, and that these developments were so very closely alike. It is natural to look for direct influences, and these can readily be found, mainly in the form of the impact of American criminological thought and law enforcement practice on Europe, and indeed on the entire world. Still, other factors must be sought to explain the relative homogeneity of European attitudes to sex offenders, in the form of the growing cultural and political unity of the European continent. These were exactly the years when Europe was moving toward something like American federalism, especially in areas like law enforcement and the workings of the mass media, and it is not surprising that images of American-style social menaces should have been constructed and disseminated in such a characteristically American way.

TOLERANCE AND REACTION

The tectonic nature of the change of attitudes toward sex offenders since the 1960s can be appreciated if we examine the attitude to sex between adults and children, generally the most sensitive area of sexual deviance in a modern society. During the 1970s, most West European societies undertook significant liberalization of their laws concerning such matters as the age of consent and homosexuality. Gay-rights movements of varying strength appeared in most nations, and at least some activists suggested that the barriers against adult-child sex would be the next to crumble: formal pedophile-rights groups appeared in Britain and the Netherlands. Meanwhile, the most liberal countries, such as the Netherlands and Denmark, were major centers for the production and distribution of child pornography broadly defined, meaning both nude images of children, and photographs of sex between adults and children, in some cases involving small toddlers (Jenkins 1992). These materials were widely available in many West European countries through the 1970s, and even after laws were generally tightened in the 1980s, European states usually had far laxer definitions of illegal pornography than did Americans. In Sweden, for instance, nude images of underage children remained permissible, although depictions of actual sex were prohibited.

While the scope of permissible sexual behavior was expanding, attitudes toward deviants were becoming more relaxed. More lenient attitudes toward sexual offenders were reflected in the popular media; this helped promote a shift away from stringent punitive sanctions. Through the 1960s, for instance, British films repeatedly depicted child molesters in a fairly benevolent light, in keeping with the generally liberal attitudes of the studios on matters like homosexuality and race. The film *Never Take Sweets From a Stranger* (1960) was an account of an elderly child molester, who unintentionally causes the death of a child he is pursuing, and *Serious Charge* (1959) concerned a false charge of sexual misconduct between a man and a teenaged boy. The Oscar-nominated film *The Mark* (1961) sympathetically portrayed a man trying to reconstruct his life after serving prison time for sexual misconduct with a young girl. The molester was again a scapegoat in the British film *Chariots of Fire* (1970), scripted by Tony Parker, who had published serious criminological studies of offenders (Parker 1969). This film examined a woman's tragic relationship with a man who had spent twenty years in prison for offenses against boys. The script argued that children in these cases suffered far more from the misplaced outrage of puritanical parents and authorities than they ever could from the sexual contact itself, while molesters were manipulated emotionally by the child objects of their affections. The main villain of the piece was the sensationalistic press, that goaded an ill-informed and malicious public. In each of these films, the notion that the molester might be a pernicious predator would have seemed quite ludicrous.

The sexual liberalism that was so marked and apparently limitless in the early 1970s suffered major setbacks by the end of that decade, for reasons that I have discussed at greater length in a study entitled *Intimate Enemies* (Jenkins 1992). (Although this book directly concerns the British experience, many of its themes apply to the other nations of Western Europe.) One major factor in the new demand for restricting tolerance was the rise of political feminism, which condemned male sexual violence against women and demanded stronger laws to suppress rape, child sexual abuse, and pornography. These attitudes became institutionalized through social-work agencies and academic departments, in which feminist and radical ideas became highly influential. Far from being seen as the cutting edge of personal liberty, the new tolerance for explicit sexual materials and child pornography was increasingly regarded as a manifestation of patriarchy and the exploitation of women.

Sexual tolerance also came under attack from the political Right, which rose to power in the age of such leaders as Britain's Margaret Thatcher, who served as Prime Minister from 1979 to 1990. Conservative ideology denounced sexual immorality and urged a return to traditional standards of behavior. Although the tolerance of homosexuality was too widely entrenched to be reversed, the major political battlefield now shifted to sex between adult men and boys, and homosexuals were regularly stigmatized as if they were pedophiles and child molesters. This conflict became all the sharper when gay-rights activists attempted to lower the age of sexual consent for males from twenty-one to sixteen, an issue that continues to be hotly debated in Parliament. The far-reaching claims emanating from both Left and Right received unprecedented coverage from a mass media that had adopted new sensational   even tabloid—standards regarding the appropriate subject matter for press reporting and the tone of coverage. Through the 1980s, virulent, irresponsible campaigns against sexual deviance and child exploitation were a frequent staple of the British media.

The new harsher attitude toward sexual deviancy became apparent during the 1977 campaign against pedophilia and child pornography (for comparable trends in the then Federal Republic of Germany, see Pfafflin 1999). In consequence, British police became more likely to arrest and press serious charges, and courts were more likely to convict: "Between 1979 and 1989, the proportion of convicted sexual offenders receiving immediate custodial sentences rose from 20 percent to 33 percent. This created a rise in the numbers of sexual offenders within the system—from 4.7 percent of the total male prison population in 1980 to 7.5 percent in 1989" (Fisher and Beech 1999; for British trends, compare Lea et al. 1999). These trends set the stage for a series of waves of panic over the next decade, each of which significantly raised the stakes in the moral debate. In the mid-1980s, successive scandals appeared to indicate a very high prevalence of child sexual abuse, far greater than had been traditionally assumed, while controversial criminal investigations pointed to the existence of extensive "child sex rings," conspiratorial criminal operations that might involve highly placed and politically powerful members of the community. The British National Society for the Prevention of Cruelty to Children has recently claimed that several hundred such "rings" operate in the United Kingdom (Smith 1998; Bibby 1996. For the Australian debate in these same years as to whether pedophilia constituted a kind of organized crime, see *Organized Criminal Paedophile Activity* 1995).

By the end of the 1980s, these diverse charges culminated in two major sets of claims that were widely publicized in numerous television programs, press exposés, and true-crime books. The more sensational was that clandestine sex rings were in fact satanic cults that inflicted ritual child abuse upon their victims, and perhaps even killed them in human sacrifices. Between 1989 and 1991, Britain experienced a satanic-ritual-abuse scare quite as intense as the one in the United States (the Netherlands also experienced such a panic in the late 1980s). As in the United States, the charges eventually collapsed, leaving a general social consensus that the whole notion had been utterly spurious (LaFontaine 1998; Jenkins 1992). Quite different, though, was the outcome of the other explosive allegation against sexual offenders, namely that secret bands of molesters were actually killing their victims, and were indeed responsible for a significant number of child murders. In this instance, although the allegations were wildly inflated, there was a core of objective truth, in that there were indeed a small number of repeat sex-killers who were also pedophiles, and in at least one notorious case, a series of murders was connected to a group, or "sex-ring" (Oliver and Smith 1993).

CHILD KILLERS

A new sensitivity to the danger of serial child-killers grew directly from the American concern with the newly defined problem of "serial murder," as defined by the U.S. federal government during 1983–84. One aspect of this was the concept of linkage blindness, the belief that multiple killers might be evading capture because police failed to recognize the similarities and connections between crimes committed in different jurisdictions.

Police agencies sought to overcome this weakness by compiling lists of unsolved cases in the hope that linkages would be drawn, and in 1986, British police took the unprecedented step of circulating details of fifteen child murders that had occurred over the previous decade. The investigation received the evocative title "Operation Stranger," presumably implying that one unknown "stranger" might be responsible for all the crimes (see Canter 1994 for the influence of American thought about serial crime).

Lengthy investigations would show that serial murder activity was indeed involved in these cases, though not solely by one offender. Three of the little girls on the Operation Stranger list were victims of Robert Black, who was arrested for a related crime in 1990, and who proved to be a violent pedophile with a strong predilection for child pornography (Wyre and Tate 1995). Some of the other victims appeared to have been killed by at least one member of a pedophile ring operating chiefly in London and southeast England: this was, incidentally, a group of very low social status, far removed from the elite pedophiles of popular mythology (Oliver and Smith 1993). During the early 1990s, attempts to elucidate the exact limits of their misdeeds led to an extensive police investigation known as "Operation Orchid," during which the media speculated that perhaps a dozen or more child victims might have been killed and buried in secret cemeteries scattered around the country. Some sources even spoke of dozens of such graveyards, and speculated that many deaths might have been recorded in "snuff" videos, though no such items ever came to light. These widely reported stories reached their height during 1990 and 1991, but remained in the news through the mid-decade thanks to retrospective news documentaries and true-crime books.

Though the group itself had existed, it should be noted that the "pedophile ring" case on which so many of the new stereotypes were based was considerably more complicated than it originally appeared, or than it is sometimes described in subsequent narratives. For all the extravagant charges about dozens of victims, members of the group were clearly connected with perhaps three fatalities, and the high media estimates for casualties may have been police disinformation intended to place pressure on ring members. The major incident that led to criminal charges by no means fitted the stereotype of an abduction murder. When Jason Swift died in 1985, he was a fourteen-year-old hustler, a "rent-boy," who perished either by suffocation or strangulation, but it was not clear if his death was intentional, or an accidental consequence of sadomasochistic sexual activity, aggravated by drug use. His body was then secretly buried. Four men were thus convicted not of murder, but of manslaughter (failing to obtain medical help) and perverting the course of justice (by concealing the body). Though the circumstances of the affair were horrible enough, these details should be borne in mind when we read misleading later accounts of the crime as "the sexual torture and murder of a 14-year-old boy" (Lyall 1998).

Multiple murder cases continued to dominate the British headlines. In 1994, the arrest of Frederick West drew attention to one of Britain's most prolific killers, who had operated for perhaps twenty years. His crimes included rape, abuse, and murder, in some cases inflicted upon members of his own family, making him clearly a "molester" or "abuser," in addition to a sex killer (Masters 1996; Burn 1998). "Pedophile" charges surfaced once more in early 1996, when Thomas Hamilton killed sixteen small children at a school in Dunblane, Scotland, an event that proved deeply traumatic for British society, with an impact comparable to that of the American shootings in Littleton, Colorado, some years afterward. Though sex charges rarely feature in such mass-murder incidents, media reports about Dunblane prominently claimed that Hamilton was "rumored to be a pedophile," and that in his last letter he denied that he was a "pervert." However tenuous the grounds, the term "pedophile" was once more contextualized among images of savage violence and murdered children. This was additional evidence, it seemed, that pedophiles killed.

The combination of these authenticated murders with the more speculative horrors of the ritual child-abuse cases contributed to a massive public reaction against sex offenders, especially those who victimized children, and these reports promoted the image of the serial pedophile as a potential killer. These deeply unsavory events also reinforced the condemnation of child pornography, which was associated with the interests of the pedophiles who were believed to abduct and kill children: there was little tolerance for the view that such materials only served to gratify sexual fantasies, without directly stimulating criminal behavior. As the British *Observer* claimed in 1996, firms distributing child pornography on the Internet were in reality "The Pedlars of Child Abuse" (Connett and Henley 1996). The image of the molester or abuser was now transformed, as the press suggested that investigations like Operation Orchid "have only just begun to illuminate the murky and savage world of pedophilia" (Boseley 1991). The terminology deserves emphasis, as a pedophile is in technical parlance an adult sexually attracted to a prepubescent child, without any implication that he or she has actually carried out any sexual acts, and certainly not of a forcible or violent nature. By the early 1990s, however, the simple term pedophile implied a persistent repeat sex criminal, a "serial offender," and terms like "a convicted pedophile" appear regularly in the news media.

TOWARD CRISIS

In 1996 and 1997, atrocity stories proliferated internationally, so that horrors like those to which the British had become so accustomed acquired a European dimension. By far the most notorious case was that of Marc

Dutroux of Charleroi, Belgium, who kidnapped a series of young girls, who were sexually abused, murdered, and secretly buried. Some of the victims were held for weeks or months in a cell built into the basement of his house, and the sexual crimes were videotaped. He may also have been selling children internationally as sexual slaves. Dutroux had a number of accomplices, making this a "pedophile ring" reminiscent of the recent British charges. The media also referred to him constantly as a "pedophile," although many of his victims were teenagers (Ryback 1997; Simons 1996).

The Dutroux case first came to light in the summer of 1996, and smoldered through the next two years. It served as a focus for political and ethnic tensions within Belgium that had already become acute following a series of bloody terrorist attacks during the mid-1980s, and a mysterious political assassination in 1991 (*New York Times* 1996; Jenkins 1991). These affairs had given rise to widespread popular suspicions about the inefficiency, or worse, of the nation's law-enforcement and political establishments. The police were denounced for their inefficiency in pursuing leads, including one incident when Dutroux's own mother reported her suspicions that her son was involved in the continuing abductions: He was a natural suspect, having been released after serving only part of a sentence for raping several teenaged girls. Moreover, families of victims had repeatedly urged police to seek evidence of a "pedophile ring," an idea that the authorities rejected in favor of the theory of a "lone psycho." The affair became almost ludicrous when Dutroux, surely one of the most dangerous criminals in Europe, managed to escape briefly in 1998, again raising damning questions about the efficiency of Belgian law enforcement. There were controversial suggestions that the affair might have even wider ramifications in the form of an elite pedophile ring involving highly placed politicians, for whom Dutroux was acting as procurer. If this were the case, then the weakness of the police investigation acquired very sinister overtones. As one Belgian child advocate remarked, "It's clear that internationally—and that includes Belgium—for sex trafficking in children to work, offenders have to have protection. There must be political and financial support. It wouldn't be surprising to discover that important people in Belgium and in Europe are implicated in the system" (Marie-France Botte, quoted in Walsh 1996). The plausibility of these charges is less significant than the fact that they were aired very publicly across the continent and in prominent media outlets. The following year, a parliamentary inquiry reported that "The commission can only conclude that there are indications of possible protection" of suspects, including Dutroux (*Sacramento Bee* 1997). Not only did pedophiles kill, it appeared, but they might be protected by powerful friends.

The coverage of the Dutroux case provided a matrix in which stories about other sex offenders could be understood, contributing to the perception of a generalized threat from serial predators, a "Dutroux phenomenon," so to speak. In 1997, France experienced a potent movement against sexual crime when it was discovered that four young women had been raped and murdered at Boulogne-sur-Mer. The killers, two brothers named Jourdain, both had records for serious crime, one for killing a young woman, the other for the rape of a minor, and both had been released quite shortly before the most recent wave of crimes (Simons 1997a). The case was regarded as not just extremely grave in its own right but as the manifestation of a deeper underlying problem of repeat violent sex offenders, and the French prime minister, Jacques Chirac, appeared on television to discuss emergency measures against predators. This was depicted as a national or international issue, perhaps even a social crisis.

Not only did sex murders seem alarmingly commonplace, but there were suggestions of linkages across borders, again indicating the thorough inadequacy of existing police responses to the crisis. The Dutroux case certainly involved an international ring, with participants in Germany and the Netherlands. Borrowing the notion of linkage blindness, police in various countries explored the idea that itinerant criminals might have left victims murdered in multiple countries: for instance, Robert Black had traveled widely across Europe in pursuit of child pornography, and there were speculations that other offenses might have occurred on these trips. As early as 1986, British police investigating a series of attacks of solitary old people in Stockwell, London, had explored a possible relationship to the contemporary and quite similar "Granny Murders" in Paris.

In addition to tales of actual violence, international cooperation between sex offenders seemed to be substantiated by the revolutionary changes occurring in the world of child pornography. At least since the early 1980s, pornographers had made use of the Internet to distribute illegal images, while information circulated through electronic bulletin boards, and these practices became massively more common following the growing use of the World Wide Web by about 1993. For these purposes, the Web had the advantage that it was all but unthinkable to impose universal legal standards on it, so that images that were quite legal in one country were utterly banned in another. Even in states where child pornography was technically banned, some police agencies turned a blind eye to enforcement. Japan, for example, continues to be a major source of commercial child porn sites that are quite legal in that country, and a fairly overt subculture glorifies the erotic appeal of the *kogal*, the high-school girl in her early or mid-teens. In addition, Japanese sites host the cosmopolitan bulletin boards that post the URL addresses for the latest child pornography images, addresses that might be based in any nation around the globe. Following the collapse of the Iron Curtain, aggressive new centers of production appeared in Russia, Poland, and the Czech Republic. Despite fierce legal restrictions in countries like Britain or the United States, access to very hard-core material was open to virtually anyone with access to the Internet and the most rudimentary technical knowledge. The availability of child pornography was burgeoning at exactly the time that popular hostility toward this material was reaching unprecedented heights.

Frustration at the inability to curb child exploitation led to major police offensives against those users and producers who could be caught, even in countries that had once been regarded as libertarian havens. In the spring of 1997, French police arrested several hundred individuals for purchasing or possessing child pornography, actions that led to a number of suicides. The event was a direct response to the recent publicity over the murders at Boulogne-sur-Mer, and suggests the power of the perceived linkage between child pornography and actual violence against children (Simons 1997b; Whitney 1997). In Germany at this same time, a senior official of the CompuServe corporation was charged criminally, not for any personal involvement in child pornography, but for failing to ensure that his company would suppress such traffic (Andrews 1997). Most remarkable perhaps was the Dutch investigation, initiated by a gangland murder, that led to the exposure of a widespread international pornography ring operating from the town of Zandvoort: the group used small children and toddlers as subjects (Traynor 1998a, b). That even the liberal Netherlands was undertaking a crackdown on pornographic materials suggested a remarkable departure from recent years. Across the continent, such investigations created further publicity about the scale of the supposed problem, that in turn fueled media pressure for further official action, launching what in effect became a self-sustaining cycle.

Especially between 1996 and 1998, there was abundant evidence of widespread support in many countries for new and stringent controls on sex offenders. In Belgium, for instance, the Dutroux case resulted in massive public protests and street demonstrations, as did the Jourdain case in France. In October 1996, a Belgian protest attracted 325,000 participants, a scale of activism not seen since the antinuclear protests of the early 1980s, when the issue at stake was the literal annihilation of Europe. There was a massive groundswell of support in these and other countries in favor of restoring the death penalty, a remarkable departure from recent trends: in most European states, capital punishment was hopelessly discredited by its association with the Nazis, and after 1945 the practice was widely abolished. However, cases like the Dutroux affair led to a major rethinking of such matters. Another consequence of the new focus on sex offenses was to encourage the identification of victims as a distinct community or interest group, as had occurred earlier in the United States and Great Britain. In 1997, one report claimed that a fifth of Belgians might have been the victims of some kind of abuse, and a delegation of victims complained of their sufferings to the king and the prime minister (Bates 1997). The existence of

such an interest group naturally gives a firmer foundation for future movements toward greater severity in treating sex offenders.

The most egregious evidence of public outrage came in Britain, following the release from custody of Robert Oliver and Sidney Cooke, members
of the "pedophile ring" involved in the death of Jason Swift (since they did
not face first-degree murder charges, their sentences for lesser offenses
were now expiring). If their crimes had been committed more recently,
then a 1991 law would have monitored them upon release and provided
supervised housing, but their crimes predated this measure, and so they
were in theory free to live where they chose. However, when the two were
released in 1997 and 1998, respectively, there was overwhelming public reaction whenever they appeared in a community where they hoped to settle, leading to violence and vigilante conduct that amounted to major
rioting (Gill 1998; Duncan 1998; *Independent* 1999b). Oliver "was hounded
from six neighborhoods as he tried to find a place to live. Apparently unable to live openly in any community, he was moved to a government
housing unit for the mentally ill in Buckinghamshire, where he has round-
the-clock protection" (Lyall 1998). Apart from the street opposition, critics
of the offenders' presence found public voice in victims' rights pressure
groups such as the White Ribbon Campaign for Justice, that forthrightly
challenged politicians and law-enforcement bureaucrats.

In addition, the popular media presented a constant diet of dema-
goguery: "The *Daily Star,* the *Sun,* the *People,* the *Mirror,* and the *Daily Mail*
all devoted at least a page each to the coverage of the released pedophile
Robert Oliver on the 26th of September 1997. The tabloids' headlines
sounded "Back on the streets, pedophile who killed schoolboy in an orgy
of terror" (*Daily Mail*) and "JASON FIEND FREED TO LIVE NEAR KID-
DIE PLAYGROUND" (*Daily Star*). The *Mirror's* front page screamed
"PURE EVIL AND FREE"; the *Sun* said, "MONSTER FREED TO PREY ON
YOUR CHILDREN"; and the *People* the following Sunday told its readers;
"FREED PEDOPHILE WILL KILL AGAIN, WARNS POLICE CHIEF."
(Bergmo 1998). Nor was this tone confined to the tabloid press: reporting
on the failure of some offenders to register, the once-sober *Times* (1997)
headlined simply "Perverts missing." There had been many precedents for
this outrage. In Manchester, a local paper named a child sex offender on its
front page. Shortly afterward, in Leicester, an elderly man suspected of sex
offenses against children was found dying from a crossbow bolt lodged in
his eye (Wavell 1996; compare Connolly 1998). In the words of the principal officer for the National Association for the Care and Resettlement of
Offenders: "There have been a spate of vigilante attacks on sex offenders
around the country. They've been physically attacked. Their houses have
been burned. Their parents have been attacked."

Public fears about predatory sex criminals were repeatedly bolstered by the sensational coverage devoted to each new horror story. The tone of media reporting is epitomized by the 1999 trial of Alan Hopkinson, who had abducted and imprisoned two young girls. The affair was aggravated by Hopkinson's criminal record, which included several similar offenses over the previous decade. He had served prison time, during which he had allegedly plotted the dual abduction. The newspapers provided alarming front-page reports, with even such quality papers as the *Daily Telegraph* and the *Independent* presenting headlines about "This most dangerous pedophile" (Buncombe and Watson-Smyth 1999) and "Fantasist with IQ of 159: Pedophile will never be free again to attack girls" (Fleet 1999; compare Finn 1999). The extensive stories prominently included police quotes claiming that Hopkinson: "is a highly motivated and dangerous pedophile, the most dangerous man I have come across. . . . I believe that, if the children had not been found, he would have been capable of killing" (Fleet 1999). Media reports often noted that the offender was a criminal "genius," a member of the high-IQ organization MENSA. The Hopkinson affair epitomized the new view of the pedophile as a highly organized predator, even a criminal genius.

POLICY RESPONSES

Against this background, governments had no alternative but to consider severe measures against sex crime, which they largely found by observing the recent American experience (for the recent British experience, see, for example, Sampson 1994; Howitt 1995; Walker 1996). Three American policies were particularly discussed, the registration of sex offenders, community notification, and some form of extended sentencing for sex criminals. Such measures naturally gained popularity during the fevered atmosphere of 1996, in the aftermath of the Dutroux horror stories (Bates 1996). A crime bill proposed in Britain in 1996 would have involved clauses making it an offense for "convicted pedophiles" to seek employment with children, again illustrating the total confusion between the psychiatric term "pedophile" and the criminological concept of the serial molester. The measure would also have extended DNA testing to allow samples to be taken from all convicted sex offenders in prison, and required convicted sex offenders to notify police of any change of address (Ford 1996). A national register of pedophiles would be compiled, which would be accessible to police, schools and social services, rather than being available to the general public, as in some U.S. jurisdictions.

Although this specific bill failed due to lack of parliamentary time, the concept of the registry was included in what became the Sex Offenders Act of 1997, under which anyone convicted of a sexual offense against children was required to register with the local police and inform them when moving. Police could then release the information to what they considered appropriate persons or institutions with a need to know (Chambers 1997). The measure was not retroactive, in that it did not apply to anyone convicted of such an offense before 1997: this aspect of the legislation became controversial during the Alan Hopkinson affair of 1999, as he was not subject to registration or reporting as his conviction had occurred several years before, and at any rate he had been convicted for offenses that were nonsexual in nature. This apparent loophole led to media pressure to make the new law apply to older cases, even though such a measure involved violating the familiar prohibition on ex post facto legislation.

The ad hoc basis of the public notification policy created much discretion for the abuse of information. In North Wales, for instance, police considered that local caravan (trailer) park owners had a need to know, on the grounds that the area was a major holiday center where many children would be present in the summer months: the owners responded by evicting a couple convicted of abusing their children, who now became homeless, and who were pursued by hostile local residents (Dyer 1997). General community notification of the sort pioneered in Washington state and since imitated in many U.S. jurisdictions continued to be opposed for fears of vigilantism, but Britain has moved far in the direction of a "Megan's Law," which was usually discussed under that very name.

More universally popular were measures to prolong the sentences of convicted sex offenders, and to extend their terms of supervision or parole. In the aftermath of the Boulogne-sur-Mer crimes, the government responded to "the demand for tougher sentences for repeat, violent sex offenders. A new bill mandating longer sentences for sex crimes was recently introduced" (Simons 1997a). Similar measures followed the exposure of the Dutroux case (compare Cowell 1996). In one popular American device, convicted offenders served their allotted prison terms and then subsequently had a special hearing to assess if they could be classified as "predators." If so, they would be detained indefinitely for the public good. Variants of this system were advocated in Britain by a number of penologists, including the country's best-known expert on sex offenders, Ray Wyre (Ahuja 1995; Wyre and Tate 1995). One modest form of the "predator" model arrived with little fanfare: life prisoners who were being considered for parole were tested with a Penile Plesythmograph or PPG, that measured their degree of sexual stimulation when shown pictures of naked children or sexual violence. If a positive reaction was found, then the inmates would remain in prison (Rose 1995). Although by no means as legally daring (or dubious) as the American concept, the British system did share the same idea about the necessity of detaining the potentially dangerous, with sex offenders being the primary targets. In the words of the

Prison Service psychologist in charge of the British scheme, Dr. David Thornton: "Ministers have placed great emphasis on protecting the public. . . . We should err in favor of the public, not the prisoner" (Rose 1995).

Over the following years, Britain drew closer to an explicit "sexual predator" model, a process made all the easier by the lack of a judiciary able or willing to challenge laws on constitutional or libertarian grounds (Cooper 1997; Sparrow 1997). In 1998, Home Secretary Jack Straw announced new legislation to permit judges to impose indefinite sentences on sex offenders deemed dangerous or likely to commit more crimes; he stated: "There is a great deal of concern about serious sex offenders who pose a threat to children. We are urgently examining ways to ensure such people are released only when they no longer impose a threat" (Lyall 1998). The following year, the release of another supposed "serial offender" made the issue still more acute, and increased demands that repeat or persistent offenders be incarcerated "until experts agree they are unlikely to attack again" (*Daily Mail* 1999).

A battery of other legal measures demonstrated the extent of concern about "predators." In 1995, Great Britain established a national DNA database in order to permit easier detection and apprehension of repeat offenders, and this was seen as a good model for the rest of Europe. It was emulated in Germany in 1998, following a number of sex killings in that country, and police agencies now proposed a Europe-wide DNA database (Schiermeier 1998). Indicating the sense of menace from sex offenders that was driving the scheme, British Home Office minister David MacLean wrote: "We are also attracted to the concept of a European DNA database for pedophiles. This could help in the detection of cross-border sex offenses committed against children. Such a database might be extended to include additional information, for example details of convictions, and therefore form the basis of a more general European pedophile register" (Dobson 1996). The assumption throughout this argument was, of course, that "pedophiles" were by definition persistent serial offenders, likely to wander between jurisdictions to elude capture. As we have seen, lost in the rhetoric was any sense that the primary sexual threat to children was likely to come not from such strangers, but from intimates and relatives. In 1999 and 2000, British authorities introduced a series of surveillance measures that were frankly advertised as a "Big Brother" system for tracking pedophiles (Waugh 1999; *Independent* 1999a; Burrell 2000).

Another ongoing area of concern was "sex tourism," in which men from wealthy countries traveled to poor Third World nations in order to have sexual contact with underage youngsters or children; Thailand, the Philippines, and Sri Lanka are traditional havens for Europeans, just as Americans visit Central American nations for these purposes. The matter was legally complex because in many cases, the men in question were not committing crimes against local laws, and it is difficult to prosecute individuals for crimes committed on foreign soil. During the crisis atmosphere of the mid-1990s, however, several nations took steps to suppress sex tourism by expanding the principle of extraterritoriality, the use of criminal law to cover acts committed outside the geographical boundaries of a particular jurisdiction. Norway, Sweden, and Finland were the first to use the idea for these purposes, and between 1993 and 1996, they were imitated by Germany, France, Australia, and Belgium. In 1996 Britain proposed a system to prosecute its citizens who engaged in this activity: the Sexual Offences (Conspiracy and Incitement) Act of 1996 allows courts to prosecute those who organize trips abroad for child abusers, and this idea was incorporated into the 1997 Sex Offenders Act. Given the immense difficulty of detecting or prosecuting these crimes, the measure was largely symbolic, but it again suggests the urgent political need to be seen to be striking at "pedophiles." The British proposal was announced at what was titled the "First World Congress Against the Commercial Sexual Exploitation of Children," meeting in Sweden ("Sex tourists to be sent packing" 1998; Kennedy 1996). The proliferation of such gatherings, no less than the intense legislative activity, could not fail to give the impression that sex offenders were an authentic international peril of immense scope and seriousness.

EUROPE AND AMERICA

When we observe the similarities between the twin "crises" over sex offenders in Europe and the United States, it is natural to suggest that this growing convergence results simply from the spread of American influence. Certainly, American influence has been as marked in recent decades in matters of law enforcement, criminology, and sociology as in any other area of culture, and such concepts as serial murder have been disseminated by American mass media no less than by academic writings and police experts. The ritual-abuse scare of the 1980s provides an excellent means of mapping these influences, to Britain and the Netherlands, and beyond, to Australia, New Zealand, and South Africa. European police institutions have been radically changed by these influences, ranging from SWAT teams to criminal profiling. The FBI Academy at Quantico, Virginia, still tends to be regarded as the Vatican of international policing.

In the case of sex offenders, it is hard to deny that the specific solutions proposed for the problem were deeply influenced by American examples: if the American states are the laboratories of democracy, then the whole United States provides the rest of the world with a vast laboratory for social experiment. From the early 1990s, British media observed Washington state's experiment with sex predator laws and community notification, which were reported in television programs and newspapers. In 1995, for example, the radio program "File on Four" reported on protection against sex offenders, emphasizing the Washington experience. The following year, a BBC team visited Seattle and used as commentator a British man whose daughter had been murdered by a repeat sex offender. The father naturally enough favored the Washington methods, and asked: "How many children have to be abused or murdered before action is taken in the United Kingdom to curb the activities of pedophiles and sex offenders?" (Cuffe 1995). The program raised doubts about the efficacy of the reporting and registry system, and community notification continued to be desperately controversial, but most other aspects of the scheme were in place in the United Kingdom by the end of the decade.

But it would be misleading to see the European developments as purely reactive or imitative. Some American trends and ideas do travel well, others do not, depending on local conditions. For instance, American antiabortion activists have enjoyed little success in exporting tactics of violent confrontation and clinic blockades, because the social and legal position of abortion is so very different in Europe from that in America, and Europeans are much more resistant to any activities that connote religious fanaticism; hence, European audiences are simply not receptive to this particular transatlantic message. Similarly, although Europe borrowed American solutions to the sex-offender crisis, it had discovered that problem quite independently. In fact, some of the influences went the other way. Under the influence of eugenic ideas, European states have since the early twentieth century favored castration as a treatment for sex offenders, and quite liberal regimes—Germany and Denmark, for example—have used this device since the 1970s. When seeking solutions to the "pedophile problem" in the 1990s, American media and officials cited the apparent success of these European examples in order to justify their own chemical-castration laws, which were introduced in Texas and elsewhere (Olsen 1996; *St. Louis Post-Dispatch* 1996).

At least from the late nineteenth century, Europeans have recognized the existence of sexually motivated and sexually violent criminals: this was the time of Jack the Ripper and such scholars as Krafft Ebing, who studied their misdeeds. Much American writing on sex crime and serial murder grows out of the work of European and particularly German scholars, especially that generation that migrated from Germany in the 1930s (Tatar 1995). However, modern perceptions represent a departure in two significant ways: in their sense of a serious and pervasive sex-crime problem, and in its geographic scope. In both areas, the growth of concern can be closely associated with political and commercial trends toward European unity. In the mass media, for instance, the last two decades have been marked by increased interpenetration of media corporations across the continent, so that such stories as the Dutroux child murders are likely to be instantly reported in every other country as if they were domestic stories. The process is accelerated by the popularity of satellite television systems spanning international boundaries.

In addition, the reduction of political differences and the weakening of internal borders has meant that individual Europeans have traveled far more widely than their ancestors might have done, so that British, Greek, or Spanish readers can be expected to have some sense of conditions in, say, Belgium, and can thus readily identify with stories about events there. In this sense, Europe has contracted to become almost a single media market very much as the United States did earlier in this century, and likewise making it easier to portray local problems as if they are national or international. The Dutroux case thus comes to be seen as relevant to the people of Manchester or Rome, and tends to escalate the significance of other local cases that can be easily associated with that affair. Symbolically, Marc Dutroux became a demon-figure in other European nations, just as Jeffrey Dahmer or Ted Bundy came to represent sadistic serial murder for all Americans, regardless of region.

The process of political unification has been a rapid affair that has particularly affected bureaucratic agencies like the police. Since the 1970s, concern about such international menaces as terrorism, drugs, and illegal immigration has led to extensive international cooperation, and linking electronic databases in major states. The reduction of internal travel controls has vastly enhanced the perceived need for such alliances, while contacts with the FBI have encouraged ideas of interjurisdictional efforts against itinerant and multinational offenders. When facing a wave of serious crimes, it has become absolutely natural for police to seek wider connections and linkages that are an obvious enough likelihood in contemporary Europe: a hypothetical sex-killer wandering between European countries is unlikely to kill all his victims in just one of the nation states he happens to visit. And while many of these problems have an authentic core of reality, it has been tempting for European police agencies to use nightmares like terrorism and drugs to enhance their own powers and resources, and to overcome the resistance from libertarian groups or foes of overcentralization. Sex crime and child pornography have both provided powerful rhetorical weapons in the creation of European police institutions. Accordingly, the last decade in particular witnessed an upsurge of international agencies and systems, such as the current scheme for a Europe-wide DNA database, and a similarly continental-scale register for missing children (Dobson 1996). Almost certainly there will soon be a register of European "pedophiles" that, from recent experience, is likely to offer a bizarre mixture of authentically dangerous, violent, repeat offenders alongside the merely annoying, inadequate, and unlucky.

European problems have thus become more "American" in part because Europe itself is now dealing with the same kinds of federal issues that dominated much of American politics during the twentieth century. Just as American social problems have increasingly become national rather than regional, and have become aggravated in seriousness in the process, so a new "nation" of Europe is experiencing very similar patterns. The likelihood is that the sex offender panic of the 1990s is just the first of a new generation of perceived European crime waves that will pervade social thought and political life well into the new century.

NOTE

1. In British usage, the word is customarily spelled "paedophile," and this is the pattern in some other English-speaking countries, like Australia. Throughout this paper, I have modified the spelling to the common American "pedophile."

REFERENCES

Ahuja, Anjana. 1995. "We Must Learn to Spot the Potential Child Killers Early." *Times* (London) (August 3).

Andrews, Edmund L. 1997. "CompuServe Official Charged in Germany." *New York Times* (April 17).

Bates, Stephen. 1996. "Belgium Hardens Abuse Laws." *Guardian* (August 31).

———. 1997. "'One in Five May Be Victims of Child Abuse' in Belgium." *Guardian* (May 26).

Bergmo, Tonje. 1998. "The Press and Pedophilia." Undergraduate dissertation, BA (Hons) Journalism, Falmouth College of Arts.

Bibby, Peter C., ed. 1996. *Organized Abuse.* Aldershot, Hants: Arena.

Boseley, Sarah. 1991. "Operation Orchid Chief Promises More Arrests." *Guardian* (June 15).

Buncombe, Andrew, and Kate Watson-Smyth. 1999. "This Most Dangerous Paedophile." *Independent* (May 29).

Burn, Gordon. 1998. *Happy Like Murderers.* London: Faber and Faber.

Burrell, Ian. 2000. "Big Brother System to Track Pedophiles." *Independent* (January 10).

Canter, David V. 1994. *Criminal Shadows.* London: HarperCollins.

Chambers, Suzanna. 1997. "Police May Warn of Pedophile Presence." *Independent* (August 10).

Connett, David, and Jon Henley. 1996. "The Pedlars of Child Abuse." *Observer* (London) (August 25).

Connolly, Shaun. 1998. "Storm Over Sex Fiends' Release: No Supervision for Violent Men." *Evening Mail* (Birmingham) (March 13).

Cooper, Glenda. 1997. "Informing on Pedophiles Was Lawful, Lords Rule." *Independent* (July 11).

Cowell, Alan. 1996. "A Child's Funeral and Germans Seek Tougher Sex Penalties." *New York Times* (September 26).

Cuffe, Jenny. 1995. "Protection: The Menace in Their Midst." *Guardian* (October 4).

Daily Mail. 1999. "Fears as Sex Pest Is Freed." (March 22).

Dobson, Roger. 1996. "European Database to Trap Pedophiles." *Independent* (December 1).

Duncan, Alan. 1998. "I Refuse to Lead a Lynch Mob." *Spectator* (July 25).

Dyer, Clare. 1997. Pedophiles in Secrecy Test." *Guardian* (July 1).

Finn, Gary. 1999. "He Carried One Girl in His Sports Bag." *Independent* (May 29).

Fisher, Dawn, and A. R. Beech. 1999. "Current Practice in Britain with Sexual Offenders." *Journal of Interpersonal Violence* 14:240–56.

Fleet, Michael. 1999. "Paedophile Will Never Be Free Again to Attack Girls." *Daily Telegraph* (May 29).

Ford, Richard. 1996. "Howard Drops Sex Offenders Register." *Times* (London) (October 22).

Gill, Alan. 1998. "Life Sentence That Starts the Moment the Pedophiles Leave Prison." *Evening Standard* (April 3).

Howitt, Dennis. 1995. *Pedophiles and Sexual Offences Against Children.* New York: John Wiley.

Independent. 1999a. "Lie Detectors Are Used to Confront Sex Offenders." (October 11).

———. 1999b. "Pedophile Admits to String of Sex Attacks" (October 5).

Jenkins, Philip. 1991. "Strategy of Tension: The Belgian Terrorist Crisis of 1982-6," *Terrorism* 13:299–309.

———. 1992. *Intimate Enemies.* Hawthorne, NY: Aldine de Gruyter.

———. 1998. *Moral Panic.* New Haven, CT: Yale University Press.

Kennedy, Dominic. 1996. "Sex Tourists to be Tried by Courts in Britain." *Times* (London) (August 27).

La Fontaine, J. S. 1998. *Speak of the Devil : Tales of Satanic Abuse in Contemporary England.* New York: Cambridge University Press.

Lea, Susan, Tim Auburn, and Karen Kibblewhite. 1999. "Working with Sex Offenders: The Perceptions and Experiences of Professionals and Paraprofessionals." *International Journal of Offender Therapy and Comparative Criminology* 43:103–19.

Lyall, Sarah. 1998. "Britons Fear Sex Offenders in Their Communities." *New York Times* (April 27).

Masters, Brian. 1996. *She Must Have Known.* New York: Doubleday.

New York Times. 1996. "Belgian Ex-Cabinet Minister Held in Murder Case." (September 8).

———. 1997. "British Impose a 'Megan's Law' of Their Own." (August 12).

Oliver, Ted, and Ramsay Smith. 1993. *Lambs to the Slaughter.* London: Warner.

Olsen, Jan M. 1996. "Chemical Castration Laws Seen as Success in Europe." *Peoria Journal Star* (August 31).

Organized Criminal Paedophile Activity. 1995. Report by the Parliamentary Joint Committee on the National Crime Authority Canberra: Parliament of the Commonwealth of Australia.

Parker, Tony. 1969. *The Hidden World of Sex Offenders*. Indianapolis: Bobbs-Merrill.

Pfafflin, Friedemann. 1999. "Issues, Incidence, and Treatment of Sexual Offenders in Germany." *Journal of Interpersonal Violence* 14:372–95.

Roberts, Leslie. 1999. "Sex List Schoolboy, 11." *Daily Mail* (February 24).

Rose, David. 1995. "Penis Test for Sexual Deviancy Keeps Lifers Behind Bars." *Guardian* (May 28).

Ryback, Timothy W. 1997. "Four Girls Abducted, Raped, Murdered: A Country on Trial." *New York Times Magazine* (February 23).

Sacramento Bee. 1997. "Police Blunders, Possible Cover-up Blamed in Belgian Child-sex Scandal." (April 16).

St. Louis Post-Dispatch. 1996. "Denmark Tries Chemical Castration." (September 1).

Sampson, Adam. 1994. *Acts of Abuse*. London: Routledge.

Schiermeier, Quirin. 1998. "German Sex Killings Prompt Decision to Create a DNA Database." *Nature* 392 (April 23):749.

"Sex tourists to be sent packing." 1998. Website http://www.britain-info.org/bistext/fordom/law/171197.htm.

Simons, Marlise. 1996. "How Belgium Blinked at Child Killer's Trail." *New York Times* (February 25).

———. 1997a. "Sex Slayings Alarm France on the Peril of Repeat Offenders." *New York Times* (February 25).

———. 1997b. "French Police Arrest 250 Men Linked to Child Pornography Ring." *New York Times* (March 14).

Smith, Geraint. 1998. "240 Child Sex Rings in UK Today." *Evening Standard* (September 29).

Sparrow,. Andrew. 1997. "No Limit Jail Plan for Sex Predators." *Daily Mail* (July 8).

Tatar, Maria M. 1995. *Lustmörd: Sexual Murder in Weimar Germany*. Princeton, NJ: Princeton University Press.

Thomas, Terry. 1999. "How Could They Let Him Live Here?" Website http://www.lmu.ac.uk/cer/metro/offender.htm.

Times (London). 1997. "Perverts missing." (December 29).

Traynor, Ian. 1998a. "Raid Uncovers Huge Child Porn Ring." *Guardian* (July 17).

———. 1998b. "'I Put the Child Porn Together with the Murder and Realized It Was Our Neighbor.'" *Guardian* (July 18).

Walker, Nigel, ed. 1996. *Dangerous People*. London: Blackstone Press.

Walsh, James. 1996. "The Terror and the Pity." *Time* (September 2).

Waugh, Paul. 1999. "Abusers to Get Lifetime Electronic Tagging." *Independent* (November 29).

Wavell, Stuart. 1996. "The Devil You Know Still Abuses Children." *Sunday Times* (October 6).

Whitney, Craig R. 1997. "French Child Porn Dragnet Is Criticized After Suicides." *New York Times* (June 24).

Wyre, Ray, and Tim Tate. 1995. *The Murder of Childhood*. London: Penguin.

9

Contemporary Youth Music and "Risk" Lifestyles

ANDY BENNETT

During the late 1980s, a form of dance music known as "house" was introduced onto the British club scene. Originally created by DJs in Chicago's gay clubs during the late 1970s (Rietveld 1997), house became a central element in the "Balearic Beat" (a style that transgresses musical boundaries by mixing elements of different music styles such as rap, jazz, soul, pop, and rock) pioneered by nightclub DJs on the Spanish island of Ibiza. There it was first heard by young British holidaymakers (Melechi 1993). House's arrival in Britain coincided with the availability of a new amphetamine-based stimulant known as Ecstasy or "E" (Rietveld 1993; Saunders 1995). The association of Ecstasy with the emergent house scene became a focus of attention for the British media. Amid a flurry of headlines such as "Bop 'til You Drop" and "Rave To The Grave" (Thornton 1994), "acid house" (a term invented by the media) was portrayed as a dark and secretive world of warehouse parties and drug taking that threatened both the physical and mental well-being of young people.

As a consequence of such media reports, house became the center of a new moral panic. Nightclubs that featured house music nights or "raves" were subject to random spot checks by the police and in some cases had their licenses revoked (Redhead 1993; Hollands 1995). In 1991, the conservative MP Graham Bright sponsored the Entertainments (Increased Penalties) Act, which outlawed the staging of large-scale unlicensed raves and warehouse parties (Garratt and Taggart 1997). This was followed by the implementation of further legal sanctions in the form of the Criminal Justice and Public Order Act 1994 that gave the police authority "to remove persons attending or preparing for a rave." Such reactions to house and related styles of dance music have not been restricted to the United King-

169

dom. On the contrary, U.K. media representations of house created international concern over dance music's potentially corrupting influence on
young people. Studies of dance music in Germany (Smith 1998) and the
United States (Champion 1997; Rushkoff 1999) document reactions on the
part of the media, the police, and other "moral guardians" similar to those
witnessed in the United Kingdom.

In this chapter I argue that such reactions to contemporary youth music result in what Epstein (1998:1) refers to as the "narrow ideation of
youth": the issues, circumstances, and problems encountered by young
people in their daily lives and the latter's articulation through music are
systematically ignored by the wider society that increasingly comes to
view youth as Generation X. I draw upon recent studies of consumption,
lifestyle, and "risk" and apply these concepts to empirical research on
dance music, rap, and punk (musical styles that have been associated with
the onset of global social problems such as drug addiction, teenage pregnancy, and the increasing incidence of teenage homicide [Martin and Segrave 1993; Epstein et al. 1990]). I illustrate how, rather than fostering the
types of pathological, self-destructive responses routinely suggested by
the media, these music styles are adopted and creatively adapted by
young people in the negotiation of risks and uncertainties (Beck 1992) imposed on the structures of everyday life by postindustrialization. Thus, I
will argue, contemporary youth music styles play a constructive role in addressing and combating social problems at an international level.

MUSIC AND MORAL PANICS

The representation of popular culture as a "threat" to young people has
a long history. For example, in 1658, Swedish poet Georg Stiernhielm's *Her-
cules* warned youth about the dangers of reading "frivolous" literature,
while in the 1870s, U.S. businessman Anthony Comstock expressed similar concern in relation to the "dime novel" (Boëthius 1995). In both instances, emphasis was laid upon popular culture's morally corrupting
influence. With the establishment of the postwar youth market during the
early 1950s, the perceived threat to youth from popular culture products
became squarely focused on popular music. In a celebrated response to the
advent of rock 'n' roll during the 1950s, the Reverend Albert Carter of the
Pentecostal Church, Nottingham, expressed the view that "Rock 'n' roll
[was] a revival of devil dancing . . . the same sort of thing that is done in a
black magic ritual" (Street 1992:305). Several years later an article by Paul
Johnson for the British journal *New Statesman* expressed similar concerns
about the Beatles, whom Johnson (1964:327) referred to as "grotesque idols"
performing to a "pathetic and listless" audience with "sagging mouths and

glazed eyes, the hands mindlessly drumming in time to the music." Scandinavian youth theorist Boëthius (1995:38) argues that such anxieties regarding young people's relationship to popular culture result from the parent culture's common perception of the popular as a "borderline area between family, school or work in which the control of guardians or supervisors has been limited or non-existent." The mass media play on such parental fears through their instigation of "moral panics" (Cohen 1987), in which isolated events, such as minor skirmishes between youth cultural groups or occasional drug-related teenage deaths, are exaggerated and distorted by the media in ways that sensitize the general public to the potentially damaging and corruptive influence of popular culture, and particularly popular music, on youth. In recent years such moral entrepreneurship on the part of the mass media has been augmented by a powerful form of grassroots censorship, the most established of which was the Washington D.C.-based Parents Music Resource Center (PMRC), formed in May 1985 by the wives of government administrators and members of Congress (Martin and Segrave 1993). Founded on the premise that popular music lyrics increasingly "glamorize graphic sex, violence and drug use" (Epstein et al. 1990:382), the PMRC began a censorship campaign that sought to "institute a record rating system" and ban from the airwaves songs by artists as diverse as Prince, Sheena Easton, and Judas Priest (Martin and Segrave 1993:292). Rap music also became a target for the PMRC following a series of violent incidents alleged to have been inspired by the lyrics of rap records (Epstein et al. 1990).

Such forms of moral entrepreneurship are problematic for several reasons. Firstly, they suggest that music can be heard only in prescribed ways and that it is essentially "preprogrammed" to elicit particular responses from young listeners. Predictably, given their interest in public scaremongering, such reports discount the audience's ability to interpret musical texts for themselves, preferring instead to cast young listeners in the role of cultural dupes. Similarly, such interpretations of youth ignore the wider public's indifference to the social circumstances that face contemporary youth and inform the everyday settings in which they select particular styles of music and use them, together with a range of other consumer commodities, to construct lifestyles (Chaney 1996) that are increasingly geared to the negotiation of risk and uncertainty.

MUSIC AND "RISK" LIFESTYLES

The concept of lifestyle first appeared in the work of Weber (1968) who argued against Marx's theory of economic determinism by suggesting that status was also a central determinant of the social strata. According to Weber, status manifested itself most readily through the "lifestyles" of different social groups. Simmel (1971) and Veblen (1949) refined the concept of lifestyle in their work on patterns of consumerism at the beginning of the twentieth century. Each of these theorists suggested that lifestyles were actively constructed by social groups whose appropriation of particular commodities enabled such groups to mark themselves off from the wider society by establishing distinctive forms of collective identity (Chaney 1996:51). Lifestyle subsequently became more readily associated with market research, where it replaced "traditional socio-economic background factors [as a means] to identify segments of buyers" (Reimer 1995:122). In a recent study Chaney (1996) redesignated lifestyle as a model for sociological inquiry arguing that, through the process of lifestyle construction, late-modern individuals inscribe products of the popular culture industries (Adorno 1991), such as music and fashion, with particularized meanings derived from the local experience of everyday life. As such, popular-culture products become key elements not only in the formation of social identities but also in the collective negotiation of local circumstances that impinge upon or oppress individuals in the course of their everyday lives.

In relation to contemporary youth, the construction of lifestyles must be seen against a social backdrop increasingly characterized by issues of risk. Risk society, a term first used by Beck (1992) to describe the ways that social action is informed by a reflexive awareness of potentially pathological circumstances arising from the late modern, postindustrial condition, has significant implications for the life experiences of the young. In particular, increasing youth unemployment has resulted in a collapse of the division between work and leisure and its replacement by indefinite periods of unstructured free time (Griffin 1993). The last two decades have also seen a sharp increase in youth homelessness and organized squatting movements, young people preferring to live "rough" on the street or in a squat rather than remain in dysfunctional family homes; others have been forced into homelessness due to unemployment and the failure of the state to provide adequate benefits. Similarly, in many parts of the western world, the economic downturn has exacerbated problems of racism and racial exclusion and, in some instances, led to a resurgence of fascism and nationalism (Fekete 1993).

Faced with such risk and uncertainty, young people have been forced to adopt new strategies for resisting or, alternatively, coping with the pressures and limitations that have been imposed upon them. In this respect one of the few powers remaining to youth, the power to consume, plays an increasingly important role. In keeping with Chaney's observations on the importance of lifestyle as a means of understanding the process of identity formation in late modern society, recent research on youth consumption practices maintains "that young people [are] capable of transforming the politics of consumption for their own ends" (Griffin 1993:141). Expanding upon this point, Willis (1990:21) argues that: "Interpretation, symbolic action and creativity are *part* of consumption." As an established medium of youth expression, and a means of marking out cultural territory, music is central to the politics of consumption engaged in by young people. Through their appropriation of musical texts and attendant sensibilities of style, young people transform their consumption practices into forms of symbolic and, in some cases, direct action in the context of a social landscape where the values, views, and basic needs of youth are increasingly ignored.

MAKING MUSIC WORK! MUSIC AND THE NEW "DO IT YOURSELF" ETHIC

It is true that local music-making in the sense of direct participation in performance is the pursuit of a minority. But this minority turns out to be a more serious and energetic one than is often imagined, whose musical practices not only involve a whole host of other people than just performers, but also have many implications for urban and national culture more generally. (Finnegan 1989:6)

In her book *The Hidden Musicians*, Finnegan provides a valuable insight into how activities readily associated with local music scenes—for example, composition, rehearsal, and performance—are supplemented by a range of extramusical pursuits such as designing posters, selling tickets, or helping to assemble staging or lighting equipment. Although primarily concerned with the social dimensions of such pursuits, that is to say, their role in the construction of community, Finnegan also notes their significance as a type of informal economic activity: many of the apparently amateur musical activities featured in her study yielded some form of financial return. In recent years music has become increasingly important as a hands-on, grassroots activity through which young unemployed people are both able to structure their time and develop new skills as musicians, producers, DJs, and so on. While conducting fieldwork for a study of contemporary youth music in Newcastle, England, and Frankfurt, Germany, I encountered a number of individuals who were pursuing "do-it-yourself" careers—for example, as rap artists, dance music producers, fanzine editors, and house party organizers (Bennett 2000). Such instances of grass-roots music-making and related activities constitute a growing network of informal entrepreneurial activities engaged in by the youth of postindustrial societies. This network's dimensions are such that it has effectively become a transnational post-Fordist music industry, coordinated by young people for whom such informal means of making a living are becoming an accepted norm as more conventional routes to vocational and economic success are increasingly blocked due to unemployment and the casualization of labor (Smith and Maughan 1997).

The rapid development of this "do-it-yourself" music industry was made possible by the digital and computer revolutions of the early 1980s and their impact upon the nature of the recording process. Whereas high-quality recording facilities were once the sole property of professional studios, digital and computer technology opened up new levels of access to the recording process. Similarly, the creative potential of "amateur" musicians and producers has also been considerably enhanced by relatively cheap, state-of-the-art technology. Important in this respect is MIDI (Musical Instrument Digital Interface), which enables a musical instrument or sound to be interfaced—electronically connected—with an infinite number of *samples*[1] with the effect that when the instrument is played or the sound produced, the sampled sounds are also simultaneously triggered. Thus, MIDI allows music to be made "within a computer's memory without the need of an acoustic environment in the studio. Hence, a composition could be produced in a confined space via the technology and the mixing desk. 'Studio' quality recording can now [therefore] take place in any location" (Negus 1992:25). Easy access to such cheap but high-quality recording equipment has resulted in growing number of *home* or *bedroom* recording enthusiasts producing music of a quality comparable with that created in professional studios. This democratization of the recording process has allowed songwriters, solo artists, and groups to record their music without the financial backing of record companies. Such grassroots musical activities have been matched by the growth of an informal infrastructure designed to give the music of home and bedroom recording artists exposure in the public sphere. Thus, as Smith and Maughan (1997:21) explain, in addition to music-making itself, the informal music industry comprises a range of support services—young people "setting up record labels, distribution companies, specialist record shops, agencies, artwork, etc."

MUSIC AND YOUTH HOMELESSNESS

In addition to its significance in providing a structure of informal entrepreneurial activities, music has also proved to be an impetus for a range of other "do-it-yourself" youth initiatives designed to combat the social problems encountered by young people in postindustrial societies. In her work on youth homelessness in Hollywood, Ruddick notes how "punk" squatters, a localized appropriation of the U.K. punk style (see Hebdige

1979), have used their image as a means of "develop[ing] a social identity which confronted their stigma" (Ruddick 1998:345). Recasting punk's spectacular resistance as a means of reterritorializing rundown, uninhabited buildings in Hollywood, the punk squatters were able to assume "a strategic control of space" (Ruddick 1998:346). Punk involvement in organized squatting movements has also been a feature of urban life in Germany since the early 1980s, when punk added its voice of protest to the Hausbesetzer-Szene (squatting-scene) of Berlin and subsequently the rest of the country (Geiling 1995). Again, the spectacular style of the punk image, together with the lyrically and musically aggressive tone of the music, performed an important role in marking out the cultural space of German squatting movements and articulating their collective cause at a national level.

Ruddick's and Geiling's studies provide a further illustration of how a youth music and attendant style cast by the media as a "social problem" have become part of a proactive strategy in the fight against a wider structural problem (homelessness) and its impact upon young people. Punk's social infamy was set in place by the British group the Sex Pistols, who became subject to particularly intense moral condemnation that was instrumental in the construction of punk as a social menace in the U.K. and Europe. In December 1976 the Sex Pistols were invited to appear on the Thames Television's news magazine show "Today." As Laing (1985:36) points out, in the space of a one-minute-and-40-second interview, interviewer Bill Grundy "managed to sketch in the popular stereotype of punk." By asking a series of rhetorical questions in quick succession, and urging the Sex Pistols to swear on TV, Grundy cemented into place the developing public image of punks as lazy, foul-mouthed degenerates. The following morning the U.K. tabloid, the *Daily Mirror* reported a wave of public outcry and disgust at the behavior of the Sex Pistols and the other punks present during the Grundy interview. As Harron (1990:199) notes, the media and by definition the general public "diagnosed [punk] not as a new music style but as a social problem." Hebdige (1979) has suggested that, seen in the wider context of Britain's socioeconomic climate during the later 1970s, punk rock simply articulated the social decay that the wider society was aware of but would not admit to. Thus, a central aspect of punk's "success . . . as spectacle" was the way in which it was able to translate the general mood of late-seventies Britain into "tangible (and visible) terms" (Hebdige 1979:87). Punk made statements that were understood not only by punks themselves but also, more importantly, by their "opponents." The expressions of outrage and disgust that punk elicited from parents, teachers, and employers, and from the moral entrepreneurs, simply served to reinforce the fact that while punk's particular mode of expression was far from commonly endorsed, it was, nevertheless, "cast in a language which was generally available" (Hebdige 1979:87). Punk's appropriation and reworking by young homeless people in the United States and Germany provides a further illustration of punk's engagement with the wider and more deep-seated social issues that are systematically ignored by the media in their attempts to portray contemporary youth music and attendant styles as spectacular examples of young people out of control and threatening the moral order of society.

A similarly misrepresented reaction on the part of young people to the issue of youth homelessness is the Exodus Collective. Originally part of the U.K. dance-party scene that organized free raves around Britain during the late 1980s, Exodus occupied a derelict old people's home and disused farm buildings near the town of Luton, in Bedfordshire, and transformed these into a housing cooperative that became known as HAZ (Housing Action Zone). Initially threatened with expulsion by the local authorities, Exodus was subsequently granted ownership of the buildings after authority inspectors visited the cooperative and noted the scale and quality of restoration work carried out by Exodus members on the occupied sites. The Exodus Collective provides a particularly effective example of how a common response to a musical text can function to produce a more concrete series of lifestyle strategies through which individuals engage with the social circumstances that confront them. Thus, as McKay (1996:124–25) states: "Exodus form[ed] a new movement of the people in the early nineties, one that originat[ed] in something as mundane as a sound system. . . . Black and white youth pull[ed] their energies together to create their own entertainment, then lifestyle, community, network of campaigns and events."

Exodus illustrates how a collective expression of musical taste can often serve as a catalyst for a more coherently structured, proactive social movement. Drawing people together into a common space—be that a club, festival field, or virtual space on the internet—music provides an occasion for sociality (Shields 1992). As individuals come together in this way to celebrate their common musical tastes and preferences, they also gain a sense of how their motives—personal, political, artistic, and so on—coalesce with those of others. Thus, loosely articulated lifestyles combine into coherent, collective lifestyle strategies. Due to the global flow of music, both through the formal networks of the leisure industries and, increasingly, the informal post-Fordist networks examined above in relation to the work of Smith and Maughan (1997), such responses are diffused across a range of regional and national settings. In each case local factors affect (and in some instances radically alter) the way in which music is responded to at a collective level and the themes and issues that are articulated through the appropriation of particular texts and genres of music. This can be seen clearly in relation to rap, a music whose global message concerning the injustice of racial prejudice is continually appropriated and reworked into particularized strategies for addressing the problem of racism as it is encountered at a local level.

RAP AND RACISM: GLOBAL ISSUES, LOCAL STRATEGIES

It is an indisputable truism that rap has been more readily associated with the incidence of youth crime and violence, and thus more rigorously censored, than any other contemporary youth music. Media images of rap center on its allegedly self-destructive characteristics to the extent that any other representation of the music and its social significance are prevented from entering into the sphere of wider public perception (Mitchell 1996). Indeed, as the African-American writer Michael Dyson (1996:178) argues, "While . . . rap takes the heat for a range of social maladies from urban violence to sexual misconduct, the roots of our racial misery remain buried beneath moralizing discourse that is confused and sometimes dishonest."

Rap, a form of rhythmic patois spoken over a continuous backbeat or "breakbeat" produced by "mixing" sections of vinyl records on a twin-turntable record player (Back 1996), developed as part of an African-American street culture known as "hip hop" in the Bronx borough of New York in the early 1970s. Aware that urban renewal programs and economic recession were leading to an increase in interracial violence and crime, an ex-street gang member, known as Afrika Bambaataa, formed the "Zulu Nation" in an attempt to "channel the anger of young people in the South Bronx away from gang fighting and into music, dance, and graffiti"[2] (Lipsitz 1994:26). Rap quickly became a community-wide means for young people to address and negotiate those socioeconomic circumstances in which they found themselves. In particular, the absence of a need for musical *skill*, in the more conventional sense of being able to play a musical instrument, gave rap an essentially hands-on quality, making it an ideal medium through which young people could spontaneously express their views or simply vent frustration regarding issues such as violence, poverty, and unemployment—issues that were exacerbated due to the effective ghettoization of the Bronx and its labeling as a "no-go" area. Beadle (1993: 77, 85) goes so far as to suggest that rap is "to the black American urban youth more or less what punk was to its British white counterpart . . . [becoming] a vehicle for pride and for anger, for asserting the self-worth of the community."

The original rap culture of the South Bronx subsequently became a "blueprint" for a range of localized rap scenes in different parts of the world. Taking the basic tenets of the rap style, young people in cities and regions across the globe have reworked the rap text in ways that incorporate local knowledge and sensibilities, thus transforming rap into a means of communication that works in the context of specific localities. A useful model for understanding the cultural mobility of rap is Lull's (1995) concept of *cultural reterritorialization*, which recasts cultural forms as malleable resources that can be inscribed with new meanings relating to the particular local context within which such products are appropriated. Perhaps because of its street-cultural, largely improvised origins, rap appears to be particularly conducive to the process of cultural reterritorialization. By the same token, however, a common thread running through localized appropriations of rap is a reflexive understanding among rap fans of the music's resonance with the risk and uncertainty that increasingly characterize their immediate socioeconomic environments and consequent life chances. Thus, as Rose (1994a:72) argues, rap's "primary properties of flow, layering and rupture simultaneously reflect and contest the social roles open to inner city youth at the end of the twentieth century." Central to the localization of rap music, then, is a process of creative adoption and adaptation, rap's core text being continually reexplored and redefined through the inscription of particular urban narratives.

Across western Europe, rap music has become a musicalized forum for a series of locally situated but thematically linked discourses concerning the related issues of racism, racial exclusion, and citizenship (see, for example, Mitchell 1996; Bjurström 1997; Bennett 1999). Primary exponents of rap in western Europe are second-generation immigrants from Africa, the West Indies, Turkey, Morocco, and parts of Asia. Originally granted entry into western Europe during the early 1950s to assist with postwar reconstruction (Foner 1978; Hebdige 1987), such immigrant populations have been forced to deal with constant racial abuse and discrimination, a situation exacerbated during the last fifteen years by the economic downturn in many parts of western Europe, mass unemployment, and the concomitant resurgence of fascism. The sociopolitical scenario within western Europe, and its particular bearing upon the lives of second-generation immigrants, has become the dominant focus for European rap. European rappers' engagement with the social tension and disruption caused by racism and racial exclusion takes a variety of localized forms, from the militant, left-wing ideology of Italian rap groups that have grown out of the *centri sociali* (social centers) formed during the 1970s by "left-wing militant students and disaffected young people" (Mitchell 1996:150) to Swedish rapper Papa Dee's tongue-in-cheek claim to be an "Original Black Viking" as a means of negotiating the hostility exhibited by white racist agitators who "celebrate the mythical Viking as an ancestor to German Nazists [sic] and their modern counterparts" (Bjurström 1997:54).

In Germany problems encountered by second-generation immigrants in relation to racism are compounded by the issue of citizenship; a child born in Germany, unlike many other countries, does not automatically receive

German citizenship. Moreover, those who acquire German citizenship often find that, in reality, such status does little to enhance their life chances in Germany and that they continue to suffer racial inequality, exclusion, and abuse. The rap group Advanced Chemistry's song "Fremd im eigenen Land" ("A Foreigner in My Own Country"), together with the video made to promote it, was one of the first German rap songs to address the issue of citizenship in Germany. Performed by three rappers, each holding German citizenship, but with respective origins in Haiti, Ghana, and Italy, the song documents the struggle of each to be accepted as German and orientates around the phrase "Ich habe einen grünen Paß, mit einem Goldenen Adler drauf" ("I have a green passport, with a golden eagle on it"—this being the design of the old German passport). In the video, each member of the group is questioned about his nationality. On one occasion group member Frederick Hahn is approached by a white German youth who asks, "Where do you come from, are you African or American?" When Hahn replies that he is German, the youth begins to ridicule him and accuses him of lying, only retreating when Hahn produces his passport and sarcastically retorts, "Is this the proof you're looking for?" In a later scene, another member of Advanced Chemistry is asked if he is "going home [i.e., back to his "home" country] later?" to which he replies: "Always the same stupid questions. . . . I've been living in this country for twenty years." In an interview for the U.K. youth magazine *ID*, Advanced Chemistry spoke of their desire to expose the racial exclusion suffered by Germany's ethnic minority groups. Thus, as one of the group explained, "We rap in German in order to reach our own public, in order that they understand our problem. . . . It's a fact of life that if you're not recognised as a full German citizen you face constant harassment and identity checks" (Harpin 1993:59–60).

Since the release of "Fremd im eigenen Land," a number of German-language rap groups have developed the song's theme and used the rap medium to explore a range of similar issues pertaining to immigrant groups in Germany. The resulting work by groups such as Fresche Fami lie has consolidated in the minds of many of those who attend their performances the link between rap as a politicized discourse and the various insecurities experienced by members of ethnic minority groups in Germany. By the same token, however, to claim that European hip hop's role in opposition to locally manifested instances of racism and fascism must in each case involve such forms of dialogic engagement with issues of nation and national identity is overly simplistic. Thus, while the lyrical themes of groups such as Advanced Chemistry may find appeal among some sections of Germany's ethnic-minority youth, for others the mutuality of German-language rap with the desire to be seen as "German" is viewed negatively and has resulted in alternative forms of rap that actively seek to rediscover and, in many cases, reconstruct notions of identity tied to traditional ethnic roots. This is particularly so in the case of Frankfurt, where the percentage of ethnic-minority inhabitants is higher than in most other German cities. While researching the Frankfurt hip-hop scene, I interviewed a group of rappers from Nordweststadt, a particularly multiethnic area of Frankfurt with a large number of Gastarbeiter families (Bennett 1999; 2000). During the interview I noticed how German-language rap groups such as Advanced Chemistry were continually criticized for their failure to acknowledge any form of ethnic identification other than that represented by their German passports, a failure that was perceived to amount to a symbolic betrayal of the right of ethnic minorities to "roots" or to any expression of cultural heritage. Thus, as a young Turkish woman put it: "I think that they [Advanced Chemistry] should be proud of their roots. When people say to me 'are you German?' I say 'no I'm not' and I'm not ashamed to say that."

Such sentiments are clearly evident in the Turkish rap styles that also are an integral part of the Frankfurt hip-hop scene. In the same way that South Asian musicians in Britain have fused Western popular music with traditional *bhangra* styles learned from cassette tapes acquired in South Asian shops (Banerji and Baumann 1990:144), so young Turkish people living in German cities are able to obtain cassette recordings of traditional songs and music very cheaply from the local shops established to cater to their cultural needs. Using rhythms and melodies learned or sampled from such cassettes, traditional Turkish musical styles have been fused with African-American rap styles to produce a distinctive variation of the rap sound (Bennett 1998). If German-language rap has come to signify the voice of the second-generation immigrant attempting to integrate into German society, then Turkish rap works to a broadly opposite effect, the whole Turkish rap movement translating into a singly defiant message aimed at white German society.

CONCLUSION

This chapter has critically engaged with media representations of contemporary youth music, its effects on youth, and subsequent impact on the international diffusion of social problems. Beginning with a consideration of media treatments of popular music and the underlying moral panic-making agenda that informs such treatments, I subsequently argued that the "cause-and-effect" explanations put forward by the media to explain music's influence on youth are not only overly simplistic but also acutely insensitive to the socially dynamic interplay between youth, music, and everyday life. Drawing on the examples of dance music, punk, and rap, I have endeavored to illustrate how contemporary youth music, rather than producing the uniformly pathological effects emphasized by the media, have become central resources in the construction of what I have termed "risk" lifestyles. Using the concept of "lifestyle strategies" identified by Chaney (1996) as integral to understanding how late-modern individuals relate their consumption practices to the wider social practices that underpin their everyday lives, I have argued that, in relation to youth, the construction of lifestyle strategies must be seen against a socioeconomic backdrop of increasing risk and uncertainty, punctuated by issues such as unemployment, homelessness, and racism. Music, as one of the dominant modes of consumption engaged in by young people is, I have argued, of central importance in the highly reflexive risk lifestyles constructed by youth. Music, I have suggested, provides an important channel for young people, not only in addressing particular social problems but also in actively engaging with and negotiating these problems.

NOTES

1. A sample is a digitally stored sound, musical or otherwise. Popular samples include orchestral and piano sounds, drum sounds, industrial noise, and everyday sounds such as traffic, birdsong, and breaking glass.

2. In addition to rap music, "graffiti" and breakdancing were also central to the hip-hop culture of the South Bronx. For an analysis of hip-hop graffiti, see Lachmann (1988), Brewer and Miller (1990), and Deppe (1997). For an analysis of breakdancing see Rose (1994b).

REFERENCES

Adorno, Theodor. 1991. *The Culture Industry: Selected Essays on Mass Culture,* edited by J. Bernstein. London: Routledge.

Back, Les. 1996. *New Ethnicities and Urban Culture: Racisms and Multiculture in Young Lives.* London: UCL Press.

Bancrji, Sabita., and G. Baumann. 1990. "Bhangra 1984–88: Fusion and Professionalisation in a Genre of South Asian Dance Music." Pp. 137–52 in *Black Music in Britain: Essays on the Afro-Asian Contribution to Popular Music,* edited by Paul Oliver. Milton Keynes: Open University Press.

Beadle, Jeremy J. 1993. *Will Pop Eat Itself? Pop Music in the Sound Bite Era.* London: Faber and Faber.

Beck, Ulrich. 1992. *The Risk Society.* London: Sage.

Bennett, Andy. 1998. "The Frankfurt Rockmobil: A New Insight into the Significance of Music-Making for Young People." *Youth and Policy* 60:16–29.

———. 1999. "Hip Hop am Main: The Localization of Rap Music and Hip Hop Culture." *Media, Culture and Society* 21:77–91.

———. 2000. *Popular Music and Youth Culture: Music, Identity and Place.* London: Macmillan.

Bjurström, Erling. 1997. "The Struggle for Ethnicity: Swedish Youth Styles and the Construction of Ethnic Identities." *Young: Nordic Journal of Youth Research* 5 (3):44–58.

Böethius, Ulf. 1995. "Youth, the Media and Moral Panics." Pp. 39–57 in *Youth Culture in Late Modernity*, edited by Johan Fornäs and G. Bolin. London: Sage.

Brewer, Devon D., and M. L. Miller. 1990. "Bombing and Burning: The Social Organization and Values of Hip Hop Graffiti Writers and Implications for Policy." *Deviant Behavior* 11:345–69.

Champion, Sarah. 1997. "Fear and Loathing in Wisconsin." Pp. 94–105 in *The Clubcultures Reader: Readings in Popular Cultural Studies*, edited by Steve Redhead, D. Wynne, and J. O'Connor. Oxford: Blackwell.

Chaney, David. 1996. *Lifestyles*. London: Routledge.

Cohen, Stanley. 1987. *Folk Devils and Moral Panics: The Creation of the Mods and Rockers*, 3rd. ed. Oxford: Blackwell.

Deppe, Jürgen. 1997. *Odem: On the Run—Eine Jugend in der Graffiti-Szene*. Berlin: Schwarzkopf & Schwarzkopf.

Dyson, Michael E. 1996. *Between God and Gangsta Rap: Bearing Witness to Black Culture*. New York: Oxford University Press.

Epstein, Jonathon S. 1998. "Generation X, Youth Culture and Identity." Pp. 1–23 in *Youth Culture: Identity in a Postmodern World*, edited by Jonathon Epstein. Oxford: Blackwell.

Epstein, Jonathon S., D. J. Pratto, and J. K. Skipper Jr. 1990. "Teenagers, Behavioral Problems, and Preferences for Heavy Metal and Rap Music: A Case Study of a Southern Middle School." *Deviant Behavior* 11:381–94.

Fekete, Liz. 1993. "Inside Racist Europe." Pp. 154–71 in *Statewatching the New Europe: A Handbook on the European State*, edited by Tony Bunyan. London: Statewatch.

Finnegan, Ruth. 1989. *The Hidden Musicians: Music-Making in an English Town*. Cambridge: Cambridge University Press.

Foner, Nancy. 1978. *Jamaica Farewell: Jamaican Migrants in London*. London: Routledge and Kegan Paul.

Garratt, Sheryl, and C. Taggart. 1997. "Fighting for the Right to Party: HM Government vs Acid House." Pp. 111–15 in *Nightfever: Club Writing in The Face*, edited by Richard Benson. London: Macmillan.

Geiling, Heiko. 1995. "'Chaos-Tage' in Hannover: Vom Ereignis zum Mythos." *Vorgänge: Zeitschrift für Bürgerrechte und Gesellschaftspolitik* 4:1–6.

Griffin, Christine. 1993. *Representations of Youth: The Study of Youth and Adolescence in Britain and America*. Oxford: Polity.

Harpin, Lee. 1993. "One Continent Under a Groove." *ID: The Europe Issue* (May 16):58–60.

Harron, Mary. 1990. "McRock: Pop as a Commodity." Pp. 173–220 in *Facing the Music: Essays on Pop, Rock and Culture*, 2nd ed., edited by Simon Frith. London: Mandarin.

Hebdige, Dick. 1979. *Subculture: The Meaning of Style*. London: Routledge.

———. 1987. *Cut 'n' Mix: Culture, Identity and Caribbean Music*. London: Routledge.

Hollands, Robert. 1995. Friday Night, Saturday Night: Youth Cultural Identification in the Post-Industrial City. University of Newcastle, Department of Social Policy Working Paper No.2.

Johnson, Paul. 1964. "The Menace of Beatlism." *New Statesman* 67 (28 February): 326–27.

Laing, Dave. 1985. *One Chord Wonders: Power and Meaning in Punk Rock.* Milton Keynes: Open University Press.

Lachmann, Richard. 1988. "Graffiti as Career and Ideology." *American Journal of Sociology* 94:229–50.

Lipsitz, George. 1994. *Dangerous Crossroads: Popular Music, Postmodernism and the Poetics of Place.* London: Verso.

Lull, James. 1995. *Media, Communication, Culture: A Global Approach.* Cambridge: Polity Press.

Martin, Linda, and K. Segrave. 1993. *Anti-Rock: The Opposition to Rock 'n' Roll.* New York: Da Capo.

McKay, George. 1996. *Senseless Acts of Beauty: Cultures of Resistance Since the Sixties.* London: Verso.

Melechi, Antonio. 1993. "The Ecstasy of Disappearance." Pp. 29–40 in *Rave Off: Politics and Deviance in Contemporary Youth Culture,* edited by Steve Redhead. Aldershot: Avebury.

Mitchell, Tony. 1996. *Popular Music and Local Identity: Rock, Pop and Rap in Europe and Oceania.* London: Leicester University Press.

Negus, Keith. 1992. *Producing Pop: Culture and Conflict in the Popular Music Industry.* London: Edward Arnold.

Redhead, Steve. 1993. "The Politics of Ecstasy [sic]." Pp. 7–28 *Rave Off: Politics and Deviance in Contemporary Youth Culture,* edited by Steve Redhead. Aldershot: Avebury.

Reimer, Bo. 1995. "Youth and Modern Lifestyles." Pp. 120–44 in *Youth Culture in Late Modernity,* edited by Johan Fornäs and G. Bolin. London: Sage.

Rietveld, Hillegonda. 1993. "Living the Dream." Pp. 41–78 in *Rave Off: Politics and Deviance in Contemporary Youth Culture,* edited by Steve Redhead. Aldershot: Avebury.

———. 1997. "The House Sound of Chicago." Pp. 106–18 in *The Clubcultures Reader: Readings in Popular Cultural Studies,* edited by Steve Redhead, D. Wynne, and J. O'Connor. Oxford: Blackwell.

Rose, Tricia. 1994a. "A Style Nobody Can Deal With: Politics, Style and the Postindustrial City in Hip Hop." Pp. 71–88 in *Microphone Fiends. Youth Music and Youth Culture,* edited by Andrew Ross and T. Rose. London: Routledge.

———. 1994b. *Black Noise: Rap Music and Black Culture in Contemporary America.* London: Wesleyan University Press.

Ruddick, Susan. 1998. "How 'Homeless' Youth Sub-Cultures Make a Difference." Pp. 343–60 in *Cool Places: Geographies of Youth Culture,* edited by Tracey Skelton and G. Valentine. London: Routledge.

Rushkoff, Douglas. 1999. "Rave Against the Machine." *THIS Magazine* (November / December):37–39.

Saunders, Nicholas. 1995. *Ecstasy and the Dance Culture.* London: Nicholas Saunders.

Shields, Rob. 1992. "Spaces for the Subject of Consumption." Pp. 1–20 in *Lifestyle Shopping: The Subject of Consumption,* edited by Rob Shields. London: Routledge.

Simmel, Georg. 1971 [1903]. "The Metropolis and Mental Life." Pp. 324–39 in *On*

Individuality and Social Form, edited by Donald Levine. Chicago: University Press of Chicago.

Smith, Fiona M. 1998. "Between East and West: Sites of Resistance in East German Youth Cultures." Pp. 289–304 in *Cool Places: Geographies of Youth Culture*, edited by Tracey Skelton and G. Valentine. London: Routledge.

Smith, Richard, and Maughan, T. 1997. Youth Culture and the Making of the Post-Fordist Economy: Dance Music in Contemporary Britain. Occasional paper, Department of Social Policy and Social Science, University of London.

Street, John. 1992. "Shock Waves: The Authoritative Response to Popular Music." Pp. 302–24 in *Come on Down?: Popular Media Culture in Post-War Britain*, edited by Dominic Strinati and S. Wagg. London: Routledge.

Thornton, Sarah. 1994. "Moral Panic, the Media and British Rave Culture." Pp. 179–92 in *Microphone Fiends: Youth Music and Youth Culture*, edited by Andrew Ross and T. Rose. London: Routledge.

Veblen, Thorstein. 1949 [1899]. *The Theory of the Leisure Class: An Economic Study of Institutions*. New York: Mentor.

Weber, Max. 1968 [1919]. "The Distribution of Power Within the Political Community: Class, Status, Party." *Economy and Society*, edited by G. Roth and C. Wittich. New York: Bedminister Press.

Willis, Paul. 1990. *Common Culture: Symbolic Work at Play in the Everyday Cultures of the Young*. Milton Keynes: Open University Press.

10

The Diffusion of Organ-Theft Narratives

VÉRONIQUE CAMPION-VINCENT

Organ-theft narratives are stories in which eyes, kidneys, and other organs are stolen from living persons (who may or not die following the theft). The spread of these tales accompanied the development of organ transplants, which became widespread in the early 1980s, with the availability of immunosuppressant drugs that mastered the recipients' rejection of the transplanted organs.

Organ-theft narratives can be sorted into three clusters that spread through different channels. The stories can be linked to social problems, different for each cluster. The Baby Parts stories (in which Third World children's organs are stolen) are linked to the traffic in children accompanying the development of international adoption. *Sacaojos* stories (involving the theft of street children's eyes) are linked to the maltreatment of the homeless poor and street children. These two clusters appeared in Latin America; they reflect the poverty and violence existing in Latin American countries, as well as the dominance exercised by the United States over the area. The third cluster, the Kidney Heist stories (in which adults have a kidney stolen) first appeared in rich countries (but are now diffused all over the world). These tales are linked both to general unease about organ transplants (and the widespread popular suspicion of the concept of brain-death that justifies organ removals), and to the existence in several Third World countries of a trade in kidneys bought from poor donors for the benefit of rich patients. All three clusters can be linked to a growing awareness of the existence of a global traffic in human beings.

This paper has four sections. First, it describes the rise and spread of organ-theft narratives since the late 1980s, following the three clusters identified, that is, Baby Parts, *Sacaojos* (Eye Robbers), and Kidney Heist stories.

Second, it then presents and analyzes the main diffusion channels through which these narratives were brought to public awareness. Rather than offering a chronological narrative, it describes the very different channels in order of their importance. Thus, it begins with TV "documentaries" of 1992–93 that used a slick presentation of proven Third World horrors (such as child kidnappings, maltreatment of patients in asylums, murders of the homeless and the poor, and the organ trade) to seemingly validate the narratives. These "documentaries" have been analyzed and proven inconsistent; furthermore, investigations have debunked their "star cases." But they generated polemics, as their conviction influenced large sectors of public opinion. This section then turns to a second channel—specialized but generally credible sources, such as politicians, nongovernment organizations (NGOs), and international organizations. A third channel involves militants, propagandists, and moral authorities, who use these narratives to exemplify the horrors of the modern world.

The paper's third section attempts to evaluate the status of organ-theft narratives in the late 1990s. They have practically disappeared from the public debate, but references to the reality of organized organ thefts still appear in the media occasionally, in a weakened mode, linked to mostly minor incidents. Although these stories have by and large dropped from public debate, they remain available as "floating myths" that can reemerge.

A final important diffusion channel, fiction, will be treated in the concluding section of this paper. It has been set aside because it presents a very different profile. Fantastic fiction describing disastrous transplants performed by malevolent "mad scientists" preceded the establishment of transplant technology; it began with Mary Shelley's *Frankenstein* (1818). Instrumental in denunciations of science that shaped American science-fiction pulp magazines, these tales were renewed in the late 1970s, using organ-theft narratives to attack the new technologies of organ transplantation. Medical thrillers—an early example is Robin Cook's *Coma*—center upon evil medical establishments and doctors. Political thrillers, very common among leftists, put the accent on the victims' condition (often they are either homeless or Third World poor). While popular fiction retains these formulas, there is a new trend—treatment of organ transplants in quality fiction.

THE NARRATIVES

Baby Parts Stories

This first cluster of stories reached the world media in early 1987 from Central America. In the Western world, these reports were limited to brief press-agency dispatches; they initially did not inspire full-length articles in the major English-language daily newspapers. However, the stories were relayed by the media of what was then the Communist bloc and by the press in developing countries.

Real cases of trafficking in children generated by the development of international adoption created an anguish-filled climate in which these stories flourished. The first four sets of accusations that reached the media involved discoveries of clandestine orphanages, called by the authorities and the Honduran media *casas de engordes* (fattening houses), a vivid expression evocative of ogres.[1] The first discoveries were made in December 1986, in Honduras's main city, San Pedro Sula, where thirteen very young children of unknown origin, kidnapped or bought from poor mothers and awaiting departure abroad for adoption, were liberated by the police. Leonardo Villela Bermúdez, secretary general of the official Honduran welfare agency JNBS [*Junta Nacional de Bienestar Social*—National Agency for Social Welfare] explained to *La Tribuna*, a Honduran daily, that foreigners pretending to adopt handicapped children for humanitarian motives were in fact selling them to be dismembered and used for organ transplants in America; he added that a child had been bought for $10,000. The article was dramatically titled "En el estrangero. Niños hondureños despezados para traficar con sus organos" [Abroad: Honduran Children Cut to Pieces for Traffic in their Organs][2] and Villela Bermúdez repeated his accusations on TV and radio. The following issue of *La Tribuna* included a denial letter from Villela Bermúdez, who explained that he had repeated to the interviewer suppositions put forward by some social workers, but without embracing them. The interviewer protested against this denial, explaining he had taped the interview, in which Villela Bermúdez clearly endorsed the accusations. A few days later Villela Bermúdez's hierarchical superior, Honduras's first lady Miriam de Azcona, honorary president of JNBS, reinforced the denial.

The second incident presented a similar structure: the February 5, 1987, discovery of fourteen children in Guatemala, eleven of them newborns; their release from the clandestine foster home where they were kept; accusations by police officer Baudillo Hichos López that these babies were to be sold abroad (for $20,000) to be butchered, their organs being used for transplant operations; and immediate denial reinforced by Hichos López's supervisors. The two cases, but not the denials, were picked up in Latin American media, and sporadically in the European press.[3] On April 5, 1987, *Pravda*'s correspondent in Mexico published an article presenting as fact that "thousands of Hondurian children were sent to the U.S. where they were used as organ donors for the children of rich families." This article was picked up by the *Tass* news agency and spread worldwide (in developing countries).

The two 1988 incidents were also very similar. In January in Guatemala, the discovery of a clandestine adoption network run by two Israelis generated accusations by policeman Miguel Aguirre (who quoted a price of $75,000 in *El Gráfico*). The policeman issued a denial the following day; it was reinforced by the U.S. and Israeli embassies, as well as by Aguirre's supervisors. In August in Paraguay, judge Angel Campos renewed the accusations while commenting on the discovery of a clandestine foster home of Brazilian babies (the price quoted for the babies was $15,000); Campos denied the accusations a few days later.

The accusations thus featured babies who were supposed to be sent abroad for adoption, asserting that they were in fact delivered to criminal clinics where they were butchered and sold as spare parts for the benefit of rich patients. The main country accused was the United States, whose dominant position in the region was close to that of a colonial power. Local middle-rank elites endorsed the assertions that a widespread murderous traffic in babies existed in their countries. While U.S. embassies and the State Department's USIA [United States Information Agency] acted fast to secure denials both from higher-level local authorities and from various U.S. agencies operating in the fields of adoption and organ transplants, these denials received far less coverage in the world media than the accusations.

Sacaojos [Eye Robbers] Stories

Sacaojos stories appeared at the end of the 1980s in big Latin American cities. The tales correspond to the widespread maltreatment of street children in countries such as Brazil, Colombia, and Peru, where homeless poor adults and street children are murdered by policemen or by militias hired by shopowners. Supported as useful policies by a vast sector of public opinion, these murders mostly go unpunished. In *Sacaojos* stories, a child is kidnapped in the street, often by Japanese or North American commandos, and released eyeless, with an ironic scribbled note ("Thank you for the eyes") in his pocket, accompanied by a ridiculously small sum of money.

Spreading through rumor, these stories usually did not reach the media, except for an isolated tale or short denials. One early short item, however, seems to be the unedited transcription of a tale just heard:

Kidnapping Children to Steal their Organs
A group of children is playing ball in a poor district of Medellin, a Colombian town at the foot of the Andes. Suddenly on the space appears a shiny Cadillac: the children stop their game, curious of this unexpected visit. From the car descend some people who, without saying a word, immobilize one of the children, carry him into the Cadillac and flee with great noises of the car's tires. The little one is back home a few days later, with a bandage and summary medication on one eye: the doctors explain that a skilled surgeon has removed his cornea. ("Rapiscono bambini per rubargli gli organi," *Corriere della Sera,* July 13, 1987.)

In Argentina, the sad story of Oscar briefly reached the world media in December 1991:

> Children Robbed of their Kidneys in Argentina
> Oscar has dark hair and a sad smile. . . . a year ago, when he was 11, he was snatched from the street, bundled into a car and whisked off to a private clinic where he was anaesthetized. . . . He was dropped off at his home, a shanty town outside Buenos Aires six weeks later with $400 (£220) in his pocket. Then he showed his mother the scar, telling her he did not feel well. It was discovered after medical checks that one of Oscar's kidneys had been removed. He had become a victim of a growing scourge in Argentina: the human organ-traffickers. . . . Such was his mother's fear that she hesitated to tell the authorities. "The same people from this town might be the ones who are handing the children over to the traffickers," she said. . . . The demand for human kidneys for transplants is so great that the traffickers can sell them for up to $45,000 each. Some organs are said to go to the United States or Europe, others to Brazil. (Maria Laura Avignolo, *Sunday Times,* December 8, 1991 and "La mafia des organes écume les bidonvilles," *Libération,* December 12, 1991.)

Persistent rumors of child kidnapping for organ theft inspired official investigations in Mexico in 1990 and 1992. These investigations identified several cases of disappearances—kidnappings—of children, but found the causes were illegal adoption or enforced prostitution, not organ theft.

Panic-rumors linked to *Sacaojos* stories spread briefly in some big Latin American cities. The best-known case was in Lima, Peru's capital, where for ten days at the end of November and the beginning of December 1988, groups of foreigners, dressed as doctors but carrying machine-guns, were said to roam the poor districts in big, shiny, black cars. These characters forced children to enter the cars and removed their eyes, releasing them with their faces hooded and the eyes bandaged, envelopes containing money and thank-you notes in their pockets. The rumor started in the El Salvador district, where four foreigners, two blacks and two whites (i.e., non-Indians) were said to have attacked a school. On the same day, November 30, 1988, the story spread to all the poor districts of the city,[4] and by 10 A.M., hundreds of parents had invaded schools and forcibly brought their children home. No bodies or mutilated kids were found and the authorities issued denials. But what was the value of such official truth compared to the words of neighbors, as the poor know that the government often lies: "Far from appeasing the population, the skeptical or ironic press articles and the solemn denial of the Health Minister on TV only exacerbate the feeling of terror: what credit is to be given to the reassuring declarations of a Minister compared to the testimony of a terrorized neighbor?" (Wachtel 1992:110). Three young French tourists barely escaped lynching in the Cantogrande district, and social workers from the Institute of Nutritional Studies specializing in the treatment of infantile diarrhea had to be protected by the police.

A few years later, novelist Mario Vargas Llosa (1996:190) recalled these panics, which his hero, the policeman Lituma, saw as a worrying symptom of the country's drop into the irrational:

> Something disturbing is happening in this country, Tomasito. . . . How can it be that a whole district of Lima swallows such a tall tale? Gringos in luxury cars, kidnapping five-year-old kids to pull out their eyes with ultra-dynamic lancets. . . . But that a whole district may believe it and that its inhabitants take their children away from school and pursue foreigners to lynch them, don't you believe this is incredible?

However, the world media largely ignored these incidents until they involved attacks on foreign tourists and scientists in Guatemala in March 1994. A surge of the by now familiar *Sacaojos* stories was noticed in the country at the end of 1993 by a good observer, an American with longstanding experience in Guatemala, John Shonder:

> In the slang of Guatemala a "bola" is a story, a rumor or a juicy piece of gossip, which purports to explain the truth behind a matter of national significance. . . . Unofficial stories, spread by word of mouth allow Guatemalans to maintain a healthy skepticism about their government. But they sometimes lead to violence, as in the case of the organ theft rumors, which lead to attacks on American citizens in two separate incidents in early 1994. . . . I first heard the story from my secretary in December of 1993 in Guatemala City. She assured me that the body of a small child had been found at the side of a road with its chest cut open and its heart and other organs missing. A note which said "Thanks for the organs" (in English of course) had been left in the chest cavity. In the next few weeks, the bodies seemed to multiply. Some people claimed that five had been found, some said seven. Other versions of the story replaced the note with U.S. currency, in amounts ranging from a few dollars to one hundred. Both the note and the money were sometimes said to have been found in the children's pants pockets instead of the chest. A completely different story concerned a street urchin found wandering around blind and dazed in Zone 1. When he was finally taken to the hospital, doctors determined that his corneas had been removed. This child's pockets had also been stuffed with American money. . . . These stories were so grotesque—and so unbelievable—that I immediately took them to be urban legends. I also reasoned that if the bodies really existed, lurid photographs would be splashed across the front page of every newspaper in the city, in full color. There is no press censorship in Guatemala. . . . The body of a child with its chest cut open would be no worse than photographs of accident victims and exhumed corpses which are published daily in *Prensa Libre, Siglo 21, El Gráfico,* and other local papers. Of course no such pictures were ever printed. (Shonder 1994:1)

On March 7, 1994, a market day in Santa Lucia Cotzemalguapa (a southern village), American tourist Melissa Larson (37, a stylist from New Mexico), accused of being a child-stealer, was arrested by the police to protect her from an angry crowd. She was transferred to a bigger town and the next day, the furious crowd (the rumor was that she had been liberated in exchange for a $36,000 bribe) burned the police station and destroyed ten cars. The army came to restore order and the riot finally caused ten casualties. Melissa Larson stayed in jail for nineteen days, before being expelled from Guatemala. The treatment of the story by sensationalist media aggravated the situation:

> The press began speculating about organ transplants. *Prensa Libre* published a chart listing various body organs and body parts along with their supposed price on the black market. One of the television stations produced a particularly irresponsible "investigative report" on the issue. The scene I recall most vividly was when the reporter went to an orphanage to investigate illegal adoptions. In a room filled with cribs and crying babies, he picked up one squirming child by the legs and asked the social worker, "How much are this one's eyes worth? His liver? His kidneys?" This program seemed to do a lot to revive the rumor. It reinforced people's beliefs, and many cited it as "proof" that babies were indeed kidnapped and killed for their organs. (Shonder 1994:1)

Ten days later, Swiss vulcanologist Thierry Stephane was slightly wounded by a crowd accusing him and the scientists with whom he was working at the volcano Acatenongo in the district of Chimaltenango of kidnapping children.[5]

The most serious incident took place on March 29, on a market day in San Cristobal Verapaz, a northeastern town. Tourist June Weinstock (52, a journalist from Alaska) took pictures and patted a child's head. Suddenly a peasant cried that her son had disappeared. A crowd assembled and started to beat up the foreigner. The child reappeared and the mother tried to stop the lynching, but in vain. Undressed and badly injured, Weinstock was saved from death by police who took her to the hospital in a comatose state. Repatriated by plane in Alaska, she had not recovered consciousness at the end of 1999. The attack was filmed and presented on television in Guatemala, and later in the United States:[6]

> The U.S. State Department issued a warning urging Americans to avoid nonessential travel to Guatemala. . . . Doctors appeared on television to explain the complicated procedures required to preserve organs for transplants, and that it was impossible for tourists to carry hearts and livers back to the United States in their luggage as some of the wilder rumors had claimed. . . . Local newspapers then began printing editorials blaming the at-

tacks and the rumors themselves on various groups. . . . Of course, as with most rumors, there was an element of truth to the organ theft stories. Children do disappear in Guatemala, and there apparently is a large trade in illegal adoptions. . . . One of the few Guatemalans I met who did not believe the rumors had this theory: he said that the country was paying the price for promoting its indigenous people as tourist attractions. . . . I think there is some truth in this. . . . Many times have I seen tourists in small villages giving candy to children, patting them on the head and filming them with video cameras. . . . There's no getting around the fact that these children are very cute, especially when dressed in colorful indigenous clothing. But I have children of my own, and I would feel very uneasy if a stranger were to touch or photograph them. Most people have sense enough not to do things like this in their own country. Indeed, I don't think many would consider going to an Indian reservation in the U.S. to photograph Native American children. We recognize that this would be patronizing, as well as an invasion of privacy. Unfortunately, some tourists who come to Guatemala seem to leave their cultural sensitivity at home. (Shonder 1994:2)

Kidney Heist Stories

Kidney Heist stories first appeared in Europe. They featured adult male tourists, honeymooners, or business travelers in the Third World. The stories vividly reported how the unhappy fellow was found wandering or lying in a hotel room after having been separated from his wife (when she went shopping or visited a museum) or from his colleagues (often because he had followed a beautiful temptress he met in a bar). He didn't know what had happened to him, was clearly not well, and had a medical checkup after he returned home. The doctors' diagnosis was unequivocal: he had had a kidney removed, and it was often stated that the scar was remarkably precise. The first printed version (February 15, 1990) was an interview in *Vestkysten,* a regional Danish daily from Jutland near the German border, in which a Lutheran pastor just returned from a Church conference in Brazil told the story:

> We heard a horrible story when we were down there. A friend of a colleague of mine had been down on the beach. When they were about to go home, one of the members of the group was missing. They immediately started to look for him, but he was gone for 24 hours before he was found on the beach, absolutely exhausted and with a stitched wound in the middle of his stomach. It turned out that he had been abducted to a hospital nearby, where one of his kidneys was snatched to be used for transplant. (Klintberg 1994:15–16)

The story appeared in Germany during the summer of 1990 and caused great concern. The mishap was said to have happened to a couple from Bremen, holidaying in Istanbul (the husband had been lost in the Bazaar and found a few days later wandering on the beach). However, after the scandal paper *Bild der Frau* reported the sad story of Luisa and Walter, a Turkish journalist checked and found that no complaint had been filed either with the police or with the German consulate in Istanbul.[7] While variants designating other locations (South America, Romania, Bulgaria) circulated, a blood donors' association advised its members not to carry their donors' cards abroad so as to make the job of kidney-nappers more difficult (Brednich 1991). Some versions involved ingenious variants, such as the story told in 1992 by a 20-year-old Swedish engineering student:

> A couple went holidaying in Brazil. While they were on the beach for a tan, a little boy asked them to sign an appeal for the movement "Save the Rain Forest." They signed. Some time later, they went in a bar by the beach for a drink. They both lost consciousness and awoke lying on an operating table. In fact, the paper they had signed had nothing to do with the rain forest. It was a consent formula saying they were ready to donate their organs for a transplant![8]

Soon First World cities were also named: New York, Las Vegas, or New Orleans for Americans, Los Angeles for Australian tourists, Paris for the Dutch and the Scandinavians. The victims also diversified and some women or children were targeted; however, men remained the most frequent victims. The stories are variations on the plot of the dangerous blonde, who lures the unsuspecting victim away from friends and tempts him with a doctored drink or a night of lust. The victim wakes up alone, missing a kidney, in the street or in a hotel room. The scar is made with surgical precision, a detail that implies the intervention of skilled professionals in the kidney removal. By March, 1991, the stories were circulating in the United States (Brunvand 1993:149–50). In the United States, the most recent versions circulate on the Internet, and often mention the victim awakening in an ice-filled bathtub, and finding scribbled instructions to dial 911. Here is an example from 1996:

> Dear Friends: I wish to warn you about a new crime ring that is targeting business travelers. This ring is well organized, well funded, has very skilled personnel, and is currently in most major cities and recently very active in New Orleans. The crime begins when a business traveler goes to a lounge for a drink at the end of the work day. A person in the bar walks up as they sit alone and offers to buy them a drink. The last thing the traveler remembers until they wake up in a hotel room bath tub, their body submerged to their neck in ice, is sipping that drink. There is a note taped to the wall instructing them not to move and to call 911. A phone is on a small table next to the bathtub for them to call. The business traveler calls 911 who have become quite familiar with this crime. The business traveler is instructed by the 911 oper-

ator to very slowly and carefully reach behind them and feel if there is a tube protruding from their lower back. The business traveler finds the tube and answers, "Yes." The 911 operator tells them to remain still, having already sent paramedics to help. The operator knows that both of the business traveler's kidneys have been harvested. This is not a scam or out of a science fiction novel, it is real. It is documented and confirmable. If you travel or someone close to you travels, please be careful.

(e-mail responses): Yes, this does happen. My sister-in-law works with a lady that this happened to her son's neighbor who lives in Houston.

Sadly, this is very true. My husband is a Houston Firefighter / EMT and they have received alerts regarding this crime ring. It is to be taken very seriously. The daughter of a friend of a fellow firefighter had this happen to her. Skilled doctors are performing these crimes! (which, by the way have been highly noted in the Las Vegas area.) Additionally, the military has received alerts regarding this. (http://www.snopes.com/horrors/robbery/kidney.htm, updated March 29, 1999.)

Kidney Heist stories are strongly linked to two quite different sets of social problems. First, social unease toward organ transplants persists, as is made clear by the refusal of about one-third of families to consent to organ removal in brain-death cases. In the late 1980s, these refusals raised stereotypical public indignation. But by the late 1990s, the facts that "some must die" (Youngner 1996), and that there is a terrible price to pay for a transplant to occur, are better appreciated by transplant specialists, who must admit that the scarcity in human body parts will remain a permanent trait of transplants, structurally linked to the rarity of brain-death conditions, rather than to relatives' refusals, which possess their legitimacy (Houssin 2000). This unease contradicts our ideology of benevolent medical care, and generates a logical conflict that largely accounts for the persistent circulation of the improbable Kidney Heist anecdotes (Campion-Vincent 1997).

Second, organ trading does occur in several Third World countries, based on "voluntary" selling of kidneys by poor local citizens, often for patients coming from foreign countries. Half the Internet page quoted above describes scandals created by sellers claiming to have been deceived and robbed of their kidneys, when they thought they were "just" selling blood, or taking tests that would procure them a coveted job. These scandals come mainly from India; they are splashed in the news deprived of all context and used for their shock value in ways that make them confusing.

All three story clusters are reinforced by the growing awareness of the traffic in human beings, for enforced labor and slavery, sexual exploitation, and prostitution. These grim realities are ageless, however, contemporary developments seem to have made them worse. The plight of children is a central concern in world opinion. Globalization has made it easy and cheap to send the exploited where they will bring the most money (thus in 1989 children from the Indian subcontinent were sent to the Middle East to work as jockeys in camel races) or to bring the exploiters to the children (the example of "sexual tourism" comes to mind, but there are numerous other cases). Spurred by NGOs and international organizations, awareness is growing, as demonstrated by such special conferences as the First Conference on the Sexual Exploitation of Children held in Stockholm in 1996.

MAIN DIFFUSION CHANNELS OF THE NARRATIVES

The great period of polemics around the reality of organ-theft narratives was 1992–96. The polemics were strongly triggered by the appearance of accusatory TV "documentaries." While the first cluster of organ-theft narratives can be situated at the junction of the realms of rumor and information, the two others clearly belong to rumor. Baby Parts stories have been used as a weapon in political debate (as more generally are other violations of human rights). NGOs dedicated to human rights adopted different strategies toward these assertions; some of them were convinced of their truth and actively promoted the tales and the "evidence." Militants, propagandists, and moral authorities have frequently made use of organ-theft narratives as a striking example of the horrors of the modern world.

Evocations of organ thefts can be indignantly descriptive or simply allusive. These two modes refer to the degree of adherence to their authenticity. While the indignant description tries to persuade, to prove the existence of alleged horrors, the allusion supposes the facts established, and refers to the stories as examples or arguments reinforcing the discourse's main point.

1992–96: TV Documentaries Create Polemics

Organ-theft narratives, or rather, unveiling the dark realities supposedly behind the narratives, became the main subject of three accusatory TV documentaries (Germany—"Organrauber. Menschen als ersatzreillanger" [Organ Thieves: Men as Spare Parts]—1992, 90 minutes; France—"Voleurs d'organes" [Organ Thieves]—1993, 60 minutes, later reduced to 40 minutes and renamed "Voleurs d'yeux" [Eye Thieves]; Great Britain and Canada—"The Body Parts Business"—1993, 60 minutes); these were widely distributed (although not in the United States due to USIA action).

The three "star examples" presented in "Voleurs d'yeux" and "The Body Parts Business" were investigated and discredited. Both films showed Pedro Reggi, whose family said that he had been blinded in an Argentinian mental asylum when he was an inmate there; in "The Body Parts

Business," Charlie Alvarado asserted that he had escaped from kidnappers in Honduras in 1993; while "Voleurs d'yeux" featured Jeison, a young blind Colombian boy. It has since been revealed that all three cases had been fabricated.

On a television show aired in Argentina on November 25, 1993, Pedro Reggi's brother publicly admitted that an infection caused Pedro's blindness and that his corneas were not missing; however, he did insist that the infection was the result of maltreatment Pedro received in the asylum (Grondona 1993.)

The Swiss consular attaché in Tegucigalpa explained that two social workers, a German and a Swiss, had been arrested after Charlie Alvarado accused them of attempted kidnapping; however, they had been cleared by the investigation and set free (Hofstetter 1994.)

And finally, Jeison's mother asserted in a very moving declaration to the TV camera that her son had been blinded by a hospital in February 1983 when he was five months old. In late 1993 and early 1994, soon after the film's release, an inquiry led by the Colombian Ombudsman proved conclusively that the blindness was the result of an infection (Colombia Defensoria 1993, 1994). But trust in the Colombian authorities is very low among the media, which may explain why no French media reported the inquiry's findings. Although the inquiry sought to cast doubt upon the mother's televised testimony by asserting that the film's director had paid her for her appearance, the argument lost its impact when it was revealed that she received an insignificant amount ($60). Furthermore, because the hospital had provided no explanation for her son's blindness in 1983, Jeison's mother was convinced in good faith that her son was the victim of medical malpractice caused, she believed, by a desire to sell the baby's eyes (Renard, Gentilini, and Fischer 1995.)

In January 1995, the shortened version, "Voleurs d'yeux," was a huge success on French TV, and the Colombians' request for insertion of a correction regarding Jeison's case was refused by the journalist in charge of the program. All the French press interviewed Marie Monique Robin, the film's passionate and convincing young writer-director, who indignantly described the campaign against the film led by the USIA (often called "the Pentagon Agency" or even "the CIA"). In May, Robin received the prestigious Albert Londres documentary prize. In August, the Colombian embassy organized the now 12-year-old Jeison's trip to France for an eye examination. Parisian medical authorities confirmed that his blindness resulted from an infection and not from criminal eye-snatching. Following publication of the medical authorities' report (Renard et al. 1995), the Albert Londres prize was suspended, but reinstated in March 1996, with an admonition urging Robin to be more careful in her assertions in the future. Ophthalmologists linked to human-rights movements continued to support the claim that Jeison's eyes had been stolen in 1983 and Robin published a book in 1996 that described the USIA's envoy as incompetent and ridiculous and the Colombian authorities (Paris embassy personnel and Bogotá doctors) as a gang of mafia characters. Titled *Voleurs d'organes. Enquête sur un trafic* [Organ Thieves: Investigation of a Traffic], the book's preface was by the president of the main French association of organ donors ADOT [*Fédération des associations pour le don d'organes et de tissus humains*]; it asserted that liberalism and the unregulated "laws of market" were the real causes of organ thefts.

A similar polemic developed in Spain in 1996 when a prize was awarded to Brazilian journalist Anna Beatrix Magno for a series published in *Correio Braziliense* (July 24–31, 1994) that treated *sacaojos* incidents and the cases of Charlie Alvarado, Pedro Reggi, and Jeison as true stories. The Spanish authorities ignored protests against this award by Spanish transplant surgeons and the U.S. embassy.

After the polemics subsided, with each side claiming victory, organ-theft narratives were no longer newsworthy. But they have not disappeared and are still widely repeated, perhaps believed, even in rich countries—thus Kidney Heist stories abound on the Internet.

Baby Parts Stories and Politics

Political forces picked up and disseminated the Baby Parts stories as a weapon against their foes. Italian radicals did not succeed in passing a 1987 European Parliament resolution concerning "traffic of children for their organs"; the project was transformed into a written question to the Commission of European Community, which denied the existence of such traffic on July 23, 1987. Later, on September 15, 1988, after more accusations from Guatemala and Paraguay had reached the media, the European Parliament, upon the motion of a French communist representative, adopted a resolution repeating the accusations against the United States and condemning "the sacrifice of children used as human spare parts." The United States protested: on September 25 and October 6, the FBI and the U.S. representative to Interpol denied the accusations; on October 8, Assistant Secretary of State William Schiffer officially protested the resolution to the European Community; and on October 21, a *New York Times* article presented the case as example of a "Soviet disinformation campaign," launching other articles debunking the story in respected European dailies such as France's reference paper *Le Monde* (October 23–24, 1988) and Germany's *Die Zeit* (October 28, 1988).

However, this denial did not kill the stories; they kept reappearing in different Latin American countries, often following some scandal concerning adoption abroad. The USIA dutifully watched and replied, encouraging high-level U.S.-inspired denials that invariably followed the assertions at the local level. The USIA also inspired denials from several U.S. agencies active in the field of organ transplantation. Several such denials, from the United Network for Organ Sharing (August 23, 1988), the FBI, the U.S. National Central Bureau (representing the United States in Interpol), and the U.S. Assistant Secretary for Health James Mason in a joint letter cosigned by U.S. Surgeon General C. Everett Koop (June 6, 1989), are listed by Todd Leventhal (1994) in a report denouncing "The Child Organ Trafficking Rumor: A Modern 'Urban Legend.'" This active stance (which characterized the United States alone—Western European countries and Israel, also frequently accused, treated the claims as "pure rumor" and did not reply to them) may have played an important role in the assertions' diffusion, as the accusations were made more visible by their very refutation.

On September 13, 1993, French representative Leon Schwartzenberg (a cancer specialist and medical celebrity who entered politics upon his retirement) presented in the European Parliament a 15-page report supporting a resolution concerning "the ban on trade in organs for transplants." This report contained passages asserting the existence of widespread criminal traffic in organs:

> Considering the recognized fact of murder and mutilations of fetuses, children and adults in some developing countries, with the aim to procure organs for transplant, exported to rich countries. . . . Illegal organized organ traffic exists just like the traffic in illicit drugs, and is often directed by the same persons. This traffic is still more monstrous when it rests upon the killing of live persons so as to take their organs sold with profit. To deny the existence of this monstrous traffic is similar to the denial of the crematoriums or the gas chambers of the last war. (Schwartzenberg 1993:5, 11)

Schwartzenberg's source, which he defended when replying to a reader's letter attacking his unproven accusations, was "Enquête sur une abomination. Enlèvements d'enfants et trafics d'organes" [Investigation into an Abomination: Children's Kidnappings and Trafficking in Organs], an article published in the August 1992 issue of the strongly leftist monthly *Le Monde Diplomatique*, always keen on attacking the United States and "World Capitalism" as *the* sources of our planet's woes. The article's author was Maïté Pinero, who thus found a much wider audience (the monthly had 125,000 subscribers) and more creditable forum than in her usual outlets, the communists' *L'Humanité* (daily) and *Viva* (monthly).

NGOs and Organ-theft Narratives

The Baby Parts and *Sacaojos* stories, and the scandals linked to international adoption, drew the attention of NGOs specializing in the defense of human rights in the Third World, admittedly a daunting task. The major NGOs, such as Amnesty International, Defense of Children International (DCI), and Human Rights Watch, examined the evidence, found it weak, and at the central level issued no endorsement of the assertions. However, some local delegates were less cautious and issued statements supporting the assertions, both in France (Amnesty's Jean-Claude Alt made public declarations supporting the reality of organized organ thefts during the 1995 polemics) and in Holland (DCI's Stan Meuwesse declared: "The accepted facts and figures about child abuse are so overwhelming that this has to be true too" [Burger 1996]).

Other NGOs, such as FIDH [*Fédération internationale des droits de l'homme*], switched position between 1988 and 1992, first denying and later supporting the assertions. In 1988, FIDH sponsored an inquest in Guatemala by lawyer Alain Feder and judge Antoine Garapon. Their report concluded that while an important traffic in children did exist, supplying illegal adoptions that involved buying or kidnapping babies,[9] no proof of organ traffic was found (Feder and Garapon 1988). In 1992, FIDH (together with other associations such as ACAT [*Association des chrétiens contre la torture*] and CIMADE [*Comité inter-mouvements auprès des évacués*] that since 1990 were researching children's disappearances in Latin America) collaborated with Marie-Monique Robin; an ophthalmologist linked to FIDH examined her film's rushes and endorsed the accusations: yes, Pedro Reggi and Jeison, shown in the Argentina and Colombia sequences, had been deprived of their corneas.

NGOs strongly influenced by communism, such as IADL [International Association of Democratic Lawyers], endorsed the assertions and repeatedly, but unsuccessfully, presented them at the yearly session of the Human Rights Commission of the U.N. in Geneva, and especially to the Working Group on the Contemporary Forms of Slavery. From 1990 to 1994 the Working Group's Special Rapporteur on the Sale of Children, Thailand's Vitit Muntarbhorn, gave increasing prominence and credence to the reality of organ thefts in his successive reports. But he did not convince his colleagues and resigned in late 1994. It is most probable that diplomatic action, overt in the case of the United States or the accused Latin American countries, and covert in the case of most Western Europe countries, caused Muntarbhorn's resignation.

The fourth volume of a multivolume series, titled *Criminalité économique et atteintes à la dignité de la personne* [Economic Crime and Attacks on Human Dignity] coedited by French and Chinese international law professors and published simultaneously in France and China, made reference to *Les trafics d'organes* [Organ trafficking] in a six-page section that quoted as proven the allegations of IADL, Vitit Muntarbhorn, and Maïté Pinero (but making no allusions to China's use of executions as a source for organ transplants) (Delmas-Marty and Gao 1997:178–83) . However, these allegations were not repeated in the fifth volume of conclusions.

A Perfect Example of the Horrors
of the Modern World

For militants and propagandists, organ-theft narratives offer a perfect, striking argument to support their causes. People from very different perspectives resort to this emblematic use, including Swiss militant antivivisectionists, an American feminist academic, and an Iranian social-science academic established in Germany.

In December 1993, the antivivisectionist Swiss bulletin *Orrizonti. Courrier de l'Antivivisection* denounced the "Traffic in Children's Organs" as a perfect example of the misdeeds of the enemy—biological medicine: "What is happening could not exist but for the complicity of surgeons, doctors, paramedical personnel and health authorities. It demonstrates clearly vivisectionist madness." The paper's conclusion totally conflates vivisection, the animal thefts said to accompany it, and theft of children's organs:

> A cat resting in the sun on a window ledge disappears, a dog attached by its leash to the door of a commercial mall vanishes, these are daily facts in Switzerland; in South America people disappear as well as animals. . . . The fate of these people is "vivisection", just like the destiny of animals for which we fight daily. Men and animals are victims of the same criminal mentality, that must be eradicated, the mentality that sets rules for vivisection instead of abolishing it. It is a proof that vivisection upon animals inevitably leads to vivisection upon humans.

A professor of women's studies and medical ethics, Janice Raymond's credentials as an academic are impeccable. Her book attacking "reproductive technologies" brings the reader into a militant universe where truth is secondary compared to the author's fight against her enemy—the new reproductive technologies: "This book is a challenge to reproductive liberalism, including its feminist variety. It is positioned against the liberal consumer movement that supports new reproductive technologies and contracts. . . . The new reproductive technologies represent an appropriation by male scientific experts of the female body, depoliticizing reproduction and motherhood by recasting these roles as fundamental instincts that must be satisfied" (Raymond 1994:xii, xix). Seeking examples of the perversity of reproductive technologies, Raymond approaches the allegations of organ theft. The question mark that ends her subtitle "A New Reproductive Traffic: Children for Organ Export?" is purely formal; the author repeats the most extreme claims with total conviction. When she talks of disinformation, she means the USIA's denials; Raymond also rejects the interpretations of academics[10] who linked the Baby Parts stories to the violence and poverty reigning in Latin America, but did not accept them as true:

> It makes just as much sense to view the allegations of organ trafficking as very much related to these factors: the widespread sexual and reproductive exploitation of women and children; the extensive traffic in adoption that is acknowledged by all governments in Latin America and by many in the West; the ravaging of indigenous resources and the culture of abject poverty; the disappearances and medical mutilation of children that occur every day; and the abandonment of children. These conditions confirm the need to view child organ trafficking not as distinct from but as part of the overall organized structure of the varied sexual and reproductive trafficking in women and children worldwide. (Raymond 1994:167)

French law bans commercial arrangements concerning surrogate motherhood, as well as the sale of sperm or human tissues, so Raymond's attack on such arrangements in the United States may seem valid as they uphold a principle widely recognized in Europe: totally banning commercial use of the human body. However, her endorsement of the most extreme allegations and her acceptance of partisan sources (IADL's Renée Bridel is thanked for her contribution to the book) weakens her credibility.[11]

In August, 1995, *Echo of Islam*, a newsletter of Islamic Iranian propaganda, published a multipart article by a professor of social economics (Ravasani 1995). An editorial titled "Decadence Devours the Guardians of Human Rights" described the article: "The dimensions of the novel western industry of dealing in human organs, children, women, human blood, hazardous pharmaceuticals, armaments, narcotics and toxic waste. . . . The following article is but a fraction of the information regarding this demoniac market" (Ravasani 1995:9–10). All extremisms are similar, and in this poorly printed and spelled document, one finds the same extreme statements as in the slick, secular, anticapitalist *Monde Diplomatique*, mixing the facts of traffic in human beings, alas not to be denied; the realities of the organ trade, systematically presented as theft; and the fables of diverted adoption (Baby Parts) and of street mutilations (*Sacaojos)*. The parts of the article that deal with the market in human organs and children are full of the most extreme assertions, rarely quoting sources except unpublished reports (unreferenced except for the IADL's 1988 document) and undated articles from the German or the Italian press:

> The charity institution which so kindly collects the homeless kids, is a supplier of body parts, in a fresh and warm state. . . . Most kidnapped Brazilian children are sent to Europe, so that there, under secure conditions and without haste, they are vivisected, their fresh body parts offered for sale piece by

piece.... An Italian newspaper accused Italy of having smuggled 5000 Brazilian children for the use of their body organs, alleging that the Napolitan Mafia Organization "Camoro" organizes the smuggling of children from Brazil, Honduras, Guatemala and Mexico. (Ravasani 1995:11–12, 15)

Moral authorities also endorse or allude to the existence of organ thefts to reinforce their message. As representative of the Brazilian Catholic bishops' conference, Paul Barruel, a religious of the Dominican order and professor of theology, in 1991 sent the U.N.'s Commission on Human Rights a report (mostly drawn from Brazilian daily papers that reported *Sacaojos*-type stories) titled "Assassinatos de crianças. Tráfico de bebês e de organos infantis" [Murders of Children: Traffic in Babies and Children's Organs].[12] The report requested an investigation, but its quotations from Brazilian daily papers were later picked up and attributed to the respected theologian, especially by Maïté Pinero in her influential *Le Monde Diplomatique* article (already discussed.)

Even the Pope alluded to organ thefts in 1994, during a trip in Brazil. He mentioned "the terrifying trade in their organs" in passing in a speech that courageously denounced the violence perpetrated against street children, but whose main subject was the denunciation of abortion: "John-Paul II has denounced Thursday, with indignant words, the murders of children, the exploitation to which they are submitted and the terrifying trade in their organs. ... The pope has denounced 'the brutal massacre of street children, the prostitution to which they are submitted, and the trade of organizations that sell organs for transplants.'"[13]

In 1995, a leaflet by a donors' association aiming to popularize the adoption of organ donors' cards in France accepted the idea of organized organ thefts in Latin America, embedding this recognition within a discourse that stressed the excellence of France's national system:

Question: Is there traffic in organs?
Answer: Traffic in organs does not exist in France. Thanks to the principle of free access to medical care, to the controlled organization and distribution of explanted organs, to the habilitation of explant and transplant centers, the French system is free from risks of traffic. Such is unhappily not the case in some countries where there is a trade in organs and even explanting from the living of essential organs. One of the most unbearable examples being that of the explanting of children's eyes in Latin America.[14]

ORGAN-THEFT NARRATIVES IN THE LATE 1990s

Organ-theft narratives still circulate, but they are increasingly viewed as unsubstantiated rumors. When the possibility of organized organ thefts arises in the quality media, it is in relation to other topics—violence linked to the maltreatment of dependents, kidnappings (successful or failed), lynching caused by fear of kidnapping, or claims of medical corruption. The idea that the narratives describe actual crimes seems to be totally discredited among political authorities and within the medical world. Thus, I found no recent examples of their use by militants or propagandists. U.S. political authorities have modified their strategy and no longer crusade against organ-theft narratives, but they recognize the legitimacy of concerns about the continuing traffic in human beings, a topic they practically ignored and left to militants ten years ago.

An Example of Treatment in the Quality Media

In a lengthy article, "The International Organ Traffic," in the *New York Review of Books*, medical ethicist David Rothman (1998:16) mentioned—and firmly dismissed—organ-theft tales:

> Medical realities make such kidnapping and murder highly unlikely. . . . However rapacious health care workers may seem, highly trained and medically sophisticated teams of surgeons, operating nurses, anesthesiologists, technicians and blood transfusers are not likely to conspire to murder for organs or accept them off the street. Had they done so, at least one incident would have come to light during the past fifteen years.

However, when the quality weekly *Courrier International* translated Rothman's article, the piece was accompanied by fairly ghoulish illustrations and sidebar stories about disturbing "news" concerning the organ trade. The items concerning organ thefts were labeled "rumor" ("Asia, Rumors, When Organized Crime Steals Your Kidneys" [an article from Pakistan that recounted a Kidney Heist story set in Australia]; "Albania, Somalia, Rumors of a Traffic in Spare Parts?" [discussed allegations presented in 1997 to the U.N. Commission on Human Rights in Geneva of a traffic in adoptions from Somalia, children being butchered, the unconfirmed announcement that a boy had been found with a missing kidney, acknowledging that other such allegations had been repeatedly disproved, quoting mostly Italian cases]). It seems these additions somewhat contradict Rothman's message: while the titles presenting organ-theft tales spoke of rumors, the illustrations and the sidebar stories probably strengthened the very suspicions the main article was trying to fight. Still, this coverage suggests that organ-theft narratives no longer receive great credence.

Recent Cases in Egypt and the Philippines

Similarly, organ thefts are sometimes offered as explanations in discussions of social problems, but they are no longer featured prominently. In

Egypt, in 1999, deaths due to neglect in an orphanage led to an official inquiry, after members of parliament linked to the ruling party filed a complaint stating that 25 children who had died in an orphanage (located in
Minufiya, 37 miles northwest of Cairo) had been killed for profit and their
body parts sold to hospitals for transplants.[15] Follow-up press coverage
blamed the deaths on neglect and embezzlement by the former orphanage's directors; according to a lawyer: "There was no evidence that the children of the two closed orphanages were actually killed and cut up for their
organs. . . . But they lived in the most appalling conditions imaginable with
no blankets, no care, no medicine and very little food. . . . They just died
because no one lifted a finger to look after them."[16] Still, the parliamentarians' complaint about organ thefts was understandable in the context of
Egypt, a country where the organ trade, with "voluntary" donors, exists
and has generated scandals:

> The sophistication of Cairo's ghoulish black market in body parts, particu-
> larly kidneys, was revealed in the paper *Al Ittiyad,* which disclosed that the
> Egyptian doctors' syndicate is cracking down on members involved in the
> macabre traffic. Each of the latest cases involved an organ from an Egyptian
> being transplanted into a foreigner for vast sums of money. In one case, the
> donor was paid 12,000 Egyptian pounds (£2,500) while the doctor received
> 100,000 Egyptian pounds. Under Egyptian law transplants are forbidden
> from Egyptians to non-Egyptians, but to overcome this, one princess from an
> oil-rich Arab country entered into a mock marriage contract with her donor.
> Other recipients of illegal kidneys in recent operations were identified only
> as an Arab businessman and a highly placed African official.[17]

In the Philippines, the triggering event was a failed abduction. When,
on January 13, 2000, it was reported that three adolescent girls had escaped
from kidnappers who had been keeping them in a warehouse with up to
50 other children, organized organ theft was offered as one explanation:
"Local officials here strongly suspect that the syndicate kidnapping children is involved either in pedophilia or in selling human organs abroad."[18]

Lynching Suspected Child Kidnappers
in Guatemala

In the Central American countries where the Baby Parts stories originated, there is evidence that fears about child kidnapping are still vivid.
There is probably good reason for this, as kidnapping (of adults and children) is not rare in these countries. Lynchings of suspected child kidnappers occur in Mexico or Guatemala, underreported when the victims are
nationals.[19] The most recent case in Guatemala involved a foreign victim,
and generated several press articles.[20] On April 30, 2000, a Japanese tourist

visiting the colorful Saturday market in the Mayan town of Todos Santos Cuchumán, in northern Guatemala, was killed when the tourists' bus was attacked by a mob branding the group as child thieves. In this case, the organ-theft motive was only briefly mentioned: "A rumour that kidnappers were stealing children to use their hearts in satanic rituals" was given prominence as an explanation by the town's mayor: "[Mayor] Mendoza said many neighbours were feeling 'nervous' that day after a local radio reported that a satanic cult had rented the town's municipal gymnasium over the weekend to carry out their bloody rites. 'This is an illiterate community and people believe in rumours. Many schools remained closed for days and women stopped venturing out of their homes.'"[21] This rumor-panic may reflect the influence of American fundamentalists, often themselves fearful of satanists, who have made numerous converts among Indian communities in Guatemala.[22]

This panic was not that different in substance from the episodes described in American communities in the 1980s (Victor 1989, 1991), although no lynchings were recorded in the American rumor-panics. This lynching needs to be placed in the general violent context of Guatemala where: "Mob justice is frequent in outlying Guatemalan towns: last year there were 71 lynching by vigilantes."[23]

Italian Controversy Accusing Doctors of Unethical Practices in Transplants

In 1999, the Italian press extensively reported on the accusations of Vito di Cosmo that he had sold a kidney in 1997 to settle his debts. (Indicted, the recipient acknowledged having given di Cosmo money after the transplant, but solely as an expression of gratitude, and categorically denied having "bought" a kidney. Di Cosmo had approached him saying he wanted to give his kidney to fulfill a vow made to the Madonna who had restored his mother's health.[24]) Magistrates from Turin indicted several persons and seized the medical files for 15 transplant operations from nonkin living donors over the previous ten years (more than 600 transplant operations took place during the same period). The press reported that another angry donor claimed he had received less than promised for his kidney, and relayed the complaints of surgeons who strongly resented being treated as criminals upon the assertions of shady characters. No further judicial action occurred, and the subject totally disappeared from the press, probably after the complaints were dismissed. However it is not impossible that a receiver and a "donor," after a private financial arrangement, fooled both the magistrates (who must approve such donations) and the doctors. All the suspect cases came from the South, where postmortem donations are extremely rare. Northern surgeons in Milan suggested that all operations between nonkin be banned, as was the practice in their city, adding that they also refused the gift of a kidney from a spouse if the two had not been married at least three years, so as to avoid marriages of convenience.

Traffic in Human Beings Legitimized as an Official Area of Concern

The USIA's crusade against the organ thefts allegations is truly a thing of the past. In the State Department's new terminology, since October 1999 the agency has been renamed *International Information Programs*; it maintains web pages[25] that ignore organ-theft accusations, except in their archival sections. But the subject of "Trafficking in Human Beings," strongly linked to the appearance of organ-theft allegations, is today recognized as important and legitimate, which was far from being the case ten years ago. Thus, the U.N. Special Rapporteur on the Sale of Children, Vitit Muntarbhorn, is still quoted, without any mention of his erroneous endorsement of the reality of organ-theft narratives.

Floating Myths and Parodies

What happens to outmoded rumors that are no longer fashionable? Having lost their capacity to raise indignation, they drop from the public debate, no longer interesting. Talking about them is passé, bringing devalued goods to the information market. Still, they have not died, but have become "floating myths" (Morin 1969) that survive as themes in parodies and popular fiction. Parodies show disbelief. Consider recent Internet parodies that include Kidney Heist stories as part of an ensemble of motifs generally recognized as unbelievable by the cool and clever types who use such texts to make fun of the ridiculous beliefs of the stupid and not up-to-date:

> Help! Craig Furr, a six-year-old British boy with a brain tumor, wanted to go to Disney World before he died. After the trip, as his parents were checking out of the hotel, they noticed they'd been charged $2,500 for chocolate chip cookies from room service. While they were arguing over the bill, a gang of kidney thieves kidnapped Craig and spirited him away through Disney World's tunnels. The kidnappers put a wig on his head (which was hairless from chemotherapy) and dressed him as a girl, but luckily, a sharp-eyed security guard noticed Craig's old-fashioned side-lacing British shoes. The hotel, though, is suing Craig's parents for the $2,500, and unless they can get enough e-mail sent to santa@northpole.org in the next month to win the Guinness Book of World Records's prize contest, they will lose their house! [Wallich 1998]

ORGAN-THEFT NARRATIVES IN THE REALM OF FICTION

Popular fiction has made extensive use of organ-theft narratives, usually as examples of elites (mostly medical) plotting against the common good. Fantastic literature, predating the existence of organ transplants, includes tales that center upon hubris-driven "mad scientists," presented as belonging to a proud oligarchy that views normal people as material for experiments, and is ready to try anything to achieve its goals (generally immortality.) Mary Shelley's *Frankenstein* (1818) was merely the first of several tales that acquired classic status.[26] In these tales, a conspiracy of evil elites supplements and enriches the basic theme of the dangers of science. The mad scientists theme inspired several stories in the science-fiction pulp magazines of the 1920s to the 1950s and strongly influenced the development of the alien abduction mythology (Meurger 1996).

The evil scientists' experiments often involve grafts that have catastrophic consequences: the creature built from cadaver pieces by Baron Frankenstein receives a stupid and criminal brain; the pianist hero of the *Mains d'Orlac* [Hands of Orlac], a 1924 film by Robert Wiene (drawn from a 1920 French novel by Maurice Renard), receives the hands of a murderer, almost driving the unhappy recipient to murder until he discovers that the murderer was in fact innocent. In the 1965 novel *Et mon tout est un homme* [And the Whole Makes a Man], a beheaded murderer ensures his survival through a succession of grafts effected with the active partnership of a criminal surgeon. Many movies exploited mad scientists themes, including multiple adaptations from the classic texts and original scripts such as *Les yeux sans visage* [The Eyes Without a Face], a classic "poetical fantasy and perverse fable concerned with creation and scientific hubris,"[27] in which a bright but mad surgeon sends his assistant-mistress to kidnap young girls in Paris, and tries (unsuccessfully) to graft their faces upon his daughter's scarred visage (his recklessness caused the car accident that disfigured her). The end is tragic: the daughter, shown with an impressive white mask hiding her disfigured features, commits suicide when she understands her father's crimes, and the mad surgeon is devoured by the wolf-dogs upon which he experimented.

Among the modern thrillers using organ-theft intrigues, the medical thrillers focus upon the evil medical establishment, while political thrillers center on the victims. The medical thriller is a prolific genre, extremely formulaic, in which doctors' greed drives individuals or organizations to murder their patients. Organ thefts are only one form these evils take, but greed and murder are always present. Robin Cook's best-known organ-theft novel is *Coma* (1977) adapted by Michael Crichton for a 1978 movie: a big hospital systematically induces comas during surgeries involving young patients who are potentially good organ sources. In Europe, several TV debates about organ transplants have quoted excerpts from the movie's two "mythical" moments: when the courageous heroine discovers that the futuristic room, where comatose patients are kept suspended by light wires and seem to float magically, is really a market place with elegant nurses conducting auctions in which Zurich and Montevideo compete for fresh hearts or lungs; and when Dr. Harris, the hospital's director and traffic organizer, explains that the future of medicine lies in the exploitation of man as merchandise. Several other medical thrillers present medical conspiracies to steal organs (*Les maîtres de la vie* [Masters of Life], Paul-Loup Sulitzer, France, 1996) or direct available organs exclusively toward the rich (*Harvest*, Tess Gerritsen, United States, 1997).

Several categories of victims appear in political thrillers using organ theft intrigues. Plots involving minorities as victims resemble the fantastic mad scientists genre: African-Americans in Chicago are pricked with poisonous syringes by a gang of organ traffickers ("The Needle Men," George M. M. Martin, United States, 1981); Third World medical students are induced into comas by the hospital where they study ("Clinical Deaths," Paul Wilson, United States, 1994); or the Portuguese employees of a health clinic are killed to rejuvenate the patients (*Traitement de choc* [Shock Treatment], Alain Jessua, France, 1972, movie).[28]

The other political thrillers try to be realistic and plausible: kidnap victims are Mexican children in Los Angeles (*Dirty Business*, Zacharias, United States, 1989, movie); or homeless adults in the United States (*Sonata for Solo Organ*, Morgenstern, United States, 1991, movie); or South America (*Le rallye des Incas*, Marc Eisenchterer, France, 1995). Several tales paraphrase the Baby Parts texts, showing Latin American children brought to the United States or Europe under the guise of adoption and murdered for their organs (*Donor*, Tomas Ross, Netherlands, 1989; *Une vie de rechange* [A Life in Exchange], François Salvaing, France, 1991; *Pièces détachées* [Spare Parts], Gérard Delteil, France, 1993; *L'enfant d'Arturo* [Arturo's Child], Paul Planchon, France, 1995, movie).

Authors of political thrillers present themselves as social commentators and their novels generally contain passages stressing the realities corresponding to the intrigues presented. *Organ Hunters* (Thomas 1994:389–90), a fairly extravagant novel featuring a gang of ex-*Stasi* that kill all over the world to procure organs for mafia types, includes a 10-page afterword that begins:

> This novel is rooted in fact. . . . I have acquired a substantial file of well-documented reports of the steps wealthy patients take to try to bypass the ever-lengthening lists of those waiting for transplants. . . . Time and again I received reports of "fattening houses" in Latin America, where undernour-

ished street children and young adults are nursed back to health so that their organs are healthy enough to be removed for transplanting. There were reports about private clinics in India, Thailand and the Philippines, as well as Central America, where such transplants are performed. There were accounts of mercenary pilots in the Pacific Rim and Central America who ferry organs from one site to another.

Prelude to a Scream presents a Kidney Heist story: after a bar encounter with a seductress, its alcoholic hero, Stanley, awakens in the middle of the Golden Gate Bridge, missing a kidney. A detective tells him:

> Right now, your kidney is in Cairo, or perhaps Calcutta, Hong Kong, Geneva or Beverly Hills. It might even be in Redwood City. . . . There are clinics, from Cairo to Zurich, from Bombay to Rio, where one can receive any organ, no questions asked. One can also have them taken away. It is equally possible to have them turned upside down, exchanged, steamed up clean, modified. One's heroin-saturated blood can be emptied and replaced by newborn's blood, one can receive bone marrow taken from ghetto children who are sold by their parents. Livers, eyes, hearts transplants. . . . The supply of replacement human organs will never meet demand. (Nisbet 1997:111–14).

The treatment of organ transplants and of organ thefts is more diversified in quality fiction. *Central do Brasil* [Central Station] (Walter Salles, Brazil, 1998, movie) alludes to organized organ thefts as one trait of Brazilian society. The selfish heroine very reluctantly takes in a young boy whose mother has been killed in a bus accident. To buy herself a new TV, she coolly sells him to a gang of organ traffickers, then feeling remorse, she returns to the apartment where she'd delivered him and successfully spirits him away. The rest of the movie shows the mutual transformation of these two loners during their trip through Brazil, in quest of the boy's father.

Spanish author-director Pedro Almodovar has twice explored the ambiguities of the medical coordinator, whose job is to convince the brain-dead's relatives to consent to an organ transplant.[29] In *Flor de mi secreto* [Flower of My Secret] (1995), the heroine participates in a role-playing session for doctors and acts the racist mother, who agrees to donate her brain-dead son's organs, "but not for an Arab." In the opening of *Todo sobre mi madre* [Everything about My Mother] (1999), the heroine, a medical coordinator, has to consent to a heart removal for transplant from her only son, killed in a car accident. In a touching scene, she sneaks into the hospital, but she cannot bring herself to speak to the organ recipient.

In Emmanuel Carrère's "La classe de neige" [Class Trip] (1995, 1998), young Nicolas lives in fear, with anguished fantasies haunted by organ traffickers. This talented short-fiction writer unveils the hero's secrets: he knows that his father, a salesman, is always away traveling, that they have recently moved in haste, and that there is strong tension between his parents. His father drives him to his winter class trip in the mountains, then drives away. Nicolas recalls a trip to EuroDisney, when his father convinced him that murderous gangs work there, kidnapping, mutilating, and killing children. When a young boy disappears from a neighboring village, Nicolas thinks he alone knows the truth: it must be the organ traffickers. Then he discovers the truth, closer to him and worse: the rapist who has murdered the young boy is his own father. Here the organ-theft narratives are the metaphor of real evil: the sadistic child killer who represents absolute evil in contemporary society.

THE FUTURE OF ORGAN-THEFT STORIES

As recent examples from around the world suggest, floating myths can be updated and revived by triggering events. Thus, early twentieth-century anti-Semitic claims about white slavery experienced a full, but brief, revival in 1969 in the French city of Orléans (Morin 1969). But such revivals are short-lived, and the rumor will not redevelop fully until a really new form emerges. Thus, several elements of white-slavery stories have been revived in organ-theft narratives. Probably tomorrow will bring a new ensemble—yet to be born—that will incorporate organ-theft narratives.

ACKNOWLEDGMENTS

The author thanks heartily those who sent her useful information, and especially Mark Glazer, Joe Goodwin, Jean-François Mayer, Frank Périgny, Jean-Luc Rivera, Bernard Strainchamp and correspondents from the "Mauvais Genres" web group (mauvaisgenres@club.voila.fr [popular fictions]), and Paolo Toselli.

NOTES

1.   Numerous folktales feature children fighting ogres (Folktales Types AA&T 327) such as "Grimm's Hansel and Gretel," in which the children are abandoned in the forest by their parents, captured in the gingerbread house, and the boy put in a cage by the witch-ogress to be fattened before the cannibal witch eats him.

2.   Danilo D. Antúnez, *La Tribuna* (January 2, 1987).

3.   *Volkskrant* (Holland—March 7, 1987); *Nin* (Yugoslavia—March 15, 1987).

4.   In 1982, the city had 5,258,000 inhabitants, roughly 25 percent of the country's population.

5.   Gianluca Bevilacqua. "'E'una mercante di bambini': linciata Morente un'a-mericana in Guatemala." *La Stampa*, March 3, 1994, Estero, 9; Martine Jacot. "Folles rumeurs sur des rapts d'enfants." *Le Monde*, April 15, 1994.

6.   On August 17, 1994, in NBC's news program *Now: FOAFTale News*, 35 (1994):3.

7.   Belkis Kiliçkaya "Alman 'kuyrukluyalan'" [Theft of German Kidneys]. *Milliyet*, September 10, 1990.

8.   Bengt af Klintberg, personal communication, December 16, 1992.

9.   Several cases of kidnapping were vividly described in the report, pages 10–13. The zeal with which the military police, seeking to improve its image after the troubles of the 1980s, raided illegal foster-homes (five during 10 days in June 1988) was also stressed, pages 8 and 15.

10.   Schepper-Hughes (1990), Palmer (1991), and Chomsky (1990, 1991) .

11.   Raymond exposed her belief in the existence of organized traffic in children's organs as she was interviewed for "Voleurs d'organes," the long version of the French TV "documentary."

12.   Geneva July–August, 1991. Quoted by Sgänger 1994:326.

13.   "Le pape dénonce les massacres et le commerce des enfants" [The Pope Denounces Massacres and Trade in Children]. *AFP Agence France Presse*, 22 décembre 1994. See also: Marco Politi. "Wojtyla a San Pietro lezione di democrazia." [Wojtyla in Saint Peter: Lessons of Democracy]. *La Repubblica*, 23 décembre 1994.

14.   "Dossier sur le don d'organes." *ADOSEN. Bulletin trimestriel d'information* n 111, juillet 1995.

15.   *AFP (Agence France Presse)*, *Reuters*, March 16, 1999; *Independent*, March 18, 20, 1999.

16.   Christopher Walker, "Egypt's Orphans Saved from Butchers," *Independent* (March 20, 1999).

17.   Ibid. A situation not very different—although of course Eygpt is much smaller—from that of India, where legislation introduced on the advice from doctors at the federal level in 1994 is being discussed during the course of its adoption by the different Indian states. The aim of this legislation is to control foreign patients, and replace the organ trade with a "cadaver program," which was still to be implemented in 1999.

18.   *Philippine Star Online* (January 13, 14, 2000) .

19.   *Associated Press*, March 27, 1998. The lynching occurred in Huejutla (state of Hidalgo); the two dead truck drivers were said to have tried to kidnap four girls aged 4 to 12.

20.   "Mob Kills Tourist, Bus Driver," *New York Times* (April 30, 2000); *Japan Times* (May 2, 3, 2000); "Two die as mob attacks Japanese tour group," *Independent* (May 2, 2000); *Asahi Shimbun* (May 1, 2000); "Satanic Rites Rumors Linked to Guatemala Attack," *Reuters* (May 4, 2000).

21.   *Reuters* (May 4, 2000).

22.   Anthropologists emphasize that conversion enables an enterprising individual to escape the yoke of community redistribution through the network of honorary (and costly) cargas (position) linked to religion.

23.   *Independent* (May 2, 2000).

24. This motive, incredible in a Northern secular environment, is a good indicator of the Italian South's "difference."

25. Cf. http://usinfo.state.gov/homepage.htm; http://usinfo.state.gov/global/traffic

26. *Dr. Jekyll and Mr. Hyde* (R. L. Stevenson, 1885) and *The Island of Dr. Moreau* (H. G. Wells, 1896) come to mind.

27. Philip French, *Observer*, April 30, 1995. The movie's writer-director was Georges Franju (1960).

28. Also very conspiratorialist was the early movie *Fleisch* [Flesh] (Rainer Erler, Germany, 1979), in which the gang capturing foreign tourists in New Mexico delivers their captives to the Roswell (yes!) airbase hospital, receiving $2,000 for each delivery made with the catch phrase, "I'm bringing meat for Dr. Jackson."

29. "Aiming to develop kidneys' grafts, far less costly than dialyses, Spain has set in hospitals since the early nineties a highly professionalized organization of organ procurement, dedicating doctors and nurses exclusively to this task. Efficiency of the accounting of brain-death conditions, strong motivation and efficient training of medical personnel interacting with the deceased's relatives have had spectacular consequences: in the whole world, the Spanish model is favorably discussed" (Houssin 2000:258).

REFERENCES

Brednich, Rolf Wilhelm. 1991. "Unfreiwillige Organspende" [Unwilling Organ Gift]. Pp. 77–80 in *Die Maus im Jumbo-Jet* [The Mouse in the Jumbo Jet]. München: C.H. Beck.

Brunvand, Jan Harold. 1993. *The Baby Train.* New York: Norton.

Burger, Peter. 1996. "Organ Snatchers," *Magonia* 56 (June):3–7, 23. (First published in *Wetenschap, Cultur en Samenleving*, April 1995).

Campion-Vincent, Véronique. 1997. Organ Theft Narratives." *Western Folklore* 56:1–37.

Carrère, Emmanuel. 1995, 1998. *La classe de neige.* Paris, POL; *Two Tales: Class Trip/ The Mustache.* New York, H. Holt.

Chomsky, Noam. 1990. "Victors I." *Z Magazine* 3 (November):15.

———. 1991. "Victors II." *Z Magazine* 4 (January):10.

Colombia. Defensoria del Pueblo and Delgado Sánchez, Fabio. 1993. *Eléments d'enquête* [Elements of Investigation]. Defensoria del Pueblo, December 27.

Colombia. Defensoria del Pueblo and Pinzon Rincon, Alejandro. 1994. *Rapport du Défenseur délégué à la Santé et la Sécurité Sociale* [Report of the Delegate to Health and Social Security]. Defensoria del Pueblo, February 4.

Delmas-Marty, Mirelle, and Gao Mingxuan. 1997. *Criminalité économique et atteintes à la dignité de la personne.* Vol 4 *Institutions internationales.* Paris: Maison des Sciences de l'Homme.

Feder, Alain, and Antoine Garapon. 1988. *Enquête sur un éventuel trafic d'organes d'enfants* [Investigation on an Eventual Traffic in Children's Organs]. Paris: FIDH.

Grondona [TV Talk Show Host]. 1993. *Hora Clave.* Argentina, November 25.

Hofstetter Münger, Barbara. 1994. "Trafic d'organes d'enfants: que font les organisations internationales?" Travail de recherche, Lausanne: IDHEAP, Institut des hautes études en administration publique, September.

Houssin, Didier. 2000. *L'aventure de la greffe* [The Adventure of Grafts]. Paris: Denoel.

Klintberg, Bengt af. 1994. *Den Stulna Njuren. Sagner och rykten i var tid* [The Wandering Kidney: Legends of our Time]. Stockholm: Norstedts.

Leventhal, Todd. 1994. "The Child Organ Trafficking Rumor: A Modern 'Urban Legend.'" Report submitted to the United Nations Special Rapporteur on the Sale of Children, Child Prostitution and Child Pornography (December). United States Information Agency:40–41.

Meurger, Michel. 1996. "Surgeons from Outside." Pp.308–21 in *Fortean Studies*, Vol. 3, edited by Steve Moore. London: John Brown.

Morin, Edgar. 1969. *La Rumeur d'Orléans.* Paris: Le Seuil. (Published in English in 1971 as *Rumour in Orléans* [Pantheon Books]).

Nisbet, Jim. 1997. *Prelude to a Scream.* New York: Carroll and Graf.

Palmer, Louise. 1991. "Baby Parts Myth Explained." *New Directions for Women* (March):12–92.

Raymond, Janice. 1994. *Women as Wombs: Reproductive Technologies and the Battle over Women's Freedom.* New York: Harper San Francisco.

Ravasani, Shahpour. 1995. "The International Market of Human Life." *Echo of Islam* 134 (August):8–30 [Editorial :8–10] .

Renard, Gilles, Marc Gentilini, and Alain Fischer. 1995. "Rapport d'examen de l'enfant Wenis Yeison Cruz Vargas." Paris: Assistance Publique, August 10 [Rapport médical] .

Rothman, David. 1998. "The International Organ Traffic." *New York Review of Books* 45 (March 26):14.

Sgänger, Jonny. 1994. *Organhandel. Kroppsdelar till salu* [Organ Traffic: Bodies for Sale]. Stockholm: Alfabeta.

Schepper-Hughes, Nancy. 1990. "Bodies, Death and the State: Violence and the Taken for Granted World," Presented at the American Ethnological Society.

Schwartzenberg, Léon. 1993. *Rapport de la commission de l'environnement, de la santé publique et de la protection des consommateurs sur l'interdiction du commerce des organes à transplanter* [Report of the Environment, Public Health and Consumer Protection Commission upon the Banning of Trade in Organs for Transplant]. Bruxelles et Strasbourg: Parlement Européen (Février).

Shonder, John A. 1994. "Organ Theft Rumors in Guatemala." *FOAFTale News* 35: 1–3.

Thomas, Gordon. 1994. *Organ Hunters.* London: Chapmans.

Vargas Llosa, Mario. 1996 [1993]. *Lituma dans les Andes.* Paris: Gallimard (published in English in 1996 as *Death in the Andes* [Faber]).

Victor, Jeffrey S. 1989. "A Rumor-Panic about a Dangerous Satanic Cult in Western New York." *New York Folklore* 15:23–49.

———. 1991. "The Dynamics of Rumor-Panics about Satanic Cults." Pp. 221–36 in *The Satanism Scare*, edited by James T. Richardson, Joel Best, and David G. Bromley. New York: Aldine de Gruyter.

Wachtel, Nathan. 1992. *Dieux et vampires. Retour à Chipaya.* Paris: Seuil (published in English in 1994 as *Gods and Vampires: Return to Chipaya* [University of Chicago Press]).

Wallich, Paul. 1998. "This Is Not a Hoax." *Scientific American* [Cyberview] (November) .

Youngner, Stuart J. 1996. "Some Must Die." Pp. 32–55 in *Organ Transplantation: Meanings and Realities,* edited by S. J. Younger, R. C. Fox, and L. J. O'Connell. Madison: University of Wisconsin Press.

11

The United States and Smoking Problems in Japan

JUN AYUKAWA

TOBACCO IN CONTEMPORARY JAPAN

Cigarette smoking in Japan displays patterns unlike those found in other industrialized countries. The consumption of cigarettes has been steadily rising in Japan due to the importation of cigarettes from the United States. In 1950, 65.3 billion cigarettes were sold; in 1960, 122.8 billion; in 1970, 222.2 billion; in 1980, 304 billion; in 1990, 322 billion; and in 1995, 334.7 billion. This represents a 413 percent rise in the consumption of cigarettes from 1950 to 1995, while the population rose only 51 percent.[1]

Who Smokes in Japan?

In 1995, Japan's smoking rate was 58.8 percent among men and 14.6 percent among women.[2] Compared to other industrialized countries, the percentage of male smokers is very high, while that of female smokers is low: in the United States, 28.1 percent of males and 23.5 percent of females smoke; in the United Kingdom, 28 percent of males and 26 percent of females; in France, 40 percent of males and 27 percent of females; and in Germany, 36.8 percent of males and 21.5 percent of females (Ministry of Health and Welfare 1993).

In recent years, the smoking rate among men has decreased somewhat, from 62.5 percent in 1986, to 58.8 percent in 1995. But smoking among women has been increasing, from 12.6 percent in 1986, to 14.2 percent in 1991. This was caused by an increase in the number of young female smokers greater than the small decrease in middle-aged and older female smokers.

In 1965, the smoking rate for men in their twenties was 80.5 percent; for women in the same age bracket it was 6.6 percent. Thirty years later, in 1995, it was 64.7 percent for men, but 23.3 percent for women. This trend is similar for males and females in their thirties. However, the smoking rate for women 40 and over decreased.

The Tobacco Enterprise Law

In order to allow for the introduction of American tobacco companies into the Japanese market, Japan Monopoly, the government agency that monopolized the manufacturing and selling of cigarettes and salt, was privatized in 1985, becoming Japan Tobacco, Inc. (JT). Since privatization, JT has had three CEOs; all were former high-ranking bureaucrats in the Ministry of Finance. The stock of JT was offered on the open market in 1992; however, two-thirds of JT stock is still held by the Ministry of Finance— that is, this "private" firm is largely owned by the government, which, therefore, has a direct stake in tobacco sales.

With the birth of JT, a new Tobacco Enterprise Law was introduced "to strive for the sound development of the tobacco enterprise and to contribute to the stability of income revenue and the sound development of the national economy." This law advocated promoting the consumption of tobacco without thinking about the health of the nation or of its youth, and recommended that the Ministry of Finance promote tobacco sales in order to increase revenue from tobacco.

Control of the Ministry of Finance

JT's first CEO was the president of Japan Monopoly, a carryover from privatization. He had retired from the Ministry of Finance as a permanent vice minister, the highest status a bureaucrat can attain below the rank of minister. The second and third CEOs directed the National Tax Administration Agency (NTAA) before retiring. The NTAA manages all tax revenues; it is closely connected to the Ministry of Finance but slightly independent from it. These two men left the NTAA to become vice presidents of the Association of Life Insurance Companies and then consultants to JT.

JT tries to keep the price of tobacco, the total sales of cigarettes, cigarette shares, and retailers' profits as high as possible. The Ministry of Finance refrains from imposing regulations on smoking and helps JT and American tobacco companies increase their sales of cigarettes. The Ministry tries to keep the revenues from the tobacco tax as high as possible. Cigarette-tax revenues total 2,800 billion yen ($24.3 billion), half of which goes to the national government and the remainder to local governments.

In the United States, tobacco companies were private from the very beginning. The U.S. government does not worry about the profit margins of these companies and it does not own stock in tobacco companies. Therefore, it is easier for the government to place restrictions on the companies.

The warning labels on packages of Japanese cigarettes consist of two sentences: "Smoking by minors is prohibited" and "Be careful not to smoke too much as it may do harm to your health." The second sentence implies that it is all right to smoke if you don't smoke too much. Before 1989, the second sentence said only, "Be careful not to smoke too much." It is the job of the Ministry of Finance to decide what kind of warning labels will be printed on cigarette packages. The Ministry of Health and Welfare has no right to put medical messages on cigarette packages.[3]

U.S. Influence on the Tobacco Market in Japan

Due to the structure of Japanese society, the United States has influenced the tobacco market more than the opposition to tobacco. The U.S. government demanded an open market because it suffered from a trade deficit with Japan. This demand was met with the enactment of the Tobacco Enterprise Law in 1985. The Reagan administration handled the negotiations: it threatened to impose "Super 301" on Japanese imports (which would have had the effect of reducing Japanese exports to the United States) in 1986. In July 1986, Senator Jesse Helms (R-North Carolina) wrote a confidential letter to Prime Minister Nakasone calling for increasing America's share of tobacco imports to 20 percent within 18 months (Isayama 1999). In response to this pressure, Japan abolished the import tax on American cigarettes. In 1985, American tobacco's share of the Japanese market was less than 3.9 percent (7.5 billion cigarettes). Ten years later, in 1995, it had risen tenfold to 71 billion cigarettes—a 21.2 percent share of the Japanese market—accounting for most of the increase in Japanese cigarette consumption.

The threat of Super 301 led to significant changes. Before 1980, the import tax on cigarettes was 90 percent; it fell to 10 percent in 1983 before being abolished in 1987. Before the import tax was abolished, a retailer who sold Japanese tobacco got 10 percent of the sale price, compared to only 8.5 percent for American tobacco sales. Abolishing the import tax resulted in identical domestic taxes on American and Japanese tobacco, and the same profit margins for retailers. Once the Japanese government announced the abolition of all import taxes, Japanese TV commercials for American tobacco increased dramatically.

Sales of American cigarettes in the United States totaled approximately 584 billion in 1986, down from their historical peak of 630 billion in 1981. In contrast, Japanese cigarette consumption continued to increase to 308 billion in 1986. American tobacco companies felt Japan was a big market that might compensate for their declining domestic sales.

INSTITUTIONAL SUPPORTS FOR TOBACCO IN JAPAN

The Ministry of Health and Welfare

The Ministry of Health and Welfare has not made any strides toward re-ducing the number of smokers or discouraging the habit. It is more correct to say that the ministry cannot afford to promote a smoke-free society, given JT and the government policy to increase tobacco imports from the United States. When cigarette manufacturing was a government-owned enterprise, it was taboo to criticize it because of the huge amounts of in-come derived from it. After the Japan Monopoly was privatized, there was very little motivation for the Ministry of Health and Welfare to promote a smoke-free society because most JT stock was owned by the Ministry of Fi-nance (which managed administrative matters concerning tobacco).

In 1964, the chief of public health within the Ministry of Health and Wel-fare made an announcement about the harmful effects of smoking on health. This announcement appeared in the same year as the first report on smoking by the U.S. Surgeon General and two years after a report on "Smoking and Health" was published by Britain's Royal Academy of Med-icine. However, in Japan, this announcement was sent only to the prefec-tural governors, and with no substantive action was required of the ministry. Only one local community office in the suburbs of Tokyo heeded this announcement by prohibiting smoking inside their city hall except in designated areas.

In 1987, a massive report, "Smoking and Health," edited by the Ministry of Health and Welfare, was published in Japan. A second edition was pub-lished in 1993. However, these two publications were not recognized as official documents; they were published privately. Finally, in 1997, per-mission was given to include smoking under the category of a "routine life disease" in the "White Paper" (annual report) of the Ministry of Health and Welfare. During this period, the Japanese government was suffering from a shortage of revenue, and needed the huge revenues from the sale of to-bacco.[4] The Ministry of Finance has the power to cut the budget for anti-smoking efforts by the Ministry of Health and Welfare. Moreover, if the Ministry of Health and Welfare persists in a policy that could threaten to-bacco revenues, it has to fear budget cuts by the Ministry of Finance for items that it considers critical, such as care of the elderly.

The Rhetoric of "Internationalization"
(Globalization)

In order to promote good public health regarding tobacco smoking, the Ministry of Health and Welfare must combat the Ministry of Finance by adopting the rhetoric of "internationalization" (Nakagawa 1995). This sim-ply means juxtaposing Japan's tobacco policies with those of the United

States, Canada, and European countries. The Japanese tend to think that better things exist abroad and that they must be imported into Japan (Ayukawa 2000). Therefore, the strategy is to use international comparisons to make the Japanese public more aware of smoking's pitfalls. Politically, it is an attempt to influence the Ministry of Finance by highlighting Japan's shameful present situation concerning smoking through criticisms of Japan by foreign countries and international organizations.

Internationalization has multiple meanings in Japan, and in this case, it means pressure or requests from legitimate international organizations to change a particular action or pattern of behavior. Although the last Director General of the World Health Organization (WHO) was Japanese, WHO's call for Japan to abolish tobacco commercials on television was ignored for a long time. The Ministry of Health and Welfare and antismoking organizations still use WHO to legitimize their claims.

However, internationalization alone will not help antismoking organizations or the Ministry of Health and Welfare. Although internationalization gave antismoking groups a strategy to fight against big tobacco, the pressure for internationalization also made Japan open the tobacco market and import huge amounts of cigarettes.

National Hospitals and the Action Plan

When the Ministry of Health and Welfare started public awareness programs on smoking, it was able to secure a budget for them by restricting their application to settings it controlled. The Ministry ordered national hospitals, for example, to make their buildings no-smoking areas in principle and to separate smoking areas from ordinary air-conditioned spaces. Although this policy affects a very small segment of the population, it is similar to the strategy that was first taken in the United States of prohibiting smoking inside federal buildings.

In 1995, the Ministry of Health and Welfare established the Action Plan on Tobacco. The plan's basic goals are threefold: (1) prevention of smoking among minors; (2) development of ways to halt or decrease the effects of passive smoking on nonsmokers; and (3) support for people who want to stop smoking and leniency for those who continue smoking. Achieving these goals requires a consensus from both smokers and nonsmokers.

In 1999, the Ministry of Health and Welfare received appropriations from the Ministry of Finance for meetings on World No Tobacco Day. It also received money to make a CD-ROM on smoking. The year before, it had not succeeded in getting any appropriations. The CD-ROM consists of three parts: (1) the history of tobacco abroad and in Japan; (2) short scientific lectures by medical doctors and researchers on smoking; and (3) "quit-smoking programs." This last section contains posters for nonsmoking campaigns from around the world, TV commercials on antismoking from the United States (including Yul Brynner, the actor, and Victor Crawford, the tobacco lobbyist who became an antagonist against tobacco companies), and a lecture on the history of tobacco by the president of the Museum of Tobacco and Salt established by JT. The inclusion of this lecture demonstrates the Ministry of Health and Welfare's ambivalence toward the Ministry of Finance, which appropriated the budget for this project.

Ministry of Labor and Local Government

In 1996, the Ministry of Labor published guidelines for the work environment. It announced that smoking should be prohibited in offices and in factories where people work and that separate rooms for smoking should be established. (These tactics of the Ministry of Labor resemble those of the Department of Health, Education and Welfare in the United States, which also tried first to make the federal government buildings smoke-free.) However, this rule was not complied with except in public office buildings. In the central government, only small numbers of public officials and scientists work for the separation of smoking and nonsmoking areas, for the prevention of juvenile smoking, and on other smoking-related matters.

Although the guidelines were established, they are not enforced by private companies. For example, employees generally smoke freely in offices at my university, as at most private universities. If a person requests a nonsmoking work space, that person might be moved into some unpopular section. Smoking during working hours is regarded in the same way as drinking tea or coffee—it is an excuse to take a rest during working hours. Also, smoking occurs when someone wants to think seriously.

Local governments also are not active in nonsmoking campaigns because they get income from cigarette sales. Approximately 60 percent of the consumer price of cigarettes in Japan goes toward taxes: half for the national government, and half for local governments. The revenue from cigarettes taxes is indispensable, especially for small local governments. Thus, they hesitate to promote nonsmoking programs.

MARKETING TOBACCO IN JAPAN

Automatic Vending Machines

There are approximately 500,000 automatic cigarette-vending machines in Japan. They stand along streets in front of small retail shops, supermarkets, and convenience stores. (If anyone asked me to identify a characteristic of the Japanese way of life, I would not hesitate to point out automatic vending machines. Cigarettes, canned juice, canned tea, Coca Cola, beer, Japanese rice wine, and even whisky are all sold through vending machines.)[5]

In Japan, cigarette-vending machines increased drastically with the U.S. government's demand for equal opportunity and treatment for American cigarettes in Japan. The number of automatic vending machines rose from 323,310 in 1980 to 499,000 in 1995. Simultaneously, sales rose from 420 billion yen in 1980 to 1,529 billion yen in 1995, with vending-machine sales accounting for 40 percent of total sales of tobacco.

Until recently, automatic vending machines worked 24 hours a day. But now their hours of nonoperation are from 11 P.M. to 7 A.M. Antismoking groups and delinquency-prevention groups argued that these machines should not be in operation when youths can buy cigarettes secretly. Still, people in Japan are more tolerant of smoking than people in America; cigarettes are more accessible to Japanese youth than to their American counterparts.

Therefore, we can see opposite trends occurring in the United States and in Japan. In the United States, regulations against tobacco were being advanced by the government in the 1980s and the 1990s. In Japan, however, the number and the length of tobacco-related TV commercials, the number of vending machines, and the number of retail stores selling tobacco increased drastically during the same period.

TV Commercials

Tobacco commercials on TV were discontinued in March 1998, when tobacco companies refrained from airing tobacco TV commercials in Japan. This action was not taken because of government pressure or the activities of the antismoking movement. It was an agreement among tobacco companies themselves. Strictly speaking, as it is self-regulation, there is no obstacle to starting TV tobacco commercials again through another agreement by the tobacco companies. After August 1987, tobacco TV commercials were permitted only after 8:54 P.M.; after January 1989, after 9:54 P.M.; and, after April 1991, after 10:54 P.M. Until March 1998, there was a great rash of tobacco commercials immediately after the end of the blackout time.[6]

Although the blackout time became longer, the number of TV cigarette commercials aired grew, especially from 1985 to 1990. In 1985, TV tobacco commercials aired in Tokyo, Japan's capital, totalled 73,200 seconds. The total grew: in 1986 (when the majority of the regulations concerning the importation of foreign cigarettes were abolished), it was 202,965 seconds; in 1987 (when the import tax on cigarettes was abolished), it was 303,390 seconds; and it reached 403,980 seconds (112 hours, 13 minutes) in 1990. The air time for tobacco commercials was approximately 5.5 times greater in 1990 than it had been in 1985; there were 6.8 times as many TV commercials for foreign cigarettes as for domestic cigarettes in 1990 (Kaneko et al. 1996).

The reason TV cigarette commercials stopped in 1998 is not clear. One hypothesis is that, among industrialized countries, only Japan was broadcasting TV tobacco commercials, and it was criticized by WHO and the antismoking movement. TV commercials may have been seen as damaging Japan's reputation. Conforming to a global standard might have been thought to be better.

Recent research indicates that juveniles sit up late and watch TV after midnight in their own rooms. Therefore, the tobacco companies anticipated requests for a further extension of the blackout time. However, extending the blackout time beyond 10:54 P.M. was deemed impossible. There was no alternative to stopping them.

According to the rule of tobacco advertising set by the Japan Association of Tobacco Companies, only new products can be advertised on TV. The term for advertising is three years from the start of the sell-date. So, tobacco companies might have been tired of producing new brands and thought it would be more rewarding to advertise their best-selling or most popular brands continuously. Since the smoking rate among juveniles had increased, tobacco companies might have been afraid of strong criticism and thought it was better to stop TV advertising before such criticism developed. Or, referring to the cultivation theory of mass communication, they may have thought TV commercials had already firmly cultivated the tendency to smoke among youth.

"Manners" Advertisements

Tobacco TV commercials stopped airing with one exception: the so-called manners advertisements. In these commercials, a famous actor or celebrity appears and says: "I'm a smoke-loving person (*Ai-en-ka*) and I don't dispose of cigarettes on the road." They recommend smokers use ashtrays along roads or even carry a handy ashtray. They also call for smokers to think about the people around them when they smoke.

It has been pointed out by antismoking groups that the manners commercials seek to create and maintain a good, positive image of smoking in both smokers' and nonsmokers' minds. The commercials intentionally showcase the phrase "Ai-en-ka", which means "smoke-loving person" instead of just "a smoker." ("Ai-en-ka" literally means "love-smoke-person.") Thus, antismoking groups point out that these commercials connote nice people, as love has a positive meaning, and the last sound "ka", which means person, is only used to show appreciation for the talent of an individual, such as an artist (*geijutsu-ka*), a novelist (*shosetsu-ka*), or an entrepreneur (*jitsugyo-ka*). This sound is never equated with a person who commits crimes or is a deviant.

"Delight" is JT's campaign catchword. JT says that it is a company that brings delight to people. In one manners commercial, a sudden shower creates an unexpected encounter between a man and a young woman. The man takes out a lighter, the young woman passes him an ashtray, but he refrains from smoking. The copy says "When you have delight, I have delight, too." It tells the smoker that there are situations where it is better to choose not to smoke. On the other hand, it implicitly requests nonsmokers to be kind to smokers. It can be said that the aim of these commercials is the symbiosis of smokers and nonsmokers. Also, this commercial encourages the habit of smoking and fosters a positive image. (You can view this TV commercial at http://www.jtnet.ad.jp/WWW/JT/JTl/delight/Welcome.html.) In magazines, one can find another kind of advertisement. It usually consists of text only; if a picture is included, it is symbolic (e.g., a curled shell with smoke coming out of the hole). The text reads "Tobacco is an adult's favorite item (*shikohin*)." There is an asterisk after "shikohin," with a note: "It depends on the person whether he likes it or not, but it takes time to find its goodness." It describes smoking as if it were a matter of taste. This mutes all criticism of smoking. People may find it good after they become dependent upon it.

Suspension of a TV Documentary Program on Smoking

In March 1992, a 25-minute documentary program on the harm caused by smoking was postponed by one of Japan's five main national networks. The program was to introduce a street campaign on the risks of smoking by people who had had throat surgery due to cancer. The program was to air on WHO's World No Tobacco Day, and would introduce the activities of the antismoking movement.

The postponement was requested by the network's sales division. The staff who made the program, the news section, and its labor union complained about the postponement to the administrators. The postponement was widely reported by the major newspapers. There was great criticism against the intervention of the sales division into the news and production sections. It appeared to be editorial interference with journalists. After the complaints gathered nationwide attention, the network announced that there was no intention of intervention and no interference from tobacco companies before airing. The program was aired two months later as a special program for WHO's World No Tobacco Day.

This episode shows how TV networks are sensitive to their sponsors and how tobacco companies have a great influence on TV companies. Tobacco companies continue to pay broadcasting companies to air manners commercials. In addition, TV programs often show smoking scenes. The number of young women smoking on the street increased after a popular female actress smoked on the street in a TV drama. According to the program's producer, this made public smoking "fashionable and stylish."

Other Methods of Promotion

By March 1998, free cigarette samples were being distributed on the streets and in public spaces by young women dressed in very sexy costumes. These women not only distributed free samples, but recommended smoking cigarettes. They would even light a cigarette between a pedestrian's lips. Such scenes cannot be seen on the streets anymore, but they occur inside buildings: when a colleague and I were having dinner at a restaurant, a beautiful young woman suddenly appeared at our table, explained a new tobacco product, and gave us a sample. Recent promotions feature handsome young men approaching young women in restaurants and bars.

Billboard advertising is common in Japan. In contrast, outside billboard tobacco ads were banned in the United States in April 1999. You can see a lot of cowboys and surfers on top of Japanese buildings and at intersections. When TV commercials stopped, the advertising money spent for newspaper and billboard advertising increased drastically. It is estimated that tobacco companies previously paid 15 billion yen to the TV networks and local broadcasting companies to broadcast TV commercials. Large amounts now flood into newspapers, magazines, billboard advertisements, premiums, incentives, and samples.

Targeting Youth and Women

Tobacco companies also offer gifts or premiums that are attractive to youngsters. When applying for gifts, applicants must write that they are at least 20 years old, but this information cannot be verified. Younger kids will be much more attracted to smoking with these premiums. For example, Marlboro's gifts are of two kinds. One kind involves a lottery: by sending in a card with eight top seals from cigarette boxes, a person can win an original Marlboro ranch coat or Marlboro gloves in a drawing. Other gifts are simply ordered through a catalog: by sending a certain number of seals and a certain amount of money, you can receive the gift you want—a Marlboro Zippo lighter costs 60 top seals plus 3,500 yen; a Marlboro duffel bag takes 40 seals and 6,000 yen. We can imagine that a boy dreaming of being a cowboy might be fascinated with these goods.

The presents offered by American tobacco companies are always more valuable and more attractive than those from Japanese companies. Because the production of American tobacco is cheaper than Japanese tobacco, American companies can channel surplus money into advertisements, incentives, and sponsorships. After American tobacco companies sponsored

Formula 1 racing, JT began sponsoring it, too. The reason seems very clear: Formula 1 racing attracts youngsters.

Virginia Slims and Salem have been big factors in the rapid increase in young female smokers in Japan. Virginia Slims conducted a campaign in which the prize was an airplane ticket to the United States. The promotional slogan for that campaign was "Visit the freedom country—the United States—by smoking Virginia Slims." Phillip Morris never mentioned that the United States was more severe in restricting and regulating smoking. Young women connected the smoking of Virginia Slims with freedom in the United States and "misunderstood" that they could enjoy smoking in the United States more freely. "Be you" is a recent Virginia Slims slogan. It means to be independent or to do what you want to break the restrictions patriarchy places on the woman; in essence, be brave and break through old customs. So, "be you" means "be yourself, be independent, be active, and be brave."

The latest strategy in the advertising of Virginia Slims is different from other female-oriented cigarettes. It advertises cigarettes on large billboards using white models. The copy reads "The love I have now is my first love." This is a charming, active-woman's message. It suggests that she takes advantage of men, but can rationalize her actions and the actions of young women who change boyfriends often: No matter how many loves she has, the love she currently has is her precious fresh love (and there is a suggestion that smoking itself may be her first love).

My university is a women's university, not large but prominent and prestigious, located in the center of Japan. Most of the students come from the upper-middle class or the upper class. We did not need ashtrays on campus four years ago. However, we recently established two smoking areas—an inside area and one outside. Frankly speaking, I cannot understand these young women's behavior. (This might be a symptom of my being older and out of touch with young people's behavior.) On the one hand, the students are health conscious with their dieting, physical exercise, sports, vegetarian menus, and vitamins. On the other hand, they smoke. However, they may want equality with males and believe that smoking is fashionable. The "Slim" in Virginia Slims also appeals to young women. Since they want to be slim, it gives them an implicit message that you will able to lose weight and keep yourself slim if you smoke.

In Japan, there is little information on the hazards of smoking. For a young woman, smoking means equality with men. This view might be seen as a byproduct of the feminist movement. The self-regulation of advertising companies says that women should not be targeted because it may make them dependent on tobacco when they are pregnant, increasing the likelihood of underweight and/or handicapped babies. However, there are only two concrete standards established for not making women targets of cigarette ads: there are no cigarette ads in magazines for women; and tobacco ads do not show female models smoking. However, there are tobacco ads targeted toward women in several kinds of TV magazines, similar to *TV Guide* in the United States. These magazines are not specifically for women, but the majority of their readers are women and youngsters. Women do not smoke in these ads—however, in one ad for Salem Pianissimo, set against the backdrop of a large picture of a beautiful young white woman, the copy reads, "Little smell and little smoke. The smell doesn't get in your hair. So just be pretty." The target of this ad is clearly young Japanese women intending to strongly motivate them to smoke. The rule prohibiting the use of women models in smoking poses in cigarette ads does not deter companies from targeting women in their cigarette ads. It is a fake rule, and it has no real impact.

Advantage of American Cigarettes

The price of tobacco is set at around 250 yen (approximately $2.45) for a pack of 20 cigarettes. American cigarettes are usually cheaper than Japanese cigarettes in Japan. Such is the American tobacco companies' strategy. According to the tobacco enterprise law, JT must buy all of the tobacco leaves cultivated in Japan (Japan Monopoly and Japan Tobacco 1964–90), which are approximately three times as expensive as those from the United States. The costs of producing cigarettes are very different between Japan and the United States: American tobacco companies have much more money to advertise, to offer incentives and premiums. American tobacco advertisements are more fashionable, sophisticated, and attractive to young people in Japan.

The commercials depict young, active people who may be sweethearts, leisure groups at the beach, pool, or on a yacht, or even cowboys riding horses in the West. The three main themes in cigarette ads are sports and action, nature, and love: Kent uses sports; Lark uses action; Parliament uses a love story. People featured in the ads and TV commercials are usually handsome young white men and beautiful white women. Since medical professionals in Japan offer no positive information on smoking, and the bad effects of smoking on the public's health are prevalent, it can be assumed that people smoke only because of the positive images from cigarette ads.

Defending Tobacco: Smoking as Culture

In a trial, JT claimed that there was no causal link between smoking and cancer. They do not make such claims outside of court. In 1980, JT published and distributed a leaflet with such a claim, but it was later recalled because of the reaction of antismoking groups.

Soon after the publication of "Smoking and Health," a lot of books with counterclaims were published. Tobacco companies emphasize the history and culture of tobacco. Japan Monopoly sold both tobacco and salt, so it established the Museum of Tobacco and Salt. A distinguished publishing company produced a series of books on "thinking about tobacco" (Japan Tobacco Research Center 1987–90). The series discusses cultural aspects of smoking, not health problems, and informs readers that, through history, human beings and smoking have been "good friends." In one recent volume, a famous play director and professor argue that smoking is a matter of choice, in which the government should not intervene. Their opinion was reported in newspapers and magazines, and many smokers approved of and were relieved by their statements.

JT also established a cultural foundation that promotes and sponsors classical music concerts. A few of JT's products are advertised with musical instruments or scores. JT does not explicitly mention smokers' right to choose but implies it through the activities of the foundation.

Now the word "light" is in vogue. Advertisements now contain the words "light," "super light," "extra light," or "ultra light," which imply that lighter cigarettes are safer because of less tar content. But, as is shown in medical experiments, a smoker tries to inhale as much nicotine as possible to reach a state of satisfaction, so more "light" cigarettes are smoked in order to get the same amount of nicotine. Lighter cigarettes do not mean safer or healthier, but the terminology is easily misunderstood.

OPPOSITION TO TOBACCO: SOCIAL MOVEMENT AND LITIGATION ACTIVITY

The Dawn of Antismoking Movements in Japan

The first Japanese antismoking group was the Circle to Protect Non-smokers, established in 1977 by lawyers in Hokkaido, Japan's northern-most island. In the following year, two similar groups, the Circle of People to Establish the Rights of Nonsmokers and the Circle of Lawyers for the Rights of Nonsmokers were established in Tokyo. Also, in 1978, a national information organization for correspondence among nonsmoking and antismoking movements was established. In 1999, there were approximately 70 antismoking groups in Japan.

"The rights of nonsmokers" is called *Ken-en-ken* in Japanese, which can be literally translated as "the rights of people who dislike smoking." It proved to be a very effective name for this kind of group because it had a strong, favorable impact on the public and drew their awareness to this problem (Best 1995:8). But because the first "ken" in the name has the connotation of very strong "hate" or "dislike," the object of this hate or dislike may be interpreted as being not only against the act of smoking itself, but smokers.

No-Smoking Areas on Super Express Trains

The first action taken by antismoking groups was in 1979, when they gathered 35,000 signatures and petitioned the Japan National Railways for no-smoking cars and no-smoking areas (Spector and Kitsuse 1977). At that time, Japan National Railways was not privatized. (It was privatized into seven private railway companies in 1987.) In April 1980, the Circle of Lawyers to Establish the Rights of Nonsmokers sued Japan National Railways in Tokyo district court to designate at least half of its Super Express coaches as nonsmoking cars. This led to one of the biggest trials on smoking in Japan, and it garnered huge mass-media attention (Isayama 1983). The trial lasted almost seven years. (One of the main characteristics of the Japanese court system is that it moves very slowly toward a judgment.) On March 27, 1987, a verdict was finally reached and the plaintiffs lost their case. The court ruled that the ill effects of smoking were tolerable, therefore the plaintiffs' suit was rejected. When the plaintiffs first filed their suit only one car of the Super Express was nonsmoking; however, by the time the verdict was finally handed down, 30 percent of the coaches on Super Express trains were nonsmoking. In light of this fact, the plaintiffs decided not to appeal their case because they felt that they had already won.

Other Activities of Antismoking Movements

During the same trial, antismoking groups and individuals carried out many other activities. They established a group for the promotion of no-smoking education in 1983. This group organizes annual meetings for schoolteachers just before summer vacation.

Two junior high school teachers requested that the Committee of Labor Relations of Nagoya City Hall make their staff office a nonsmoking area. The committee refused in 1983. The following year, the teachers requested a smoking room separate from the staff office area. This request was also turned down with the ruling that the density level of carbon monoxide was within the safe level according to the environmental guidelines of 1985. The teachers then filed a suit against the city's decision in the district court, but the court dismissed the case in 1991, saying that the level of smoking did not go beyond the accepted level of tolerance. The teachers appealed their case to the superior court, but it was dismissed again in 1992. An appeal to the Supreme Court was dismissed in 1993.

There have been several suits filed demanding a separation of working space and smoking space. With the exception of two cases, all were defeated. In one case, an individual who filed a suit in 1992 succeeded in making his work space a nonsmoking area in 1994. In the other case filed in 1991, the individual agreed to move to another, nonsmoking working environment in 1993. It is interesting to note that the majority of people who filed suits were public employees, whose employment was insured by law.

People in Japan are less inclined to bring cases to court than in the United States. Thus far, there has been only one case in which a group of people who smoked and suffered from cancer brought a suit against a tobacco company. No family of a deceased person who smoked and died of cancer has sued a tobacco company in Japan.

One achievement of the antismoking movement was the abolition of commemorative cigarette packaging by national and local governments. The governments were in the habit of printing cigarette packaging to commemorate their anniversaries and then distributing the cigarettes to people who had made great contributions to that local government. This practice stopped in 1992.

The Product Liability Case

The second biggest lawsuit by the antismoking movement was initiated in May 1998. The antismoking movement sued JT using the product liability law, which was passed in the Diet and implemented in 1997.

A preparatory group for the trial was established in November. Initially, the group tried to find individuals who would become plaintiffs but failed. They started a "Dial 110 for tobacco disease" campaign through the mass media. (The number 110 is an emergency call number in Japan, much like 911 in the United States.) Eighty-four people called, including 35 serious cases. Seven people were selected as the plaintiffs. They were mostly old, long-term smokers. One was a dentist born in 1927 who began smoking just after World War II, when cigarettes, along with rice, were distributed by the government because of a shortage of goods. After having smoked 50 or 60 cigarettes per day for years, the dentist was diagnosed with lung cancer when he was 54 and had his right lung removed. Since then, he has had to use a portable oxygen tank. Another individual was 72 years old and had been smoking for 50 years. Eight years earlier, he was diagnosed with emphysema and it was now difficult for him to breathe or climb steps and hills.

The lawyers cooperated with antismoking movement members, medical doctors, and scientists. They requested that social movement groups manage ordinary meetings, meetings for opinion gathering and exchange, fund raising, and the organization of meetings to report on the progress of cases.

The lawyer group brought "the case to demand compensation for tobacco disease" to Tokyo District Court on March 15, 1998. It sued JT, three past and present CEOs of JT, the Ministry of Finance, and the Ministry of Health and Welfare within the government. The suit made six demands: (1) payment of $86,000 for each of the seven plaintiffs (a total of 70 million

yen); (2) stop the sale of tobacco through vending machines; (3) stop tobacco advertising; (4) stop tobacco-company sponsorship of sports, concerts, and Japanese chess events; (5) stop tobacco advertising under the
guise of manners advertisements; and (6) print labels with explicit warnings about tobacco's dangers on cigarette packages (Isayama 1999).

Sixteen lawyers participated in the case. The lawyers claimed that the
link between smoking and cancer had been proven. In particular, the plaintiffs claimed that the warning labels on the package were incorrect and had
manipulated them into smoking. The suit targeted JT and its leaders and
the Ministry of Finance.

JT fought the claim linking smoking with cancer. The other defendants,
the Ministry of Finance and the Ministry of Health and Welfare, demanded
an explanation of the text of the petition to try to escape from responding
to it and delay the trial. Because the petition referred to reports ("Smoking
and Health" and the "White Paper of Health and Welfare 1997") edited by
the Ministry of Health and Welfare itself, both ministries could not dispute
the claim without contradicting government reports.

Importation of Law and Strategy

In Japan, most new laws are proposed by the cabinet to the Diet. After
lengthy committee discussions and careful consideration of the possibility
of unnecessary suits or disturbances to ordinary enterprise, the Ministry of
Justice proposed the Product Liability Law and it passed through the Diet.
Product liability laws had been used to bring many suits against tobacco
companies in the United States (Tanase 1999). As the Japanese product liability law became effective only recently, it is not easy to tell how often
people and lawyers will make use of it. But, at present, few lawyers are interested in suing tobacco companies.

In this sense, the United States exported to Japan a weapon for fighting
tobacco companies. But the ways of utilizing this weapon are different in
the two countries. Product liability law is used only by a small number of
Japanese lawyers who consider themselves responsible for restricting antisocial activities or for protecting the public's health. In the beginning,
lawyers were hesitant to sue but the pressure from antismoking movements finally persuaded them.

Although the leading lawyer of the product liability suit also had been
the chief lawyer in the unsuccessful suit against Japan National Railway,
the antismoking movement needed a new approach for the product liability case. In the suit against the national railway and in other efforts to separate fresh-air space and smoking space, the antismoking movement
portrayed nonsmokers as victims and smokers as the perpetrators. But the
product liability suit required viewing smokers as victims; the movement
had to ally itself with smokers (Best 1999).

How is it possible to see smokers as the movement's co-plaintiffs in the tobacco war? To nonsmokers, it is the smokers' fault if they suffered from lung cancer, heart disease, or emphysema because they chose to smoke, made little effort to stop smoking, and probably caused ill effects on their nonsmoking neighbors. The movement might see such smokers as enemies (selfish, weak-minded, cowardly, or sly) who try to shift the responsibility for their illness onto others.

In order to reconcile the relationship between nonsmokers and the defendants in this case, the lawyers pointed out that most smokers were also victims because they had begun smoking through curiosity or the influence of friends, and had become habitual smokers because of the addictive nature of nicotine. Thus, smokers were victims of misinformation propagated by the tobacco manufacturers (Best 1999; Holstein and Miller 1990).

It is not easy to collect money to try a case. In order to file the product liability suit, the plaintiffs managed to collect six million yen, of which two million yen was donated by the lawyers who filed the suit. The lawyers cannot expect any monetary reward from this case because, in Japan, there is no class-action system. It is not easy get lawyers to commit to cases such as these because they do not think there is profit in helping people sue tobacco companies. In Japan, ambitious lawyers who wish to gain large profits do not organize class-action suits. There are fewer lawyers in Japan than in the United States; 700,000 in the United States and 14,000 in Japan; per 100,000 inhabitants, there are 15.6 lawyers in Japan compared with 363 lawyers in the United States. Because of the demand (latent cases) and supply (lawyers) relationship, Japanese lawyers are not as competitive as their counterparts in the United States, since they have prestigious social status and income. They do not need to "chase ambulances." Most lawyers who commit to class-action suits are like missionaries following their "calling"— what Max Weber (1947:214) designated *Beruf*—or "noble obligation." Some lawyers will join these cases for ideological reasons; that is, in pursuit of "social justice" and punishment of the government's antisocial activities.

Another suit sought to sue one CEO of JT for having committed murder. However, the prosecutor's office refused to take the case. The lawyers turned it into a civil case, claiming that it should be against the law to sell tobacco with health warning labels. They argued that selling tobacco should be banned. The court decided that damage from tobacco was tolerable and refused the demand. In the ruling, the court recommended that JT add a sentence to the warning label that secondhand smoke is harmful to people.

Grassroot Movements: The Japanese Way

It is no exaggeration to say that no one profits from antismoking actions in Japan. People who are committed to the antismoking movement know

that they will be donating their time and labor and cannot expect any
material reward. So far, only one person who works for the movement full-
time receives a subsidy. He has established the Tobacco Problem Information Center, edits and publishes an eight-page monthly newsletter, and is
the general director of the Capital Metropolitan Area Council of Smoking
Problems. The Tobacco Problem Information Center is the most popular
information center for antismoking activists, and the newsletter, with 1,500
subscriptions, is the movement's only periodical (a one-year subscription
costs 6,000 yen). He also publishes several books and gives nonsmoking
education lectures at high schools (Watanabe 1996). However, the movement cannot afford to maintain his subsidy. (In contrast, the leading U.S.
activist, John Banzaf, earned more for his activities as president of Action
on Smoking and Health [ASH] than from his faculty salary at Georgetown
University's law school [Troyer and Markle 1983].)

The Japanese nongovernmental organization (NGO) and nonprofit organization (NPO) law was passed in the Diet in 1998, but only one of each
were established as part of the antismoking movement. The Tobacco and
Health Problem NGO Council coordinates the main health organizations,
while the Council for a Nonsmoking Environment for Children became an
NPO in Osaka in 1999. Approximately ten volunteers work for this organization without payment. The Tobacco Problem Information Center is not
expected to become a nonprofit organization; people pay to support this
organization. According to the Japanese law, donations to an NPO will not
result in a tax reduction. The economic base for the antismoking movement—and social movements in general—is weaker in Japan than in the
United States.

In order to organize the international meeting of the Asian Pacific Conference on Tobacco and Health (APACT) in 1993 in Omiya, another activist
quit her job as a junior high school English teacher two years before her retirement and lives only on her pension. She has been the representative for
the Council on Smoking and Women, which may be a council in name only
(she may be the only worker there). The council may have been established
to be recognized internationally, to act easily, to get better responses from
public organizations, and to get an advantage in negotiating with local and
national governmental organizations. Although there are fewer social resources that can be mobilized for antismoking movements in Japan than in
the United States, the movement is vital to promoting nonsmoking, as the
Japanese government is handicapped in executing a nonsmoking policy.

The Use of Numbers

The large number of deaths linked to tobacco is sometimes cited by antismoking groups (Best 1990). In 1994, WHO announced that 3 million peo-

ple die every year from smoking. In 1996, it proclaimed that, at the beginning of the twenty-first century, the number of deaths because of smoking will increase to 10 million a year. U.S. newspapers also quoted President Clinton's announcement that 400,000 Americans are killed yearly by smoking. He declared that smoking should be treated as a drug and controlled by the Food and Drug Administration.

But in Japan, where the majority of adult males smoke, and where antismoking movements do not rely on statistics, there is cognitive dissonance between the proclaimed huge number of deaths and the the tolerance of smoking. The number of smoke-related deaths seems unbelievable and exaggerated to the general public: on the one hand, one hears about the dangers of smoking, on the other hand, one sees older smokers who are healthy. Because smoking in public places is not strictly regulated, the majority of adult males still smoke and people are forced to breathe air contaminated with cigarette smoke in the workplace and other locations. It is difficult to persuade people of the fatal effects of smoking through numbers alone. Japanese antismoking movements do not rely on statistics.

Prevention of Juvenile Smoking

In the United States, restrictions on tobacco are often justified as protecting the health of vulnerable children and youth. By contrast, in Japan, youth smoking is seen as a kind of delinquency. Almost a century ago "the law prohibiting smoking by youth" was passed in Japan; Christian women were active in establishing this law.[7] Although the law prohibits juveniles (people under twenty in Japan) from smoking, there is no punishment for juvenile smokers. Under the law, adults who make juveniles smoke or who sell tobacco to them are punished, but even this was rare: in 1997, only eight parents and four shop owners were punished under this law. And because there is no supervision, juveniles are able to purchase cigarettes from vending machines easily.

One of the main aims of the antismoking movement is to separate smoking areas from clean-air spaces to prevent passive smoking. Another goal, although not particularly popular with the public, is to prevent juveniles from smoking. Several organizations have been established for this purpose. The Tobacco Problem Information Center, for example, provides estimated data on juvenile smoking. In 1998, sales of cigarettes totaled 336.6 billion. Of this, the number of cigarettes smoked by juveniles was calculated to be 54.9 billion. This exceeds the number of cigarettes smoked by female adults, and represents 16.3 percent of cigarettes sold in 1998. Also according to JT, 26.5 million Japanese male adults smoke; the average number of cigarettes smoked by males per day is 24.1, compared to 17.1 per day for females.

Dr. Minowa (1996) of the Research Institute of Public Health in the Ministry of Health and Welfare researched the smoking habits of junior and senior high school students, asking how often they smoked in the last 30 days. Among male high school students, 25.4 percent of the first grade (15–16 years old), 31 percent of the second grade (16–17 years old), and 36.9 percent of the third grade (17–18 years old) had smoked cigarettes at least once in the previous 30 days, while 10.5 percent of the first grade, 18.3 percent of the second grade, and 25.4 percent of the third grade had smoked cigarettes daily during the previous 30 days. Among female high school students, 9.2 percent of the first grade, 13.3 percent of the second grade, and 16.6 percent of the third grade had smoked cigarettes at least once in the previous 30 days.

American tobacco is very popular with young people in Japan because Japanese youth yearn for the spirit of freedom in the United States. This yearning may reflect an admiration of American and European people because the individuals appearing in American tobacco ads in Japan are white. Presumably, advertising agencies chose these models after much market research into how to increase sales. Moreover, the packaging of American tobacco is quite fashionable; the hardcover, squared-box format contrasts with Japanese tobacco's soft-cover paper wrapping.

Although research by Dr. Minowa and other researchers was publicized, the Japanese do not seem to view preventing juveniles from smoking as urgent, and prevention programs are not taken as seriously as in the United States. In this sense, antismoking groups do not get people's attention, do not get the national or local government's endorsement to prevent juvenile smoking, and do not succeed in using juvenile smoking problems to score public-relations points against the tobacco companies.

In Japan, smoking by juveniles tends to be seen as a delinquency problem, a kind of "status offense," rather than a health problem. Although prohibited by law, there is no penalty for juvenile smoking, so policemen only issue warnings to juveniles who smoke and make short reports. The reports list the number of juveniles who smoked and who were cautioned about not smoking. While the number of juveniles warned about smoking has decreased, few people believe that the number of juvenile smokers is decreasing; more juveniles are seen smoking in public spaces such as on roads, in front of retail shops, and at parks.

Although smoking used to be seen as a form of delinquency, it has now become popular for youth. Adults cannot see it as a vice. Therefore, people have become rather tolerant of youth smoking; in particular, parents are very tolerant of their children's smoking. Parents fear that their children will think it too much of an intervention into trivial matters to be cautioned about smoking. Parents feel that their children will become hostile and more disobedient if they are scolded about smoking or have their cigarettes confiscated. If smoking was defined as a health problem, a different reaction might be taken.

Because it is seen as a behavioral problem, parents think juvenile smoking is a rite of passage. Parents hope that their children will stop smoking when they become adults. People are not nervous about the dependence upon nicotine because alcohol, which also creates dependent behavior, is not regulated severely either. (Remember, vending machines also sell beer and Japanese rice wine along the streets in Japan. Needless to say, there is no need for young people to show identification at a shop before buying alcohol.)

Health Organizations

Medical and health-related associations are not active in antismoking campaigns in Japan. The Japan Association of Medical Doctors and Dentists for Tobacco Control was established in 1992. It is estimated that approximately 20 percent of Japanese doctors smoke. So, doctors themselves do not acknowledge the increasing risks of smoking on health.

The Tuberculosis Prevention Association, the Japan Cancer Association, Mother-Child Health Association, Cancer Research Promotion Association, the Making of a Healthy Strong Body Association, and the Japan Eating-Life Association constitute the Tobacco and Health Problem NGO Council. They sponsor the conference on World No Tobacco Day. But their activities are not so vibrant as those of the American Cancer Association or the American Lung Association. One of the reasons why they are not so active in Japan is that these organizations are more professionally oriented than publicly oriented. Ordinary citizens seldom donate to these organizations or become members. Medical-equipment and pharmaceutical companies do donate. Ironically, the donors might profit if the number of people suffering from smoke-related cancer increases, thus increasing the demand for the equipment and the medicine being sold by the doctors.

Some labor unions try to promote the separation of smoking and non-smoking workplaces. But, according to research by the Tobacco Problem Information Center, the percentage of smokers among union leaders is higher than that of ordinary union members. Also, as JT's labor union is well organized and powerful in the Japan Trade Union Confederation, the country's largest confederation of labor unions is not inclined to make claims or to appeal to politicians for laws regulating smoking.

Technology Advancement

The Ministry of Health and Welfare and the Ministry of Labor and other foundations are not powerful enough to control or decrease the number of smokers in Japan. But the advancement of technology may help reduce the number of smokers. The CAT scan is one example. The kinds and the number of diseases linked to smoking have increased. In addition to X-rays, which have been used to detect lung cancer, CAT scans of the entire human body have become popular. The damage to the lungs can be shown clearly and vividly by a CAT scan. A smoker is able to witness with his or her eyes the damage smoking does to the lungs. Also, these pictures can be used by the antismoking movement as evidence of the danger of smoking and of the need to regulate it. CAT scans may change the psychological condition of smokers who deny the bad effects of smoking or refuse to quit smoking.

A second advance is the growing popularity of the Internet. Antismoking movements find it easier to make claims for regulation and disseminate information on the dangers of smoking via the Internet. Also, it can be effective in helping people quit smoking—that is, people who want to quit smoking and who have access to the Internet can participate in a group with medical doctors, former smokers, and smokers who want to quit. When individuals try to stop smoking and want to smoke again, they can express their pain and promptly find someone who has conquered this experience and, through this person, find ways to manage the situation and not backslide. This quit-smoking "marathon" is very effective and is publicized by antismoking groups. It is one way to avoid making enemies of smokers. By providing smokers with ways to quit, antismoking groups can avoid the antipathy of smokers and get support from people who have quit smoking—sometimes even from current smokers.

Micropolitics of Workplace Smoking

Antismoking policies are being introduced in Japan. Smoking on subways, local trains, and local buses is prohibited; people can smoke only at designated places on station platforms (at subway stations, smoking is prohibited). In late 1998, all domestic airlines and two major Japanese international airlines became nonsmoking. The number of hospitals that have a smoking room with strong ventilating machines segregated by clear glass partitions from other spaces is on the increase. According to research by the Tokyo Metropolitan government in 1995, 68 percent of district halls, 39 percent of city halls, and 22 percent of town and village halls have a designated smoking spot separated from ordinary nonsmoking space.

However, there is no research on the separation of smoking and nosmoking areas at work places because this idea has not become widespread in Japan. Whether smoking problems occur at the workplace depends on the constellation of workers and the circumstances of the physical environment.

The smoking rate among middle-aged males is as high as 50 percent in Japan. Although guidelines for smoking in working spaces were published, there are no penalties for companies or people who do not follow the guidelines. So, the politics of particular situations shape whether the guidelines are followed. Not all public offices obey the guidelines; it depends on the ministry, the prefecture, or the city. For example, a branch office of Nagoya City Hall in Moriyama Ward has a "no smoking time" system, which means only a 90-minute suspension of smoking at the office from 1:30 to 3:00 P.M. During the majority of the time, public employees can smoke inside the building.

There are no statistics concerning no-smoking or separate smoking places at workplaces. Therefore, I will use my university as an example in discussing smoking in the workplace (Holstein and Miller 1990). At this university, workers who smoke, with the exception of faculty members, do not appear to be anxious about the nonsmoking people in their offices. The only exception is the meeting rooms, where it is a tradition not to smoke. It is rather rare in Japan for a white-collar worker to have his own individual office; more commonly, three to ten or more people work together in the same office. If the boss is a heavy smoker, it is not easy to ask to change the working space into a no-smoking area or to even set up "no-smoking times."

The structure of the building is also a factor. In new office buildings, there may be a space at an entrance or a room for smoking where strong ventilating systems are in place. This space does not make smokers feel segregated. Some bosses voluntarily go outside the building to smoke and other employees follow suit. This happens only when they can easily go outside and return. When a smoking room is established in an old building, it is sometimes a small space that fills with smoke when a few smokers smoke there. Smokers often complain of feeling imprisoned when they smoke in a room separated from the working space and filled with condensed smoke. Even smokers usually do not like to inhale the smoke of other smokers.

Americans may wonder about the influence of labor unions. Few labor unions are vigorous on smoking problems. As the smoking rate among union members is high, labor unions may lose the support of their members and create conflict if they support smoking-free zones. It is said that the rate of smoking among union leaders is higher than that among rank and file. (According to research done by the Smoking Problem Information Center about ten years ago, the rate of smoking among the representatives of the Diet who belonged to the Socialist party was higher than that among the representatives belonging to the Conservative party.)

When a woman becomes pregnant, her office will become a nonsmoking area as long as she is pregnant. Generally speaking, however, newly hired young men or women who do not like passive smoke hesitate to make demands because they are afraid of creating tension between themselves and their smoking superiors. When people ask to make the work space smoke-free, they may be told that they are too nervous or too sensitive; the request might be attributed to the claimsmaker's individual character. Even worse, the claimsmaker might receive bad or insulting comments if he / she tries to expel the smokers or create a confrontation inside the work space. He / she might be said to be selfish, not being cooperative with others, not friendly, or too demanding. In order to avoid being labeled, people often refrain from making claims.

When a person calls for no smoking in a situation where this is not easily accomplished, others' typical reaction might be "Don't make trouble." He / she might be told: "This is company tradition, so you should conform or adapt to it." As group integration or harmony is highly valued in Japan, group pressure is applied to persuade someone not to request a nonsmoking area at the office. Would-be claimsmakers may refrain from making requests, for fear of being moved to another section, office, or place. Although lifelong employment at one company is no longer a certainty, it is still a tradition in Japanese employment. So, prospective claimsmakers fear being disadvantaged in the company at some point. If he / she wants to be promoted quickly and stay in the same company as long as possible, it is wise not to make trouble, especially against the bosses. A worker who advocates no-smoking might be recommended for transfer to another section by a boss. Thus, would-be claimsmakers feel intimidated.

The rhetoric of rights is also used to suppress no-smoking claimsmaking: The rights of smokers should be protected, too. At some offices, the virtues of smoking may be espoused, as it makes the work progress or it makes workers more productive or creative. (This makes smoking sound as if it is a kind of drug.)

There are some exceptions. A few companies encourage smoking employees to become nonsmokers. One gives a bonus to an employee if he / she succeeds in quitting. Others make no-smoking a condition for promotion.

At my university, faculty meetings in the junior college became no-smoking more than 20 years ago because of the demands of a woman professor of music who is also a singer. At the Faculty of Human Sciences, a nonsmoking, forty-something faculty member was elected dean of the department. By Japanese standards, he was rather young to be elected to this position. One of his first acts was to rid the faculty meeting room of all ashtrays without consulting the faculty members. He was criticized by the members and the ashtrays were set out on the tables again. He has since lost all support of the department members because of his independent action. In 1990, a 60-year-old smoking faculty member was elected dean. He proposed making the meeting a no-smoking gathering. The majority of the faculty supported it. The time was different, but the most important factor seemed to be who made the proposal. Nonsmokers prefer that (elder) smokers propose making the conference room or work space no-smoking. Sometimes it takes time, and sometimes their wish may not be fulfilled.

At present there are seven faculty members in the Department of Sociology and Social Work, including one woman. There is only one smoker in the department, and the department's faculty meeting is a no-smoking meeting. None of the faculty requested that smoking be prohibited; that the meeting would be no-smoking was considered a matter of manners. When the formal faculty meeting of the department is finished and the woman professor has departed, the smoker rushes into an adjoining office, brings out an ashtray, and begins smoking as if it were natural to smoke there in front of the remaining male faculty. None of the remaining occupants of the room try to stop him from smoking.

Administrators at this university smoke as often as they like in their offices. But they refrain from smoking when they attend meetings where the primary participants are faculty members. Smoking at my university is contingent; it depends upon the context.

CONCLUSION

Japan's unique social structure and culture shape the construction of tobacco as a social problem. Most important, through its ownership of a majority of Japan Tobacco, Inc.'s stock and through the collection of taxes on tobacco sales, the Japanese government—and particularly the powerful Ministry of Finance—has a strong vested interest in the tobacco business. The Ministry of Health and Welfare and other government agencies that might be expected to promote antismoking policies therefore must proceed cautiously. At the same time, the Japanese legal system's tendency to move slowly, and the difficulties of mounting class-action suits, limit the courts' influence on tobacco policy. Perhaps because the antismoking movement has had difficulty influencing either the government or the courts, the movement remains small. And, because the Japanese respect hierarchy and value harmony, reforms (such as changes in workplace smoking rules) depend more on decisions from the top than claims from below.

This does not mean that Japan's treatment of tobacco exists in isolation. The United States and other Western nations do affect what occurs in Japan, both encouraging and discouraging tobacco use. American tobacco companies have aggressively entered the Japanese market. The U.S. government used the threat of trade sanctions to open Japan to U.S. tobacco sales, and American firms have used a variety of marketing strategies to capture a growing share of the Japanese market. Much of this marketing plays upon the prestige of the United States, through the use of cowboy imagery, slogans about individualism, white models, and so on.

At the same time, the United States and other Western nations offer examples of effective antismoking efforts. Their governments—particularly public-health agencies—have been active claimsmakers, first in detailing the health risks to smokers, and later in constructing second-hand smoke as a social problem (Troyer 1989). A variety of regulations—restrictions on television commercials and other forms of tobacco advertising, restrictions on smoking in public places and the workplace, and so on—increasingly constrain smoking. In addition, the success rate of liability claims against tobacco companies is increasing. All of these tactics serve as resources, models the Japanese antismoking campaign can consider adopting. Perhaps the most powerful of these resources is the idea of globalization—the concern that Japan's treatment of tobacco is increasingly out of step with policies in Western nations.

Japan's treatment of tobacco, then, is subject to contradictory pressures, both from within the country and abroad. In recent years, these pressures have produced slow progress toward antismoking.

POSTSCRIPT: JAPAN TOBACCO'S STRATEGIES
FOR THE FUTURE

One of the biggest pieces of news concerning tobacco in 1999 was the purchase of the international section of RJR (a major American tobacco firm) by JT. The general public was surprised and pondered this move by JT. It seems that JT has two main aims with this purchase: to retain its share of the Japanese market in the face of drastic increases in the sales of American tobacco, and to snare the market in Russia and the other post–Soviet Union Eastern European countries.

Upon its establishment, JT announced that it would diversify its operations by making a 20 percent profit from its life sciences divisions by the end of the twentieth century. The purchase of the international section of RJR highlights the failure of this policy and is a catalyst in the decline of JT. When the announcement of the purchase was made, JT stock fell approximately 6 percent on the Tokyo Stock Exchange. Although JT paid $7.83 billion for this purchase, it may eventually have to sell at a great loss if huge amounts in compensation are awarded to smokers in the event of international lawsuits. Until JT clearly states what it intends to do with the purchase of the international section of RJR, we must wait and see what the outcome of this purchase will be.

ACKNOWLEDGMENT

The author thanks Sanford Taborn for valuable comments, suggestions, and advice on earlier drafts of this paper. Without his help, this paper could not have been written. I greatly appreciate his help and accept responsibility for any remaining inadequacies.

NOTES

1.   These statistics come from the Japan Tobacco Association, as reported by the Ministry of Finance.

2.   The smoking rate in Japan is reported by Japan Tobacco, Inc. The Ministry of Health and Welfare collected similar data from 1989 to 1997, which showed slightly lower rates of smoking.

3   There are four kinds of warnings placed on packages of cigarettes by the Surgeon General in the United States, the American counterpart of the Japanese Ministry of Health and Welfare. The ease with which the Surgeon General can execute antismoking programs is one of the biggest differences between these two ministries.

4.   Some people may say that revenue could be assured through increased taxes on cigarettes even if the consumption of cigarettes is reduced. But the major political party, which is supported by tobacco farmers and gets political donations from tobacco companies, blocks tax increases on cigarettes. Also, that party does not want to lose the votes of smokers at elections.

5.   Although the Japanese association of retail stores selling alcohol announced that it would stop selling alcohol through vending machines by the end of May 2000, most of the vending machines were still working in the first month after the deadline.

6.   In comparison, TV tobacco commercials were banned in Great Britain in 1965, in the United States in 1971, in West Germany in 1974, and in France in 1976.

7.   Christianity is a minor religion in Japan; approximately one percent of the population (including both Catholics and Protestants) is Christian.

REFERENCES

Ayukawa, Jun. 2000. "The Sociology of Social Problems in Japan." *American Sociologist* 31(3):15–26.

Best, Joel. 1990.   *Threatened Children.* Chicago: University of Chicago Press.

———, (ed.). 1995. *Images of Issues.* 2nd ed. Hawthorne, NY: Aldine de Gruyter.

———. 1999. *Random Violence.* Berkeley: University of California Press.

Holstein, James A., and Gale Miller. 1990."Rethinking Victimization." *Symbolic Interaction* 13:101–20.

———. 1993. "Social Constructionism and Social Problems Work." Pp. 131–52 in

Constructionist Controversies, edited by Gale Miller and James A. Holstein. Hawthorne, NY: Aldine de Gruyter.

Isayama, Yoshiro. 1983. *Ken'en ken wo kangaeru* (Thinking About the Right to Dislike Smoking). Tokyo: Iwanami-shoten.

———. 1999. *Gendai tabako senso* (Modern Tobacco Wars). Tokyo: Iwanami-shoten.

Japan Monopoly and Japan Tobacco. 1964–80. *Tabaco sembai shi* (The History of Japan Monopoly). 6 vols. Tokyo: Japan Monopoly and Japan Tobacco.

Japan Tobacco Research Center (ed.). 1987–90. *Tabako wo ganaeru* (Thinking about Tobacco) Vol.1–4. Tokyo: Heibon-sha.

Kaneko, S., Muramatsu, T., et al. 1996. "Terebi tabako CM no hoei to mondaiten" (Some problems with tobacco advertisements). *Bulletin of the Faculty of Engineering* (Chubu University) 28.

Ministry of Health and Welfare (ed.). 1993. *Kitsuen to kenko—Kitsuen to kenko mondai ni kansuru hokokusho* (Smoking and Health—Reports Concerning Smoking and Health Problems). 2nd ed. Tokyo: Hokendojin-sha.

Ministry of Labor. 1996. *Shokuba ni okeru kitsuen taisaku no tameno gaido rain* (Guidelines for Regulating Smoking in the Workplace). Tokyo.

Nakagawa, N. 1995. "Social Constructionism in Japan." *Perspectives on Social Problems* 7:295–310.

Osaki, Y., M. Minowa, et al. 1996. "1996 nendo miseinen-sha no kitsuen-kodo ni kansuru zenkoku chosa" (National Survey on Smoking Behavior among Juveniles in 1996). *Kosei no Shihyo* (Indexes on Welfare) 46(13):16–22.

Smoking Problem Information Center. 1990–. *Kin'en janaru* (No Smoking Journal).

Spector, Malcolm, and John I. Kitsuse. 1977. *Constructing Social Problems*. Menlo Park, CA: Cummings.

Tanase, Takao. 1999. "Beikoku tabako sosho on tenkai to tabako seisaku" (The Development of Lawsuits Concerning Smoking and Policy on Smoking in the U.S.). *Jurisuto* (Jurist), No.1149:66–74.

Troyer, Ronald. 1989. "The Surprising Resurgence of the Smoking Problem." Pp. 159–76 in *Images of Issues*, edited by Joel Best. Hawthorne, NY: Aldine de Gruyter.

———, and Gerald E. Markle. 1983. *Cigarettes: The Battle over Smoking*. New Brunswick, NJ: Rutgers University Press.

Watanabe, Fumisato. 1996. *Tabako no gaito tatakatte* (Fighting Against the Hazard of Tobacco). Tokyo: Dainihon-tosho.

Weber, Max. 1947. *The Theory of Social and Economic Organization*. Glencoe, IL: Free Press.

12

The Legal Problem of Sexual Harassment and Its International Diffusion

A Case Study of Austrian Sexual-Harassment Law

MIA CAHILL

In 1980, sexual harassment, the social problem, was translated by feminist legal activists, the Equal Employment Opportunity Commission (EEOC), and others into sexual harassment, the legal problem. That year, the EEOC, the government agency charged with enforcing Title VII under the 1964 Civil Rights Act, issued regulatory guidelines defining sexual harassment as a type of sex discrimination. While the EEOC Guidelines did not have the force of law, the regulatory embodiment of the concept of sexual harassment fostered the diffusion of *this particular conceptualization* of sexual harassment. The dominance of this particular legal embodiment of sexual harassment was not limited to the United States. The basic legal model was soon disseminated abroad by activists, governmental actors, and media involved in the publicizing the social problem of sexual harassment. As European countries began to legislate about of sexual harassment, the ways they addressed it were greatly affected by the U.S. legal codification and the subsequent diffusion of this legal form. European countries varied in the degree to which they relied on the U.S. legal conception. Some followed the U.S. model entirely, others shifted its frame away from discrimination, and still others used the U.S. model as a foil against which to define their own law. By the late 1980s in Europe, the U.S. influence over the legal form of sexual harassment was undeniable. At the turn of the next decade, whatever significance sexual harassment had as a social problem was joined and perhaps even overshadowed by the view that it was a legal problem with a legal definition and a solution in law.

In this chapter, I use Austria as a case study to explore the consequences of the legal diffusion of sexual-harassment law. I suggest that Austria ultimately adopted a sexual harassment provision to their Equal Treatment Act based on a mix of internal pressure and the availability of this institutionalized, external legal model. I argue that the diffusion of the U.S. sexual-harassment-law model to the European Union, and ultimately to Austria, had three main consequences. First, the international community provided pressure (or perceived pressure) to conform to the laws of the economic First World. This sped the success of internal feminist attempts to obtain sexual-harassment protections. Second, the diffusion of this form narrowed the definition of what comprises sexual harassment according to the law. Finally, because the external legal model—and the issue of sexual harassment—were so closely associated with the United States, the *use* of law by victims of sexual harassment is rejected as nonindigenous by many Austrians in both formal and informal dispute resolution. The global legal diffusion of a sexual-harassment-law model added fuel for critics who charged that the *problem* of sexual harassment is nonindigenous, as well as the law.

THE CREATION OF THE BASIC LEGAL MODEL

The United States

In the United States, sexual harassment was not originally conceived in the passage of the 1964 Civil Rights Act, when Congress included protections for sex discrimination along with the hard-fought racial discrimination protections sought by the civil rights movement. The word "sex" was added late in congressional debate by Representative Howard Smith in what was likely an ill-fated attempt to kill the bill benefiting minorities. However, discrimination protections for women were not completely without support inside and outside of Congress. Representative Smith had supported (white) women's rights in the past and the ban on sex discrimination was supported in earnest by a coalition of five congresswomen and women's rights groups outside Congress (Saguy 1999; Bird 1997). Title VII of the act states:

> It shall be an unlawful employment practice for an employer—(1) to fail or refuse to hire or to discharge any individual, or otherwise to discriminate against any individual with respect to his compensation, terms, conditions, or privileges of employment because of such individual's race, color, religion, *sex*, or national origin. (Civil Rights Act of 1964, 42 U.S.C. Sec. 2000e-2 (1988)—emphasis added)[1]

Nevertheless, the statute makes no mention of sexual harassment. This came later, through case law.

The first legal claims of sexual harassment appeared in the mid-1970s, with the rise of the modern feminist movement in the United States. Prominent movement groups, such as the National Organization for Women and the National Women's Political Caucus, supported the work of two activist groups opposed to sexual harassment that worked to increase its recognition as a social problem. The first, Working Women United, and its research branch Working Women's Institute, was organized in 1975 to protest sexual harassment and later, to counsel victims (Weeks et al. 1986). The following year, the Alliance Against Sexual Coercion (AASC) similarly worked to raise media awareness and aid sexual harassment victims (Weeks et al. 1986; Elman 1996).

With the issue of sexual harassment gaining media coverage, victims began turning to the courts and asking them to define sexual harassment as a legal wrong. Because the Civil Rights Statute addressed discrimination in *employment*, the first sexual-harassment cases arose out of employment relations. Their legal arguments were initially rejected. In *Barnes v. Train*,[2] for example, an Environmental Protection Agency clerk claimed that her job had been eliminated because she refused to have sexual relations with her supervisor, a claim we know today as quid pro quo sexual harassment. Reasoning that she was fired because of her refusal to have sexual relations rather than because of discrimination based on sex, as Title VII of the 1964 Civil Rights Act requires, the trial judge ruled against her claim. Similar claims were made and initially lost at the trial level (e.g., *Tomkins v. Public Service Electric and Gas Co.*).[3] However, by the end of the 1970s, appeals courts began to recognize a legal claim of sexual harassment. In a 1977 appeal of the *Barnes v. Train* case, the Appeals Court in *Barnes v. Costle* found that the plaintiff was indeed a victim of sex discrimination in employment, and ruled in her favor.[4] The appeals courts in the fourth and third circuits made similar rulings, finding that sexual harassment was covered under Title VII of the Civil Rights Act of 1964 as a type of sex discrimination, and were soon followed by other circuits.[5]

In the late 1970s, two studies added to the legitimacy and publicity for sexual harassment as a social and legal problem. They foreshadowed waves of sexual harassment research and cases to come. In the book *Sexual Shakedown*, Lin Farley (1978) described incidents of sexual harassment (or sexual bribery) and brought the issue of sexual harassment to the attention of researchers. The first congressional hearing on sexual harassment was conducted the following year, before the House Committee on Post Office and Civil Service. At this hearing, plans to conduct a systematic study of the sexual harassment of federal workers were developed (Weeks et al. 1986). The ensuing study, the U.S. Merit Systems Protection Board's (1981) survey of approximately 20,000 male and female federal workers, provided the basis for much of the scholarly research on sexual harassment through the 1980s.

The first widely publicized study of sexual harassment was based on the responses of *Harvard Business Review* and *Redbook Magazine* subscribers. The study's findings became a media sensation when it reported that 90 percent of the female respondents had been sexually harassed—and declared sexual harassment a pervasive problem in the workplace (Collins and Blodgett 1981). The study reported the responses of those magazine subscribers who bothered to return the survey—surely raising the specter of response bias.[6] With media attention focused on the issue, activists against sexual harassment lobbied states to make victims who left or were dismissed from their jobs as a result of sexual harassment eligible for unemployment benefits (Elman 1996).

Soon, plaintiffs began to challenge the courts in earnest with sexual-harassment cases, laying the groundwork for the definition that would dominate global debates on sexual harassment. In doing so, they relied on a legal argument set out by Catharine MacKinnon (1979) in her book, *Sexual Harassment of Working Women*. Early drafts of her legal argument circulated in the legal community prior to the book's publication and were even used by a law clerk in the *Barnes v. Costle* decision (Saguy 1999; Weeks et al. 1986). MacKinnon argued that sexual harassment in employment contributed to the sexual coercion of women by men, and was therefore sex-based discrimination as understood within Title VII of the 1964 Civil Rights Act. Central to MacKinnon's legal argument is that sexual harassment is *group-based* harm, falling under the discrimination statute rather than *individual harm*, which would fall under state tort law. As a type of discrimination based on sex, women as a group should receive the protections of civil rights law. In 1980, 75 sexual-harassment lawsuits were filed (Feary 1994).

MacKinnon's (1979) path-breaking legal argument distinguished two types of sexual harassment: *quid pro quo* and *hostile environment* harassment. These categories soon formed the foundation of the EEOC's 1980 regulatory guidelines, the first U.S. Supreme Court decision on sexual harassment, and over a decade later, actions by parliaments around the world. While the EEOC Guidelines were meant as the commission's interpretation of the Civil Rights Act and do not have the force of law, the act of a government body writing the legal definition allowed—and indeed began—the diffusion of *this particular legal form* of sexual harassment.[7]

According to the EEOC guidelines,[8] for sexual harassment to be illegal as a type of sex discrimination in *employment*, it needs to be behavior of a *sexual nature* and *unwelcome*. Two main types of harassment were defined in the 1980 guidelines: quid pro quo (1 and 2 below), and hostile environment (3 below). The guidelines state in part:

Unwelcome sexual advances, requests for sexual favors, and other verbal or physical conduct of a sexual nature constitute sexual harassment when:
(1) submission to such conduct is made either explicitly or implicitly a term or condition of an individual's employment,
(2) submission to or rejection of such conduct by an individual is used as the basis for employment decisions affecting such individual, or
(3) such conduct has the purpose or effect of unreasonably interfering with an individual's work performance or creating an intimidating, hostile or offensive working environment.

Six years later, in the first major decision on sexual harassment, the U.S. Supreme Court relied heavily on the EEOC guidelines and MacKinnon's original argument in their opinion. The legal form of sexual harassment had now been imprinted on the domestic and international consciousness. The EEOC guidelines acted as a legal form book for the embodiment of sexual-harassment law worldwide. When the European Union considered the issue of sexual harassment, they drew heavily on the U.S. model, far expanding its dissemination and legitimacy.

European Union

The European Union first addressed the issue of sexual harassment in the context of the Equal Treatment Directive. In 1976, the European Council of Ministers passed this directive outlawing sex discrimination at work and in worker training.[9] While making no mention of the concept of sexual harassment, it set the stage for the legal arguments to come (Carter 1992; McCrudden 1993; Earle and Madek 1993; Webb 1994; Bernstein 1994, 1997). In 1983, the Industrial Tribunal in the U.K. decided the issue of sexual harassment in favor of a female apprentice in a car mechanic shop in Northern Ireland[10] (Collins 1996). The tribunal found that her treatment constituted unlawful discrimination and this led to the mounting pressure "for a Union-wide response to the problem" (Collins 1996:26).

Voluntary measures in the 1980s followed the Equal Treatment Directive. First, in 1984, the Council of Ministers passed a resolution calling for "dignity for women at the workplace" and for action policies to eliminate inequalities affecting women.[11] The European Union took two more steps in 1986, the year of the *Meritor Savings Bank v. Vinson* decision in the United States. First, the European Commission agreed to the request of the Council of Ministers on Women's Issues to begin research into sexual harassment in the European Communities (Collins 1996). This resulted in a widely cited study on sexual harassment in the European Communities by Michael Rubinstein (1988). Rubinstein recommended that the European Union adopt a directive on sexual harassment that would require legal conformity of the member states. In the second voluntary measure that year, the European Parliament adopted a resolution on violence against women.[12] Including sexual harassment within the category of violence, the resolution called for the assessment of the legal protections against sexual harassment in labor and antidiscrimination law (Collins 1996). In 1989, Spain became the first European Union country to adopt a sexual-harassment law (Valiente 1998, 2000).

Finally, in 1990 the Council of Ministers addressed sexual harassment directly in a resolution calling for the protection of the dignity of men and women at work (Bernstein 1997).[13] The resolution defined sexual harassment, under some circumstances, as contrary to the principle of equal treatment (Carter 1992). Soon after, a recommendation and code of practice were enacted, which further elaborated the legal meaning of sexual harassment. It called on member states to pursue measures aimed at creating a climate of respect for men and women in the workplace and explicitly stated that sexual harassment is contrary to the already existing Equal Treatment Directive.[14] Interestingly, the European Union law places sexual harassment in the contexts of both dignity and equal treatment.

The EU definition of sexual harassment relied greatly on the U.S. EEOC guidelines for its legal structure, even though it was established within the context of the "dignity" of the worker, a frame absent in U.S. law. The U.S. context is one of civil-rights law, or antidiscrimination. The conception of *worker dignity* reflected the requirement in EU law (under the Treaty of Rome) that equality provisions remain within the economic domain. Just as the U.S. law was limited to the employment context because it falls under the Civil Rights Act, the European Union legal conceptualizations were similarly limited to the economic context. This is one of the key features of sexual-harassment law.

Like U.S. law, the recommendation did not provide specific examples of behavior considered sexual harassment and initiatives to do so were quickly killed in the consultation process (Collins 1996). Instead, the recommendation and code of practice used the broad EEOC formulation of quid pro quo and hostile-environment sexual harassment, as well as retaining the employment context. The European Union defines sexual harassment:

> (1) conduct of a sexual nature, or other conduct based on sex affecting the dignity of women and men at work, including conduct of superiors and colleagues, constitutes an intolerable violation of the dignity of workers or trainees and is unacceptable if:
> (a) such conduct is unwanted, unreasonable and offensive to the recipient;
> (*Quid Pro Quo*)(b) a person's rejection of, or submission to, such conduct on the part of employers or workers (including superiors or colleagues) is used explicitly or implicitly as a basis for a decision which affects that person's access to vocational training, access to employment, continued employment, promotion, salary or any other employment decisions;

and/or
(*Hostile Environment*)(c) such conduct creates an intimidating, hostile or humiliating working environment for the recipient.[15]

Although neither the recommendation, resolutions, nor the code of practice are binding on member states, they may have a role in national courts. The European Court of Justice ruled that national courts must use recommendations to clarify or supplement the binding measures of the European Union, such as directives (Collins 1996).[16] This means that the recommendation on sexual harassment can be used by plaintiffs in national courts to argue that the Equal Treatment Directive of the European Union includes sexual harassment.

This European Union attention to sexual harassment law provided impetus to a feminist push for sexual-harassment laws in several European countries (Valiente 1998, 2000; Elman 1996, 2000; Saguy 1999). While some countries explicitly rejected the U.S. model, it is the EEOC definition that forms the foundation of international debates on sexual harassment.

In the latter parts of this chapter, I discuss the consequences of this diffusion for Austrian sexual-harassment disputes. First, in addition to domestic issues, perceived pressure from the international community led Austrian elites to speed the adoption of a sexual-harassment law. Second, the legal model of sexual harassment narrowed the definition of what comprises sexual harassment. Finally, the global legal diffusion of a sexual-harassment-law model, initially derived in the United States, added fuel to Austrian critics who charged that the *problem* of sexual harassment is foreign, as well as the solution. I begin with Austria's adoption of a sexual harassment law.

THE ADOPTION OF THE BASIC LEGAL MODEL IN AUSTRIA, VIA THE EUROPEAN UNION

Austrian feminists had already achieved legalized abortion (1974), and revisions to the conservative Family Act[17] (1975) when the Austrian Equal Treatment Act was passed in 1979 (Appelt 1998). The Equal Treatment Act prohibited discrimination in the salaries of men and women.[18] Although only weakly defined as "disadvantageous differentiation which is undertaken without material justification" (Rosenberger 1998:113), the act uses the term "discrimination" to reflect the social problems it purports to address. This discrimination terminology was carried through to the sexual-harassment provision (when it was added in 1992).[19]

The 1979 Equal Treatment Act also established an Equal Treatment Commission (GBK)[20] to hear claims and make nonbinding recommendations under the statute. By law, the GBK consists of representatives of Austrian unions, industry, and government (the "social partners"). Without the enforcement powers of the courts, the GBK's opinions[21] are treated as suggestions or proposals rather than enforceable legal decisions. However, in discrimination cases, it is the GBK that sees by far the largest number of disputes. Although there were minor amendments to the Equal Treatment Law in 1985,[22] and again in 1990,[23] the most fundamental change came in 1992 with the addition of the sexual-harassment and other provisions.

Like many other European countries, the issue of sexual harassment was brought to national attention through the trade unions and labor movement, but by drawing on institutionalized models abroad. By the mid-1980s, union members raising concerns about sexual harassment were a small but vocal minority. The problem of sexual harassment was facing trade union staff representatives (within companies) who knew first-hand of the sexual harassment working women faced. The staff representatives raised these issues within the internal hierarchy of the trade unions. In response to the rising significance of sexual harassment to working women in Austria, feminists within the trade unions promoted the issue internally and were eventually approached by the Ministry for Labor and Social Affairs about disseminating surveys for a study they intended to conduct.[24]

In 1986, the Women's Office of the Ministry for Labor and Social Affairs commissioned a study on sexual harassment in the workplace, *Sexuelle Belästigung am Arbeitsplatz* (Hopfgartner and Zeichen 1988). This was the first major study of sexual harassment in Austria and certainly the best-known study today (Zippel 1999). It was designed to examine the prevalence of sexual harassment in the workplace, and the impact that sexual harassment has on women's lives. This report relied explicitly on the U.S. legal definition of sexual harassment in both defining the problem and describing its scope. In addition to a 1983 definition by the Health and Research Employees Association of Australia, and the United Kingdom's "Charter for Equality for Women Within Trade Unions (TUC)," the authors cited law and research focused on the United States. All of these English-language texts remained true to the original EEOC guidelines in the United States.

The international legal model of sexual harassment in the late 1980s was the U.S. EEOC model (in whatever guise), just as it also was the source of most of the available scholarly research on sexual harassment:

> In 1980, few people in Europe discussed sexual harassment as a problem; it did not have a name, and those subjected to it had no legal protection. By contrast, in the United States, discussion on the nature of the problem and ways to deal with it had begun in the 1970s. By the decade's close, activists on both sides of the Atlantic were aware that the Equal Employment Op-

portunities Commission had developed guidelines and a legal position on what constituted sexual harassment (Collins 1996:25).

Hopfgartner and Zeichen (1988), the authors of the Austrian report, reviewed the EEOC Guidelines on sexual harassment, research from the Merit Systems Protection Board study, MacKinnon's *Sexual Harassment of Working Women*, Farley's *Sexual Shakedown*, the Working Women's Institute publications, as well as research in U.S. academic publications.

Indeed, the Hopfgartner and Zeichen (1988) study showcases the U.S. *Redbook Magazine/Harvard Business Review* study that found that over 90 percent of women had been sexually harassed (Collins and Blodgett 1981). Their own study shares that survey's problem of unrepresentative sampling, although it is equally dramatic in its findings. Hopfgartner and Zeichen found that 81 percent of women in their study had been sexually harassed.[25] The findings were used prominently in the political debate over the inclusion of sexual harassment in the Equal Treatment Law. While the methodology of this study—like that of *Redbook Magazine* in the United States—is certainly suspect, Hopfgartner and Zeichen's findings were important in establishing sexual harassment as a problem of *Austrian* women and linking it to *legal* regulation already in existence, albeit across the ocean.

At this time, sexual harassment was also becoming an issue of the International Labour Organization (ILO) (of the United Nations). However, it was not until 1988 that the ILO publicly raised the issue. Its Committee of Experts listed examples of sexual harassment as unwelcome and associated with the conditions of employment (Aeberhard-Hodges 1996)—again modeling the U.S. legal form. This and other more minor initiatives of the ILO regarding sexual harassment were not disseminated broadly in the 1980s but, because of the ILO's reporting requirement, government officials in Austria knew it was a rising issue of international concern.

In 1990, a ruling by the Constitutional Court (*Verfassungsgericht*) mobilized women's-rights activists and eventually led to the adoption of a sexual-harassment provision two years later. After several failed attempts to overturn it (Peterka 1987), the gender-specific retirement age for state benefits was finally struck down by the Constitutional Court as a violation of the equal treatment law. This meant that Parliament would have to amend the law and provide equality in retirement ages, essentially raising the retirement age for women. Proponents of women's rights took this legislative opportunity to demand the long-touted de facto equality. Feminists in Austria had been raising the issue of sexual harassment for some time without much success. In response to an impending change in the retirement ages, the Minister of Women's Affairs (Johanna Dohnal) and other women politicians presented a list of equality demands to the government and industry that included workplace equality. The demand for a sexual-harassment provision within the equal treatment act was high on their list.

As the "package of equality," as it would come to be known, was debated within Austria, the government was preparing to define its post–Cold War future. The negotiations occurred against the backdrop of a declining Soviet Union and strengthening European Union. Schally described the dramatic political and economic shifts in the region at the time:

> Europe, a continent which only a few years ago seemed to be frozen in time, is presently experiencing a complete and dramatic change of history. As the present events bring Europe back into the international spotlight, the bipolar system of the postwar era is about to be replaced by multipolarism. . . . Since 1986 two previously unimaginable developments have changed the course of events in Europe. The first of these developments is the European Community's attempt to create a single European market. The second is the end of Communist domination in the Eastern European Countries. (Schally 1991:267–68)

Austrian participation in the European Union was not something to be taken lightly. Joining the EU would require legislative conformity in accordance with its laws, and a shift to the West. Kennedy and Specht (1990:409) warned that "joining the European Communities means a large-scale and largely irreversible transformation of a state's substantive law, governmental structure and international status. . . . Membership would so dramatically transform both the constitutional structure of Austrian government and its legal capacity for an independent defense that Austria's international legal status as a 'permanent neutral' would be jeopardized."

In addition to concerns about giving up the increasingly irrelevant "neutrality," Austrians were concerned about joining a European Union controlled by their larger and more economically powerful neighbor, Germany: "Austrians no longer seek an Anschluß [the German/Austrian unification of WWII]—indeed, many of them fear absorption into a German-dominated Europe—but Germany is always on their minds, whereas Austria is a topic of almost no sustained interest in Germany itself" (Judt 1998:135).[26] In seeking to retain Austria's unique culture apart from Germany, many in Austria feared a second Anschluß, albeit largely economic. Given Austria's history, geography, and culture, even if economic pragmatism demanded the joining of the European Union, it would not be without concern about their northern neighbor.

It was within this context—the end of the Cold War, the rising importance of the European Union, and concerns about a strong Germany—that industry, union, and government leaders in Austria eventually supported sexual-harassment legislation. While the issue of sexual harassment had been raised before by Austrian feminists in government and the trade unions, industry leaders had strongly resisted it. However, these same leaders of industry generally supported joining the EU, and they used the negotiations over the equal treatment act to do two things: first, they agreed to a sexual-harassment law that they believed they would eventually be subject to anyway, under EU law; and second, they voluntarily adopted their own law, in their own manner, before Germany did.[27]

While the European Union had not issued a *mandatory* requirement that member states have a specific prohibition against sexual harassment, at the time of the equal-treatment packet negotiations in Austria, it looked as though a sexual harassment directive was likely to be adopted by the European Union. Although this ultimately would not be the case, the Austrian industry representatives who were negotiating equal treatment domestically were also hopeful partners in a European Union that had several equality policies, as well as a sexual-harassment recommendation largely modeled on U.S. law.

After two years of negotiations sparked by the ruling on unequal retirement ages, the Austrian "Equal Treatment Packet" was adopted. It included the provision on sexual harassment long sought by women's-rights activists in Austria.[28] To some in Austrian politics, the passage of the sexual-harassment provision and Austria's joining of the European Union were linked. Reflecting concern over how Austria would appear to a European Union that Austrian industry wanted to join, one Austrian representative of industry who participated in the equal-treatment negotiations described the "voluntariness" of the provision. But, he added, "we have our peace in Brussels [the headquarters of the European Union] in this field. We wouldn't have it, still having a law without a sexual harassment paragraph" (interview).[29] Another government official also involved in the negotiations explained why they supported the sexual harassment provision: "First thing, it was mostly to comply with the [European Union] and second, [it was] to show that they supported woman's wishes in this respect" (interview). The Austrian law went into effect on January 1, 1993, over a year before Germany addressed the issue of sexual harassment with the Employee Protection Act.

THE FORM OF THE LAW: CONCEPTUALIZING THE SCOPE OF WHAT IS SEXUAL HARASSMENT

Like U.S. law, the logic of Austrian law places sexual harassment within the context of discrimination (Bei and Novak 1997; Aeberhard-Hodges 1996). Also like the U.S. law, the Austrian provision of sexual harassment defines two types of sexual harassment, or *Sexuelle Belästigung am Arbeitsplatz,* as a type of discrimination that arises out of the employment relationship.[30]

While there might be many ways to define sexual harassment, the legal definition limits sexual harassment to: (1) things that are within the context of employment, (2) that fall into one of the two legal categories, and (3) are unwelcome. While potentially there are many other ways to conceptualize sexual harassment, any other formal or informal conceptualization must overcome this legal model.

The United States and Austria make similar conceptual distinctions in sexual harassment law between the two main types of sexual harassment— quid pro quo harassment and hostile-environment harassment. Quid pro quo harassment involves "the conditioning of concrete employment benefits on sexual favors" (*Vinson* at 2403). Under Austrian law, this is behavior "that typically includes the promise of [employment] advantages for the tolerance, as well as the threatening of [employment] disadvantages on the rejection of sexual acts" (Bei and Novak 1997:127). For example, quid pro quo harassment would include the situation where an employer demands sex from an employee, threatening the loss of the employee's job. It would still be considered sexual harassment whether or not the employee submitted to the demands, assuming the other conditions of a sexual-harassment case were met.

The second category, hostile environment, creates a hostile or abusive work environment for the victim. It is similarly defined in Austrian law as behavior that "creates an intimidating, hostile or humiliating work environment" (GBG Sec. 2(1 b (1))). First described by the Supreme Court in *Vinson,* the court elaborated the definition of hostile environment sexual harassment in *Harris v. Forklift Systems, Inc.* 114 S. Ct. 367 (1993). In this case, a unanimous court stated that the conduct contributing to a hostile environment must be "severe" and "pervasive,"[31] but exactly what such conduct is can be determined only "by looking at all of the circumstances."[32] Austria's standard draws here on the concept of dignity, but is equally ambiguous, requiring that the conduct (for any type of sexual harassment) impair personal dignity and affect the work atmosphere.[33]

Yet, even given differences in the context of the U.S. and Austrian legal systems,[34] feminists and activists in Austria relied on the research and law from the United States. Feminists in the United States had already successfully defined sexual harassment as a social problem with a legal solution when Austrians attempted to establish their law of sexual harassment.[35] They relied on the narrowed definition of sexual harassment and adopted it as a type of discrimination in employment with two major categories: quid pro quo and hostile environment.

While I do not suggest that all countries adopted exactly the same U.S. law, the U.S. model is fundamentally the starting point for both popular debates and legislative negotiation. For example, the European Union rejected the discrimination frame in part by placing sexual harassment within equal treatment, but also placing it in the larger context of worker dignity. Yet, even in shifting the context, the EU retained the basic definition of sexual harassment. Spain and Sweden rejected the concept of coworker hostile-environment sexual harassment, but maintained the concept of quid pro quo harassment in employment. This was likely the result of Socialist party attention to hierarchical abuses of power, as is exemplified in quid pro quo harassment, and the Socialist party's inattention to power relationships between male and female coworkers (Elman 1996, 2000; Valiente 1998, 2000). Yet, the basic model of sexual harassment is the same. In France, the U.S.-derived vision of sexual harassment was specifically rejected in the presentation of their sexual harassment legislation (Saguy 1998, 1999). France defined sexual harassment more narrowly as abuse of authority in ways most commonly associated with quid pro quo harassment. Even as foils, the U.S. legal framework and definition of sexual harassment globally influenced both the adoption and the implementation of sexual-harassment law.

Austria's adoption of the external model of sexual harassment also implied acceptance of an individual rights–based model. The government was not charged with spot-checking employers; rather, individual sexual-harassment victims were given the right to bring a lawsuit against the harasser and the employer, and ask for monetary compensation. Within a minimum Austrian schillings value set for each act of sexual harassment found in law, victims of sexual harassment were encouraged by the Ministry for Women's Affairs and others to bring their experiences of sexual harassment to the legal system, use a state-funded equal treatment lawyer, and find their remedy in law.

CONSEQUENCES OF THE ADOPTION OF THE U.S. MODEL FOR AUSTRIAN CLAIMS OF SEXUAL HARASSMENT

Austrian victims of sexual harassment face the consequences of the diffused U.S. legal model in two places. First, at the formal level of legal complaints, victims risk appearing un-Austrian if they rely too heavily on the legal model, even as adopted in the act. Second, at the informal level within firms, victims of sexual harassment also risk association with things foreign if they raise the issue of sexual harassment. Some Austrian managers reject sexual harassment as an American topic, and this has consequences for sexual-harassment disputes. Below, I consider each of these levels, drawing on Austrian interviews conducted in the course of my larger study (Cahill 2000a).

The Formal Level

While the model for the Austrian law came from foreign sources, it attracted Austrian feminists because it challenged the existing patriarchal patterns in the workplace. However, actual use of the law by sexual harassment victims occurs within the context of the labor courts or most often, the GBK. From the inception of the law, the equal treatment act (Sec. 4–5) provided for a GBK to hear complaints under the law, and when the sexual-harassment provision was adopted, the GBK had little idea that this issue would soon overshadow all others in its work. The GBK mediates equal treatment law claims. An employer, an employee, or an institution represented in the membership of the GBK, or the state-funded equal treatment lawyer (*Gleichbehandlungsanwältin*)[36] can bring a case before the GBK (Sec. 6(1)). The State provides an equal treatment lawyer[37] to bring the claims of sexual harassment victims to the GBK. At the end of a hearing, the GBK makes a recommendation, rather than a decision, on the outcome of the case.[38]

Feminists encouraged victims to use the GBK because it is generally viewed as a friendlier and more private forum for sexual-harassment victims than the labor courts. This is not to say that women making claims to the GBK do so without reprisals. As of 1997, there had not yet been a victim of sexual harassment who had made a claim to the GBK and was also able to keep her job.

The establishment of the GBK draws on the value of consensus, or reaching an agreement amenable to all without a formal decision. Yet, by its very definition, sexual harassment is a legal wrong, a discrimination. Even in its formal structure, Austrian sexual-harassment victims face the formidable challenge of using an individual rights–based law within a consensus-building commission. Filing a claim about sexual harassment, even with the GBK, with membership likely to be sympathetic to the wrongs of sexual harassment, threatens this consensus. As one equal treatment GBK member explains, the issue of sexual harassment is especially disruptive and even taboo in social life. Women who do bring it to the attention of the law are not well received either in their firms or in the courts:

> There are not many legal decisions. It's a taboo. The women are afraid and also the judges don't like this problem. [They are afraid] because they lose their work, and also they have a black mark on their head when they are looking for new work. Austria is a small country and you hear about everything. "That's the woman who goes to court because of sexual harassment." (interview)

The reliance on the law, and the legal frame that dominates the field of sexual harassment is further limited in its implementation by attempts to delegalize the legal process of bringing disputes before the GBK.

The GBK members and the equal treatment lawyer work hard to present the GBK as a safe place to bring sexual-harassment complaints. This is often done in contrast to the courts, which they generally see as outright hostile to sexual-harassment victims. Often analogized to rape trials, one commission member agrees that, "[I]t's more difficult for the women in court than before the commission. She is often harshly questioned, sometimes they try to insinuate certain things about the woman. She is asked about her way of life, that's rarer in the commission" (interview). As another member describes it, lawyers only add to this problem of legalizing the disputes and increasing the conflict:

> If they have a lawyer and they ask him what to do, he will never say, "Talk about the situation." He will say, "You can do this and that and we have to do this or write a letter to the woman and tell her she must apologize and she will say that she is wrong." That's the first thing he will tell him. And then he will tell him, "And we have the paragraph so and so and she will have to pay." That's what the lawyer will tell you. (interview)

While most the lawyers appearing before the commission represent the harasser or employer, lawyers and the lawyerly assertiveness associated with the formal assertion of rights violate the idea of consensus. Because the commission draws on the value of consensus, the actual use of the right-based approach in law limits the possibilities for victim success within the legal definition of sexual harassment.

The Informal Level

Most instances of sexual harassment in the workplace never involve courts or judges. Many lawsuits are settled before reaching a court decision. Other complaints are never presented in court. They are resolved within the organization, through a private disputing process such as mediation or arbitration. Still other complaints are resolved even more informally, within the organization. Some legal wrongs are never claimed because of fear of retribution (Prager, Pichler and Staudacher 1996), difficulties associated with leaving the firm or other sociopsychological reasons (Buhmiller 1987). Many other potential cases of sexual harassment are never even characterized by the victims as legal wrongs (Felstiner, Abel and Sarat 1980). This suggests that we should also turn to the individuals and organizations struggling with sexual-harassment law both inside and outside the courts in order to understand how it is implemented

Because sexual harassment law was drawn from law outside Austria, its implementation is intertwined with conceptions of national autonomy. For example, in an interview, the CEO of a domestic Austrian pharmaceutical firm rejected the conceptualization of sexual-harassment law as a legal problem, and redefined it as a political issue. This CEO rejected the liberal legal assumption of law as distinct from politics and replaced it with a critical assessment of the U.S. export of legal concepts: "Sexual harassment is not an Austrian problem. It's an American problem imposed on Austria. The United States tells countries they should do something according to the law, but then does whatever they want—regardless of the law" (interview).

Just as this CEO challenged the legitimacy and relevance of sexual harassment law, the Austrian manager of a U.S. multinational in Austria similarly described sexual harassment law as nonindigenous to Austria, and irrelevant to Austrian society: "I have to say it's not at all covered in our company policies because it is not really an issue in our thinking and behavior. It's not even mentioned. I think sexual harassment has never been an issue in Austria" (interview). The theme of American dominance in the world is one that strikes a nationalistic chord in Austrian culture, and easily shifts the dispute to something other than sexual harassment. Recast as an expression of American colonialism, this manager shifted discussion of sexual-harassment law to predictable cultural battle lines of U.S. imposition. What it is not, according to this view, is an issue relevant to Austrians or Austrian organizations. The implied challenges to the primacy of consensus over conflict within Austria's sexual-harassment law make it problematic for sexual-harassment victims who rely on the U.S.-inspired legal model, even as it gives Austrian officials the symbolic gain of having a sexual-harassment law (Cahill 2000b).

CONCLUSION

The broad dissemination of the legal definition of sexual harassment, initially derived in the United States, had implications that went far beyond the dissemination of the legal words. First, the existence of an external model, an embodiment of legal words, was important in legitimizing the cause of feminists working against sexual harassment. Austria, at the very least, looked outside for legitimation as well as the legal words to use when they codified a sexual harassment law. However, once codified, the use of sexual harassment law remained intertwined with its origin.

As does all legislation, sexual-harassment law specifies the circumstances under which it takes place. In the United States and Austria, sexual harassment was limited to things that happened in employment (and some specific educational settings), and to fact-patterns that met the criteria of one of two types of sexual harassment: quid pro quo and hostile-environment. While this is not problematic per se, squarely positioning sexual harassment in the legal realm and within the context of victim-asserted rights, could limit the societal definition of sexual harassment and its connection to societal patterns. Because sexual harassment is so intertwined with its legal definition or the possibilities of legal success under the law, policymakers may overlook other, more broad-based remedies because they consider the issue a legal matter and, essentially, resolved.

Finally, while the law relies on victims to assert their legal claims, overt legalistic appeals tend to be rejected at the formal level of the GBK, which draws more heavily on the value of consensus. While Austrian victims of sexual harassment are encouraged to use the law, they are discouraged from acting in a way that disrupts the consensus-building function of the GBK. Second, because the law and the concept of sexual harassment are so closely associated with the United States, victim use of the law in informal settings, such as the firm, risks raising the specter of foreignness. While the problem of sexual harassment is cross-cultural, the law of sexual harassment is closely associated with the United States and its legal definition. To use sexual-harassment law is to risk becoming entangled with perceptions of the United States.

Indeed, as countries such as Argentina (1993), Costa Rica (1995), the Philippines (1995), New Zealand (1993), and others outside North America and Europe prohibit sexual harassment under their own laws, each might reflect carefully on the law's implementation. As the basic legal model of sexual harassment is further diffused around the world, one must ask not only what the same legal words will mean in different local settings, but what are the implications of framing national law alongside or against this legal model. Drawn from the civil rights context of individual, rights-based enforcement in the United States, this enforcement model is ever present underneath the regulatory words of the basic legal model. The adoption of sexual harassment law without strong formal and informal enforcement of the law leaves sexual harassment victims to struggle with the norms and values that sustain the social problem of sexual harassment in both their underlying dispute and in the implementation of the law.

ACKNOWLEDGMENT

I wish to thank Lauren Edelman, Howard Erlanger, Marc Galanter, Charles Halaby, Nancy Reichman, Abigail Saguy, Joyce Sterling, Mark Suchman, and Kathrina Zippel for their comments on earlier drafts of this chapter. I am grateful to the National Science Foundation, the University of Wisconsin, and the Institute for Law and Society at New York University for their generosity in support of this larger project.

NOTES

1.   Sexual harassment claims based on Title VII are also affected by the statute's limitations. Importantly, under the statute, the term "employer" is restricted to those employing 15 or more employees. Title VII of the Civil Rights Act of 1964 also exempts Congress, Native American tribes, private-membership clubs, and religious groups. While some state laws define employers covered by sex-discrimination law more expansively, this is not the case under federal civil-rights claims. In addition, plaintiffs must file prior to the expiration of the statute of limitations, which is 180 days after the sexual harassment occurred (42 U.S.C. Sec. 2000e-5(e)(1988)).

2.   13 Fair Empl. Prac. Cas. (BNA) 123 (D.D.C) 1974.

3.   568 F. 2d 1044 (3d Cir 1977).

4.   *Barnes v. Costle,* 561 F. 2d 983 (D.C. Cir. 1977).

5.   *Garber v. Saxon Business Products,* 552 F. 2d 10132 (4th Cir. 1977); and *Tomkins v. Public Service Electric and Gas Co.,* 568 F. 2d 1044 (3rd Cir. 1977).

6.   Other studies with more reliable sampling methods have found that about one-half of working women experience some type sexual harassment at work (U.S. Merit Systems Protection Board 1981; Gutek 1985; Fitzgerald and Shullman 1993; Bioarsky et al. 1995; Griffin-Shelley 1985), with somewhat higher rates for women in predominately male workplaces (Gruber 1998). In an analysis of the results of 18 studies, Gruber (1997) estimates that 44 percent of women have been sexually harassed, although the range extends from 28 to 75 percent.

7.   There might have been other legal forms, such as a worker's compensation law for sexual harassment, or the legal form could have been shaped under existing tort law. Or, the courts might have rejected sexual harassment as a legal claim at all, leaving it purely in the social sphere.

8.   29 C.F.R. 1604.11 (1980).

9.   Directive 76/207, 1976 OJ (L 39/40).

10.   *M v. Crescent Garage Ltd* IT Case 23/83/SD.

11.   1984 OJ (L 331).

12.   OJC 176/79, 14 July 1986.

13.   Council Resolution of May 29, 1990, on the protection of the dignity of women and men at work, OJ C 157) 3–4, June 27, 1990. In addition, the Code of Practice recognizes sexual harassment as "contrary to the principle of equal treatment" under the 1976 directive, meaning that sexual harassment may be actionable under a member nation's equal treatment law that does not specifically mention sexual harassment (Earle and Madek 1993:87n325).

14.   Commission Recommendation of 27 November 1991 (C(91) 2625) on the protection of the dignity of women and men at work (92/C 27/04, OJ (C27)), 4.2.92, 4.

15.   1990 OJ © 157, cited in Earle and Madek (1993:76).

16.   *Grimaldi v. Fonds de Maladies Professionnelles* (Case 322/88 [1990] IRLR 400).

17.   The Family Act, dating from 1811, legally reiterated the conservative social norm of "the father as the head of the family" (Rosenberger 1998:108). Among other things, the amendments did away with the requirement that a wife obtain her husband's permission in order to work.

18. GBG Sec. 2 (2). The law at this point only included private employers.

19. Using the concept of discrimination makes Austrian law more like the U.S. legal context; the European Union stopped short of calling sexual harassment "discrimination."

20. *Gleichbehandlungskomission* (hereinafter referred to as GBK) Sec. 3 (1)–(6) and Sec. 4–6.

21. Written opinions resulting from GBK cases are not entitled *"Bescheid"* or "decision," as are court opinions; rather, they are entitled *"Vorschlag,"* meaning a suggestion or a proposal.

22. These amendments increased its jurisdiction, required equality in vocational training, fringe benefits, and gender-neutral job advertising. They also limited state subsidies to those companies in compliance with the act (Rosenberger 1998).

23. These amendments prohibited sex discrimination in the working relationship and in job dismissal, and also established an *Anwältin für Gleichbehandlungsfragen,* or a state-subsidized lawyer, to assist plaintiffs with equal-treatment claims and facilitate conciliation between employers and employees regarding equal-treatment violations.

24. Personal communication with trade union official, February 15, 1997.

25. Although grand in design, only 14 percent of the survey's 10,000 questionnaires sent to labor unions for distribution were returned. More recent studies of sexual harassment in Austria report lower rates of sexual harassment (see Zippel 1999).

26. Holzer (1998:148) makes a similar point: "True, Germany plays a very important role, both in real terms and in the memory of many Austrians. Many have retained a partly fearful, partly jealous, partly self-righteous inferiority complex. The benign neglect of Austria by many Germans, the imbalance in degree of mutual attention, is, however, quite normal between neighbors of such disproportionate size and power."

27. For a comparison of German sexual harassment law, see Zippel (2000).

28. *Gleichbehandlungskomission* Sec. 12. The package also included extension of paid leave for a relative's illness and shifted the focus of discrimination under that statute from equal pay to comparable worth (Rosenberger 1998). In 1993, an affirmative-action program for women was instituted, although two years later the European Supreme Court rejected it (Rosenberger 1998; Decision of the European Supreme Court of 17 October 1995, Nr. C-450/93 related to Provision 177 EC-Treaty). A provision subjecting federal employees to an equal treatment law was eventually required for conformity to the laws of the European Union. This occurred in 1993 and provided for a federal Equal Treatment Law and Commission.

29. Names of subjects in author-conducted interviews are withheld to maintain anonymity.

30. Sexual-harassment law in Austria also covers apprenticeships associated with educational programs and training. In the United States, sexual harassment in education is covered under Title IX.

31. *Harris v. Forklift Systems, Inc.* 510 U.S. 17, 22(1993) and *Vinson.*

32. Judges are directed to consider four factors, including: (1) the frequency and (2) severity of the conduct, (3) whether it is physically threatening or humili-

ating, or mere offensive utterances, and (4) whether it unreasonably interferes with an employee's work performance. (Psychological injury might be considered a fifth factor, but is not necessary to a claim of hostile-environment sexual harassment.) *Harris* at 22(1993).

33.   When considering a hostile-environment case, behavior might not reach the threshold of impairing personal dignity, but could still be considered sexual harassment if it was frequent or continuous, not unlike the U.S. conceptualization. The crucial aspect, however, "is whether the work atmosphere has become unbearable for the victim" (Bei and Novak 1997:127).

34.   As a civil-law country, Austria's law is based on statutory law. It is the equal treatment statute and accompanying motives, rather than individual cases, that provide the primary basis for judicial decision making. This is in contrast to the U.S. system of case law, which is based on both statutory law and judicial interpretation of statutory and nonstatutory law. Thus, Austrian legal protection of sexual harassment could not develop through case law, as it did in the United States, but must occur through the political system in the form of new legislation: to create a new legal protection, a new law must be passed. One might wonder if a "sexual harassment law" could have been passed in 1986 in the United States, the year of the Supreme Court decision in *Meritor Savings Bank v. Vinson* 477 U.S. 57, 106 S.Ct. 2399, 91 L.Ed.2d 49 (1986), when President Ronald Reagan would have had to sign the law.

35.   Indeed, Austria's main text is virtually indistinguishable from the EEOC guidelines. This is particularly fascinating considering the quirk in U.S. sexual-harassment law—it is defined by case law under a statute passed with its primary emphasis on ending racial discrimination in the workplace.

36.   The "in" ending connotes the female sex in German. Her duties include appearing before the GBK with cases and conducting investigations on behalf of the GBK (Bei and Novak 1997). The equal treatment lawyer (and one lawyer serving as a vice-equal treatment lawyer) represent claims to the GBK throughout Austria. She is nominated by the Ministry for Social Affairs "for the consultation and support of persons who feel discriminated against in the sense of [the Equal Treatment Act.]" Her duties include appearing before the GBK with cases and conducting investigations on its behalf (GBG sec. 3a). The equal treatment lawyer is institutionally supported by the Department of Women's Affairs in the Federal Chancellery and appointed for an unspecified term.

37.   The equal treatment lawyer is required by statute to hold office hours for consultation with individuals claiming violations of the GBG, BGBI Nr 108/1979, idF BGBI Nr 290/1985, 410/1990 and 833/1992 sec. 3a(2).

38.   While GBK decisions may be used in the labor courts, they do not hold precedential value.

REFERENCES

Aeberhard-Hodges, Jane. 1996. "Sexual Harassment in Employment: Recent Judicial and Arbitral Trends." *International Labour Review* 135:499–533.

Appelt, Erna M. 1998. "Women in the Austrian Economy." Pp. 83–103 in *Women in Austria,* edited by Guenter Bishof, Anton Pelinka, and Erika Thurner. New Brunswick, NJ: Transaction.

Bei, Neda, and Renate Novak. 1997. "Frauen und Recht Rechtswissenschaft." Pp. 84–157 in *Handbuch der Frauenrechte,* edited by Ulrike Aichorn. Wien: Springer Verlag.

Bernstein, Anita. 1994. "Law, Culture and Harassment." *University of Pennsylvania Law Review* 142:1227–1311.

———. 1997. "Treating Sexual Harassment with Respect." *Harvard Law Review* 111:446–527.

Bird, Robert C. 1997. "More Than a Congressional Joke: A Fresh Look at the Legislative History of Sex Discrimination of the 1964 Civil Rights Act." *William and Mary Journal of Women and the Law* 3:137–61.

Boiarsky, Carolyn, Laurel Grove, Barbara Northrop, Marianne Phillips, Felicity Myers, and Patricia Earnest. 1995. "Women in Technical/Scientific Professions: Results of Two National Surveys." *IEEE Transactions on Professional Communication* 38:68–76.

Buhmiller, Kristin. 1987. "Victims in the Shadow of the Law: A Critique of the Model of Legal Protection." *Signs* 12:421–39.

Cahill, Mia. 2000a. *The Social Construction of Sexual Harassment Law: The Role of the National, Organizational and Individual Context.* Dartmouth, NH: Ashgate.

———. 2000b. "Now You See It, Now You Don't: The Disappearance and Reappearance of External Legal Models in the Implementation of Austrian Sexual Harassment Law." Paper presented at the Law and Society Association.

Carter, Victoria A. 1992. "Working on Dignity: EC Initiatives on Sexual Harassment in the Workplace." *Northwestern Journal of International Law and Business* 12: 431–53.

Collins, Eliza G. C., and Timothy B. Blodgett. 1981. "Some See It . . . Some Won't." *Harvard Business Review* 59 (March):76–96.

Collins, Evelyn. 1996. "European Union Sexual Harassment Policy." Pp. 23–33 in *Sexual Politics and the European Union,* edited by Amy Elman. Oxford: Berghahn Books.

Earle, Beverley H., and Gerald A. Madek. 1993. "An International Perspective on Sexual Harassment Law." *Law and Inequality* 12:43–91.

Elman, R. Amy. 1996. "Feminism and Legislative Redress: Sexual Harassment in Sweden and the United States." *Women and Politics* 16:1–26.

———. 2000. "Sexual Harassment Policy: Sweden in European Context." Paper presented at the Twelfth International Conference of Europeanists.

Farley, Lin. 1978. *Sexual Shakedown.* New York: McGraw-Hill.

Feary, Vaughana Macy. 1994. "Sexual Harassment: Why the Corporate World Still Doesn't 'Get It.'" *Journal of Business Ethics* 13:649–62.

Felstiner, William L. F., Richard L. Abel, and Austin Sarat. 1980. "The Emergence and Transformation of Disputes." *Law and Society Review* 15:631–54.

Fitzgerald, Louise, and Sandra L. Shullman. 1993. "Sexual Harassment: A Research Analysis and Agenda for the 1990s." *Journal of Vocational Behavior* 42:5–27.

Griffin-Shelley, Eric. 1985. "Sexual Harassment: One Organization's Response." *Journal of Counseling and Development* 64:72–73.

Gruber, James. 1997. "An Epidemiology of Sexual Harassment: Evidence from North America and Europe." Pp. XX in *Sexual Harassment,* edited by William O'Donohue. Needham Heights, MA: Allyn & Bacon.

———. 1998. "The Impact of Male Work Environments and Organizational Policies on Women's Experiences of Sexual Harassment." *Gender and Society* 12: 301–20.

Gutek, Barbara A. 1985. *Sex and the Workplace.* San Francisco: Jossey-Bass.

Holzer, Gabriele. 1998. "Haider Business." Pp. 141–57 in *Women in Austria,* edited by Guenter Bishof, Anton Pelinka, and Erika Thurner. New Brunswick, NJ: Transaction.

Hopfgartner, Andrea, and Maria Magdalena Zeichen. 1988. *Sexuelle Belaestigung am Arbeitsplatz.* Wenen: Bundesministerien fuer Arbeit und Soziales, Frauenreferat.

Judt, Tony. 1998. "Austria and the Ghost of the New Europe." Pp. 126–40 in *Women in Austria,* edited by Guenter Bishof, Anton Pelinka, and Erika Thurner. New Brunswick, NJ: Transaction.

Kennedy, David, and Keopold Specht. 1990. "Austrian Membership in the European Communities." *Harvard International Law Journal* 31:407–61.

MacKinnon, Catharine. 1979. *Sexual Harassment of Working Women.* New Haven: Yale University Press.

McCrudden, Christopher. 1993. "The Effectiveness of European Equality Law: National Mechanisms for Enforcing Gender Equality Law in the Light of European Requirements." *Oxford Journal of Legal Studies* 13:320–67.

Peterka, Josef. 1987. "Equality of Treatment of Men and Women in the Pension Insurance Scheme in Austria." Pp. XX in *Equal Treatment in Social Security.* International Social Security Association, Studies and Research No. 27.

Prager, Tessa, Petra Pichler, and Anita Staudacher. 1996. "Die Grapscher Sind Ueberall." *New nr.* 19:28–32.

Rosenberger, Sieglinde Katharina. 1998. "Politics, Gender, and Equality." Pp. 104–19 in *Women in Austria,* edited by Guenter Bishof, Anton Pelinka, and Erika Thurner. New Brunswick, NJ: Transaction.

Rubinstein, Michael. 1988. *The Dignity of Women at Work: A Report on the Problem of Sexual Harassment in the Member States of the European Communities* 19.

Saguy, Abigail. 1998. "French and U.S. Lawyers Define Sexual Harassment." Pp. XX in *Symposium on Sexual Harassment,* edited by Catharine MacKinnon and Reva Siegal. New Haven: Yale University Press.

———. 1999. "Discrimination or Abuse of Authority: Making Sexual Harassment Law in France and the United States." Unpublished paper.

Schally, Hugo. 1991. "Austria and the Central European Countries." *Whittier Law Review* 12:267–71.

U.S. Merit Systems Protection Board. 1981. *Sexual Harassment in the Federal Workplace: Is It a Problem?* Washington: Government Printing Office.

Valiente, Celia. 1998. "Sexual Harassment in the Workplace: Equality Policies in Post-Authoritarian Spain." Pp. 169–79 in *Politics of Sexuality,* edited by Terrell Carver and Veronique Mottier. New York: Routledge.

———. 2000. "Left or Right: Does It Make Any Difference? Central-State Sexual

Harassment Policies in Spain." Paper presented at the Twelfth International Conference of Europeanists.

Webb, Susan L. 1994. *Shock Waves: The Global Impact of Sexual Harassment.* New York: MasterMedia Limited.

Weeks, Elaine Lunsford, Jacqueline M. Boles, Albeno P. Garbin, and John Blount. 1986. "The Transformation of Sexual Harassment from a Private Trouble into a Public Issue." *Sociological Inquiry* 56:432–55.

Zippel, Kathrina. 1999. "Austria." Pp. 47–55 in *Sexual Harassment at the Workplace in the European Union,* edited by Directorate-General for Employment European Commission, Industrial Relations and Social Affairs. Luxembourg: Office for Official Publications of the European Communities.

———. 2000. Policies Against Sexual Harassment: Gender Equality Policies in Germany, the European Union and the United States. Ph.D. dissertation, Department of Sociology, University of Wisconsin-Madison.

13

Successful and Unsuccessful Diffusion of Social Policy

The United States, Canada, and the Metric System

GRACE ELLEN WATKINS AND JOEL BEST

The metric system of measurement offers an especially clear example of cultural diffusion. Prior to the system's spread, most societies used their own peculiar units of measure. These often had their roots in folk practices (e.g., a "foot" was originally the length of a man's foot). Initial pressures to standardize measures came from governments (because taxes were often to be paid in standard units of grain, etc.) and traders (who needed to agree on measures in order to set prices). Over time, measures became more precise and their relationships to one another were spelled out, but the resulting systems could be complicated (e.g., 12 inches to a foot, three feet to a yard, 1,760 yards to a mile).

The metric system was, quite literally, revolutionary. It was a byproduct of the French Revolution, first adopted in 1795 as a rational, coherent set of measures based on multiples of ten.[1] The meter (originally believed to be one 10,000,000th of the distance from the North Pole to the Equator) was multiplied or divided by powers of ten to create longer or shorter units of length (e.g., 1,000 meters equal a kilometer; 1/1000th of a meter equals a millimeter). Units of volume and weight were derived from measures of length (e.g., a liter is a cubic decimeter; while a kilogram is the weight of a liter of water). Anyone seeking to convert one measure to another finds the metric system far easier to use that any of the traditional systems that had been cobbled together from folk measures.

The French were proud of the metric system, and they promoted its adoption—called *metrication*—in other nations (Zupko 1990). The first countries to adopt the system tended to border on or trade with France. France also had a large colonial empire, and it pressed its colonies to adopt the metric system. Scientists, who formed their own international network and who were particularly likely to need to make precise measurements and to calculate conversions among measures, quickly adopted metric measures as the standard for scientific discourse. Other countries began to adopt the system because of its ease of use, and to facilitate trade with countries that had already adopted metric measures. By 1950, the only serious rival to the metric system was the English—or imperial—system, used in England, the British Commonwealth, and the United States. In 1965, Great Britain, which increasingly saw its future linked to (otherwise metric) Western Europe, surrendered and announced it would begin adopting metric measures.

Suggestions that the United States adopt the metric system date back to George Washington's presidency. There have been cycles of interest in adopting metric measures (Watkins 1998). These cycles begin when reformers approach the federal government (charged by the Constitution with maintaining a system of weights and measures); they argue that there would be substantial advantages to adopting the metric system (e.g., the system is easier to use, its adoption will foster increased trade with metric nations, etc.). Congress often seems to bend to the inevitability of metric adoption—until opponents mobilize and warn that conversion will be terribly expensive (a common example is that most American machines are designed to use screws with English-system threads—imagine the cost of reconfiguring every screw in the United States). In response, Congress often passes some piece of largely symbolic legislation, in effect praising the metric system without requiring the nation to adopt it. In 1866, for example, Congress legalized the use of the metric system, but did not require anyone in the United States to use it, and in 1875, the United States signed the "Treaty of the Meter" that made the metric system the standard international system of measurement, but again there was no requirement that the system be adopted for domestic use. These cycles of considering—yet never adopting—the metric system have left the United States one of only three nonmetric countries in the world.

This chapter examines the most recent metric reform cycle in the United States. In the 1970s, the federal government finally seemed to commit itself to metrication. At almost the same time, Canada announced that it, too, would adopt the metric system. By 1980, Canada had all but completed the transition. Twenty years later, the United States remains wedded to English measures. Why? Comparing the U.S. and Canadian campaigns to adopt the metric system reveals a good deal about the diffusion of social policies.

THE UNITED STATES ALMOST GOES METRIC, 1971–82

In 1968, in response to yet another campaign by metric system advocates, Congress passed the Metric Study Act. This law authorized the Secretary of Commerce to conduct what became a mammoth, three-year study of the costs and benefits of conversion. The resulting report, entitled *A Metric America: A Decision Whose Time Has Come* ran to 170 pages; it was supplemented by twelve specialized volumes that totaled more than 2,200 pages (U.S. Department of Commerce 1971a). *A Metric America* recommended phasing in metrication over a ten-year period. Congress pondered the matter in further hearings, but eventually passed the Metric Conversion Act of 1975.

The Metric Conversion Act seemed to commit the United States to metric conversion, but it neither required metrication nor set a deadline for completing the process (Watkins 1998). The act did establish the United States Metric Board to oversee the process of voluntary conversion, but the board lacked either compulsory powers or governmental support. The 17-member board was to be appointed by the president, but the president was required to appoint two board members to represent organized labor and two to represent small business interests (labor and small business tended to oppose conversion because they believed they would bear disproportionate shares of the costs), as well as representatives from big business, education, science, and so on.

There were early signs that metrication was on its way: new signs posted on some interstate highways gave distances in kilometers; soft-drink manufacturers introduced two-liter bottles; and the U.S. Office of Education awarded $2 million in metric education grants (Watkins 1998). However, the Metric Board's members were not appointed by President Carter until 1978. By that time, public opinion polls showed that metrication's supporters were not only a small minority but their numbers were declining, and that many more people—nearly half the population—opposed adopting the metric system. Any momentum for metrication had dissipated. In 1979, the Metric Board—the body supposedly overseeing the conversion process—passed a resolution that it would remain neutral on the question of metrication. In 1982, the Reagan administration dissolved the board, and the *Los Angeles Times* reported that eliminating:

all funding for the U.S. Metric Board . . . is arguably the only Reagan budget cut that hardly anyone squawked at. . . . With a few minor exceptions, the voluntary changeover to the metric system that began with the Metric Conversion Act of 1975 is dead in the water, and at present, there seems little impetus to revive it. (Dembart 1982:5)

Although Congress continues to promote metrication within federal agencies (in the Technology Competitiveness Act of 1987) and U.S. industry (in the Omnibus Trade and Competitiveness Act of 1988), conversion remains a voluntary, gradual process.

CANADA CONVERTS, 1970–80

Like the United States and other English-speaking countries, Canada began considering—and postponing—metrication in the nineteenth century. However when, in 1965, the British government announced plans to gradually adopt the metric system (the process was essentially completed thirty years later), Canadians began to view adoption as inevitable. The prime minister established a committee to study the issue in 1967, and this led, three years later, to a *White Paper on Metric Conversion in Canada* that called for adopting the metric system (Canadian Minister of Industry, Trade and Commerce 1970). The Canadian government responded by establishing Metric Commission Canada in 1971 (Watkins 1998). The commission's 17-member board first met in January of the following year; by that time, the commission had a 40-member staff.

The Commission set 1980 as a target date for metric conversion, and went about mobilizing the many elements of Canadian society that would need to confront new measures. It "divided the economy into 100 different sectors and established committees comprised of some 2,000 volunteers from sectors as diversified as retail and wholesale trade, industry, consumers, government, and education" (Johnston 1997:1). It invited over 200 Canadian national associations to become part of the massive planning effort. There were ten steering committees, each responsible "for coordinating a group of related economic sectors" (Keller 1975:14). Each steering committee was charged with submitting a conversion plan to the Metric Commission, as well as helping to coordinate implementation of all the conversion plans. In addition, the commission created more than 50 sector committees, "each responsible for a particular industry, group or interest" (Keller 1975:16). The Canadian government had its own interdepartmental committee to coordinate and plan metrication.

Significantly, a public information program committee was created to maintain high public awareness of the Canadian metrication process. This committee created and distributed various publications and created a logo—a "stylized M with a maple leaf . . . to become a national symbol for metric conversion in Canada"—that could denote metric products (Keller 1975:22). Other public-information tools included outreach presentations, exhibits, posters, films, and a free newsletter. The committee particularly sought to involve Canadian print and broadcast media in publicizing information about the adoption process.

The commission organized a series of transformations, and highlighted symbolically important changes (Watkins 1998). In 1974—only two years after the commission first met—toothpaste became the first consumer item sold in metric units (presumably it was chosen in part because few consumers care about exactly how much toothpaste is in a tube). In 1975, weather reports began using metric units; in 1976, all prepackaged food had to display metric units; in 1977, speed limit signs were converted to metric and new cars were required to have metric speedometers; and so on. In 1977, Parliament empowered the government to set cutoff dates, after which it would be illegal to use imperial measures for different purposes. By 1980 (the campaign's target date), the metric system was relatively well integrated into Canadian life. Although the Conservative government disbanded Metric Commission Canada in 1985, it was too late to halt conversion. When a 1986 Gallup Poll asked Canadians to estimate the day's highest temperature, three times as many gave responses in Celsius degrees as answered using Fahrenheit (*Toronto Star* 1986).

In other words, by the early 1970s, the federal governments in both the United States and Canada recognized the need to move toward adoption of the metric system, and both devised national commissions intended to guide the transition. Yet, in the United States, the effort barely began before it collapsed, whereas the Canadians managed to make the metric system standard. What accounts for this difference?

INERTIA AND METRIC'S OPPONENTS

Opposition to metric conversion came from essentially the same quarters in both the United States and Canada. Conversion is, of course, both inconvenient and costly. Systems of measurement are woven into the fabric of daily life in countless, taken-for-granted ways: when we look at a weather forecast to decide whether to wear a coat, or decide to shed some weight, or follow a recipe to prepare a meal, or measure a room to see whether it is big enough to hold some furniture, we use standard measures of temperature, weight, volume, distance, and so on. Adults who have grown up using imperial measures have an intuitive sense of what it means to say that the temperature is 78°, that someone is 5'11" tall, or that a car gets 23 miles per gallon. The equivalent metric measures seem, at least at first, difficult to master. Moreover, the imperial system works perfectly well for most of these everyday purposes. Metric's advocates point to the difficulties of converting, say, inches to miles or grains to tons, but most people probably pass through life without ever needing to make such calculations.

Howard S. Becker (1995) notes that social arrangements have inertia. Ordinary U.S. citizens own rulers and tape measures that show inches, bathroom scales that show pounds, speedometers calibrated in miles per hour, and kitchen utensils that measure cups and teaspoons (and cookbooks that call for those measures). Imagine replacing the huge number of U.S. road signs that use English measures, not just those setting speed limits in miles per hour or showing the number of miles to the next town, but the mile markers (and the freeway exits numbered according to those mile markers), the signs that give overpass clearances in feet, and so forth. The examples go on and on: buildings use standard—imperial-measured— sizes of lumber and pipes; a standard sheet of paper is $8\frac{1}{2}$" by 11". Conversion to the metric system would require countless adaptations. Some would take years, during which the two measurement systems would have to coexist (when a 3" pipe bursts, a plumber cannot simply insert a metric replacement). Adopting the metric system carries real costs—costs in time and effort to learn and master a new system of measurement, costs in new equipment (new rulers, bathroom scales, etc., etc.), and costs in maintaining two systems during the period of transition (plumbing-supply stores would need to maintain inventories of both imperial and metric pipes). In the short run, it is always easier not to change such complex social arrangements:

> Each piece of the package presupposes the existence of all the others. They are all connected in a way that, when you choose any one of them, you find it enormously easy to take everything that comes with that choice, and enormously difficult to make any substitutions. It's the package that exerts the hegemony, the inertial force. (Becker 1995:304)

Such inertia is at the root of opposition to adopting the metric system.

One source of opposition to metrication comes from ordinary individuals who do not want to be bothered with learning a new system of measurement. In the United States, an October 1977 Gallup Poll not only found that Americans who claimed to be familiar with the metric system opposed its adoption by almost two to one, but that opposition had actually been growing over the previous six years (Gallup 1992). Worse, as revealed in Table 1, between 1971 (when the Secretary of Commerce recommended adopting the metric system) and late 1977 (before President Carter even managed to appoint the Metric Board), the percentage of Americans who reported being unfamiliar with the metric system or having no opinion fell from 62 percent to 30 percent, and more than fourth-fifths of those newly opinionated citizens opposed adoption.[2] There was evidence that metrication was also unpopular with many Canadians.

Table 1.　U.S. Gallup Polls on Metrication, 1971–91

Date of Poll	Favor	Oppose	Not Aware	No Opinion
1971	19%	19%	56%	6%
1973	29%	19%	46%	6%
1977 (January)	29%	40%	25%	6%
1977 (October)	25%	45%	26%	4%
1991	26%	51%	20%	3%

Source: Gallup (1992: 201)

In the United States, popular opposition to the Metric Conversion Act coalesced around half-serious/half-playful social movement organizations: in New York, artist Seaver Leslie organized Americans For Customary Weights and Measures; while syndicated *Chicago Tribune* columnist Bob Greene wrote several columns about his "movement" WAM! (We Ain't Metric!) (Watkins 1998). Letters to newspaper editors regularly denounced metrication as another instance of big government intruding into citizen's lives. In California, where the State Superintendent of Public Instruction announced in 1973 that the state's public schools would teach only the metric system by 1976, the momentum for metrication soon slowed. Governor Jerry Brown appointed Stewart Brand (publisher of *The Whole Earth Catalog* and a vocal metric opponent) to the state's Metric Conversion Council; Brand attended a council hearing wearing a t-shirt that said "Stop Metric Madness" and blamed "international corporations" for the metrication campaign (*Los Angeles Times* 1977). Resistance to what was portrayed as metric pressure from big government and business struck a populist chord.

Parallel efforts to mobilize popular opposition appeared in Canada (Watkins 1998). In addition to complaints about government intrusion in its citizens' lives, opponents pointed to the metric system's French origins, and the fact that the metrication process was organized by Prime Minister Pierre Trudeau's Liberal government. The president of the Canadian Federation of Retail Grocers explained metrication: "The people who are running this country are French and feel an allegiance to France" (Meisler 1982).[3] Metric opponents complained that the media covered the government's prometric public relations campaign but paid little attention to opposition. Still, polls showed that once the process was well under way, most Canadians favored completing metrication—although there was support for letting the rest of the transition occur gradually.

However, the most serious opposition in both countries came from groups that expected to bear the costs of change—particularly small business. Enthusiasm for metrication has always been greatest among those who often communicate with—and particularly among those who seek to export to—metric nations. Large corporations, particularly those with substantial exports, often find it necessary to adopt metric measures for foreign markets. These firms can at least hope that the costs of metrication— of learning a new system, of redesigning and manufacturing products in metric measures—will be covered by increased profits. In contrast, small businesses that have no foreign markets usually see few benefits in adopting the metric system. For example, a butcher who is ordered to weigh cuts of meat in kilograms rather than pounds will have to buy a new metric scale, and probably cannot expect profits to increase enough to cover the cost of the new equipment. Not surprisingly, many small businesses—in both the United States and Canada—argued that they had little to gain and at least something to lose from metrication.[4]

In both countries, representatives of small business and organized labor did not so much stand opposed to voluntary metrication, as they worried about bearing the costs of mandatory conversion, particularly if they would be required to make the change fairly suddenly (Watkins 1998). In Canada, complaints centered on enforced metrication: "The government has threatened to begin prosecuting merchants who have not adopted the metric standard, and 26 opposition members of Parliament promptly challenged the move by taking over a filling station for the purpose of selling gasoline by the gallon" (*New York Times* 1982). Of course, in some sectors of the economy, metrication had already occurred. Science and medicine had long ago adopted metric measures as standard, but other familiar products used metric measures (e.g., virtually all pharmaceuticals [including vitamins and over-the-counter medications], and photographic equipment and film), and in other sectors English and metric measures coexisted (e.g., many socket-wrench sets accommodate both systems, and firearms ammunition is available in both metric and imperial calibers). These examples suggested that voluntary metrication, while found unevenly across the economy, can occur.

THE ISSUE OF FOREIGN TRADE

Metric's advocates argued that common standards would encourage foreign trade, and that maintaining different standards might impede it. As more and more countries switched to the metric system, this argument seemed increasingly compelling. However, its significance was different in the United States and Canada.

The United States, of course, boasts the world's largest economy. This— and probably this alone—has allowed it to continue to resist metrication. U.S. manufacturing continues to be powerful enough to set the standards for some new products (computer disks offer a nice example—even in metric nations, computer users refer to "3½ inch disks"). Although U.S. exports make up a substantial share of world trade (17 percent in 1971), they account for a relatively small proportion (4 percent in 1971) of the country's gross national product (GNP) (U.S. Department of Commerce 1971b:5). The U.S. Metric Study concluded that retaining English measures did not endanger U.S. trade:

> The notion that the U.S. is losing exports to metric countries because its products are not designed and manufactured in metric units and standards appears to be ill-founded. U.S. exports of MSS [metric standard-sensitive] products to metric countries are more than double exports to nonmetric countries. Furthermore, some of the fastest growing markets for U.S. MSS products are the metric countries. (U.S. Department of Commerce 1971b:3)

Although metric advocates warned that using English standards inhibited U.S. foreign trade, and promised that metrication would increase trade, it was difficult to find the evidence to make their arguments convincing.

Canada's pattern of foreign trade was very different. At the time the *White Paper* was being prepared, recent economic data showed that exports accounted for a much larger share—17.5 percent—of Canada's GNP (Canadian Minister of Industry, Trade and Commerce 1970; Keller 1975). About a quarter of these exports went to metric nations, and another tenth went to Great Britain (which had announced it would adopt the metric system). However, Canada's principal trading partner was the United States: most Canadian exports went to the United States; roughly half of the capital invested in Canada came from the United States; and the two countries had a number of reciprocal commitments to use common measurement standards (e.g., in the production of defense and automobile products). In the early and middle 1970s, when both countries seemed to have made commitments to metrication, there appeared to be a clear economic advantage to Canada's adopting metric measures. But, as the decade proceeded, and Canada's metrication progressed while the U.S. campaign stalled, Canadians confronted a dilemma: should they slow their efforts and lose the momentum they had built for conversion; or should they adopt measurement standards different from their principal trading partner? Canada continued to convert. By the 1980s, the Canadian industries that continued to resist metrication were those most dependent on the U.S. market (Watkins 1998). For example, 85 percent of Canadian wood industries reported that their U.S. customers were impeding their efforts to convert.

EXPLAINING THE DIFFERENCES

What happened to metrication? In the early 1970s, the United States and Canada were among the last countries in the world to cling to nonmetric measures—even England had decided to abandon the English system. The shift to a worldwide standard seemed inevitable and, at least in the long run, desirable. Metrication's inevitability was acknowledged in authoritative government reports (*A Metric America* produced by the U.S. Secretary of Commerce; and the *White Paper on Metric Conversion in Canada* by the Canadian Minister of Industry, Trade and Commerce). In both countries, legislators established special entities—the United States Metric Board and Metric Commission Canada—to guide their nations toward metrication, although neither law mandated adoption of metric measures. An observer in, say, 1973 might easily have concluded that the United States and Canada were at the same stage in the same process: both countries had defined nonmetric weights and measures as a problem; both acknowledged metrication as the solution; and both had established administrative entities—the commissions—to lead the conversion efforts. The similarities seemed obvious. And yet, in spite of these similarities, the two countries' metrication campaigns took very different paths: Canada converted to metric measures; while the United States retained imperial measures and thereby became the world's last major nonmetric nation (Liberia and Myanmar [Burma] were the only other holdouts).

Obviously, the national commissions had very different histories. Metric Commission Canada's chairman was appointed only a month after the commission was authorized, and its seventeen members held their first meeting six months later. In contrast, it took almost three years following the authorization of the United States Metric Board to appoint its seventeen members. That is, during the years that Canada's commission organized its metrication efforts, inaugurated its public relations campaign, and announced highlights of symbolic progress (e.g., toothpaste sold in metric units), the United States accomplished nothing. By delaying the board's starting date, U.S. officials gave the metric system's opponents time to campaign against metrication, and thereby turned a largely uninformed public into one that was mostly opposed to adopting the metric system. By requiring that the board contain representatives from the interest groups most likely to oppose metrication (small business and organized labor), Congress insured that the board would remain a forum for debating metrication, rather than an organization committed to change. Whereas the Canadian commission mobilized an elaborate network of volunteers to oversee change in specific economic sectors, and engineered favorable media coverage of the transition, the U.S. board abdicated any role in guiding the nation through metrication and, instead, announced its neutrality.

Accounting for the different pathways taken by the two countries requires understanding the differences in their cultures and social structures. Consider, for example, comments from an interview with Joseph Reid, President Emeritus of the Canadian Metric Association:

Canada is a modest country with a great deal to be modest about. We do not feel that we are world leaders and that we have nothing to learn from other countries. Per capita we travel a lot more than Americans do. A much larger proportion of our population was born abroad. A quarter of our population speaks French and looks to France as the Mother Country rather than Britain.

Our constitution has fewer checks and balances than the American Constitution. Also, party discipline is stronger in Canada. Politicians of the ruling party do not attack the government and administration because it is their government and the administration is completely subservient to the government. By 1969, all the countries in the British Commonwealth had decided to go metric and the National Bureau of Standards had started a comprehensive study in preparation for the United States to go metric. A proposal from our civil service to the government that Canada should follow was accepted by our cosmopolitan Prime Minister, Pierre Elliott Trudeau, and the government. (Reid 1997)

Three themes run through Reid's explanation. First, he argues that Canada has stronger ties to foreign countries than the United States: Canadians travel more; they are more often foreign-born; a quarter identify with France; and they were led by a "cosmopolitan Prime Minister." These external ties linked Canada to the larger, metric-using world. Second, as a "modest country," Canada was prepared to follow the rest of the world—including France, the British Commonwealth nations, and (it seemed) the United States—in adopting metric standards. (Of course, Reid's statement can be read as implying that the United States is not modest, that it perceives itself as a world leader, and that it doubts it can learn from other nations.) Third, he suggests that the organization of Canadian parliamentary government—and particularly the importance of party discipline—made adoption possible.

Seymour Martin Lipset's *Continental Divide: The Values and Institutions of the United States and Canada* (1990) offers a broader interpretation of U.S.-Canadian structural and cultural differences, a context within which Reid's explanation for Canadian metrication can be understood. The observation that parliamentary systems produce government, while the United States has politics explains the national differences between the two countries. Lipset argues that Canadians are more likely to support their national government's policies. "Americans, from the days of the Revolution, have resisted authority, demanded their rights, and preferred weak government, while Canadians have complained less, been less aggressive, and desired a strong paternalistic government" (Lipset 1990:44). These differences are reflected in a 1987 survey that compared Canadian and U.S. attitudes toward liberty and authority. Asked to respond to the statement "It is better to live in an orderly society than to allow people so much freedom they can become disruptive," 65 percent of Canadians—but only 51 percent of U.S.

respondents—agreed. To the item "The idea that everyone has a right to their own opinion is being carried too far these days," 37 percent of Canadians—but only 19 percent of Americans—agreed (Lipset 1990; 110–11). The two nations' histories, their governmental structures, and their citizens' attitudes show consistent differences.

In other words, Canada's metrication campaign can be seen as business as usual. The government—presumably guided by individuals with considerable expertise—concluded that the country should adopt the metric system. The policy was announced, an organizational network was devised to guide the process, the media promoted the transformation, most economic sectors made the shift reasonably quickly, and, although the public perceived the inconvenience the change created, there was little organized opposition. Although the government initially framed metrication as a voluntary process—the greatest opposition arose when, after a few years, the government tried to set penalties for people who would not comply—metric standards were soon used so widely that opposition became impractical.

In contrast, the United States continued to treat metrication as a subject for debate. Although the secretary of commerce recommended conversion, it took years for Congress to establish and the president to staff the U.S. Metric Board. During those years, opponents testified before Congress, and Congress made sure that the board would contain members who could present opponents' arguments. When the U.S. government announced that metrication would be voluntary, Americans assumed that they could continue to resist—and they did. Opponents made vocal objections, and public opinion shifted against metrication. The metric board caved in and announced its neutrality; this virtually insured that only piecemeal changes would occur.

IMPLICATIONS

The long-standing differences in culture and social structure, then, insured that the United States and Canada—however much they may both have seemed poised to adopt the metric system—would follow different paths. This example reminds us that claims do not occur in a vacuum. Sociologists must locate the construction of both social problems and social policies within their contexts.

The rhetoric adopted by the metric system's proponents in both the United States and Canada was essentially the same: (1) the system was easier to use; and (2) adopting the system would help foster trade with what was becoming an otherwise all-metric world. (Of course, these were the same arguments that American metric advocates—without much success—had been making since the nineteenth century.) For that matter, the rhetoric of opposition in both countries evoked similar themes: conversion would be costly and inconvenient, and it was unnecessary. If rhetoric determines the adoption of social policies, both countries should have come to the same decision, either to adopt or reject the metric system.

Obviously, the similarities in the claims cannot explain the differences in the outcomes. The claims and counterclaims were debated within very different societal contexts. Contemporary U.S. political culture, suspicious of big government, fostered debate, dithering, and eventual defeat of metrication.

This should offer a useful reminder to sociologists of social problems. There is a large body of constructionist case studies demonstrating how this set of claimsmakers, promoting that set of claims, managed to draw attention to some particular social problem. These analyses routinely overlook the narrow focus of many of these campaigns: often, claims emerge within particular segments of the population (e.g., conservative Protestants, or feminists, or whatever); even when some fairly general alarm is aroused through national media coverage, many social problems do not touch directly on the lives of most citizens. Even most social policies do not touch most people—except indirectly in the form of higher taxes. In a world of increased media outlets—24-hour cable news stations, talk-show proliferation, Internet news coverage, and so on—it becomes relatively easy to make claims and—at least to some degree—get them heard.

But this does not necessarily mean that it is easy to overcome broad-based social inertia. Adopting the metric system would prove inconvenient to virtually all Americans. In a culture that celebrates freedom and often deplores government intrusion in citizen's lives, proposals for metrication inevitably attract opposition. Changing measurement standards requires organization, coordination, and firm direction by some central authority. Canadian culture and social structure made this possible; the U.S. context did not.

Will the United States eventually adopt the metric system? In an essentially all-metric world, the transformation seems inevitable. But then, generations of science teachers have warned their students that they would spend adulthood in a metric world, and those predictions have not come to pass. Clearly, we can anticipate that more industries will, one by one, choose to convert, that more and more products will feature metric (and in some cases, also English) labels. But it is harder to foresee when U.S. tape measures and scales will show only metric units.

NOTES

1. Following the French Revolution, France also adopted the French Republican Calendar as part of the effort to establish a new social order. The revolutionary calendar featured twelve 30-day months, each divided into three 10-day cycles, that

were in turn divided into ten hours—each 100 "decimal minutes" long. The new calendar failed, of course. Zerubavel (1977:875) argues that it was too uncompromising, that it sought to obliterate the familiar systems of date keeping, but he then remarks: "the metric reform of the system of weights and measures, which was introduced in France at about the same time, clearly achieved a tremendous success despite its absolute obliteration of the traditional order. . . . The failure of the calendrical reform . . . cannot be fully accounted for only by the totality of the obliteration of the old order." However, acceptance of the metric system took time: it did not become the sole legal measurement system in France until 1840; metric and traditional measures coexisted for decades (Zupko 1990). Zerubavel also argues that calendar reform failed because it refused to acknowledge dates of religious significance, and because it was overtly French (e.g., the new year began on the anniversary of the founding of the French Republic) and held little appeal for other countries.

2. Table 1 shows that the trend continued into the 1990s: as more people claimed familiarity with the metric system, the margin by which opponents outnumbered advocates continued to grow.

3. However, metric conversation may have encountered less Canadian opposition because it had symbolic appeal for both francophones (for whom the metric system could be seen as a stunning accomplishment of French culture) and anglophones (who knew that Great Britain had also begun the process of conversion). In addition, Canadians could take pride in their successful metrication campaign, contrasted with its bungled counterpart in the United States.

4. The recurring debates over metrication have featured conflicting estimates of the economic benefits and costs of adopting the new system (Watkins 1998). Proponents argue that the refusal to adopt metric measurements impedes foreign trade (one 1972 estimate argued that not using metric measures cost the United States $600 million annually in potential trade benefits); they insist that metrication will stimulate the economy by vastly increasing commerce. In response, opponents warn that metrication will involve hideous costs (a 1972 estimate for conversion costs was $6–14 billion over ten years).

REFERENCES

Becker, Howard S. 1995. "The Power of Inertia." *Qualitative Sociology* 18:301–9.

Canadian Minister of Industry, Trade and Commerce. 1970. *White Paper on Metric Conversion in Canada.*

Dembart, Lee. 1982. "Idea Whose Time Has Come." *Los Angeles Times* (May 15):5.

Gallup, George, Jr. 1992. *The Gallup Poll: Public Opinion 1991.* Wilmington, DE: Scholarly Resources, Inc.

Johnston, Alan. 1997. Letter to James McCracken (April 9).

Keller, J. J. 1975. *Metric Yearbook.* Neenah, WI: International Technical Publishers.

Lipset, Seymour Martin. 1990. *Continental Divide: The Values and Institutions of the United States and Canada.* New York: Routledge.

Los Angeles Times. 1977. "Going Backward by the Numbers" (March 3):4.

Meisler, Stanley. 1982. "Oppose Its Frenchness: Canadians Gripe at Metric Conversion." *Los Angeles Times* (February 11):9.

New York Times. 1982. "Canada Threatens to Fine Non-Metric Users" (December 19):17.

Reid, Joseph. 1997. Personal interview with Grace Ellen Watkins (June 13).

Toronto Star. 1986. "Canadians Becoming Familiar with Celsius, Poll Shows" (December 15): A3.

U.S. Department of Commerce. 1971a. *A Metric America: A Decision Whose Time Has Come: U.S. Metric Study.*

————. 1971b. *U.S. Metric Study Interim Report VIII: International Trade.* National Bureau of Standards, special publication 345-8.

Watkins, Grace Ellen Grove. 1998. "Measures of Change: A Constructionist Analysis of Metrication in the United States." Unpublished Ph.D. dissertation, Southern Illinois University at Carbondale.

Zerubavel, Eviatar. 1977. "The French Republican Calendar: A Case Study in the Sociology of Time." *American Sociological Review* 42:868–77.

Zupko, Ronald. 1990. *Revolution in Measurement: Western European Weights and Measures Since the Age of Science.* Philadelphia: American Philosophical Society.

14

Child Protection without Children— or Finnish Children without Problems?

TARJA PÖSÖ

Within the European Union, Finland, like the other Nordic countries, is seen as having "child-friendly" public policies—a conclusion borne out by a number of comparative analyses of the EU countries (Millar & Warman 1996; Pringle 1998). These studies recognise the degree to which Finland supports parenting by various means through the state's family policy and has also addressed the rights of children—to some extent more so than in any non-Nordic country. Finland banned the parental use of corporal punishment in the 1980s; this law has been celebrated as an essential symbol of child-friendly state policies.

There are, however, a growing number of doubts about the actual position of children. The vast public day-care system is seen as technocratic; the public education system does not treat children as individuals but more or less as a group. In addition, the recession of the early 1990s strongly eroded services for children and families, even giving rise to the term "the children of recession." This meant that the children who grew up during those years were deprived of proper social services and proper parental care due to the high unemployment and depressive mental attitude of those years (cf. Salmi, Huttunen, and Yli-Pietilä 1996). In the late 1990s, a new social problem emerged—children's alcoholism—as medical studies of school children revealed a high consumption rate of alcohol and drugs. Also the general public became concerned about the high number of drunk children in the streets. Not surprisingly, social workers, teachers and psychiatrists expressed strong concern about the well-being of these children, and several parental groups sought to increase control over children's free time and street life and also to have more influence on school life and other formal institutions of childhood and youth.

Keith Pringle's (1998) analysis of Nordic social welfare policies for children questioned how well Nordic welfare principles worked in practice. He argued that the glowing image of Nordic social solidarity conceals essential power relations associated with gender, race, age, and poverty (Pringle 1998: 107). In particular, he criticized the ways child abuse is treated and debated as unfair to children. Pringle's discussion of Nordic social practices dealing with children at risk or in need asks whether there is trouble in paradise.

Is it Pringle's contention that child-friendly Nordic welfare excludes the most threatened children from public care? What is the role of child protection as a distinctive social institution in a strong welfare state? Sharing some of the concerns in his analysis, I will look in more detail at the issue of the role of child protection in the Finnish welfare state. My main argument is that child protection is geared to look after children mainly through parents, and that this approach tends to construct and keep the formulations of social problems in a family context. I will argue later that the construction of child protection issues as family issues ignores the children as actors involved in child-protection issues; as a matter of fact, children become "unheard voices." Thus, Pringle's thesis will serve to guide this article which is, therefore, not only about Finnish child protection but also about national and cultural practices in viewing social troubles, in this case particularly troubles in families.

I begin by describing the system of child protection and its role in dealing with children's problems, before discussing actual child-protection practices. Child protection's political character and history will be described but this should not be read as an explanation for its present practices. Rather, the focus is on describing and analyzing the practices that construct the "family" as the main target for child protection and their implications for children's position. A thorough description of the system of child protection is important because it plays a crucial role in shaping the cultural notion of children in need and is in turn influenced by that notion. My arguments are based on research in this area. The reader should know that Finland is small, both in its population (around 5 million inhabitants) and also in its academic communities, thus a few studies in this area might become more influential[1] than in countries with larger research literatures and readership. Such studies can be used to construct a picture of the recent practices dealing with troubled children.

THE STRUCTURE OF THE CHILD WELFARE SYSTEM

In the United States, the history of child protection is often described in terms of child-saving movements (Platt 1969; Smith and Merkel-Holguin

1996; Gordon 1988). In Finland, however, the roots of child protection can be understood in terms of the growth and expansion of public social welfare, especially on the local level, and the laws shaping the relationships between children, parents, and the state. There is, and always has been, considerable voluntary and charity interest in children's issues; as a matter of fact, some highly influential national organizations have affected the well-being of children and families, as well as the public policies to deal with them. Most recently, several nongovernmental projects concerning the inclusion of marginalized youth, children, and families have flourished due to EU-supported research activities and priorities. Nevertheless, the core of child protection has remained a legal, public, municipal issue.

The basic structure for municipal child protection was established in the late nineteenth century when poor relief became a collective responsibility of local (municipal) government. Those duties had previously belonged to the Lutheran parishes but, after 1879, local government was obliged to look after minors under insufficient protection and care as well as after adults who could not support themselves. There was no specific legislation concerning children's well-being as such before the Child Welfare Act of 1936.[2] There had, however, been serious debates and proposals made in Parliament to pass legislation concerning, for example, delinquent children. Finnish society was changing rapidly due to the late industrialization and the first steps of urbanization, and new actions were needed to combat new children's and families' problems. Also, political restlessness in the early decades of this century, related to Finland's becoming independent from the Soviet Union and coping with its internal tensions, created pressure to ensure the "right" upbringing of children (Satka 1995). Child protection was needed to resolve the conflicts between different social classes and their ways of upbringing. Tove Stang Dahl (1985) describes this kind of approach to children as social defense. Only in the late 1930s, however, was there enough collective and political agreement on this sensitive issue to enable the first child-protection law to be passed. Only then was it possible to remove neglected and abused children from the custody of their parents to public care. Before that, public care had been only for orphaned or totally abandoned children. In addition, delinquency among youth was now defined first and foremost as a child-welfare issue, the juvenile justice system only coming into play for adolescents 15 or more years of age. Even at that age range, the juvenile justice system was supposed to cooperate with the child welfare system in order to encourage a change in the offender's behavior, skills, attitudes, and social environment (Pösö 1991).

However, a new shift occurred in the 1980s, when legislation concerning children was introduced, including a new Child Welfare Law in 1983, that emphasized children's rights. Children were given the right to express their opinion in custody issues in the cases of parental divorce as well as in child-protection issues. The best interests of the child now became the leading principle for any social policy concerning children. Corporal punishment was also finally forbidden in the same piece of legislation. The Finnish welfare state has long been described as woman-friendly and, at this historical stage, a new discourse of child friendliness emerged as well.

As laws concerning children were increased, municipal (local) government remained the central actor for providing services, education, and care for children in general, and children at need or risk in particular. The Finnish system of municipal government is ideologically based on the principle of local self-government, according to which local authorities have the autonomy to create and implement policies (Kröger 1999:56–57). Full autonomy in local democratic decision making was to be the *sine qua non* of local government, and central government control and subordination were to be avoided. Practice, however, never fully matched this ideology in Finland. The central state has from the very beginning sought at least some power and control over local government. The central state also had a direct impact on families, as some social benefits—such as child benefits—came under its jurisdiction. Nevertheless, local authorities enjoyed discretionary powers that are quite unusual in other, non-Nordic countries. Although the expansive welfare state brought with it elements of intense central steering, local decision making retained a good part of its significance.

Local government structure places a lot of essential decision making in the hands of politically chosen lay representatives. In child protection, these representatives comprise the social welfare board, and the law gives child-protection duties to that board. In practice, however, child-protection work is actually done by social workers employed by the municipal government. Early legislation required that most of the decisions were to be confirmed by the social-welfare board, but, since the 1980s, decision-making authority has been given to a large extent to social workers. In other words, professional assessment now has priority over lay or communal knowledge when making decisions about intervention in the lives of individual children and families. Compared to practices outside the Nordic countries, the social work profession gained the decision-making power over the courts in matters of child protection.

Child protection refers to a distinctive practice provided by the municipal governments and their social-welfare boards, regulated by legislation, mainly by child welfare law. Its task is to look after the well-being of the children within the municipality. With threats that could harm the well-being or health of children, it has the right and duty to intervene, including removing the child from his/her home ("taking the child into care").

This approach to child protection is preventive rather than reactive. One is supposed to provide welfare and thereby protection is guaranteed. The

criterion for action is "the best interest of the child." Recent Finnish legislation emphasizes prevention and measures that can occur within the community to support families in better looking after their children. Such
measures might mean financial assistance, family guidance, home help
services, and such like. This is called "open care." Only in the most severe
cases is the child allowed to be taken into care with the proviso that the
placement of the child in a foster home or children's home should be as
short as possible. In 1998, 12,132 children were placed out of their homes,
this is 1.1 percent of the child population below the age of 18. The number
of children under supervision in open care was three times more than that
(38,632 children) (Muuri 1999.) The parents do not lose their parental rights
during the placement and the duty of the social workers involved in each
particular case is to help the (biological) parents and the child to strengthen
their psychological attachment in order to make it possible for the child to
return to his/her parents. Adoption is extremely rare as a child-protection
measure and the law does not encourage it (but does not prohibit it, either).

The legislation regulating child protection is a skeleton law, meaning
that the regulations leave a lot to the discretion of municipal social workers who have the right to make decisions, even about taking the child into
care. The legal apparatus becomes involved only in those cases when the
parents or children object or make a complaint. Self-evidently, this means
great variation in the practices across the country, as the local authority and
individual social workers can construct their own interpretations of risks,
harms, and threats to the well-being of children, as well as definitions of
the best interest of the child. However, this is not only an issue of discretion but also of the resources available: child-protection practice relies
heavily on the social services available within the community, and here
there is wide discrepancy among municipalities. Regional inequality has
been, as a matter of fact, identified as a key problem in present child-protection practice (*Lastensuojelusta* . . . 1995; Kivinen 1994:62–63).

The way Finnish child protection is organized on the policy level carries
several implications. First, the tasks of child protection are defined so
broadly that in principle, all children below the age of 18 could be seen as
possible clients. Any possible risks and harms to the healthy, balanced development of the child are seen as potential problems requiring child protection. However, the actual child-protection practice treats only severe
problems; minor problems are treated by other institutions in the field of
family and social welfare. The question of what problems are considered
severe is an issue of special interest in this chapter. Second, the way problems are approached in child-protection practice focuses on support
through services; this links child protection heavily with the welfare state
and the services provided by it or in conjuction with it. There, the needs of
families and children at risk or in need are understood in terms of the run-

ning of everyday life and material needs. Third, the role of families (parents) is essential as they are the main partner for child protection and through whom most of the open-care interventions are led.

On the policy and system level, the Finnish approach to child protection can be characterized as family service orientation, to use Gilbert's (1997) terminology, based on a comparative analysis of child-protection practices in different countries. He suggests that wealthy Western countries vary in the extent to which their child-abuse reporting systems emphasize child-protection or family-service orientations. In the child-protective orientation, a frame of individual or moralistic problems is evident, as well as an emphasis on legalistic or investigatory interventions. The relationship between the state and parent is seen as adversarial and out-of-home placements are involuntary. In the family-service orientation, however, the problem definition often emphasizes social and psychological aspects and the interventions aim at assessing the clients' therapeutic needs. The relationship between the state and the parents is based on a partnership of some kind. Voluntarism even characterizes the out-of-home placements.

Most countries do not fit neatly into those orientations, but the Finnish child-protection system can, without any doubt, be defined as representing the family-service orientation. Family and social policies support that orientation as well, emphasizing either financial benefits or nonmaterial social services to families with children (Takala 1992).[3] In this chapter, I will examine in detail how the social problems of families and children are viewed within this approach.

CHILD-PROTECTION PROBLEMS

Inevitably, child abuse and neglect are the heart of child-protection problems globally. The meanings of abuse and neglect vary from extremely brutal violence against the child's physical and sexual privacy and self-respect to a lack of support for the child's psychosocial development. Thus, the vocabulary of the problems tends to cover a wide range of troubles, while being constructed in every national and local practice in a particular way.

In Finland, the politics of child protection have been such that the vocabulary of abuse and neglect has been used only occasionally. Instead of abuse and neglect, child protection rhetoric defines troubles that focus more on the family situation (e.g., parental or family conflicts), parents' behavior (e.g., mental health issues, substance abuse), or in the case of adolescence, the inappropriateness of the adolescents' behavior (e.g., delinquency, running away).

When the first child welfare law was introduced in 1936, the reasons for child-protection intervention were established in terms of lack of parental care or of proper care and the child's antisocial behavior. During the era of that law, child abuse was also used as a category for defining child-protection troubles both in the law and in the actual practices of child protection. It was expected that certain troubles should be recognized in the child before child protection could intervene. Self-evidently, that still meant a lot of negotiations and interpretations in each individual case, but the ideology was to locate the child-protection troubles within this framework and exclude those that did not match it. The second Child Welfare Act in 1983, still valid today, took a more general approach to describing problems. That act emphasizes every child's right to proper care, a balanced upbringing, health, and a good social environment. Any risk in those areas entitles the community to initiate child-protection activities. Naturally, the activities required in those cases are of general nature, that is, to improve the environment and services (among others) in terms of prevention. The conditions that require child-protection inteventions in the form of taking the child into care are: (1) when failure in the care of the child or the conditions at home seriously threaten the health or development of the child, or when the child him / herself seriously threatens his or her health or development by using drugs, committing more than a minor offence, or any other action equivalent to the ones mentioned; (2) when open care measures turn out to be inappropriate, impossible, or insufficient; or (3) when an out-of-home placement is seen to promote the best interest of the child. The legislation does not specifically define how the well-being or health of the child could be threatened. It is left to the actual practitioner to decide.

As a matter of fact, the problem definitions are far from random or endless. There are obviously certain routine definitions that emerge from, for example, the statistics describing child protection on the national and municipal level. This information is mainly about the nature of interventions (their number, length, regional differences, etc.). There is still very little statistical information available about the causes for interventions but what there is suggests that the main reason is family conflicts and parents' drug-related (and associated psychiatric) problems. What is most important is that the main problems are with the parents (Kivinen 1994) and the terminology emphasizes their social behavior (substance abuse, multiple social problems, marginalization, etc.). Distinctive diagnoses or exact categorizations are avoided. Also, the terminology very rarely recognizes the children. Child abuse referring to violence of any kind experienced by children, internationally so widely known as the main justification for child protection, is seldom used and when it is, it refers to abuse diagnosed by a medical doctor (Pösö 1995).

There is a certain logic in how information is collected and factualized in the statistics: the reasons for child-protection interventions are seen as being so complicated that they cannot be categorized into simple definitions (Kivinen and Heinonen 1990). This logic applies not only to statistical data, but to the actual practices documented in child-protection case records and formal decisions. The forms used encourage social workers to describe the problems in their own words, instead of guiding their judgment by providing ready categories. The way the social workers complete these forms seems to follow the definitional pattern described in the statistics as well (Kähkönen 1993). This type of professional reasoning is seen as sufficient for the bureaucratic needs of the child protection system as well as for the rights of their clients. This is evidence for the strong position of social work in Finnish child protection; still, it is not without tensions.

When Tine Egelund (1996) analyzed Danish child-protection practice, she concluded that too much of the practice reflected the needs of the bureaucratic system—that is, the rules that the law and local administration set for the practice. Her analysis was based on records, observations of social work, and interviews with families, her starting point being that both rules and professional knowledge are necessary in street-level bureaucrats' practice. Professional knowledge turned out to be marginalized by the rules, and the freedom of discretion seemed constrained. According to her view, the treatment of families was politically rather than professionally determined.

Similar concerns are known with regard to Finnish child protection. Several researchers have pointed out that local administration and its bureaucratic and political organization of social welfare, not to mention the expansive social-welfare legislation, regulate how individual citizens' needs are met by the social welfare system (Mäntysaari 1991). Tarja Kivinen (1994) sees that the service structure in child protection, more than the needs and wishes of the clients, determines to a large extent the services provided to the families and children in need or at risk. However, more recent analysts claim that social-work activities are grounded in knowledge constructed within the practice, and that that knowledge is more tacit than based on distinctive social-work theories or bureaucratic or legal norms (Heino 1997). Tarja Heino tried to trace the nature of tacit knowledge by reviewing case histories with social workers, in order to make the actual decision-making process verbal. She found strong emotional and ethical reasoning combined with awareness of the facts of the case. These three elements played different roles, but when all three appeared to be present, the social worker was most likely to intervene.

Heino's (1997) study illustrates well the collective nature of social workers' reasoning. Social workers work in pairs or teams in child protection, except in small municipalities, where one social worker is supposed to take care of all the social-welfare needs of the citizens. In those cases, even the most fundamental child-protection decisions are made by just one individual social worker, with the result that she has no chance (and no pressure) to share her reasoning with colleagues. This occurs in a good number of Finnish municipalities, the smallest of which have only one social worker or even none at all (Marjamäki, Mäntysaari, and Ristimäki 1998).

The tacit knowledge used in child-protection decision making is also interesting in the sense that the work is done by professional social workers who, in order to work in the public systems, should gain professional qualification through university training. The most common degree for social workers is an M.A. in Social Work or in Social Sciences. Social work has been taught at the universities since the late 1970s and it has been an independent academic discipline since the 1980s, with its own doctorate degree. Due to its very special history and character (Karvinen, Pösö, and Satka 1999), Finnish social-work training has favored a very flexible, sociopolitical approach, and has consequently not encouraged any direct or mechanistic applications of theories into practice. The fiercest critics claim that social-work training has not succeeded in creating appropriate skills for practice; this is the reason why social-work practice relies so heavily on routine everyday knowledge, rather than bureaucratic and legal norms or social work methods (Satka 1997). If that critique is taken seriously, the extent of tacit knowledge might seem problematic.

On a societal level, social-work expertise has recently been challenged by other expert institutions such as law and psychiatry. The legal experts have been concerned about the legal aspects of interventions into family and children's lives when children are taken into care. They argue that social-work knowledge and practice as such do not guarantee that the rights of the clients are protected (*Lapsioikeudellista* . . . 1995). They suggest, therefore, that the actual decision about taking the child into care should be made by the courts (as in the United Kingdom and United States, for example). According to this proposal, social workers would prepare the case for the court and they would work with the case after the court's decision. This proposal has been warmly welcomed by some social workers who experience conflict between their roles as a giver of support and as the person who chooses extreme interventions. However, others say that the issues connected with a child-protection case are so diverse and so social by their nature that they cannot be dealt with within legal discourse and terminology. Although decision making has not yet been given to the courts, it is obvious that the legal experts' role has grown in child protection. More lawyers and solicitors have become involved in cases on behalf of clients, thereby influencing and legalizing social-work practice.

RECOGNIZING THE TROUBLES

The route to child protection is twofold: either the clients—parents or children—turn to the child-protection agency to ask for help; or a report of a lack of appropriate care is made by the authorities or other members of the community. Legally, every authority working for social and health-care agencies—the educational system, the police, the church—is required to inform the child-protection agency (in other words, the social welfare board) if they have any reason to suspect a child of lacking care. The duty to report is beyond any case-bound consideration. In addition, every citizen should make a report if they have any doubts or concerns about any child's well-being or the quality of care.

About half of all child-protection referrals come from other authorities (Saikku 1998:44). This illustrates the strong interauthority and interorganizational nature of child-protection work, especially the links between the child protection and the health, education, and day-care systems. However, community members, parents, and children themselves actively search for help as well. In their referrals, community members express their concern about the maltreatment of a child, whereas parents and children (teenagers in most cases) actively contact the child-protection agency if they feel troubled about family or upbringing conflicts or the parents' psychiatric problems (Kivinen 1994:73–74).

It is, however, most likely that not all child-protection concerns are reported to the child-protection agency. Some authorities deal with their concerns and doubts themselves, or choose to approach the concern by following the case themselves because they trust their own methods (Forssen 1997a). The community members as well as the parents often avoid contacting the child-protection agency because its image is rather negative; there is a belief that there is a great likelihood of the child being taken into care as a solution to the problem presented. In other words, in a legal and administrative frame, the mandatory reporting system does not function in the way it should.

According to Tarja Heino (1997), there is no clear administrative definition of child-protection clienthood. The route through referrals might sound clear but it does not seem so in practice. Heino's study revealed that child-protection reports do not necessarily lead to any action by social workers. Legally and administratively they should act, but in practice social workers might decide that the report can wait or that it is not urgent or based on real facts—or that they do not have enough resources or time to check the report. This means that some reports are practically ignored. Another reason for the administratively obscure definition of child-protection clienthood is organizational. Child-protection issues are most often dealt with in the municipal social welfare agency by social workers who also deal with other social welfare issues, such as substance abuse and income support. Child protection is not separate, but actually a part of a wider agency, as the municipality, the local administration, is responsible for providing social welfare services of different kinds. From the client's point of view, this organization of services might mean that he/she is seeking help for his/her financial or drug-related problems but is treated as a child-protection case instead (sometimes without his/her knowing—a point which has been so sarcastically pointed out in Weightman & Weightman's (1995) analysis of Swedish child protection practice). It also tends to be difficult for social workers to draw the line between when the client is treated as a child-protection client and when not. Categorization as a child-protection client most often becomes clear only when the concerns about family life and parental care have become "obvious" (and this can be tricky to define) (Heino 1997).

One gains the "status" of a child-protection client through processes of social-work practice that are only slightly determined by administrative and legal regulations. Heino (1997) shows that social workers' reasoning in that process is manyfold and consists of different ethical, cognitive, and emotional elements. Other studies and reports do, however, examine the process of the selection to clienthood by analyzing the clients' characteristics. In the studies by Forssen (1993, 1997a) and Kivinen (1994), child protection seems to deal with many parents who have long (generational) histories of social problems. Single mothers are overrepresented in relation to their numbers in the population in general. In those studies, as also in many agency recording systems, "client" means parents (a child-protection case is registered under the name of the parent; the name of the child is used as a registration unit mainly only in the case of out-of-home placements).

On a more general level, the routes to clienthood seem be constructed in ways that are to some extent arbitrary in an administrative sense, but not in a social sense. Social workers play an active part in selecting, excluding, and institutionalizing cases. This is a familiar finding in any of the ethnomethodological studies on social work or welfare practices (e.g., Pithouse 1987; Hall 1997). What is essential in Finland, however, is that the organizational arrangements are not geared to restrict that variety.

What follows from the categorization of someone as a child-protection case also varies. The Child Welfare Act (1983) asks social workers to establish open care or, if it proves to be inadequate, to take the child into care. Open care is meant to support and guide the families and children so that problems can be settled and no tougher interventions will be required. This could involve anything "between heaven and earth" (Kivinen 1989) the social worker could dream up—within the constraints of existing resources, of course. Most often, open care means providing home help, financial assistance, use of family support centers, or lay/therapeutic support.

When analyzing child-protection practices, Katja Forssen (1993, 1997a) concluded that the practitioners most often just "keep an eye" on their cases. This approach implies that the social worker does not have any immediate concern about the case and also that the case could be scrutinized by collecting information from different sources. This approach is possible because no exact regulations exist about the length of time during which cases should be treated. It also depends on many sources of information, including the (municipal) home helpers, day-care personnel, school teachers, health nurses, and doctors at schools and child clinics—in other words, people working in the public-welfare services. They are asked to give reports about the well-being of the children they meet in their work and, if something alarming turns up, to contact the child-protection workers. To function, child protection needs other welfare practitioners to serve as informants. Gathering information requires networking among welfare professionals. Sometimes networking involves clients and their social networks as well (Karjalainen 1996).

Other welfare practitioners are needed, as they are the main actors in providing open-care measures. The child-protection worker often coordinates the activities of other service providers, limiting his/her own active role to a great extent. Also, the actual contacts with the child-protection clients more often are carried out by other practitioners than by the social worker in charge. From the point of view of the clients, this can mean quite a wide network of professionals around them. This network can be experienced as a net of surveillance by some parents, with the result that control replaces support (Laakso 1998).

The purpose of child protection functioning in strong cooperation with welfare service providers is to provide general, rather "soft," supportive measures to the clients. They are encouraged to deepen their family ties and home life by teaching them practical and interactional skills and providing them with financial resources. The professional understanding of family problems emphasizes everyday life and the clients are supported to cope with it. If everyday life functions well, it provides a better social environment for the child; that is, the child is helped through the improvements in family life.

Annually, approximately 250 children are taken into care as emergency measures (Heino 1998:124). In those cases, the supportive approach is replaced by something else, most often by the need of protection. Then, the children are to be protected from a total lack of care. But in other cases, protection plays a secondary—or a temporarily limited—role. Even in the cases of taking the child into care, the child's right to return to the families is emphasized even though there is no clear understanding whether that principle is in the best interest of the child or the parents. To some, this emphasis means that the rights of parents are protected at the expense of the children (Forsberg 1998). Whether the children are protected, however, is not the main issue in the present child-protection policy. The government set its guidelines in 1995; these were quite widely debated and prepared in Parliament and by other parties involved in family and child policy. The main message was that protecting children is not enough for a developed welfare society; instead, one should strengthen the right of children to participate in different social activities where decisions concerning their position are made. The emphasis was also on sharing the resources in society more equally between the different generations and strengthening the participatory rights and possibilities of children (*Lastensuojelusta* . . . 1995). The terminology of child protection or child welfare was criticized as narrow and old-fashioned; therefore, the term "child policy" was introduced to cover practices for protection, participation, and equal sharing of resources. The government report adds, however, that society should also guarantee protection and care for those children who live in unsafe or risky conditions. The protection tasks remain but they are placed even more within the frame of child policy (as a part of general social and cultural policies).

That particular report essentializes the different present discourses: on the one hand, there are social policies to protect the children; on the other hand, we have policies aiming to strengthen the children's position. Neither is very clear or unproblematic. Child-protection policy is focused on protecting children through families, whereas "child policy" aims to treat children as individuals and equal citizens in society, responsible also to some extent for their own well-being. Neither policy is likely to make the present practices for recognizing child-protection problems more focused on the children's experiences than they are at the moment.

WHERE ARE THE CHILDREN?

In the present era of child policy, the rights of the children are the key issue (*Lastensuojelusta* . . . 1995). Finland established children's rights in its legislation in the 1980s, especially the sections concerning children and custody and child protection. Finland ratified the UN Convention on the Rights of the Child in 1991. That convention is viewed as the most significant recent policy development intended to promote and protect children's rights (Franklin 1995:16). The convention incorporates civil, economic, social, and cultural rights, including the most basic right to life, the right to adequate health care, food, clean water, and shelter, rights to protection against sexual abuse, neglect, and exploitation, rights to education, privacy, and freedom of association, expression, and thought.

The emphasis on rights has introduced three essential features to the rhetoric of the practices and policies about children. First, when rights are emphasized, children are seen as independent subjects who might have interests and needs that conflict with the parents' and families' needs. Second, children are given the right to be heard and their wishes and opinions should be taken into account (taking into consideration the age and developmental stage of the children) when the parents and authorities make decisions concerning the children; and third, the best interest of the child should guide all the decisions made in relation to the children. According to the principles of the rights of children, every child has to be consulted— "heard"—when it is a question of taking him/her into care, especially if the child is 12 years of age or more. This should be routine in all child-protection cases.

Academic discourse has joined legal discourse in viewing children as independent subjects, with the "child question" being explored in more detail both in sociology and in other subjects (Alanen 1992). At the end of the 1990s, a growing number of studies done from the perspective of "childhood studies" looked at institutions such as families, schools, play culture, or services (e.g., Törrönen 1999; Ritala-Koskinen 1997; Kalliala 1999) as arenas for children's activities and tried to view them from the children's point of view. These studies share an interest in "hearing the child's voice" and giving the child the status of a speaker and creator of his/her own life. Special research units and programs have also been established to support this research agenda (Lyytinen & Lyytinen 1996).

However, the studies looking at the position of children in child protection give a contradictory picture about the practice's relations with children. Small in size but important in terms of its impact, Törrönen and Mäenpää's study (1995) on child-protection case records showed that hardly any professional attention had been given to the children, that is, no notes had been made about them. Even in some long-term relationships, the social worker's notes have focused on the adult's behavior or the actions they had taken; there were very few descriptions of the children. The social workers did not report their own interviews with children. Most descriptions of the child's situation had been given by other parties, such as teachers and health nurses involved in that case. According to this study, the focus changed only if the child had been taken into care and placed in a children's home; in that context, more notes had been made about the child. That was the arena where children played a role important enough for social work notification.

Another study by Hannele Forsberg (1998) also showed the children's roles as clients to be minor. This ethnographic research examined the child-protection practices in a social-welfare office as well as in a family-support center. Looking especially at the encounters between the practitioners and clients, she realized that most of the work involved the adults in both contexts. Family-support centers are expected to help families and children cope with their problems so that there would be no need to take the child into care. This work seems to be done mostly through and among adults. Interestingly, both agencies proclaimed their methods to be child-centered as well as family-centered. Child-centeredness is obviously a rhetorical frame for practice with adults. Family-centeredness, on the other hand, does not necessarily mean working with the families as a whole but working with mothers. Both of these strong professional discourses, nowadays strongly flavored by solution-focused therapies as well, and radical in their approach to avoid too narrow or individualistic a problem definition, tend, however, to exclude children in practice (Forsberg 1994, 1998).

One could go so far as to say that children are not necessarily needed as speaking subjects in child-protection practices because much professional work can be carried out just by speaking with adults (speaking being the main tool of social work) (Forsberg 1998; Hurtig 1999). In an ongoing study of ours (Hearn et al. 1999), sixteen interviews have been conducted in three regional social-welfare offices about referral practices in child-protection cases and in none of them has the social worker interviewed the child. The main discussants or informants for the social workers have been adults, either the child's parents or people working in the welfare services. Only in a couple of cases had the social worker even seen the child when paying a home visit. As we followed up the cases, we found that in the following six or more months, contact remained mainly between the social worker and adults. A personal relationship with the parent was established only in rare cases. Based on that, one could say that the child is not even seen in the practice—or indeed that the child is not needed even as a physical being.

The legal frame positions children differently from what can be learned about social-work practice through the studies. The status of independent citizen seems to have a very vague role in practice but a strong one in the legal frame; as a matter of fact, child-protection practice seems to emphasize the adults (parents) more than children, giving the children a role very difficult to define in terms of the present child-protection vocabulary.

DO FINNISH CHILDREN HAVE ANY PROBLEMS (EXCEPT THOSE OF THEIR PARENTS)?

As stated previously, on the one hand child-protection problems are constructed as family problems in current child-protection practice, but on the other hand they are viewed as general social and citizen policy issues in child-policy discourse. The legal and administrative discourse supports both and can be used for promoting either. The growing public (media and professional) concern about drug abuse among teenagers and early youth exclusion from the educational and labor markets, among other troubles, adds some complications to the picture. Some view children as having social problems, but this view is less common among those whose social role as part of the Finnish welfare state is to promote and look after children's well-being. On the other hand, the welfare state is celebrated as an active

instrument in equalizing economic inequalities among the child population: Finland has the lowest incidence of child poverty among several
OECD countries (Forssen 1997b). Should we therefore think that Finnish
children do not suffer from abuse and neglect to the extent that they do not
"need" a concept and practical framework of their own? The answer is
hesitant.

In terms of abuse, we do know different phases in the problem's history.
As child abuse became a widely debated issue internationally in the late
1960s and 1970s, the same concern hit Finland as well. Physicians declared
that they met abused children in their work and some NGOs became active in providing shelter for those who had been battered in their homes
(Peltoniemi 1984). Typically for Finland, the phenomenon was conceptualized as "family violence" (*perheväkivalta*). This concept did not include
any gender or generational aspects, even though it was known from practical work that it was mainly women with their children who sought a
place of shelter (Peltoniemi 1984). By using that concept, a holistic and sys-
temic approach to the problem of intimate violence was emphasized. Intimate violence at home was seen as an outcome of family problems of
different types and therefore, family interventions and concepts were emphasized. Most interestingly, Riitta Leskinen (1982) published a research
report about the "family violence" experienced by the children staying in
the shelters. That report was met with interest but it did not establish any
different ways of treating the issue to give special emphasis to children.
Even in the mid-1990s, child-protection workers did not use any conceptual framework for children's experiences of violence at home (except for
sexual abuse, which has been given a fair amount of special attention in
multiprofessional and multiagency professional practices). Social workers
preferred to call the abuse issues "family conflicts" or "parents' drinking,"
"coping," or "psychiatric problems," and those definitions were also used
in the case reports (Pösö 1995).

It took almost twenty years to introduce new conceptual approaches to
"family violence." In the late 1990s, "family violence" was reconceptual-
ized by some scholars and practice agencies as gendered intimate violence
or violence at home, and researchers were encouraged to study the gendered nature of the phenomenon. Simultaneously, in the field of social welfare, a nation-wide NGO project, "Time for Children," was established to
introduce methods of working with and for children, and to sensitize practitioners to recognizing the needs of abused children or children who have
witnessed violence in their homes. The first years of the project have, however, frustrated the project's workers. Mikko Oranen (1999), the project
leader, writes about the anger they have experienced due to the invisibil-
ity of children in the field of social welfare. The project workers have met
children suffering from severe violence and abuse at their homes, and

some of them have been clients of different social-welfare and health services, but the professionals have not paid any attention to the children's traumatic state. According to Oranen, the children are neither heard nor seen and their interests are too often given second priority after the parents' needs and interests in the general welfare and health services, including child protection. The project workers themselves have also lacked approaches, concepts, and methods that are sensitive to the (abused) children; establishing ways of dealing with these cases has been a very slow process (Forsberg 2000).

This project suggests that abuse exists as an experience of children, but that professional practices keep it from being noticed and visible (Oranen 1999). This statement is supported, on the one hand, by retrospective studies of the early childhood of prisoners and adults in child protection (Haapasalo 1999) that draw a picture of rather severe violence experienced by those groups and, on the other hand, by prevalence studies that suggest that violence against children is widespread but generally mild (Sariola & Uutela 1992). Although the problems of comparisons are obvious, Sariola and Uutela gathered that the overall frequency of violence toward children in Finland is significantly lower than in the United States, but identical to the (low) level in Sweden. In the context of criminal homicide, the risk of being killed by another person is highest during the first year of a person's life, whereas later during childhood and puberty the risk is very low (Kivivuori 1999:141). That risk is not, however, debated much at all.

Abuse and violence—like any other social problems—are dependent on definitional practices. Therefore it is difficult and even risky to make any statements about the situation of Finnish children in terms of their experience of social problems, troubles, and conflicts. I do, however, take seriously the view that there is some confusion in this area. On the one hand, there are social practices focusing on families' problems that ignore the children's position as the main focus of intervention and problem definition, by trying to construct a holistic approach to social problems. On the other hand, there are actors who claim that children do suffer from maltreatment at the hands of adults and that they should be given a more central status in the protective welfare services. This diffusion could be a social problem. From a normative standpoint, however, it should also be an issue, whether someone—troubled children and their mothers first and foremost—experiences unnecessary pain due to the diffusion.

DISCUSSION

In Finland, social problems concerning children are in the process of reformulation. However, in the context of child protection there seem to be firmly institutionalized frames for recognizing and treating children's social problems. As argued before, the problems are framed as family problems and the interventions and the service system as a whole are geared to supporting the family and its adult members. Simultaneously, there are different legal, administrative, and social discourses that intend to strengthen the role of children as independent actors. The process of reformulation is therefore rather confusing.

The Finnish version of the family-service orientation of child protection (Gilbert 1997) is rooted in the strong role of the welfare state: it is based on the services provided by the public sector, and thereby on a coalition. In that coalition, services to families, surveillance of appropriate parenthood, and judgments of good-enough care of children are closely tied together; the duty of social workers is to find a balance between those tasks in actual client work (Eräsaari, Julkunen, and Silius 1995). In order to function, child protection needs cooperation with the clients—that is, the parents. Therefore the parents cannot be challenged too much in terms of their parenthood (Kuronen 1994). One way to challenge the parents is to express concern about the well-being of children. That seems to be avoided since, as stated previously, the recognition of children's problems is almost missing and vague family problems are categorized instead. This cooperative coalition is not so much needed in the work done outside the public sector and there, at the moment, child-based problem formulations and treatment programs are flourishing more than in public child protection. In this sector, coalitions between the professionals and troubled children replace those made between practitioners and parents.

The strong link between the welfare services and child protection is typical not only of Finland but of Sweden as well. Weightman & Weightman (1995) compared Swedish and English child-protection practice and concluded that the practices were fundamentally different even though they both proclaim "the best interest of a child" as their main aim. English child protection tended to be reactive, intervening only when severe problems had occurred, whereas the Swedes preferred to work in a supportive, preventative way, providing care and services at the early stages of possible problems. The English system was not geared to provide care, services, or prevention but it was efficient in cases of actual harm to the children. In contrast, Weightman and Weightman claim that the Swedish system was incapable of functioning in those situations. Also, the English system tended to define the problems of the children in a detailed, regulated way, whereas the Swedish system preferred a general and loose definition of those situations requiring child protection. This reflected different approaches to the role of the state and its welfare duties. Swedish universalist welfare thinking views child protection as a nonthreatening resource available equally but, in the residualist British welfare state, the autonomy of citizens is highly respected and any state intervention into the privacy of families or citizens is viewed with suspicion. In Sweden, the welfare state and child protection create a coalition as well.

Is there trouble in the Nordic welfare-state paradise, was the question put (at the beginning of this chapter) by Keith Pringle, whose interest was the status of troubled children. My answer is twofold. No, there is no trouble if you consider only children who can be helped together with their parents. But yes, there is trouble if the child's life is threatened in a more serious way, possibly by his/her parents. They might be those children who suffer "in the paradise" created by the family-based services and child protection since their experiences and voices are heard in such a limited way. They are also excluded from the agenda of proper financial resources since in the dynamics of the welfare state, child-protection functions, especially taking the child into care and out-of-home placements, are restrained by the lack of municipal resources. On a more general level, any hegemonic trouble definitions could be seen as threatening paradise as well, and the new diffusions could be warmly welcomed.

However, to give that answer, one has to agree that the child could have some agency on his/her own. The main question is not whether the "hidden problems" that children experience are found, or whether families should play an active role in child protection, but it is about the focus of the looking eye—it should reach children and their experiences even in the contexts of abuse and neglect, and it should be strong enough to look past the parents and their importance to the functioning of the welfare state. To be honest, it is not yet known what we could gain from a more child-focused approach, since the experiences of other national practices cannot be directly applied as the social, cultural, and welfare state contexts and actors are different. Thus, the claim is more or less ideological and moral.

NOTES

1. Child protection has long been a neglected subject in the Finnish social sciences Not until the 1990s did child protection appear on the agenda of academic research. The period is also known for renewed interest in research on children and families.

2. The legislation on child protection has been formally translated into English as "Child Welfare Acts." Child welfare is also used in many formal translations. However, internationally the term "child protection" is more often used. Yet "Child Welfare Acts" can still be considered an appropriate translation as it makes the Finnish emphasis on welfare issues in child protection explicit. In this article I have preferred to use the internationally more neutral term "protection."

3. The start of the expansion of the welfare state in the 1960s marked a turning point in policies aimed at family and gender relations (Pfau-Effinger 1999:148–49).

REFERENCES

Alanen, Leena. 1992. *Modern Childhood? Exploring the "Child Question" in Sociology.* Institute for Education Research Publication Series A, Research Report 50. Jyväskylä: University of Jyväskylä.

Dahl, Tove Stang. 1985. *Child Welfare and Social Defence.* Oslo: Norwegian University Press.

Egelund, Tine. 1996. "Bureaucracy or Professionalism? The Work Tools of Child Protection Services." *Scandinavian Journal of Social Welfare* 5:165–74.

Eräsaari, Leena, Raija Julkunen, and Harriet Silius (eds.). 1995. *Naiset yksityisen ja julkisen rajalla.* Tampere: Vastapaino.

Forsberg, Hannele. 1994. *Yksi ja monta perhettä* (Research report 42). Helsinki: Stakes.

———. 1998. *Perheen ja lapsen tähden.* Helsinki: Lastensuojelun Keskusliitto.

———. 2000. *Lapsen näkökulmaa tavoittamassa—Arviointitutkimus turvakotien lapsikeskeisyyttä kehittävästä projektista.* Helsinki: Ensi-ja Turvakotien Liitto.

Forssen, Katja. 1993. *Suojaverkon lapsiperheet* (Sarja A:2). Turku: Turun yliopisto. Sosiaalipolitiikan laitos.

———. 1997a. "Lastensuojelun asiakastyö: Tukea, kontrollia ja viranomaisyhteistyötä." Pp. 161–82 in *Tehdä itsensä tarpeettomaksi?* (Sosiaalityö 1990-luvulla, Report 213), edited by Riitta Viialainen and Maisa Maaniittu. Helsinki: Stakes.

———. 1997b. "Lapsiköyhyys ja perhepolitiikka OECD-maissa." Pp. 57–89 in *Onko sosiaalipolitiikalla vaikutusta?*, edited by Kari Salavuo. Helsinki. Sosiaali-ja terveysministeriö.

Franklin, Bob. 1995. "The Case for Children's Rights: A Progress Report." Pp. 3–24 in *Handbook of Children's Rights: Comparative Policy and Practice,* edited by Bob Franklin. London: Routledge.

Gilbert, Neil. 1997. "A Comparative Perspective." Pp. 232–40 in *Combatting Child Abuse: International Perspectives and Trends,* edited by Neil Gilbert. New York: Oxford University Press.

Gordon, Linda. 1988. *Heroes of Their Own Lives: The Politics and History of Family Violence.* New York: Penguin.

Haapasalo, Jaana (ed.). 1999. *Väkivallan kierre* (Report 5). Helsinki: Vankeinhoidon Koulutuskeskus.

Hall, Chris. 1997. *Social Work as Narrative: Storytelling and Persuasion in Professional Texts.* Aldershot: Ashgate.

Hearn, Jeff, Johanna Korpinen, Tarja Pösö, Carole Smith, and Sue White. 1999. "What is a Case?: History, Methodology and Preliminary Empirical Findings in the Lastensuojelu/Child Protection Research Project." Paper presented at the conference of European Association of Schools of Social Work, Helsinki.

Heino, Tarja. 1997. *Asiakkuuden häämäryys lastensuojelussa* (Research Report 77). Helsinki: Stakes.

———. 1998. "Selvitys lastensuojelun keskeisistä käsitteistä ja toimintamuodoista." Pp. 122–29 in *Hyvä huostaanotto?* (Aiheita 28), edited by Riitta Laakso and Peppi Saikku. Helsinki: Stakes.

Hurtig, Johanna. 1999. *Huvitusta, yyvitystä vai hyödyllistä: Perhekuntoutuksen arviointi.* Rovaniemi: Lapin Yliopisto.

Kähkönen, Päivi. 1993. *Vanhemmuuden murtuminen: Lapsen huostaanotto sosiaalitoimen asiakirja-aineiston valossa*, (Lisensiaatin tutkimus). Jyväskylä: Jyväskylän yliopiston psykologian laitos.

Kalliala, Marjatta. 1999. *Enkeliprinsessa ja itsari liukumäessä*. Helsinki: Gaudeamus.

Karjalainen, Vappu. 1996. *Verkoston lupaus* (Research Report 68). Helsinki: Stakes.

Karvinen, Synnöve, Tarja Pösö, and Mirja Satka (eds.). 1999. *Reconstructing Social Work Research*. Jyväskylä: SoPhi.

Kivinen, Tarja. 1989. *Viimeinen pari verkosta ulos* (Julkaisuja 11). Helsinki: Sosiaalihallitus.

————. 1994. *Valikoituminen lastensuojelun asiakkaaksi* (Research Report 45). Helsinki: Stakes.

————, and Pekka Heinonen. 1990. *Lastensuojelu 1987*, (Report 11). Helsinki: Sosiaalihallitus.

Kivivuori, Janne. 1999. *Suomalainen henkirikos* (Research Report 159). Helsinki: Oikeuspoliittinen Tutkimuslaitos.

Kröger, Teppo. 1999. "Local Historical Case Study: The Unique and the General in the Emergence of Social Care Services." Pp. 54–90 in *Reconstructing Social Work Research*, edited by Synnöve Karvinen, Tarja Pösö, and Mirja Satka. Jyväskylä: SoPhi.

Kuronen, Marjo. 1994. *Lapsen hyväksi naisten kesken* (Research Report 35). Helsinki. Stakes.

Laakso, Riitta. 1998. "Ehdot selviksi." Pp. 4–41 in *Hyvä huostaanotto?* (Aiheita 28), edited by Riitta Laakso, and Peppi Saikku. Helsinki: Stakes.

Lapsioikeudellista päätöksentekomenettelyä selvittäneen toimikunnan mietintö. 1995. (Komiteamietintö 12). Helsinki: Sosiaali- ja terveysministeriö.

Lastensuojelusta kohti lapsipolitiikkaa. 1995. (Report 5). Helsinki: Sosiaali- ja terveysministeriö.

Leskinen, Riitta. 1982. *"Kuka kuulisi minua"—Perheväkivalta lapsen silmin* (Report 2). Helsinki: Ensi Kotien Liitto.

Lyytinen, Paula, and Heikki Lyytinen. 1996. *Lapsi ja tutkimus*. Atena: Jyväskylä.

Mäntysaari, Mikko. 1991. *Sosiaalibyrokratia asiakkaiden valvojana*. Tampere: Vastapaino.

Marjamäki, Pirjo, Mikko Mäntysaari and Tero Ristimäki. 1998. *Sosiaalityöntekijät Suomessa 1998—Tehtävät, koulutus, määrä ja riittävyys* (Selvityksiä 9). Helsinki: Sosiaali- ja terveysministeriö.

Millar, Jane, and Andrea Warman. 1996. *Family Obligations in Europe*. London: Family Policy Studies Centre.

Muuri, Anu. 1999. *Lastensuojelu 1998* (Tilastoraportti 33). Helsinki: Stakes.

Oranen, Mikko. 1999. "Raivo tekee näkyväksi." *Esikko* 4:2.

Peltoniemi, Teuvo. 1984. *Perheväkivalta*. Helsinki: Otava.

Pfau-Effinger, Birgit. 1999. "Change of Family Policies in the Socio-Cultural Context of European Societies." *Comparative Social Research* 18:135–59.

Pithouse, Andrew. 1987. *Social Work: The Organisation of an Invisible Trade*. Aldershot: Gower.

Platt, Anthony. 1969. *The Child Savers: The Invention of Delinquency*. Chicago: University of Chicago Press.

Pösö, Tarja. 1991. "Troublesome Youth in the Finnish Residential Child Welfare System." Pp. 98–120 in *Youth, Crime and Justice* (Scandinavian Studies in

Criminology, Vol. 12), edited by Annika Snare. Oslo: Norwegian University Press.

———. 1995. "Lasten pahoinpitely lastensuojelussa - Ollako vai eikö olla?" Pp. 32–53 in *Sosiaalityö, asiakkuus ja sosiaaliset ongelmat,* edited by Arja Jokinen, Kirsi Juhila,and Tarja Pösö. Helsinki: Sosiaaliturvan Keskusliitto.

Pringle, Keith. 1998. *Children and Social Welfare in Europe.* Buckingham: Open University Press.

Ritala-Koskinen, Aino. 1997. "Stepfamilies from the Child's Perspective: From Stepfamily to Close Relationships." Pp. 135–51 in *Stepfamilies From Various Perspectives,* edited by Irene Levin and Marvin B. Sussman. New York: Haworth Press.

Saikku, Peppi. 1998. "Yhdessä Suunnitellen." Pp. 42–77 in *Hyvä huostaanotto* (Aiheita 28), edited by Riitta Laakso and Peppi Saikku. Helsinki: Stakes.

Salmi, Minna, Jouko Huttunen, and Päivi Yli-Pietilä. 1996. *Lapset ja lama* (Report 197). Helsinki: Stakes.

Sariola, Heikki, and Antti Uutela. 1992. "The Prevalence and Context of Family Violence against Children in Finland." *Child Abuse & Neglect* 16:823–32.

Satka, Mirja. 1995. *Making Social Citizenship.* Jyväskylä: SoPhi.

———. 1997. "Sosiaalityö ajassa - Ydinkysymysten äärellä." Pp. 27–38 in *Tehdä itsensä tarpeettomaksi* (Sosiaalityö 1990-luvulla, Report 213), edited by Riitta Viialainen and Maisa Maaniittu. Helsinki: Stakes.

Smith, Eve P., and Lisa A. Merkel-Holguin. 1996. *A History of Child Welfare.* New Brunswick, NJ: Transaction.

Takala, Pentti. 1992. "Kohti postmodernia perhettä—Perhepolitiikan muuttuvat käsitykset." Pp. 577–600 in *Sosiaalipolitiikka 2017,* edited by Olavi Riihinen. Juva: WSOY.

Törrönen, Maritta. 1999. *Lasten arki laitoksessa* Helsinki: Helsinki University Press.

———, and Johanna Mäenpää. 1995. *Lapsen tie laitokseen* (Aiheita 5). Helsinki: Stakes.

Weightman, Keith, and Annika Weightman. 1995. "Never Right, Never Wrong: Child Welfare and Social Work in England and Sweden." *Scandinavian Journal of Social Welfare* 4:75–84.

INDEX

305